HARR...

DICTIONA...

ENGLISH
SPELLING

HARRAP'S
DICTIONARY OF
ENGLISH SPELLING

Editors: Bud Wileman, Robin Wileman

HARRAP
London

First published in this edition
in Great Britain 1990
by HARRAP BOOKS Ltd
Chelsea House, 26 Market Square,
Bromley BR1 1NA

ISBN 0 245-60035-3

Printed and bound in Great Britain by
Richard Clay Ltd, Bungay, Suffolk

In gratitude to all those children and adults who helped
with the spelling in this dictionary.

Foreword

This is a book that deals with an age old problem.

"Please, how do you spell 'inconceivable'?"
"Why don't you look it up in the dictionary?"
"I did, but it's not there!"

Of course it was there, but not in the form sought by the puzzled inquirer, who was trying to find "inconseavable".

In English, there is no simple relationship between speech sounds and their graphic representation: a single sound may be written in a number of different ways. However, far from being a haphazard arrangement, English spelling is based on a complex system of rules which govern the interrelationship of a word's visual appearance, sound and meaning. Sometimes, as in the K sound in *skip* (Scandinavian) and *schizoid* (Greek), the word's origin determines the spelling. On other occasions it is the grammatical function, as in "there" and "their", which both derive from Old English.

The visual patterns also impose limitations on meaning, and they may give readers significant clues. For example, the homonyms "to", "too", and "two" have differing syntactic and semantic functions; "night" and "knight" are both nouns, but mean different things.

For struggling readers and writers, the whole system can be bewildering, and the rules difficult to learn. What can be done to help? One possibility is to reform spelling so that it becomes phonetically regular. G.B. Shaw left a legacy to that end, and some beginning reading and writing schemes such as the Initial Teaching Alphabet have attempted the task. However, such alleged reforms would result in considerable problems for those who have already learnt to read and write, and would deprive all readers of the valuable clues to meaning inherent in the present system.

The alternatives are, firstly, to find more efficient ways of teaching spelling in context as a system of auditory and visual patterns that contribute to our understanding of the printed word and, secondly, to provide writers with a key to correct spellings of incidental words as they need them.

Word Spell provides such a key. It consists of a lexicon of words commonly used in English, containing not only their correct spelling but also common misspellings, so that the reader can look up "inconseavable" or "inconceivable" and find the accepted form of the word. The incorrect spellings are easily identified both by indention and a pale blue lettering.

The misspellings have been drawn from a range of spelling tests, lists of commonly misspelt words, and the editors' own experience. An additional advantage is the provision of a set of simple guidelines to help inexperienced or erratic spellers to improve their mastery of written language.

Word Spell is designed to help those people who, although their oral conversation is adequate, may not be able to spell all the words they know. It will be an invaluable reference for the many children and adults with problems in this area, as well as for the teachers who are endeavouring to help them.

Dr. Patricia Long,
Chairperson
Special Education Department,
Melbourne College of Advanced Education.

Introduction

How To Find a Word.

If possible, write down what you think is the spelling of the word you wish to find. Decide what are the first two or three letters.

Find these in the dictionary by looking at the left hand column. If you have the correct spelling you will find the word printed in **black**.

If you have the incorrect spelling you will find the word printed in **blue**, in the second left hand column. You will then find the correct spelling in **black** in the right hand column.

If you do not find the word, check any directions that may be given e.g.

> Look under **de-** if the
> word is not under **di**.

Then proceed as above. Check how close you were to the correct spelling and if necessary learn the correct spelling.

How To Learn the Correct Spelling.

Say the word and the letters.

Look at the word carefully.

Write the word three times.

Close your eyes and think of the word. **Write it down** with your eyes closed.

Check to see you are correct.

Write the word in a sentence so that you will remember its meaning as well as its spelling.

Consult a standard dictionary if you are unsure of the meaning.

About the Dictionary.

You will see that all the words, correct spellings and incorrect spellings are listed in alphabetical order.

Nouns

To form the plural of most nouns add "**s**" to the word.

> e.g. rabbit, rabbits.

Where the plural may be difficult, you are given help.

> e.g. injury, -ries (for 'injuries')
>
> > goose, geese
> >
> > piano, pianos

You will find hints to help you with plurals on page ix.

Verbs

Verbs listed in the dictionary give the endings for the past tense, the past participle and the present participle. Most verbs have the same word for the past tense and the past participle.

> e.g. reach, -ed, -ing for reach, reached, reaching.

Where difficulty could occur with the spelling, you are given further help.

> e.g. collide, -lided, -liding for collide, collided, colliding.
>
> > erase, erased, erasing

Where the past tense and the past participle are different, the words are given in full.

> e.g. sing, sang, sung, singing.

Adjectives

Where there may be difficulty in spelling the comparative and superlative forms, further help is given.

> e.g. dizzy, dizzier, dizziest.

Adverbs

Where the ending -**ly** is given, it is added to the word.

   e.g. mythical, -ly for '**mythically**.'

Where there is a change in spelling, further help is given.

   e.g. haste, -tily for '**hastily**'.

   palpable, -bly for '**palpably**'.

SOME SPELLING HINTS

1. For short sounding words (one syllable words) *that do not end in* **e**, double the last letter when adding -ed, -er or -ing, e.g. ban, banned; jog, jogger; fit, fitting.

2. In short words *that end in* **e** where the central vowel sound is said the same way as the letter name — e.g. make — drop the **e** when -ed, -er or -ing are added, e.g. cope, coped; make, maker; bite, biting.
   Short words keep the **e** when -ly is added, e.g. tame, tamely; time, timely.

3. Short words (one syllable) ending in **y**, preceded by a vowel, keep the **y** when -ed, -er or -ing are added, e.g. key, keyed; buy, buyer; toy, toying.
   If the **y** is preceded by a consonant, when -ed, or -er are added, the **y** is changed to **i**, e.g. try, tried; fly, flier.
   The **y** is kept when adding -ing, e.g. try, trying.

4. Longer words ending in **y**, change the **y** to **i** when adding other parts, e.g. berry, berries; marry, marriage; happy, happiness; hurry, hurried; funny, funnily; heavy, heavier and heaviest.
   However, when adding -ing, the **y** is kept, e.g. hurry, hurrying; bury, burying.

5. Vowels that can be doubled are **e** (been) and **o** (moon) and sometimes **u** (vacuum); **a** and **i** are not doubled in English words.

6. Letters that can be doubled in the middle of a word are **b, d, f, g, m, n, r, s, t**, and **z**.

7. In short words, **f, l, s** and **z** at the end of a word are doubled, e.g. cuff, doll, pass, buzz.

8. If **full** is added to the end of a word, one **l** is dropped, e.g. helpful, until.

9. When **all-** or **well-** are added to the front of a word, one **l** is dropped, e.g. already, welcome.

10. When **dis-** and **mis-**, meaning 'not', are placed in front of a word, the **s** is not doubled — e.g. disable, misbehave — unless the main word begins with **s**, e.g. disservice, misspell.

    Also when **un-** is placed in front of a word, the **n** is not doubled — e.g. unmade — unless the main word begins with **n**, e.g. unnecessary.

    Similarly, when **in-** is placed in front of a word, the **n** is not doubled — e.g. insane — unless the main word begins with **n**, e.g. innumerable.

PLURALS

1. Most words ad **s** to form the plural — e.g. cat, cats, but words that end in a sibilant sound (-s, -sh, -ss, -tch, -x) add **es**, e.g. gases, wishes, masses, catches, foxes.

2. Most words ending in **f** change the **f** to **v** and add **es**, e.g. thief, thieves. There are some exceptions, so check the word.

3. Most words ending in **o** add **es**, e.g. potato, potatoes. Exceptions are foreign words, so check the word if you are unsure.

4. Words ending in **y**, *preceded by a consonant*, change the **y** to **i** and add **es** — e.g. ferry, ferries, but words ending in **y**, *preceded by a vowel*, add **s**, e.g. day, days; monkey, monkeys.

5. Words ending in **ful** usually put the **s** after the stem word, e.g. cupful, cupsful. However the placement of **s** at the end of the word is now becoming acceptable, e.g. cupful, cupfuls.

6. Some words add **en** or **ren** to the stem word, e.g. ox, oxen; child, children.

7. Some foreign words change the ending and add **a**, **ae**, **i**, e.g. compendium, compendia; formula, formulae; bacillus, bacilli.

POSITION OF LETTERS

1. In 'ee' sound words, **c** is always followed by **ei**, e.g. receive, ceiling. Most others have **ie**, e.g. believe, priest. However, there are many exceptions so check the word if you are unsure.

2. **q** is always followed by **u** in English words.

3. No English words end in **j** or **v**.

4. If **g** and **h** come together, **g** is always before **h**, e.g. eight, enough.

5. **ck** never starts a word.

SOUND

1. If a long word (more than one syllable) ends in the sound '**shun**', it could be spelt -tion, -sion, -cion.

2. **ti**, **si** and **ci** make the '**sh**' sound, but not at the beginning of a word.

3. A long word ending in the '**j**' sound could be -age, -ege, -ige, -dge. Check the word if you are not sure.

4. A long word ending in the '**ree**' sound could be -ary, -ery, -ory, -ury or -ry. Check if you are not sure.

5. Very short words (one syllable) ending in **y** make the '**i**' sound as in sly, pry, sky.

6. Words ending in the '**ul**' sound could be spelt -ble, -al, -el, -il, -ol, -le. Check if you are not sure.

7. Most words ending in the '**ize**' sound are usually spelt -ise, e.g. analyse, paralyse. Some exceptions are capsize, prize.

Aa

aback

abacus, abaci, abacuses

abait — abate

abakus — abacus

abalone

abalonie — abalone

abandon, -ed, -ing

abandonment

abase, abased, abasing

abasement

abashed

abate, abated, abating

abatement

abators — abattoirs

abattoirs

abatwaz — abattoirs

abayance — abeyance

abbess (nun)

abbess — abyss (hole)

abbey, -beys

abbie — abbey

abbot

abbreviate, -ated, -ating

abbreviation

abcence — absence

abdacate — abdicate

abdicate, -cated, -cating

abdication

abdomen

abduckshun — abduction

abduct

abduction

abductor

abel — able

aberation — aberration

aberrant

aberration

abet, abetted, abetting

abeyance

abeyense — abeyance

abhor, abhorred, abhorring

abhore — abhor

abhorent — abhorrent

abhorrent, -ly

abidance

abidanse — abidance

abide, abode, abided, abiding

abilitee — ability

abilitey — ability

ability, -ties

abismal — abysmal

abiss — abyss

abject, -ly

abjective — objective

abjekt — abject

abjure, -jured, -juring

ablaze

able, abler, ablest

able-bodied

ablushun — ablution

ablution

abnegashun — abnegation

abnegate, -gated, -gating

abnegation

abnormal, -ly

abnormality, -ties

aboard

abode

abolish

abolishment

abolishun — abolition

abolitionary

abolitionist

abollish — abolish

A-bomb

abominabel — abominable

abominable

abominably

abominate, -nated, -nating

abomination

abord — aboard

aboriginal

Aborigine

aborshun — abortion

abort, -ed, -ing

abortion
abortive, -ly
abound, -ed, -ing
about
above
aboveboard
  abowt   about
abracadabra
abradant
abrade, abraded, abrading
abrasion
abrasive
abreast
  abrest   abreast
abridge, abridged, abridging
abridgment
  abrige   abridge
abroad
abrogate, -gated, -gating
abrupt, -ly
abruptness
  absail   abseil
abscess
abscond, -ed, -ing
absconder
abseil, -ed, -ing
absence
  absense   absence
absent, -ed, -ing
absentee
absenteeism
absent-minded
  absess   abscess
absinth
  absolushun   absolution
absolute, -ly
absolution
absolutism
absolutist
absolve, -solved, -solving
absorb, -ed, -ing
absorbency
  absorbensy   absorbency
absorbent
  absorbshun   absorption
absorption
absorptive

abstain, -ed, -ing
  abstane   abstain
abstemious, -ly
  abstemius   abstemious
  abstenshun   abstention
abstention
abstinence
  abstinense   abstinence
abstinent, -ly
abstract, -ed, -ing
abstraction
  abstrakshun   abstraction
  abstrakt   abstract
abstruse, -ly
absurd, -ly
absurdity
abundance
abundant, -ly
  abundence   abundance
  abundent   abundant
  abusave   abusive
abuse, abused, abusing
abusive, -ly
abut, abutted, abutting
abuttal
abysmal, -ly
abyss (hole)
acacia
academic
academician
  academishun   academician
academy, -mies
  accacia   acacia
  accademic   academic
  accademy   academy
accede, -ceded, -ceding (agree)
  accede   exceed
              (surpass)
accelerate, -rated, -rating
acceleration
accelerator
accent, -ed, -ing
accentual, -ly
accentuate, -ated, -ating
accept, -ed, -ing
  acceptabel   acceptable
acceptability

acceptable, -bly
acceptance
  acceptense   acceptance
access
  accessable   accessible
accessary, -ries (crime)
  accessibel   accessible
accessibility
accessible, -bly
  accessibul   accessible
accession
accessory, -ries (extra)
accident
accidental, -ly
acclaim, -ed, -ing
acclamation
acclimatise, -tised, -tising
accolade
accommodate, -dated, -dating
accommodation
  accomodation   accommodation
accompaniment
accompanist
accompany, -nied, -nying
  accompanyment   accompaniment
accomplice
accomplish, -ed, -ing
accomplishment
  accompliss   accomplice
accord, -ed, -ing
accordance
  accordanse   accordance
accordant, -ly
accordingly
accordion
accordionist
accost, -ed, -ing
account, -ed, -ing
  accountabel   accountable
accountability
accountable
accountably
  accountabul   accountable
accountancy
accountant
  accoustic   acoustic
accredit, -ed, -ing

accreditation
  accreshun   accretion
accretion
  accrew   accrue
  accross   across
accrual
accrue, -crued, -cruing
  accult   occult
  accumen   acumen
accumulate, -lated, -lating
accumulation
accumulative
accumulator
accuracy
  accurasy   accuracy
accurate, -ly
accurateness
accursed
accusation
accuse, -cused, -cusing
accuser
accustom, -ed, -ing
  accute   acute
ace
  acelerate   accelerate
  acerage   acreage
  acerbait   acerbate
acerbate, -bated, -bating
acerbic
acerbity
  acerige   acreage
acetate
acetic (acid)
  acetic   ascetic (hermit)
  acetilene   acetylene
acetylene
ache, ached, aching
  acheivable   achievable
  acheive   achieve
  achievabel   achievable
achievable
  achievabul   achievable
achieve, achieved, achieving
achievement
achiever
acid
acidic

acidify, -fied, -fying
acidity
ackers
acknowledge, -edged, -edging
acknowledgment

> For other **ack-** words,
> look under **ac-** or **acc-**.

aclaim	acclaim
aclamation	acclamation
acme	
acne	
acolade	accolade
acommodate	accommodate
acommodation	accommodation
acompanist	accompanist
acompany	accompany
acomplice	accomplice
acomplish	accomplish
acord	accord
acordion	accordion
acorn	
acost	accost
acount	account

acoustic
acoustical, -ly
acoustics
acquaint, -ed, -ing
acquaintance

acquaintanse	acquaintance

acquiesce, -esced, -escing
acquiescence
acquiescent, -ly

acquiess	acquiesce

acquire, -quired, -quiring
acquisition
acquisitive, -ly
acquit, -quitted, -quitting
acquittal
acre
acreage

acredit	accredit

acrid, -ly
acrimonious, -ly
acrimony, -nies
acrobat
acrobatic

acrobatically
acrobatics

acrofobia	acrophobia

acrophobia
acropolis
across
acrylic

acryllic	acrylic

act, -ed, -ing

acter	actor

acting
action

actionabel	actionable

actionable

actionabul	actionable

activate, -vated, -vating
active
activism
activist
activity, -ties
actor
actress
actual, -ly
actuality, -ties
actually
actuarial, -ly
actuary, -ries
actuate, -ated, -ating
acuity
acumen
acupuncture
acupuncturist

acupunshur	acupuncture

acute, -ly
acuteness
adage
adagio

adajio	adagio

adamant

adament	adamant

adapt, -ed, -ing

adaptabel	adaptable

adaptability
adaptable

adaptabul	adaptable

adaptation
adaption

adaptive, -ly
adaptor
  adda   adder
addendum, -da
adder
  addicshun   addiction
addict, -ed, -ing
addiction
addictive
  addishun   addition
addition (add)
  addition   edition (book)
additional, -ly
additive
addled
address, -ed, -ing
adduce, -duced, -ducing
  adducibel   adducible
adducible

> For other **add-** words,
> look under **ad-**.

adenoid
adept, -ly
adeptness
adequacy
  adequasy   adequacy
adequate, -ly
  adherant   adherent
adhere, -hered, -hering
adherence
  adherense   adherence
adherent, -ly
  adheshun   adhesion
adhesion
adhesive, -ly
adjacent, -ly
  adjasent   adjacent
adjectival, -ly
adjective
  adjetival   adjectival
  adjetive   adjective
adjoin, -ed, -ing
adjourn, -ed, -ing
adjournment
adjudicate, -cated, -cating
adjudication

adjudicative, -ly
adjudicator
adjunct
adjure, -jured, -juring
  adjurn   adjourn
  adjurnment   adjournment
adjust, -ed, -ing
  adjustabel   adjustable
adjustable, -bly
  adjustabul   adjustable
adjustment
  admeral   admiral
administer, -ed, -ing
  administrabel administrable
administrable
  administrabul administrable
administrate, -trated, -trating
  administrater administrator
administration
administrative, -ly
administrator
admirable, -bly
admiral
admiralty, -ties
admiration
admire, -mired, -miring
admirer
  admishun   admission
  admissable   admissible
  admissibel   admissible
admissible, -ly
  admissibul   admissible
admission
admit, -mitted, -mitting
admittance
  admittanse   admittance
admittedly
admonish, -ed, -ing
  admonishun   admonition
admonition
ad nauseam
ado
adobe
adolescence
adolescent
  adolesense   adolescence
  adolesent   adolescent

adopshun   adoption
adopt, -ed, -ing
adoption
adoptive, -ly
adorabel   adorable
adorable
adorably
adorabul   adorable
adoration
adore, adored, adoring
adorn, -ed, -ing
adornment
adorrable   adorable
adorre   adore
adrenalin
adress   address
adrift
adroit, -ly
adroyt   adroit
adulate, -lated, -lating
adulation
adulatory
adult
adulterate, -rated, -rating
adulteration
adulterer
adulteress
adulterous
adultery, -teries
adulthood
adultry   adultery
advacate   advocate
advance, -vanced, -vancing
advancement
advanse   advance
advansement   advancement
advantage, -taged, -taging
advantageous, -ly
advantaje   advantage
advenscher   adventure
advenshur   adventure
advent
adventure, -tured, -turing
adventureous   adventurous
adventurer
adventuresome
adventurous, -ly

adverb
adverbial, -ly
adversary, -saries
adverse, -ly
adversery   adversary
adversity, -ties
advert, -ed, -ing
advertise, -tised, -tising
advertisement
advertiser
advertisment   advertisement
advice (opinion)
advice   advise (give advice)
advisabel   advisable
advisability
advisable, -bly
advisabul   advisable
advise, -vised, -vising (give advice)
advise   advice (opinion)
advised, -ly
adviser
advisery   advisory
advisory
advocacy
advocasy   advocacy
advocate, -cated, -cating
advokate   advocate
adze
aegis
aeon
aerate, -rated, -rating
aerator
aerial, -ly
aerobatics
aerobics
aerodrome
aerodynamics
aeronautical, -ly
aeronautics
aeronortics   aeronautics
aeroplain   aeroplane
aeroplane
aerosol
aerospace
aesthetic

aetiologist	
aetiology	
afable	affable
afadavit	affadavit
afair	affair
afar	
afasia	aphasia
afect	affect (pretend)
afect	effect (result)
afectation	affectation
afected	affected
afected	effected
afection	affection
afectionate	affectionate
afective	affective
afeild	afield
affabel	affable
affability	
affable	
affableness	
affably	
affabul	affable
affadavit	affidavit
affair	
affare	affair
affecshun	affection
affect, -ed, -ing (pretend)	
affectation	
affection	
affectionate, -ly	
affective, -ly (emotion)	
affective	effective (actual)
affidavit	
affiliate, -ated, -ating	
affiliation	
affilliation	affiliation
affinity, -ties	
affirm, -ed, -ing	
affirmation	
affirmative, -ly	
affix, -ed, -ing	
afflicshun	affliction
afflict, -ed, -ing	
affliction	
afflictive, -ly	
affluence	

affluense	affluence
affluent, -ly	
afford, -ed, -ing	
affordable	
affordabul	affordable
affraid	afraid
affray	
affresh	afresh
affro	afro
affront, -ed, -ing	
afield	
afinity	affinity
afirm	affirm
afirmative	affirmative
afix	affix
aflict	afflict
afliction	affliction
afloat	
afluent	affluent
aford	afford
afraid	
afray	affray
afresh	
afro	
afront	affront
aft	
after	
afterbirth	
afterglow	
afterlife	
aftermath	
afternoon	
afters	
afterthought	
afterwards	
again	
against	
agape	
agate	
age, aged, ageing or aging	
agency, -cies	
agenda, -das	
agensy	agency
agent	
agghast	aghast
aggrandise, -dised, -dising	
aggrandisement	

aggrandiser
aggravate, -vated, -vating
aggravation
aggravator
  aggreeved   aggrieved
aggregate, -gated, -gating
aggregation
aggregative
  aggreived   aggrieved
  aggreshun   aggression
aggression
aggressive, -ly
aggressor
  aggreved   aggrieved
aggrieved
aggro
  agground   aground
aghast
agile, -ly
agility
  agis   aegis
agist, -ed, -ing
agistment
agitate, -tated, -tating
  agitater   agitator
agitation
agitative
agitator
agnostic
agnosticism
ago
agog
agonise, -nised, -nising
agonisingly
agony, -nies
  agorafobia   agoraphobia
agoraphobia
  agraculture   agriculture
agrarian
  agravate   aggravate
  agravation   aggravation
agree, agreed, agreeing
  agreeabel   agreeable
agreeable, -bly
agreeableness
  agreeabul   agreeable
agreement

  agregate   aggregate
  agression   aggression
  agressive   aggressive
  agressor   aggressor
agricultural, -ly
agriculturalist
agriculture
  agrieved   aggrieved
agronomist
agronomy
aground
ahead
  ahed   ahead
ahoy
aid (help)
aide (assistant)
ail, -ed, -ing
  ail   ale (beer)
aileron
  ailias   alias
ailment
aim, -ed, -ing
aimless, -ly
aimlessness
ain't (am not)
  aint   ain't
air, -ed, -ing
  air   hair
  airate   aerate
  airborn   airborne
airborne
air-brake
  air-break   air-brake
airbus
  air condishun   air-condition
air-condition, -ed, -ing
aircraft, -craft
  airfeild   airfield
airfield
airforce
airgun
air hostess
  aireal   aerial
  airial   aerial
airily
airlift
airline

airliner
airlock
airmail
airman, -men
   airobatics   aerobatics
   airobics   aerobics
   airodrome   aerodrome
   airodynamics   aerodynamics
   airoplane   aeroplane
   airosol   aerosol
air-pocket
airport
air-pressure
airship
airspace
airspeed
airstream
airstrip
air terminal
airtight
   airtite   airtight
airwaves
airy, airier, airiest
airy-fairy
aisle (path)
aitch
ajar
   ajis   aegis
akimbo
akin
alabaster
   alabi   alibi
   alacart   à la carte
à la carte
   alackrity   alacrity
alacritous
   alacritus   alacritous
alacrity
   Alah   Allah
alarm, -ed, -ing
alarmist
alas
alaska
   albatros   albatross
albatross, albatrosses
   albeeit   albeit
albeit

albino, -nos
albinism
album
albumen (egg white)
albumin (protein)
albuminous
   albuminus   albuminous
   alcali   alkali
   alcaline   alkaline
alchemist
alchemy
alcohol
alcoholic
alcoholism
alcove
alderman, -men
ale (beer)
   ale   ail (ill)
   alege   allege
alert, -ed, -ing
   alfa   alpha
   alfabet   alphabet
alfalfa
alfresco
alga, -gae
algebra
algebraic, -ally
alias, aliases
alibi, -bis
alien
alienate, -nated, -nating
alienation
alienator
alight, alighted, alighting
align, -ed, -ing
alignment
alike
aliment (food)
   aliment   element (part)
alimentary (food)
   alimentary   elementary
                (basic)
alimony
alive
   alkaholic   alcoholic
alkali, -lis, -lies
alkaline

alkalinity

alkeline	alkaline
alkohol	alcohol
alkoholic	alcoholic
alkoholism	alcoholism
alkove	alcove

all (every)

| all | awl (tool) |
| allabaster | alabaster |

Allah

allay, -layed, -laying

| allbatross | albatross |
| alledge | allege |

allegation

allege, -leged, -leging

allegiance

| allegianse | allegiance |

allegorical, -ly

allegory, -ries

allegro

alleluia

allergic

allergy, -gies

| allert | alert |

alleviate, -ated, -ating

alleviation

alleviator

alley, alleys

alliance

allied

| alliense | alliance |

allies

alligator

all-in

alliteration

alliterative, -ly

| allmanac | almanac |
| allmost | almost |

allocate, -cated, -cating

allocation

| alloft | aloft |
| allone | alone |

allot, -lotted, -lotting

allotment

all-out

allow, -ed, -ing

| allowabel | allowable |

allowable

| allowabul | allowable |

allowance

| allowense | allowance |

alloy

all right

| allrite | all right |

all-rounder

| allso | also |

allude, -luded, -luding (refer)

| allude | elude (avoid) |

allure, -lured, -luring

| allushun | allusion |

allusion (mention)

| allusion | illusion (trick) |

allusive, -ly (mentioned)

| allusive | elusive (avoid) |

alluvial

ally, -lies

ally, -lied, -lying

| ally | alley |

almanac

almanack

almightily

almightiness

almighty

almond

almoner

almost

alms (gifts)

| alocate | allocate |

aloe

aloft

alone

along

alongside

| alood | allude |

aloof

| alot | a lot (of) |
| alot | allot (give) |

aloud (speak)

aloud	allowed (permit)
alow	allow
alowable	allowable
alowance	allowance
aloy	alloy

alp		amaize	amaze
alpaca		amalgam	
alpacka	alpaca	amalgamate, -mated, -mating	
alpha		amalgamation	
alphabet		amalgum	amalgam
alphabetical, -ly		amass, -ed, -ing	
alphebet	alphabet	amassabel	amassable
alpine		amassable	
already		amassabul	amassable
alredy	already	amatcher	amateur
Alsatian		amatchur	amateur
also		amater	amateur
altar (church)		amateur	
altatude	altitude	amatory	
altenate	alternate	amaze, -mazed, -mazing	
alter (change)		amazement	
alterable, -bly		Amazon	
alteration		ambaguity	ambiguity
altercation		ambassader	ambassador
altercative		ambassador, -ial	
alter ego		ambel	amble
alternate, -nated, -nating		amber	
alternately		ambiance	ambience
alternation		ambiant	ambient
alternative, -ly		ambidexterity	
alternator		ambidextrous, -ly	
alterration	alteration	ambience	
although		ambiense	ambience
altimeter		ambient	
altitude		ambiguity, -ties	
alto, -tos		ambiguous, -ly	
altogether		ambiguus	ambiguous
altrooism	altruism	ambishen	ambition
altrueism	altruism	ambishus	ambitious
altruism		ambit	
altruistic, -ally		ambition	
alturnate	alternate	ambitious, -ly	
alude	allude	ambivalence	
alumina		ambivalense	ambivalence
aluminium		ambivalent	
aluminum	aluminium	amble, -bled, -bling	
alumminum	aluminium	ambul	amble
alure	allure	ambulance	
alurt	alert	ambulanse	ambulance
alushun	allusion	ambush, -ed, -ing	
alusive	allusive	ame	aim
always		ameanable	amenable

ameba	amoeba

ameliorate, -rated, -rating
amelioration
amen

amenabel	amenable

amenable, -bly

amenabul	amenable

amend, -ed, -ing
amendment
amends
amenity, -ties
America

ameter	ammeter
amethist	amethyst

amethyst

> For **amf-** words, look
> under **amph-**.

amiabel	amiable

amiability
amiable, -bly

amiabul	amiable
amicabel	amicable

amicability
amicable, -bly

amicabul	amicable

amid
amidst
amigo
amiss
amity, -ties
ammeter
ammonia
ammunition

> For other **amm-** words,
> look under **am-**.

amnesia, -iac
amnesty, -ties
amnesty, -tied, -tying
amoeba, -bae, -bas
amoebic
amok
among
amongst
amoral, -ly

amorfous	amorphous

amorous, -ly
amorphism
amorphous, -ly

amorphus	amorphous

amortise, -tised, -tising
amount, -ed, -ing

amownt	amount
ampair	ampere
ampel	ample

amperage
ampere
amphetamine
amphibian
amphibious, -ly
amphitheatre
ample, -pler, -plest (enough)

amplefy	amplify

amplification
amplifier
amplify, -fied, -fying
amplitude
amply
ampoule (bottle)

ampul	ample (enough)
ampul	ampoule (bottle)

amputate, -tated, -tating
amputation
amuck

amuk	amok
amuk	amuck

amulet

amung	among
amungst	amongst
amunition	ammunition

amuse, amused, amusing
amusement
anachronism
anachronistic

anackronism	anachronism
anackronistic	anachronistic

anaconda
anaemia
anaesthesia
anaesthetic
anaesthetisation
anaesthetise, -tised, -tising

anaesthetist

anagram

   anaky   anarchy

anal

analgesia

analgesic

   analise   analyse

   analisis   analysis

   analist   analyst

analog (electric)

   analog   analogue

                (similar)

analogous, -ly

analogue (similar)

   analogue   analog

                (electric)

analogy, -gies

analyse, -lysed, -lysing

analysis, -ses

analyst

analytical, -ly

anarchical, -ly

anarchism

anarchist

anarchy

anathema, -mas

anatomical, -ly

anatomist

anatomy, -mies

ancestor

ancestral, -ly

ancestry, -tries

anchor, -ed, -ing

anchorage

anchorman, -men

anchovy, -vies

ancient

ancillary, -aries

anecdotal

anecdote

   anemia   anaemia

   anemic   anaemic

   anesthesia   anaesthesia

   anesthetic   anaesthetic

   anesthetise   anaesthetise

   anesthetist   anaesthetist

aneurism

anew

   anewity   annuity

angel (spirit)

   angel   angle (fishing)

angelic

   angellic   angelic

anger, -ed, -ing

angina

angle, angled, angling (fishing)

   angle   angel (spirit)

angler

Anglican

Anglicanism

Anglo-Catholic

   Anglo-Sacksen   Anglo-Saxon

Anglo-Saxon

angora

   angree   angry

   angrie   angry

angrily

angry, angrier, angriest

   angsiety   anxiety

anguish, -ed, -ing

angular, -ity

   anguler   angular

   angwish   anguish

   anigma   enigma

animal

animate, -mated, -mating

animatedly

animation

   animel   animal

animosity, -ties

aniseed

   aniversary   anniversary

   anjel   angel

   anjelic   angelic

   anjina   angina

   anker   anchor

   ankerage   anchorage

   ankeridge   anchorage

   ankerije   anchorage

ankle

anklet

annals

anneal, -ed, -ing

annex, -ed, -ing (join)

annexation
annexe (building)
  annialate   annihilate
annihilate, -lated, -lating
anniversary, -ries
Anno Domini
annotate, -tated, -tating
annotation
announce, announced, announcing
announcement
annoy, annoyed, annoying
annual, -ly
annuity, -ties
annul, annulled, annulling
annulment
annulus, -li, or -luses
annunciate, -ated, -ating
annunciation

> For other **ann-** words,
> look under **an-**.

anode
  anodine   anodyne
anodyne
anoint, -ed, -ing
  anomaley   anomaly
anomaly, -lies
anon
  anonimity   anonymity
  anonimous   anonymous
anonymity
anonymous, -ly
anorak
  anorecksia   anorexia
anorexia
another
  anoynt   anoint
  anser   answer
  anserable   answerable
  anserabul   answerable
  ansestor   ancestor
  ansestral   ancestral
  ansestrul   ancestral
  ansestry   ancestry
  ansilary   ancillary
answer, -ed, -ing
  answerabel   answerable

answerable, -bly
  answerabul   answerable
antacid
antagonise, -nised, -nising
antagonism
antagonist
antagonistic, -ally
Antarctic
  antasid   antacid
  anteak   antique
anteater
antecedent
antechamber
  anteclimax   anticlimax
  antecyclone   anticyclone
antedate, -dated, -dating
  antediloovian   antediluvian
antediluvian
  anteek   antique
antelope, antelopes
  antena   antenna
antenatal
  antenatel   antenatal
  antenatul   antenatal
antenna, -tennae, -tennas
anterior
anteroom
anthem
anthill
anthology, -gies
anthracite
  anthracks   anthrax
  anthrasite   anthracite
anthrax, -thraces
anthropoid
  anthropologey anthropology
anthropologist
anthropology
antibiotic
antibody, -bodies
antic
  anticeptic   antiseptic
  antichamber   antechamber
Antichrist
  anticiclone   anticyclone
anticipate, -pated, -pating
anticipation

anticipatory	
anticlimacks	anticlimax
anticlimactic	
anticlimax	
anticlockwise	
anticyclone	
anticyclonic	
antidate	antedate
antidepressant	
antidotal	
antidote	
antifon	antiphon
antifreeze	
antigen	
antihisstamine	antihistamine
antihistamine	
antikwarian	antiquarian
antikwated	antiquated
antikwitey	antiquity
antilope	antelope
antimony	
antinatal	antenatal
antinatul	antenatal
antinewklear	antinuclear
antinuclear	
antipathy, -pathies	
antiperspirant	
antiphon	
antipodes	
antipodies	antipodes
antiquarian	
antiquary, -quaries	
antiquated	
antique	
antiquity, -quities	
antiroom	anteroom
anti-Semitic	
anti-Semitism	
antiseptic, -ally	
antisiclone	anticyclone
antisipation	anticipation
antisocial, -ly	
antithesis, -theses	
antithisis	antithesis
antitoksic	antitoxic
antitoksin	antitoxin
antler	

antonim	antonym
antonym	
anus	
anuther	another
anvil	
anvul	anvil
anxiety, -ties	
anxious, -ly	
any	
anybody	
anyhow	
anyone	
anything	
anyway	
anywear	anywhere
anywere	anywhere
anywhere	
Anzac	
aorta, -tas, -tae	
apace	
apart	
apartheid	
apartied	apartheid
apartite	apartheid
apartment	
apase	apace
apathetic, -ally	
apathy	
ape, aped, aping	
apeace	apiece
apease	apiece
apeice	apiece
apeks	apex
apercher	aperture
apergee	apogee
apergey	apogee
aperitif	
aperture	
apex, apexes, apices	
aphasia	
aphid	
aphorism	
aphrodisiac	
apiary, apiaries	
apiece	
apissul	epistle
apistle	epistle

aplom	aplomb
aplomb	
aply	apply
apocalipse	apocalypse
apocalypse	
apocalyptic	
apocrifal	apocryphal
apocryphal, -ly	
apogee	
apologetic, -ally	
apologey	apology
apologise, -gised, -gising	
apologist	
apology, -gies	
apoplectic	
apoplexy	
aposle	apostle
apostasy, -sies	
apostel	apostle
apostle	
apostolate	
apostolic	
apostrofy	apostrophe
apostrophe	
aposul	apostle
apothecary, -ries	
apoynt	appoint

> For other **ap-** words,
> look under **app-**.

appal, -palled, -palling	
apparatus, -tus, -tuses	
apparel	
apparent, -ly	
apparishun	apparition
apparition	
appart	apart
appeal, -ed, -ing	
appealing, -ly	
appear, -ed, -ing	
appearance	
appearense	appearance
appease, -peased, -peasing	
appeasement	
appelant	appellant
appellant	
appellate	

appellation	
append, -ed, -ing	
appendacitis	appendicitis
appendage	
appendectomy, -mies	
appendicitis	
appendige	appendage
appendiks	appendix
apperatus	apparatus
appertain, -ed, -ing	
apperture	aperture
appetiser	
appetite	
applaud, -ed, -ing	
applause	
applawd	applaud
applaws	applause
apple	
appliance	
applianse	appliance
applicability	
applicable, -bly	
applicant	
application	
applie	apply
applied	
applique	
apply, -plied, -plying	
appoint, -ed, -ing	
appointment	
apporshun	apportion
apportion, -ed, -ing	
apportionment	
apposishun	apposition
apposite, -ly	
apposition	
appraisal	
appraise, -praised, -praising	
appraysal	appraisal
apprayse	appraise
appreciabel	appreciable
appreciable, -bly	
appreciabul	appreciable
appreciate, -ated, -ating	
appreciation	
appreciative, -ly	
apprehend, -ed, -ing	

apprehenshun	apprehension	arable	
apprehensibel	apprehensible	arabul	arable
apprehensible		araign	arraign
apprehensibul	apprehensible	arain	arraign
apprehension		arange	arrange
apprehensive, -ly		aray	array
apprentice		arber	arbour
apprenticeship		arbiter	
apprentise	apprentice	arbitrary	
appricot	apricot	arbitrate, -trated, -trating	
apprise, -prised, -prising		arbitration	
approach, -ed, -ing		arbor (axis)	
approachabel	approachable	abor	arbour (shade)
approachable		arboreal	
approbation		arboricultural	
approch	approach	arboriculture	
approchabul	approachable	arbour (shade)	
approove	approve	arbour	arbor (axis)
appropos	apropos	arc, arced, arcing (curve)	
appropriate, -ated, -ating		arc	ark (boat)
appropriation		arcade	
approval		arcane	
approve, -proved, -proving		arch	
approvel	approval	archaeological, -ly	
approximate, -mated, -mating		archaeologist	
approximately		archaeology	
approximation		archaic	
apricot		archaism	
April		archangel	
apron		archary	archery
apropos		archbishop	
apt, -ly		archer	
aptitude		archerfish	
aptley	aptly	archery	
aqualung		archetypal	
aquamarine		archetype	
aquaplane		archipelago, -gos, -goes	
aquarium		architect	
Aquarius		architectural, -ly	
aquatic		architecture	
aqueduct		architrave	
aqueous		archival	
aquiline		archives	
arabel	arable	archivist	
arabesk	arabesque	arcipelago	archipelago
arabesque		arcipeligo	archipelago
Arabic numerals		arcitect	architect

arcitectural	architectural	arival	arrival
arcitecture	architecture	arive	arrive
arcives	archives	ark (boat)	
arc light		ark	arc (curve)
arctic			
Arctic Circle			
ardent, -ly			

For other **ark-** words, look under **arc-**.

arder	ardour	arm	
ardour		armacher	armature
arduous, -ly		armachur	armature
arduus	arduous	armada	
are		armadillo, -los	
area		Armageddon	
arears	arrears	armament	
arena		armature	
aren't		armchair	
arent	aren't	armed	
arest	arrest	armer	armour
argent		armey	army
argew	argue	armistice	
argon		armistise	armistice
arguabel	arguable	armoner	almoner
arguable, -bly		armour	
arguabul	arguable	armoured	
argue, -gued, -guing		armourer	
arguement	argument	armoury, -ries	
argument		armpit	
argumentation		arms (weapons)	
argumentative, -ly		arms	alms (gifts)
argus		army, -mies	
arguw	argue	arogance	arrogance
argy-bargy, -bargies		aroganse	arrogance
aria (melody)		arogant	arrogant
aria	area (piece)	aroma	
arial	aerial	aromatic	
arid, -ly		arora	aurora
aridity		arose	
Aries		around	
arina	arena	arousal	
arise, arose, arisen, arising		arouse, aroused, arousing	
aristocracy, -cies		arow	arrow
aristocrasy	aristocracy	arownd	around
aristocrat		arowroot	arrowroot
aristocratic		arowse	arouse
arithmetic		arpeggio	
arithmetical, -ly		arpejio	arpeggio
arithmetician		arraign, -ed, -ing	

arraignment
arrange, -ranged, -ranging
arrangement
arrant, -ly
arras
array, -ed, -ing
arrears
arrest, -ed, -ing
arrival
arrive, -rived, -riving
arrogance
   arroganse   arrogance
arrogant, -ly
arrogate, -gated, -gating
   arrouse   arouse
arrow
arrowroot
arsenal
arsenic
arsenical
   arsnic   arsenic
arson
art
   artachoke   artichoke
artefact
arterial
artery, -teries
artesian bore
artful, -ly
arthritic
arthritis
   articel   article
artichoke
article, -cled, -cling
   articul   article
articulate, -lated, -lating
articulation
artifact
artifice
artificer
artificial, -ly
artificiality
   artifise   artifice
   artifishial   artificial
artillery
artisan
artist (painter)

artiste (actor)
artistic
artistry
   artizan   artisan
artless, -ly
arvo (afternoon)
   arwry   awry
asbestos
ascend, -ed, -ing
ascendancy
ascendant
   ascenshun   ascension
ascension
ascent (upward)
   ascent   assent (agree)
ascertain, -ed, -ing
   ascertainabel   ascertainable
ascertainable, -bly
   ascertainabul   ascertainable
ascertainment
ascetic, -ally
asceticism
ascribe, ascribed, ascribing
   ase   ace
   asend   ascend
   asendancy   ascendancy
   asendansy   ascendancy
   asendant   ascendant
   asenshun   ascension
   asent   ascent (upwards)
   asent   assent (agree)
aseptic, -ally
   asershun   assertion
   asertain   ascertain
   asertane   ascertain
   asertayne   ascertain
   asetic   ascetic
   aseticism   asceticism
asexual, -ly
   asfalt   asphalt
   asfelt   asphalt
   asfixia   asphyxia
   asfixiate   asphyxiate
ash
ashamed, -ly
   ashaymed   ashamed

ashfelt	asphalt	assault	
ashore (beach)		assaulter	
ashore	assure (certain)	assay, -ed, -ing (analyse)	
aside		assay	essay (try)
asidity	acidity	assayer	
asign	assign	assemblage	
asilum	asylum	assemble, -bled, -bling	
asimetrical	asymmetrical	assembly, assemblies	
asimetry	asymmetry	assembul	assemble
asine	assign	assend	ascend
asinement	assignment	assendancy	ascendancy
asinine, -ly		assendansy	ascendancy
asininity		assendant	ascendant
asitic	ascetic	assenshun	ascension
ask, -ed, -ing		assension	ascension
askance		assent (agree)	
askanse	askance	assent	ascent
askew			(upward)
askue	askew	assention	ascension
asleep		assershun	assertion
asma	asthma	assert, -ed, -ing	
asmatic	asthmatic	assertion	
asp		assertive, -ly	
asparagus		assess, -ed, -ing	
aspect		assessabel	assessable
aspen		assessable	
aspershun	aspersion	assessabul	assessable
aspersion		assessment	
asphalt		assessor	
asphyxia		asset, assets	
asphyxiate, -ated, -ating		assiduous, -ly	
asphyxiation		assign, -ed, -ing	
aspic		assignable, -bly	
aspirant		assignation	
aspirate, -rated, -rating		assignee	
aspiration		assignment	
aspirator		assine	assign
aspirayte	aspirate	assinment	assignment
aspire, aspired, aspiring		assist, -ed, -ing	
aspirin		assistance	
asprin	aspirin	assistant	
ass, asses		associate, -ated, -ating	
assail, -ed, -ing		associashun	association
assailant		association	
assassin		associayte	associate
assassinate, -nated, -nating		assonance	
assassination		assonanse	assonance

assonant
assort, -ed, -ing
assortment
   assoshiate   associate
assuage, -suaged, -suaging
assume, -sumed, -suming
assumption
   assumshun   assumption
assurance
   assuranse   assurance
assure, -sured, -suring (certain)
   assure   ashore (beach)
aster
asterisk
astern
asteroid
asthma
asthmatic
astigmatism
astir
astonish, -ed, -ing
astonishment
astound, -ed, -ing
   astownd   astound
astral
astray
astride
astringency
astringent, -ly
astrologer
astrological, -ly
astrology
   astronaught   astronaut
astronaut
astronautics
   astronort   astronaut
   astrul   astral
   astur   astir
   asturn   astern
astute, -ly
astuteness
asunder
asylum
   asymetry   asymmetry
asymmetric
asymmetrical, -ly
asymmetry

ate (food)
   ate   eight (number)
   ateen   eighteen
   atey   eighty
atheism
atheist
atheistic
   athiesm   atheism
   athiest   atheist
   athiestic   atheistic
   athleet   athlete
athlete
athletic
atlas
   atmosfear   atmosphere
   atmosfere   atmosphere
   atmosferic   atmospheric
atmosphere
atmospheric
   atol   atoll
atoll
atom
atomic
atomiser
atone, atoned, atoning
atonement
atrocious, -ly
atrocity, -ties
atrophy, -phied, -phying
   atroshus   atrocious
attach, -ed, -ing
attaché
attachment
attack, -ed, -ing
attain, -ed, -ing
attainable
attainment
attempt, -ed, -ing
attend, -ed, -ing
attendance
attendant
attention
attentive, -ly
attenuate, -ated, -ating
attest, -ed, -ing
attic
attire, -tired, -tiring

attitude

attorney

attract, -ed, -ing

attraction

attractive, -ly

attribute, -uted, -uting

attrishun — attrition

attrition

attune, -tuned, -tuning

atune — attune

aturney — attorney

For other **at**- words,
look under **att**-.

---

atypical, -ly

aubergine

auburn

aucshun — auction

auction, -ed, -ing

auctioneer

audacious, -ly

audacity

audasity — audacity

audeo — audio

audibel — audible

audibility

audible

audibly

audibul — audible

audience

audiense — audience

audio

audiometer

audiometric

audiometry

audiovisual

audishun — audition

audit, -ed, -ing

audition

auditor

auditorium, -toriums, -toria

auditory

auditree — auditory

auditry — auditory

auger (tool)

auger — augur (foretell)

aught (any part)

aught — ought (should)

augment, -ed, -ing

augmentation

augur (foretell)

augur — auger (tool)

augural

august (majestic)

August

aukward — awkward

aunt

auntie

aunt sally

aunty

aura

aural, -ly (hearing)

aural — oral (spoken)

aureole

auricle

auricular

auriferous

auriole — aureole

aurora

auspice, auspices

auspicious, -ly

auspise — auspice

Aussie

austeer — austere

austere, -ly

austerity, -ties

austral

Australasia

Australia

Australian

Australiana

Australien — Australian

australight — australite

australite

Australorp

autamatic — automatic

autamobile — automobile

authentic

authenticate, -cated, -cating

authentication

authenticity

authentisity — authenticity

author

authoress

authorisation
authorise, -rised, -rising
authoritarian
authoritative, -ly
authority, -ties
autism
auto
autobiographical, -ly
autobiography, -phies
autocracy
   autocrasy   autocracy
autocrat
autocratic
autocue
   autograf   autograph
autograph
automatic
automation
automative
automobile
automotive
   autonomee   autonomy
autonomous, -ly
   autonomus   autonomous
autonomy
autopilot
autopsy, -sies
   autum   autumn
autumn
autumnal, -ly
auxiliary, -ries
avail, -ed, -ing
   availabel   available
availability
available
   availabul   available
   avalable   available
   avalanch   avalanche
avalanche
   avale   avail
   avaliable   available
avant-garde
   avarey   aviary
avarice
avaricious, -ly
   avaris   avarice
   avarishus   avaricious

   avenew   avenue
avenge, avenged, avenging
avenger
avenue
aver, averred, averring
average, -raged, -raging
   avericious   avaricious
   averidge   average
   averige   average
   averishus   avaricious
   averiss   avarice
averse, -ly
   avershun   aversion
aversion
avert, -ed, -ing
   avery   aviary
avgas
aviary, aviaries
   aviater   aviator
aviation
aviator
avid, -ly
   avinue   avenue
   avlanch   avalanche
avocado, avocados
avoid, -ed, -ing (evade)
   avoid   ovoid (egg)
avoidable, -ably
avow, -ed, -ing
avowal
   avoyd   avoid
   avridge   average
   avrije   average
   avud   avid
   avur   aver
   avurse   averse
   avurshun   aversion
   avursion   aversion
   avurt   avert
await, -ed, -ing
awake, awoke, awaking
awaken, -ed, -ing
award, -ed, -ing
aware
awareness
away
   awayte   await

awb	orb
awe, awed, awing (fear)	
awe	oar (boat)
awear	aware
awesome, -ly	
awful, -ly	
awgy	orgy
awksilary	auxiliary
awkward, -ly	
awkwud	awkward
awl (tool)	
awl	all (every)
awning	
awoke	
awry	
axe, axes	
axe, axed, axing	
axel	axle
axial, -ly	
axident	accident
axidental	accidental
axiom	
axiomatic	
axis, axes	
axle	
axsede	accede
axseed	accede
axsel	axle
axsellerate	accelerate
axsent	accent
axsentuate	accentuate
axsept	accept
axseptable	acceptable
axseptabul	acceptable
axseptance	acceptance
axsesary	accessary
axsesory	accessory
axsess	access
axsessable	accessible
axsessabul	accessible
axsessible	accessible
axsessibul	accessible
ay, ayes (yes)	
ayatollah	
aye (ever)	
aysure	azure
azalea	

azalia	azalea
azure	
azury	

Bb

babbel	babble (chatter)
babble, -led, -ling (chatter)	
babboon	baboon
babbul	babble (chatter)
babe	
babel (confusion)	
babel	babble (chatter)
babey	baby
babie	baby
baboon	
babul	babble (chatter)
baby, babies	
baby-sitter	
baccarat	
bach	batch
bacheler	bachelor
bachelor	
bacillus, bacilli	
back, -ed, -ing	
backbencher	
backblocks	
backbone	
back-burn	
backer	
backfire, -fired, -firing	
backgammon	
background	
backhand	
backing	
backlash	
back-pedal, -alled, -alling	
backroom	
back-seat driver	
backstage	

backstitch, -ed, -ing	
backstop, -stopped, -stopping	
backstroke, -stroked, -stroking	
back-to-back	
backwards	
backwash	
backyard	
bacon	
bacteria	
bad, worse, worst (not good)	
bade (ask)	
badge	
badger	
badly	
badminton	
baffel	baffle
baffle, -fled, -fling	
bag, bagged, bagging	
bagatelle	
baggage	
baggidge	baggage
baggy, baggier, baggiest	
bagman, -men	
bagpipes	
baige	beige
bail (court)	
bail	bale (bundle)
bailif	bailiff
bailiff	
bairn	
bait (fishing)	
bait	bate (hold)
baize, baized, baizing	
baje	badge
bake, baked, baking	
bakelite	
baker	
bakery	
bakshee	
balaclava	
balad	ballad
balalaika	
balance, -anced, -ancing	
balanse	balance
balast	ballast
balay	ballet
balcony, -conies	

bald (hairless)	
bald	bawled (cried)
balderdash	
balding	
baldness	
bale, baled, baling (bundle)	
bale	bail (court)
baleful, -ly	
balefull	baleful
balerina	ballerina
balero	bolero
balet	ballet
baliff	bailiff
ball (round)	
ball	bawl (cry)
ballad	
ballast	
ball-bearing	
ballerina	
ballet	
ballistics	
balloon	
balloonist	
ballot, balloted, balloting	
ballpoint	
ballsa	balsa
ballsam	balsam
ballyhoo	
balm	
balmy, balmier, balmiest (good)	
balmy	barmy (stupid)
balonee	baloney
baloney	
baloon	balloon
balot	ballot
balsa	
balsam	
balustrade	
balyhoo	ballyhoo
bamboo	
bamboozle, -zled, -zling	
ban, banned, banning	
banal, -ly	
banana	
banana republic	
band, banded, banding (strip)	
band (group)	

band	banned (forbidden)
bandage, -daged, -daging	
bandanna	
bandey	bandy
bandicoot	
bandige	bandage
bandit	
bandoleer	bandolier
bandolier	
bandsaw	
bandwagon	
bandy, -died, -dying	
bandy-legged	
baner	banner
bangalow	
bangel	bangle
banger	
bangle	
bang-on	
banish, -ed, -ing	
banishment	
banister	
banjo, banjos	
bank, -ed, -ing	
bankbook	
banker	
banknote	
bankrupcy	bankruptcy
bankrupsy	bankruptcy
bankrupt	
bankruptcy	
banksia	
bankwet	banquet
banned (forbidden)	
banned	band (strip)
banner	
banns (notices)	
banquet, -queted, -queting	
bans (forbids)	
bans	banns (notices)
bantam	
bantamweight	
banter, -ed, -ing	
bantum	bantam
banyan	
baonet	bayonet

bap

baptise, -tised, -tising

baptism

baptismal

Baptist

bar, barred, barring

barack	barrack
baracouta	barracouta
barage	barrage

barb

barbarian

barbaric

barbarism

barbarous, -ly

barbarus	barbarous

barbecue, -cued, -cuing

barbed wire

barbell

barbeque, -qued, -quing

barber

barbiturate

bard (poet)

bard	barred (stopped)

bare, bared, baring (uncover)

bare, barer, barest

bare	bear (animal)

bareback

barefaced

barefoot

bareheaded

barel	barrel

barely

baren	baron (noble)
baren	barren (sterile)
bareskin	bearskin

bargain, -ed, -ing

bargainer

bargan	bargain

barge, barged, barging

bargee

bargen	bargain
baricade	barricade
barier	barrier

baring (uncovering)

baring	barring (stop)
baring	bearing (hold)

barister	barrister

baritone

barium

bark, -ed, -ing

barley

barlie	barley
barm	balm
barmade	barmaid

barmaid

barman, -men

barmy, barmier, barmiest (stupid)

barmy	balmy (good)

barn

barn	bairn
barnacel	barnacle

barnacle

barnacled

barnacul	barnacle

barney

barnicul	barnacle

barnstorm

barometer

barometric

baron (noble)

baron	barren (sterile)

baronet

baronial

baroque

barow	barrow

barrack, -ed, -ing

barracker

barracouta

barracuda

barrage, -raged, -raging

barramundi

barrel, -relled, -relling

barren (sterile)

barren	baron (noble)

barrenness

barricade, -caded, -cading

barrier

barring (stop)

barring	baring (uncovering)

barrister

barrow

barrul	barrel

barter, -ed, -ing
  barul   barrel
basal, -ly
basalt
base, based, basing (support)
base, baser, basest
  base   bass (low tone)
baseball
basement
  baset   basset
bash, -ed, -ing
bashful, -ly
basic
basilica
  basillus   bacillus
basin
  basinette   bassinette
basis, bases
  basit   basset
bask, -ed, -ing (enjoy warmth)
  bask   basque (garb)
basketball
  baskit   basket
  basoon   bassoon
basque (garb)
bas-relief
bass (low tone)
  bass   base (support)
bass clef
basset
bassinette
bassoon
bastard
  bastardisashun   bastardisation
bastardisation
bastardry
baste, basted, basting
  basterd   bastard
bastion
bat, batted, batting
batch
bate, bated, bating (hold breath)
  bate   bait (fishing)
  baten   baton (stick)
  baten   batten (timber)
  bater   batter
  baterey   battery

bath
bathe, bathed, bathing
bathers
bathroom
batik
  batle   battle
  batler   battler
batman, -men
baton (stick)
  baton   batten (timber)
batsman, -men
batt (insulating)
  batt   bat (cricket)
battalion
  battaliun   battalion
  battel   battle
batten (timber)
batter
battering ram
battery, -ries
battle, battled, battling
battleaxe
battledress
battler
battleship
batty, battier, battiest
  batul   battle
  baty   batty
  baubel   bauble
bauble
  baubul   bauble
baulk, -ed, -ing
bauxite
  bawble   bauble
  bawdie   bawdy
bawdiness
bawdy, -dier, -diest
bawl, -ed, -ing (cry)
  bawl   ball (round)
  bawlsa   balsa
bay
  bayliff   bailiff
  baynet   bayonet
bayonet
  baythe   bathe
bazaar (market)
  bazaar   bizarre (odd)

bazar   bazaar
bazooka
be, been, being (exist)
  be   bee (insect)
beach, -ches (shore)
  beach   beech (tree)
beachcomber
  beachcomer   beachcomber
beacon
bead, -ed, -ing
beady, beadier, beadiest
  beaf   beef
  beafeater   beefeater
  beafy   beefy
  beagel   beagle
beagle
beak
beaker
beam, -ed, -ing
bean (vegetable)
  bean   been (be)
beanie
beano
bear (animal)
bear, borne, bearing (carry)
  bear   bare (uncover)
  bearback   bareback
beard
bearer
  bearfaced   barefaced
  bearfoot   barefoot
  bearheaded   bareheaded
bearing (hold)
  bearing   baring
                   (uncovering)
bearskin
beast
beastliness
beastly, beastlier, beastliest
beat, beaten, beating (strike)
  beat   beet (food)
  beatel   beetle
beater
beatific
beatify, -fied, -fying
beatitude
  beatle   beetle

beatnik
  beatroot   beetroot
  beatul   beetle
beau, beaus, beaux (suitor)
beaut
beauteous, -ly
beautician
  beautie   beauty
beautiful, -ly
beautify, -fied, -fying
  beautishun   beautician
beauty, beauties
beaver
becalmed
became
  becarmed   becalmed
because
beck
beckon, -ed, -ing
become, became, becoming
  becon   beacon
  becos   because
bed, bedded, bedding
bedeck, -ed, -ing
  bedevel   bedevil
bedevil, -illed, -illing
  bedevul   bedevil
bedlam
bedouin
  bedowin   bedouin
bedpan
bedraggled
  bedraguled   bedraggled
bedridden
  bedriden   bedridden
bedrock
bedside
bed-sitting room
bedspread
  bedspred   bedspread
bedstead
  bedsted   bedstead
bed-wetting
bee (insect)
  bee   be (exist)
beech (tree)
  beech   beach (shore)

beechcomber	beachcomber
beechcomer	beachcomber
beecon	beacon
beed	bead
beef	
beefeater	
beefy, beefier, beefiest	
beegel	beagle
beegle	beagle
beehive	
beeline	
beem	beam
been (be)	
been	bean (food)
beenie	beanie
beep	
beer (ale)	
beer	bier (coffin)
beerd	beard
beest	beast
beeswaks	beeswax
beeswax	
beet (food)	
beet	beat (strike)
beetel	beetle
beetle	
beetle off	
beetroot	
beetul	beetle
beever	beaver
befall, -fell, -fallen, -falling	
befit, -fitted, -fitting	
befor	before
before	
beforehand	
befuddle, -dled, -dling	
befudul	befuddle
beg, begged, begging	
began	
begar	beggar
beger	beggar
beggar	
beggarly	
begger	beggar
begile	beguile
begin, began, begun, beginning	
beginner	

begone	
begonia	
begrudge, -grudged, -grudging	
begruge	begrudge
beguile, -guiled, -guiling	
begun	
behalf	
beharf	behalf
behave, -haved, -having	
behavior	behaviour
behaviour	
behavioural	
behead, -ed, -ing	
behed	behead
beheld	
behest	
behind	
behive	beehive
beige	
beije	beige
being	
bekos	because
bekweath	bequeath
bekwest	bequest
bel	bell (ring)
bel	belle (girl)
belabor	belabour
belabour, -ed, -ing	
belated, -ly	
belay, -layed, -laying	
belbird	bellbird
belch, -ed, -ing	
beleaf	belief
beleavabul	believable
beleave	believe
beleif	belief
beleive	believe
belfrey	belfry
belfry, -fries	
Belgian	
beli	belie
belicose	bellicose
belie, -lied, -lying	
belief	
believable, -bly	
believe, -lieved, -lieving	
beligerence	belligerence

beligerency belligerency
beligerense belligerence
beligerent belligerent
beline beeline
belittel belittle
belittle, -tled, -tling
bell (ring)
bellbird
belle (girl)
bellicose, -ly
belligerence
belligerency
belligerent, -ly
bellow, -ed, -ing (roar)
   bellow below (under)
bellows
belly, bellies
belly, bellied, bellying
bellyache
belong, -ed, -ing
belongings
   belose bellows
beloved
   belovid beloved
below (under)
   below bellow (roar)
   belows bellows
belt, -ed, -ing
belt-up, belted-up, belting-up
   bely belly
bemoan, -ed, -ing
bemused
bench, benches
benchmark
bend, bent, bending
bender
beneath
benediction
benefactor
benefactress
benefice
beneficence
beneficent, -ly
beneficial, -ly
beneficiary, -aries
   benefis benefice
   benefisense beneficence

   benefisent beneficent
   benefishal beneficial
   benefisharey beneficiary
benefit, -fited, -fiting
benevolence
   benevolense benevolence
benevolent, -ly
benign, -ly
   benine benign
bent
   benum benumb
benumb
benzene (coal tar)
benzine (petroleum)
bequeath
   bequeeth bequeath
bequest
berate, -rated, -rating
   beray beret
bereave, -reaved, -reaving
   bereeve bereave
bereft
beret
   bereve bereave
   berglar burglar
   beri berry (fruit)
   beri bury (in earth)
   berial burial
beri-beri
   berie berry (fruit)
berley (bait)
   berley burly (large)
   berli berley (bait)
   berli burly (large)
berry, berries (fruit)
   berry bury (in earth)
berserk
berth (ship)
   berth birth (born)
   bery berry (fruit)
   bery bury (in earth)
   beseach beseech
beseech, -seeched, -seeching
   beseige besiege
beset, -set, -setting
beside
besides

besiege, -sieged, -sieging
besotted
best
bestial, -ly
bestiality
bestir, -stirred, -stirring
bestow, -ed, -ing
bestowal
bet, bet, betting
beta
beta particle
betel nut

| betel | beetle |
| betle | beetle |

betoken, -ed, -ing
betray, -ed, -ing
betrayal
betrayer
betrothal
better
betterment

| betul | beetle |

between
betwixt
bevel, -elled, -elling
beverage

beveridge	beverage
bevarije	beverage
bevie	bevy

bevy, bevies
bewail
beware

bewayl	bewail
bewear	beware
bewhere	beware
bewhich	bewitch

bewilder, -ed, -ing
bewilderment
bewitch

| bewty | beauty |

beyond

| bezerk | berserk |

biannual, -ly (twice a year)

| biannual | biennial (every two years) |

bias, biased, biasing
bias binding

biass	bias
biassed	biased
Bibel	Bible

Bible

| bibliografy | bibliography |

bibliographer
bibliography, -phies

| Bibul | Bible |
| bicame | became |

bicameral
bicarbonate

| bicarmed | becalmed |

bicentenary
bicentennial
biceps

| bich | bitch |
| bicicle | bicycle |

bicker, -ed, -ing
bicycle
bid, bade, bidding

| biday | bidet |

biddy, -dies
bide, bided, biding
bidet

| bidevil | bedevil |

biennial, -ly (every two years)

| biennial | biannual (twice a year) |

bier (coffin)

| bier | beer (ale) |
| bifell | befell |

bifocal
bifurcate, -cated, -cating
big, bigger, biggest
bigamist
bigamy

| bigan | began |
| biggot | bigot |

bight (bay)

bight	bite (cut)
bight	byte (computer)
bigile	beguile
bigin	begin
biginer	beginner
bigining	beginning
bigon	begone

bigone	bygone	billycan	
bigot		billygoat	
bigoted, -ly		bilong	belong
bigotry		bilow	below (under)
bigrudge	begrudge	bilow	billow (wave)
bigun	begun	bilyards	billiards
		bilyon	billion
		bilyus	billious
		bimoan	bemoan
bikameral	bicameral	bimuse	bemuse
bike		bin, binned, binning	
bikini		bin	been
bikweath	bequeath	binary	
bikwest	bequest	bind, bound, binding	
bil	bill	binder	
bilaber	belabour	bineath	beneath
bilated	belated	binevolent	benevolent
bilateral, -ly		binge	
bilaw	by-law	bingo	
bilay	belay	binine	benign
bild	build	binoculars	
bilding	building	binomial, -ly	
bile		binumb	benumb
bileavabul	believable	biochemist	
bileave	believe	biochemistry	
bileif	belief	biodegradable	
bilet	billet	biografer	biographer
bilge		biografical	biographical
biliards	billiards	biografy	biography
bilief	belief	biographer	
bilingual, -ly		biographical, -ly	
bilingwal	bilingual	biography, -phies	
bilion	billion	biokemist	biochemist
bilious, -ly		biologey	biology
biliousness		biological, -ly	
bilittul	belittle	biologist	
bilius	bilious	biology	
bilk, -ed, -ing		biopsey	biopsy
bill, -ed, -ing		biopsy	
billabong		biorhythm	
billet, -eted, -eting		bipartisan	
billiards		bipartite	
Billingsgate		bipartizen	bipartisan
billion		bipass	by-pass
billit	billet	biped	
billow (wave)		biplane	
billy, billies		biproduct	by-product

For **bih-** words, look under **beh-**.

birate	berate	bisy	busy
birch		bit	
bird		bitch, -ches	
birdie		bitchiness	
bird's-eye		bitchumen	bitumen
bireave	bereave	bitchy	
bireft	bereft	bite, bitten, bit, biting (cut)	
biro		bite	bight (bay)
birth (born)		bite	byte
birth	berth (ship)		(computer)
birthday		biter	bitter
birthrate		bitoken	betoken
biscet	biscuit	bitray	betray
biscuit		bitrayal	betrayal
biscut	biscuit	bitrothal	betrothal
bisecshun	bisection	bitser	
bisect, -ed, -ing		bitten (bite)	
bisection		bitten	bittern (bird)
bisector		bitter, -ly	
biseech	beseech	bittern (bird)	
biseege	besiege	bitterness	
biseige	besiege	bitters	
biseksual	bisexual	bitumen	
bisen	bison	bituminous	
bisentenary	bicentenary	bitween	between
bisentenyal	bicentennial	bitwixt	betwixt
biseps	biceps	biuld	build
biset	beset	bivalve	
bisexual, -ly		bivouac, -acked, -acking	
bisexuality		bivuac	bivouac
bishop		biwail	bewail
bishopric		biway	byway
bisicle	bicycle	biwear	beware
biside	beside	biwich	bewitch
bisier	busier	biwilder	bewilder
bisily	busily	biwitch	bewitch
biskit	biscuit	biword	byword
bismuth		bizar	bazaar (fair)
bisness	business	bizar	bizarre (odd)
bison, -son		bizarre, -ly (odd)	
bisotted	besotted	bizier	busier
bistander	bystander	bizily	busily
bistir	bestir	bizmuth	bismuth
bistow	bestow	bizness	business
bistowal	bestowal	bizy	busy
bistro		blab, blabbed, blabbing	
bisun	bison	blabber, blabbered, blabbering	

blabbermouth
  blaber — blabber
black
blackberry, -ries
blackbirding
blackboard
  blackbord — blackboard
blackbutt
blackcurrant
  blackcurrent — blackcurrant
blacken, -ed, -ing
blackfellow
blackguard
blackhead
blackjack
blackleg
blackmail
  blackmale — blackmail
blackout
blackshirt
blacksmith
blacktracker
bladder
blade
  blader — bladder
  blaggard — blackguard
  blaid — blade
  blaim — blame
  blaimless — blameless
  blair — blare
  blaise — blaze
  blaiser — blazer
blame, blamed, blaming
blameless, -ly
blameworthy
  blamonge — blancmange
blanch, -ed, -ing
blancmange
bland, -ly
blandish
blandishment
blank
blanket
blare, blared, blaring
blarney, -neyed, -neying
  blarny — blarney
  blasay — blasé

blasé
  blasfeem — blaspheme
  blasfemus — blasphemous
  blasfemy — blasphemy
blaspheme, -phemed, -pheming
blasphemous, -ly
blasphemy, -mies
blast, -ed, -ing
blast-off
blatancy
blatant, -ly
blather
blaze, blazed, blazing
blazer
blazon
bleach, -ed, -ing
bleachers
  blead — bleed
bleak, -ly
bleakness
blear, -ed, -ing
blearily
bleary, blearier, blearist
bleat, -ed, -ing
  bleech — bleach
bleed, bled, bleeding
bleeder
  bleek — bleak
bleep
  bleer — blear
  bleet — bleat
blemish, -ed, -ing
blench, -ed, -ing
blend, -ed, -ing
blender
  blert — blurt
bless, blessed, blessing
blew (to blow)
  blew — blue (colour)

> For other **blew-** words, look
> under **blue-**.

blight, -ed, -ing
blighter
Blighty
blimey
blimp

blind, -ed, -ing

blind, -ly

blindfold

blindman's buff

blindness

blink, -ed, -ing

blinker

blip

bliss

blissful, -ly

blister, -ed, -ing

blistery

blite	blight
bliter	blighter

blithe, -ly

blithering

blits	blitz

blitz, -ed, -ing

blizard	blizzard

blizzard

blo	blow

bloat, -ed, -ing

bloater

blob

bloc (group)

block, -ed, -ing (stop)

blockade, -kaded, -kading

blockage

blockaid	blockade

blockbuster

blockidge	blockage
blok	bloke

bloke

blond, blonde

blone	blown

blood

bloodbath

bloodcurdling

blooded

bloodless

blood-poisoning

blood pressure

bloodshed

bloodshot

bloodstream

bloodthirsty

bloody, bloodied, bloodying

bloody, bloodier, bloodiest

bloom, -ed, -ing

bloomers

blosom	blossom

blossom

blot, blotted, blotting

blot	bloat

blotch, -ed, -ing

blotchy

bloting	blotting

blouse

blow, blew, blown, blowing

blower

blowfly

blowhole

blowlamp

blow-out

blowpipe

blowse	blouse

blow-up

blu	blue (colour)
blu	blew (to blow)

blubber

blubbery

bluber	blubber

bludge, bludged, bludging

bludger

bludgeon

For all other **blud-** words, look
under **blood-**.

blue (colour)

blue	blew (to blow)

blue, bluer, bluest

bluebird

bluebottle

blue-collar

blueprint

blue-ribbon

blues

blue-tongue

bluey

bluf	bluff

bluff, -ed, -ing

bluish

blummers	bloomers

blunder, -ed, -ing

blunt, -ed, -ing
blur, blurred, blurring
blurb
blurt, -ed, -ing
blush, -ed, -ing
bluster, -ed, -ing
blustery

  blustry   blustery

boa
boa constrictor
boar (pig)

  boar   boor (rude)
  boar   bore (drill)

board, -ed, -ing
board (wood)

  board   bored (drill)

boarder (lodger)

  boarder   border (edge)

boast, -ed, -ing
boastful, -ly
boat
boater
boat-house
boating
boat people
boat-race
boatswain
bob, bobbed, bobbing

  bobbel   bobble
  bobbie   bobby

bobbin
bobble

  bobbul   bobble

bobby, -bies
bobby-dazzler
bobby pin, bobby pins
bobcat

  bobie   bobby
  bobin   bobbin
  boble   bobble
  bobslay   bobsleigh

bobsled
bobsleigh

  boby   bobby
  boch   botch
  boddy   body

bodgie

bodice

  bodie   body
  bodigard   bodyguard
  bodiley   bodily

bodily

  bodis   bodice

body, bodies
body, bodied, bodying
body corporate
bodyguard
body language
bodywork
boffin
bog, bogged, bogging
bogey, bogies (golf)

  bogey   bogy (evil)
  boggel   boggle

boggle, -gled, -gling

  bogul   boggle

bogus
bogy, bogies (evil)

  bogy   bogey (golf)

bohemian

  boi   boy (male)
  boi   buoy (afloat)
  boiancy   buoyancy
  boiant   buoyant
  boicot   boycott

boil, -ed, -ing
boiler
boilermaker
boilersuit
boisterous, -ly

  boisterus   boisterous
  boks   box
  bolairo   bolero
  bolard   bollard
  bolaro   bolero

bold, -ly (brave)

  bold   bowled (ball)

bolder (braver)

  bolder   boulder (rock)

bole (trunk)

  bole   bowl (ball)

bolero
bollard
Bolshevik

Bolshevism
bolshie
bolster, -ed, -ing
bolt
    bom   bomb
bomb, -ed, -ing
bombardier
bombardment
bombastic
bomber
    bomberdeer   bombardier
bombora
bombshell
    bomer   bomber
bona fide
bonanza
bonbon
bonce
bond, -ed, -ing
bondage
bone, boned, boning
    bonet   bonnet
bonfire
    bonie   boney
    bonie   bonny
    bonit   bonnet
bonk, -ed, -ing
bonny, bonnier, bonniest
bonsai
bonus
bony, bonier, boniest
bonzer
boo, booed, booing
boob
    boobie   booby
boo-boo
booby, -bies
    boodwar   boudoir
    boofant   bouffant
boogie-woogie
book, -ed, -ing
    bookay   bouquet
bookcase
    bookeeping   bookkeeping
bookie
bookish, -ly
bookkeeping

bookmaker
bookstall
bookworm
    boolevard   boulevard
boom, -ed, -ing
boomer
boomerang
boon
boor (rude)
    boor   boar (pig)
    boor   bore (drill)
    boorjwah   bourgeois
    boorjwahzey bourgeoisie
boost, -ed, -ing
booster
boot
bootee (shoe)
    bootee   booty (plunder)
    booteek   .boutique
booth
    bootie   bootee (shoe)
    bootie   booty (plunder)
    bootik   boutique
bootleg, -legged, -legging
bootlegger
bootstrap
booty, -ties (plunder)
    booty   bootee (shoe)
booze, boozed, boozing
boozer
bora
boracic
    boraks   borax
    borasic   boracic
borax
    borbon   bourbon
    bord   board (plank)
    bord   bored (tired)
border (edge)
    border   boarder
                  (lodger)
border, -ed, -ing
borderline
    bording   boarding
    bordom   boredom
    bordy   bawdy
bore, bored, boring (drill)

bore · boar (pig)
bore · boor (rude)
boredom
boree
borer
born (birth)
born · borne (carry)
born · bourn (limit)
borne (carry)
borne · born (birth)
borne · bourn (limit)
boronia
borough (town)
borough · burrow (hole)
borow · borrow
borrow, -ed, -ing
borrower
Borstal
bort · bought
bos · boss
bosie · bossy
bosily · bossily
bosn · bosun
bosom
boss, -ed, -ing
bossom · bosom
bossy, bossier, bossiest
bosun
bosy · bossy
bot · boat
botaney · botany
botanical, -ly
botanist
botany
botch, -ed, -ing
botchy
boter · boater
both
bother
bothersome
bothersum · bothersome
botom · bottom
bottel · bottle
bottle, -tled, -tling
bottlebrush
bottleneck
bottler

bottom -ed, -ing
bottomless
botul · bottle
botulism
boudoir
bouffant
bougainvillea
bough (branch)
bough · bow (bend)
bought
bouillon
boukay · bouquet
boulder (rock)
boulder · bolder (braver)
boulevard
bounce, bounced, bouncing
bouncer
bound, -ed, -ing
boundary, -ries
boundry · boundary
bounteous, -ly
bountiful, -ly
bountious · bounteous
bounty, -ties
bouquet
bourbon
bourgeois
bourgeoisie
bourgwah · bourgeois
bourgwahzey · bourgeoisie
bourn (limit)
bourn · born (birth)
bourn · borne (carry)
bout
bouteek · boutique
boutique
bovine
bow, -ed, -ing (bend)
bow · bough (branch)
bow · beau (dandy)
bowel
bower
bowerbird
bowie knife
bowl (ball)
bowl · bole (trunk)
bowleg

bowler
bowline
bownce	bounce
bownd	bound
bowndary	boundary
bownse	bounce
bouwnser	bouncer
bownteous	bounteous
bowntiful	bountiful
bowt	bout

bowyang
box, -ed, -ing
boxer
box-frame
boy (child)
boy	buoy (float)
boyansy	buoyancy
boyant	buoyant
boycot	boycott

boycott, -ed, -ing
boykot	boycott
boyle	boil
boysterus	boisterous

bra, bras (brassiere)
brace, braced, bracing (clamp)
bracelet
bracken
bracket, -ed, -ing
brackish
brackit	bracket
braclete	bracelet
brade	braid

brag, bragged, bragging
| bragart | braggart |

braggart
bragger
Brahma
Brahman, -mans
braid
| brail | braille |

braille
brain
brainstorm
brainwash, -ed, -ing
brainy, brainier, brainiest
braise, braised, braising (cook)
| braise | braze (solder) |

braisen | brazen
brakage | breakage
| brakaway | breakaway |
| brakdown | breakdown |

brake, braked, braking (stop)
brake	break (divide)
braken	bracken
brakeneck	breakneck
braker	breaker
brakewater	breakwater
brakidge	breakage
braking	breaking
brakish	brackish
brale	braille
brambel	bramble

bramble
brambly
| brambul | bramble |
| bramin | Brahman |

bran
branch, -ches
branch, -ed, -ing
brand, -ed, -ing
brandish, -ed, -ing
brand-new
brandy, -dies
| brane | brain |
| braney | brainy |

bras (brassieres)
| bras | brass (metal) |
| brase | brace (clamp) |

brash
brasier	brassiere (bra)
brasier	brazier (burner)
braslet	bracelet

brass
brassiere (bra)
brassy, brassier, brassiest
| brasy | brassy |

brat
bravado, -does, -dos
brave, braver, bravest
bravely
bravery, -ries
| bravly | bravely |

bravo, -voes, -vos
| bravrey | bravery |

brawd broad
brawl, -ed, -ing
brawn
brawny, brawnier, brawniest
bray, -ed, -ing
  brayd braid
  brayn brain
braze, brazed, brazing (solder)
  braze braise (cook)
brazen, -ly
brazenness
brazier (burner)
  brazier brassiere (bra)
brazil nut
breach, -ed, -ing (break)
  breach breech (gun)
bread (food)
  bread bred
      (produced)
breadline
breadth
breadwinner
break, broke, broken, breaking
(divide)
  break brake (stop)
  breakabel breakable
breakable
  breakabul breakable
breakage
breakaway
breakdown
breaker
breakfast
break-in
breakthrough
breakwater
bream (fish)
breast
breastbone
breastfeed, -fed, -feeding
breastplate
breast stroke
breath (air)
  breath breadth (wide)
  breathaliser breathalyser
breathalyser
breathe, breathed, breathing

breather
breathless, -ly
breathtaking
bred (produced)
  bred bread (food)
  bredth breadth
  bree brie
breech, -ches (gun)
  breech breach (break)
breed, bred, breeding
breeder
breeding
  breef brief
breeze, breezed, breezing
breezily
breezy, breezier, breeziest
  breif brief
  brest breast
  brest stroke breast stroke
  breth breath (air)
  breth breadth (wide)
  brethalyser breathalyser
  brethless breathless
brethren
  brethtaking breathtaking
breve
brevity, -ties
brew, -ed, -ing (beer)
  brewed brood (worry)
brewer
brewery, -ries
  brews bruise (hurt)
  breze breeze
  brezy breezy
briar
bribe, bribed, bribing
bribery, -ies
bric-a-brac
brick, -ed, -ing
brickbat
  brickette briquette
bricklayer
brick veneer
brickyard
bridal (marry)
  bridal bridle (horse)
bride

bridegroom
  bridel — bridal (marry)
  bridel — bridle (horse)
  bridesmade — bridesmaid
bridesmaid
bridge, bridged, bridging
bridle, -dled, -dling (horse)
  bridle — bridal (marry)
brie
brief, -ly
briefcase
briefs
brig
brigade, -gaded, -gading
  brigadeer — brigadier
brigadier
brigalow
brigand
  brige — bridge
bright, -ly
brighten, -ed, -ing
brightness
brilliance
brilliant, -ly
brilliantine
  brilyanse — brilliance
  brilyansy — brilliancy
  brilyant — brilliant
brim, brimmed, brimming (edge)
  brim — bream (fish)
brimstone
brindled
brine, brined, brining
  briney — briny
bring, brought, bringing
brink
brinkmanship
briny, brinier, briniest
bri-nylon
briquette
  brisel — bristle
brisk, -ly
brisket
  brisle — bristle
bristle, -tled, -tling
bristly
Britain

brite — bright
briten — brighten
British
  britle — brittle
brittle, brittler, brittlest
brittleness
broach, -ed, -ing (mention)
  broach — brooch (pin)
broad, -ly
broadcast, -cast, -casting
broadcaster
broaden, -ed, -ing
broad-minded
broadsheet
brocade, -caded
broccoli
  broch — broach (mention)
  broch — brooch (pin)
brochure
  brocoli — broccoli
  brog — brogue
brogue
broil, -ed, -ing
broken, -ly
broken-hearted
broker
brokerage
  brokeridge — brokerage
brolly, -lies
bromide
bromine
bronchial
bronchitis
bronco, -cos
  bronkial — bronchial
  bronkitis — bronchitis
bronze, bronzed, bronzing
brooch, -ches (pin)
brood (worry)
  brood — brewed (beer)
broody, broodier, broodiest
brook, -ed, -ing
broom
  broonette — brunette
  broose — bruise
  broot — brute

brootal — brutal
brootality — brutality
brootish — brutish
brorn — brawn
brort — brought
broshure — brochure
brosure — brochure
broth
brothel
brother
brotherhood
brother-in-law, brothers-in-law
brotherliness
brotherly
brow, brows (eyebrow)
browbeat, -beat, -beaten, -beating
brown
   brownee — brownie
brownie
   brows — browse (read)
browse, browsed, browsing
browser
bruise, bruised, bruising (hurt)
   bruise — brews (beer)
bruiser
brumby, brumbies
brunch
   brunet — brunette
brunette
   bruse — brews (beer)
   bruse — bruise (hurt)
brush, -ed, -ing
brushwood
brushwork
   brusk — brusque
brusque, -ly
brusqueness
brutal, -ly
brutality, -ties
brute
brutish
   bubbel — bubble
bubble, -bled, -bling
bubble-and-squeak
   buble — bubble
   bubly — bubbly
bubonic plague

bubul — bubble
bucaneer — buccaneer
buccaneer
buccaneering
   bucher — butcher
buck, -ed, -ing
   buckaneer — buccaneer
   buckel — buckle
bucket, -ed, -ing
bucketful, bucketfuls
buckjump, -ed, -ing
buckjumper
buckle, -led, -ling
buckshot
buckskin
bucktooth, -teeth
   buckul — buckle
bucolic
bud, budded, budding
Buddhism
Buddhist
buddy, -dies
budge, budged, budging
   budgereegar — budgerigar
budgerigar
budget, -eted, -eting
budgetary
budgie
   budgrigar — budgerigar
   Budhism — Buddhism
   Budhist — Buddhist
   buf — buff
   bufalo — buffalo
   bufay — buffet
   bufer — buffer
buff
buffalo, -loes, -los
   buffay — buffet
buffer
buffet (food)
buffet, -ed, -ing (hit)
buffoon
buffoonery, -eries
   bufit — buffet
   bufoon — buffoon
   bufoonery — buffoonery
bug, bugged, bugging

bugbare	bugbear
bugbear	
bugel	bugle
bugerigar	budgerigar
buget	budget
buggy, -gies	
bugie	buggy
bugle, -gled, -gling	
bugler	
bugy	buggy
build, built, building	
builder	
build-up	
buisness	business
bukshee	

For **buk-** words, look under **buc-**.

bul	bull
bulb	
bulbar	bull-bar
bulbous	
bulbul	
buldog	bulldog
buldoze	bulldoze
bulet	bullet
buletin	bulletin
bulfight	bullfight
bulfrog	bullfrog
bul-headed	bull-headed
bulion	bullion
bulk	
bulkhead	
bulky, bulkier, bulkiest	
bull-bar	
bulldog	
bulldoze, -dozed, -dozing	
bulldozer	
bullet	
bulletin	
bullfight	
bullfrog	
bull-headed	
bullion	
bullock	
bullring	
bullroarer	

bullrush	
bullseye	
bull-terrier	
bullwark	bulwark
bully, -lies	
bully, -lied, -lying	
bulock	bullock
bulring	bullring
bulroarer	bullroarer
bulrush	
bulseye	bullseye
bulwalk	bulwark
bulwark	
buly	bully
bulyun	bullion
bum, bummed, bumming	
bumbel	bumble
bumble, bumbled, bumbling	
bumf	
bump, -ed, -ing	
bumper	
bumpey	bumpy
bumpiness	
bumpkin	
bumpshus	bumptious
bumptious, -ly	
bumptiousness	
bumpy, bumpier, bumpiest	
bumshus	bumptious
bunch, -ches	
bunch, -ed, -ing	
buncum	bunkum
bundel	bundle
bundle, -dled, -dling	
bundul	bundle
bundy	
buney	bunny
bung, -ed, -ing	
bungaloe	bungalow
bungalow	
bungel	bungle
bunger	
bunghole	
bungkum	bunkum
bungle, -gled, -gling	
bungler	
bungul	bungle

bunie — bunny
bunion
bunk, -ed, -ing
bunker, -ed, -ing
bunkum
bunny, -nies
  bunnyip — bunyip
Bunsen burner
bunt
bunting
  buny — bunny
bunyip
  bunyon — bunion
buoy, -ed, -ing (float)
  buoy — boy (child)
buoyancy
  buoyansy — buoyancy
buoyant, -ly
  burbel — burble
burble, -bled, -bling
  burbul — burble
  burch — birch
  burd — bird
burden, -ed, -ing
burdensome
  burdensum — burdensome
  burdie — birdie
  burdseye — bird's-eye
bureau, -eaus, -eaux
bureaucracy, -cies
  bureaucrasy — bureaucracy
bureaucrat
bureaucratic
  buret — burette
burette
  burgandy — burgundy
  burgel — burgle
burgeon, -ed, -ing
  burger — burgher
burgess
burgher
burglar
burglary, -ries
burgle, -gled, -gling
  burgler — burglar
  burgul — burgle
burgundy

burial
burke, burked, burking
burl, -ed, -ing
burlap
  burlesk — burlesque
burlesque, -lesqued, -lesquing
  burlie — burly (large)
burly, -lier, -liest (large)
  burly — berley (bait)
burn, burnt, burned, burning
burnable
burn-back
burner
burnish, -ed, -ing
  buro — bureau
  buro — burro
  burocrasy — bureaucracy
  burocrat — bureaucrat
  burow — bureau
  burow — burrow (hole)
burr, burred, burring
  burra — borough (town)
burro, -ros (donkey)
  burro — bureau
  burrocracy — bureaucracy
  burrocrat — bureaucrat
burrow, -ed, -ing (hole)
  burrow — borough (town)
  burrow — burro (donkey)
bursar
bursary, -ries
  burser — bursar
  bursery — bursary
burst, burst, bursting
  burth — berth (ship)
  burth — birth (born)
bury, buried, burying (cover)
  bury — berry (fruit)
bus, buses, busses
bus, bused, busing or bussed, bussing
  busbie — busby
busby, -bies
  busel — bustle
bush, -ed, -ing
bushcraft
bushel
bushfire

bushie (farmer)
  bushie   bushy
bush-lawyer
bushman, -men
bushranger
bushranging
bushwalk
bushy, bushier, bushiest
busier
busily
business
businesslike
businessman, -men
businesswoman, -women
busk, -ed, -ing
busker
bust, -ed, -ing
bustard
  busted   bustard
  bustel   bustle
buster
bustle, -tled, -tling
bust-up
  busul   bustle
busy, busied, busying
busy, busier, busiest
busybody, -bodies
but (contrary)
  but   butt (end)
butane
butcher, -ed, -ing
  buteek   boutique
  buten   button
  buter   butter
  buterfly   butterfly
  butey   beauty
  butician   beautician
  butify   beautify
  butique   boutique
  butishun   beautician
butler
  butock   buttock
  buton   button
  butress   buttress
butt, -ed, -ing (end)
  butt   but (contrary)
butter, -ed, -ing

butter-fingers
butterfly, -flies
butterscotch
buttock
button
buttonhole, -holed, -holing
buttress, buttresses
buxom, -ly
buy, bought, buying (purchase)
  buy   by (near to)
  buy   bye (sport)
buyer
  buz   buzz
  buzard   buzzard
  buzer   buzzer
  buz-saw   buzz-saw
buzz, -ed, -ing
buzz, -es
buzzard
buzzer
buzz-saw
by (near to)
  by   bye (sport)
  by   buy (purchase)
bye (sport)
  bye   by (near to)
  bye   buy (purchase)
bye-bye, bye-byes
by-election
  byennial   biennial
  byer   buyer
  byer   byre (shed)
  byfocal   bifocal
bygone
  bying   buying
  byke   bike
by-law
  byle   bile
  bylore   by-law
  bymetallic bimetallic
  bymonthly bimonthly
  bynominal binominal
  byopsey   biopsy
  bypartisan bipartisan
  bypartite   bipartite
bypass
  byped   biped

byplane	biplane
by-product	
byre (shed)	
bysecshun	bisection
bysect	bisect
byseksual	bisexual
bystander	
byte (computer)	
byte	bite (chew)
byway	
byword	
Byzantine	

Cc

cab
cabal, -balled, -balling
  cabaray   cabaret
cabaret
cabbage
  cabbidge   cabbage
cabby, cabbies
  cabel   cable
  cabey   cabby
  cabie   cabby
  cabige   cabbage
cabin
cabinet
cable, -bled, -bling
caboose
  cabul   cable
cacao, -caos
  cach   cache
  cach   catch
  cachay   cachet
cache, cached, caching (hide)
  cache   cash (money)
cachet
  cachou   cashew
  cachword   catchword
  cackel   cackle
cackle, -led, -ling
  cacktus   cactus
  cackul   cackle
  cacofony   cacophony
cacophony, -nies
cactoblastis
cactus, -ti, -tuses
  cacul   cackle
cad
cadaver
cadaverous, -ly
  caddey   caddie (golf)

  caddey   caddy (tea)
caddie, -died, -dying (golf)
  caddie   caddy (tea)
caddy, -ies (tea)
  caddy   caddie (golf)
cadence
  cadense   cadence
cadenza
cadet
cadetship
cadge, cadged, cadging
  cadjole   cajole
cadmium
Caesar
caesarean section
  cafay   cafe
cafe
  cafeen   caffeine
cafeteria
caffeine
  caffeteria   cafeteria
  cafiene   caffeine
  cafiteria   cafeteria
caftan
cage, caged, caging
cagey, cagier, cagiest
  cagy   cagey
cahoots
  cain   cane
cairn
caisson
  caje   cage
cajole, -joled, -joling
cake, caked, caking
calabash
calamari
calamine
calamitous, -ly
calamity, -ties
  calarie   calorie
calcareous
  calcarious   calcareous
calcification
calcify, -fied, -fying
calcium
calculable
  calculabul   calculable

calculate, -lated, -lating
calculation
calculative
calculator
  calculaytor   calculator
calculus, -luses
Caledonian
calendar (time)
calender (roll)
calendula
calf, calves
calfskin
  caliber   calibre
calibrate, -brated, -brating
calibration
calibrator
calibre
  calicks   calyx
calico, -coes, -cos
  calif   caliph
  caligraphy   calligraphy
  caling   calling
caliper
caliph
  calipso   calypso
calisthenics
  calix   calyx
  calk   caulk
call, -ed, -ing (cry out)
  call   caul
               (membrane)
  callamity   calamity
  calldron   cauldron
caller
callgirl
calligrapher
calligraphy
calliper
callistemon
callisthenics
callosity, -ties
callous, -ly (cruel)
  callous   callus (skin)
callousness
callow
callus, calluses (skin)
  callus   callous (cruel)

calm, -ly
calmness
calorie
calorific
calorimeter
  calory   calorie
  calow   callow
  calsify   calcify
  calsium   calcium
calumniate, -ated, -ating
calumniation
calumnious, -ly
  calumnius   calumnious
calumny, -nies
  calus   callous (cruel)
  calus   callus (skin)
Calvary
calve, calved, calving (give birth)
  calve   carve (cut)
Calvinism
Calvinist
calypso, -sos
calyx, calyces, calyxes
cam
  camaflage   camouflage
camaraderie
camber
cambric
came
camel
camelhair
camellia
  camelya   camellia
  camember   camembert
camembert
cameo, -os
camera
cameraman
  camerardery   camaraderie
  camfer   camphor
  camio   cameo
camisole
  camle   camel
camouflage, -flaged, -flaging
camp, -ed, -ing
campaign
  campain   campaign

campanology
camper
campervan
  campher   camphor
camphor
campus, -es
camshaft
  camul   camel
can, could (able to)
can, canned, canning (tinned)
  canabis   cannabis
Canadian
canal
canape
canary, -ries
canasta
cancan
cancel, -celled, -celling
  cancelation   cancellation
cancellation
cancer
cancerous
  cancerus   cancerous
  candel   candle
candelabrum
  candellight   candlelight
  candelstick   candlestick
  cander   candour
  candey   candy
candid (open)
  candid   candied (sugar)
candidate
candied (sugar)
  candied   candid (open)
candle
candlelight
candlestick
candour
  candul   candle
  candulstick   candlestick
candy, -dies
candy, candied, candying (sugar)
cane, caned, caning (hit)
  caned   canned (tinned)
  canee   canny
  canery   cannery
cane-sugar

  canibal   cannibal
  canibalism   cannibalism
  canie   canny
canine
canister
cannabis
  cannary   canary
canned (tinned)
  canned   caned (hit)
cannelloni
cannery, -ries
cannibal
cannibalism
canniness
cannon (gun)
  cannon   canon (law)
cannot
canny, -nier, -niest

For other **cann-** words, look under **can-**.

canoe, -es
canoe, -noed, -noeing
canoeist
canon (law)
  canon   cannon (gun)
canonical
canonisation
canonise, -nised, -nising
  canoo   canoe
canoodle, -dled, -dling
  canooist   canoeist
canopy, -pies
  cansel   cancel
  canser   cancer
  canserous   cancerous
cant (insincere)
can't (cannot)
cantaloup
cantaloupe
cantankerous, -ly
  cantankerus cantankerous
cantata
canteen
canter, -ed, -ing
cantilever
canto, -tos

canton

cantor

  canue   canoe

canvas, -es (tent)

  canvas   canvass
               (gather)

canvass, -ed, -ing (gather)

  canvass   canvas (tent)

  cany   canny

canyon

cap, capped, capping

capability, -ties

capable, -bly

  capabul   capable

capacious, -ly

capacitor

capacity, -ties

  capasitor   capacitor
  capasity   capacity
  capchure   capture

cape

caper, -ed, -ing

  capilary   capillary

capillary, -laries

capital

capitalisation

capitalise, -lised, -lising

capitalism

capitalist

capitalistic

capitulate, -lated, -lating

capitulation

capon

cappuccino

> For all other **capp-** words,
> look under **cap-**.

caprice

capricious, -ly

capriciousness

Capricorn

  caprise   caprice
  caprishus   capricious
  capshulate   capsulate
  capshun   caption
  capshus   captious

capsicum

capsize, -sized, -sizing

capstan

capsule

captain, -ed, -ing

captaincy

  capter   captor
  captin   captain

caption

captious, -ly

captiousness

  captius   captious

captivate, -vated, -vating

captivation

captive

captivity, -ties

captor

capture, -tured, -turing

  caracter   character
  caracteristic   characteristic

carafe

  caraffe   carafe

caramel

  caramul   caramel

carat (weight)

  carat   carrot (food)
  carate   karate

caravan, -vanned, -vanning

caraway

carbine

carbohydrate

carbon

carbonate, -nated, -nating

carbon dioxide

carbonise, -nised, -nising

carbon monoxide

carbuncle

  carbuncul   carbuncle

carburettor

carcase

carcass

carcinogen

carcinogenic

carcinoma, -mata, -mas

card, -ed, -ing

  cardagan   cardigan

cardboard

  cardbord   cardboard

cardiac
cardigan
cardinal, -ly
  cardiograf   cardiograph
cardiologist
cardiology
cardiovascular
cardsharp
care, cared, caring
careen
career, -ed, -ing
carefree
careful, -ly
careless, -ly
carelessness
caress, -ed, -ing
caressingly
caret (mark)
  caret   carat (weight)
caretaker
cargo, -goes
caribou, -bou
caricature, -tured, -turing
caricaturist
  caricter   character
  caricteristic   characteristic
  caridge   carriage
  carie   carry (bear)
  carier   carrier
caries (decay)
  caries   carries (bear)
  carillion   carillon
carillon
  carillyon   carillon
  carion   carrion
  carisma   charisma
  carkey   khaki
  carki   khaki
  carm   calm
carmine
carnage
carnal, -ly
carnality
carnation
  carnidge   carnage
  carnije   carnage
carnival

carnivore
carnivorous, -ly
carol, -rolled, -rolling (song)
  carol   carrel (study)
  carol   corral (yard)
caroller
  carot   carat (weight)
carousal (feast)
  carousal   carousel
             (merry-go-round)
carouse, -roused, -rousing
carousel (merry-go-round)
  carousel   carousal (feast)
carp, -ed, -ing
carpenter
carpentry
carpet, -ed, -ing
carrel (study)
  carrel   carol (song)
  carrel   corral (yard)
carriage
carriageway
carrier
carries (bears)
  carries   caries (decay)
carrion
carrot (food)
  carrot   carat (weight)
carry, -ried, -rying
  carryon   carrion
  carsinoma   carcinoma
cart, -ed, -ing
carte blanche
cartel
cartilage
  cartilege   cartilage
  cartilidge   cartilage
  cartografy   cartography
cartographer
cartographic
cartography
carton
cartoon, -ed, -ing
cartoonist
cartridge
  cartrige   cartridge

cartrije — cartridge
cartwheel
carve, carved, carving (cut)
carve — calve (give birth)
cary — carry
casava — cassava
cascade, -caded, -cading
case, cased, casing
caseen — casein
casein
casement
caserole — casserole
casette — cassette
casock — cassock
casowary — cassowary
cash, -ed, -ing (money)
cash — cache (hide)
cashay — cachet
casheer — cashier
cashew
cashier
cashmear — cashmere
cashmere
cashoo — cashew
casia — cassia
casing
casino, -nos
cask
caskade — cascade
casket
caskit — casket
casock — cassock
cassava
cassel — castle
casserole, -roled, -roling
casset — cassette
cassette
cassia
cassock
cassowary, -ries
cast, cast, casting (fling)
cast — caste (class)
castanet
castaway
caste (class)
caster or castor (sugar)

caster — castor (oil)
castigate, -gated, -gating
castigation
cast-iron
castle, -tled, -tling
castor (oil)
castrait — castrate
castrate, -trated, -trating
castration
castrayte — castrate
casual, -ly
casuality — casualty
casualty, -ties
casuarina
casuistic
casuistry, -tries
casulty — casualty
catachism — catechism
cataclysm
cataclysmic
catacomb
catalise — catalyse
catalist — catalyst
catalitic — catalytic
catalog — catalogue
catalogue, -logued, -loguing
cataloguer
catalyse, -lysed, -lysing
catalyst
catalytic
catamaran
catapiler — caterpillar
catapult
catar — catarrh
cataract
catarh — catarrh
catarrh
catarrhal
catastrofic — catastrophic
catastrofy — catastrophe
catastrophe
catastrophic, -ally
catcall, -ed, -ing
catch, caught, catching
catcher
catchment
catchword

catchy, catchier, catchiest
catechise, -chised, -chising
catechism
catechist
categorical, -ly
categorise, -rised, -rising
categorist
category, -ries

catel	cattle

cater, -ed, -ing
caterer
caterpillar

caterpiller	caterpillar
caterwall	caterwaul

caterwaul
catfish, -fishes, -fish
catgut
catharsis
cathartic
cathedral
catheter
cathode
catholic (universal)
Catholic (religion)
Catholicism
Catholicity

caticise	catechise
catigoric	categoric
catigorise	categorise
catigory	category
catikism	catechism
catish	cattish

catkin

catle	cattle

catnap, -ed, -ing
cat-o'-nine-tails

cattel	cattle
catterpillar	caterpillar

cattle
cattlegrid
cattle-run
cattish, -ly
catty, -ier, -iest

catul	cattle

catwalk
Caucasian
caucus, -ed, -ing

caught (did catch)

caught	court (law)
cauk	caulk

caul (membrane)

caul	call (cry)

cauldron

cauliflour	cauliflower

cauliflower
caulk, -ed, -ing
causal, -ly

causal	casual

causality, -ties
causation
causative, -ly
cause, caused, causing
causeway
caustic, -ally
cauterise, -rised, -rising
caution, -ed, -ing
cautionary
cautious, -ly
cavalcade, -caded, -cading

cavaleer	cavalier

cavalier
cavalry, -ries
cavalryman, -men
cave, caved, caving
caveman, -men
cavern
cavernous
caviar
cavil, -illed, -illing
cavity, -ties

caw	core (heart)
caw	corps (group)
cawcas	caucus
Cawcasian	Caucasian
cawcus	caucus

cay
cayenne
cease, ceased, ceasing
cease-fire
ceaseless, -ly
cedar
cede, ceded, ceding (yield)

cede	seed (plant)
ceder	cedar

ceeling — ceiling (roof)
ceese — cease
cefalic — cephalic
ceiling (roof)
ceiling — sealing (close)
celebrant
celebrate, -brated, -brating
celebration
celebrity, -ties
celerity
celery (food)
celery — salary (wage)
celestial, -ly
celibacy, -cies
celibasy — celibacy
celibate
celibrant — celebrant
celibrate — celebrate
cell (prison)
cell — sell (goods)
cellar (basement)
cellar — seller (goods)
cellarman, -men
celler — seller (goods)
cellist
cello, -los
cellofane — cellophane
cellophane
cellular
celluler — cellular
celluloid
cellulose
celofane — cellophane
Celsius
cement, -ed, -ing
cemetary — cemetery
cemetery, -teries
cemical — chemical
cemist — chemist
cemistry — chemistry
cenotaf — cenotaph
censer (incense)
censer — censor (books)
censership — censorship
censhure — censure
censor (books)
censor — censer (incense)

censorious, -ly
censorship
censurable
censurabul — censurable
censure, -sured, -suring
census
cent (coin)
cent — scent (perfume)
cent — sent (away)
centaur
centenarian
centenary, -ries
centenery — centenary
centennial, -ly
center — centre
Centigrade
centimeter — centimetre
centimetre
centipede
centor — centaur
central, -ly
Centralia
centralisation
centralise, -lised, -lising
centralism
centralist
centrality
centre, -tred, -tring
centreboard
centrefold
centrepiece
centrifugal, -ly
centrifuge
centripetal, -ly
centupel — centuple
centuple, -pled, -pling
centupul — centuple
centurion
century, -ries
cephalic
ceramic
ceramicist
ceramics
ceramist

For any cerc- words,
look under **circ-**.

cereal (grain)
  cereal   serial (part)
  cerebelum   cerebellum
cerebellum, -bella
cerebral
cerebrate, -brated, -brating
cerebration
cerebrum, -bra
ceremonial, -ly
ceremonious, -ly
  ceremonius   ceremonious
ceremony, -monies
  cerial   cereal (grain)
  cerial   serial (part)
  ceribellum   cerebellum
  ceribrum   cerebrum
cerise

> For any **cerk-** words,
> look under **circ-**.

certain, -ly
certainty, -ties
  certanty   certainty
  certen   certain
  certenty   certainty
certifiable, -fiably
  certifiabul   certifiable
certificate, -cated, -cating
certification
certifier
certify, -fied, -fying
  certinty   certainty
certitude
cervical
  cervicul   cervical
  cerviks   cervix
cervix, cervixes, cervices
  cesation   cessation
  ceshun   session (time)
  cesion   cession (yield)
  cespit   cesspit
  cespool   cesspool
cessation
cession(yield)
  cession   session (time)
cesspit
cesspool

chablis
cha-cha
  chacoal   charcoal
chafe, chafed, chafing (rub)
  chafe   chaff (straw)
chaff (straw)
chaffinch, -es
chagrin, -ed, -ing
chain
chain-drive
chain-reaction
chainsaw
chain-smoke, -smoked, -smoking
chain-stitch, -ed, -ing
chain-store
chair, -ed, -ing
chairlift
chairman, -men
chairperson
chairwoman, -women
  chaise   chase
chalet
chalice
  chalinge   challenge
  chalis   chalice
chalk, -ed, -ing
challenge, -lenged, -lenging
challenger
  chamba   chamber
chamber
chamberlain
  chamberlin   chamberlain
  chambermade   chambermaid
chambermaid
chameleon
  chamee   chamois
chamfer, -ed, -ing
  chamie   chamois
chamois
champ, -ed, -ing
champagne
  champaign   champagne
champers
champignon
champion, -ed, -ing
championship
  champiun   champion

chance, chanced, chancing
chancel
  chanceler   chancellor
  chancelery   chancellery
  chanceller   chancellor
chancellery, -ries
chancellor
chancellorship
chancery, -ceries
chancy, chancier, chanciest
  chandeleer   chandelier
chandelier
chandler
  chane   chain
  chane-drive   chain-drive
  chanel   channel
  chane-reaction chain-reaction
  chanesaw   chainsaw
change, changed, changing
changeable, -bly
  changeabul   changeable
changeling
changeover
channel, -nelled, -nelling
  chanse   chance
  chansel   chancel
  chanseler   chancellor
  chanselery   chancellery
  chansey   chancy
chant, -ed, -ing
chaos
chaotic, -ally
chap, chapped, chapping
chapel
chaperone
  chaple   chapel
chaplain
chaplaincy
chaplet
  chaplin   chaplain
chapter
char, charred, charring
character
characterise, -rised, -rising
characteristic, -ally
charade
  charaid   charade

charcoal
  chare   chair
  chareman   chairman
  chareperson   chairperson
  charewoman   chairwoman
  charey   chary
charge, charged, charging
charger
chariot
charioteer
charisma
charismatic
charitable
charitableness
charitably
  charitabul   charitable
charity, -ties
charlady, -ladies
charlatan
charleston
charm, -ed, -ing
charmer
chart, -ed, -ing
charter, -ed, -ing
chartreuse
  chartroos   chartreuse
chary, charier, chariest
chase, chased, chasing
chased (follow)
  chased   chaste (pure)
  chasen   chasten
chaser
  chasis   chassis
chasm
  chassie   chassis
chassis, chassis
chaste (pure)
  chaste   chased (follow)
chasten, -ed, -ing
chastener
chastise, -tised, -tising
chastisement
chastiser
chastity
chat, chatted, chatting
chateau, -teaus, -teaux
  chatel   chattel

chater	chatter
chatily	chattily
chatiness	chattiness
chattel	
chatter, -ed, -ing	
chatterbox, -boxes	
chattily	
chattiness	
chatty, -tier, -tiest	
chaty	chatty
chauffer	chauffeur
chauffeur	
chauvinism	
chauvinist	
chauvinistic, -ally	
cheap (price)	
cheap	cheep (sound)
cheapen, -ed, -ing	
cheapish, -ly	
cheapskate	
chear	cheer
chearful	cheerful
chease	cheese
cheat, -ed, -ing	
cheater	
check, -ed, -ing (stop)	
check	cheque (money)
Check	Czech (person)
checkers	
checkmate, -mated, -mating	
checkout	
checkpoint	
checkup	
chedar	cheddar
cheddar	
cheder	cheddar
cheef	chief
cheeftan	chieftain
cheekily	
cheekiness	
cheeky, cheekier, cheekiest	
cheep, -ed, -ing (sound)	
cheep	cheap (price)
cheer, cheered, cheering	
cheerey	cheery
cheerful, -ly	
cheerfulness	

cheerie	cheery
cheerily	
cheeriness	
cheerio, -os	
cheery, -rier, -riest	
cheese	
cheesecake	
cheesecloth	
cheesed-off	
cheeseparing	
cheesy, -sier, -siest	
cheet	cheat
cheeta	cheetah
cheetah	
cheeter	cheetah
chef	
chef-d'oeuvre, chefs-d'oeuvre	
cheif	chief
cheiftan	chieftain
chelist	cellist
chelo	cello
chemical, -ly	
chemise	
chemist	
chemistrey	chemistry
chemistry, -tries	
chemotherapist	
chemotherapy	
chenille	
cheongsam	
cheque (money)	
cheque	check (stop)
Cheque	Czech (person)
cheque-book	
chequer	
chequered	
cherie	cherry
cherio	cheerio
cherish, -ed, -ing	
cheroot	
cherp	chirp
cherry, -ries	
cherub, cherubim, cherubs	
cherubic, -ally	
chery	cheery
chery	cherry
ches	chess

chesbord   chessboard
chess
chessboard
chessnut   chestnut
chest
chesterfield
chestnut
chevalier
chevon (goat meat)
chevron (stripe)
chew, -ed, -ing (eat)
chewie
chewing gum
chews   choose (select)
chewy
chiack, -ed, -ing
chic (stylish)
chicanery, -ries
chick (young bird)
chickenfeed
chickenpox
chickpea
chickweed
chicle
chicory, -ries
chide, chided, chiding
chidingly
chief, chiefs
chiefly
chieftain
chieftaincy
chiffon
chiffonier
chifon   chiffon
chignon
chihuahua
chil   chill
chilblain
chilblane   chilblain
child, children
childbaring   childbearing
childbearing
childberth   childbirth
childbirth
childhood
childish, -ly
childlike

childproof
chili, -ies (fruit)
chili   chilly (cold)
chill, -ed, -ing
chilli, -ies (fruit)
chilli   chilly (cold)
chilliness
chilly, -ier, -iest (cold)
chilly   chilli (fruit)
chimbly   chimney
chime, chimed, chiming
chimera, -ras
chimeric, -ally
chimnee   chimney
chimney, -neys
chimpanzee
chin
china
chinchilla
Chinese
chink, -ed, -ing
chintz, chintzes
chintzy
chip, chipped, chipping
chipboard
chipmonk   chipmunk
chipmunk
chipolata
chiropodey   chiropody
chiropodist
chiropody
chiropracter   chiropractor
chiropractic
chiropractor
chirp, -ed, -ing
chirpily
chirpy, -pier, -piest
chisel, -elled, -elling
chiseller
chit
chitchat
chivalrous, -ly
chivalrus   chivalrous
chivalry
chive
chivvy, -ied, -ying
chloride

chlorinate, -nated, -nating
chlorination
chlorine
   chlorofill   chlorophyll
chloroform, -ed, -ing
chlorophyll
chock, -ed, -ing
chock-a-block
chock-full
chocks
   choclat   chocolate
chocolate
choice, choicer, choicest
choir (singers)
   choir   quire (measure)
   choise   choice
choke, choked, choking
choker
choko
choler (anger)
   choler   collar (neck)
cholera
choleric
cholesterol
   choo   chew
chook
choose, chose, chosen, choosing
  (select)
   choose   chews (eats)
choosy
chop, chopped, chopping
chopper
choppy, -pier, -piest
   chopsooey   chop suey
chopstick
   chopy   choppy
choral, -ly (sing)
   choral   chorale (tune)
chorale (tune)
   chorale   choral (sing)
chord (music)
   chord   cord (string)
chore
   choreograf   choreograph
choreograph, -ed, -ing
choreographer
choreographic

choreography
chorister
chortle, -tled, -tling
   chortul   chortle
chorus, -ruses
chorus, -rused, -rusing
chose
chosen
chow
chowder
chow mein
   chrisalis   chrysalis
chrism
   Chrismas   Christmas
Christ
   Christain   Christian
christen, -ed, -ing
christendom
Christian
Christianity
Christmas
chromatic, -ally
chrome
chromium
chromosome
   chronalogical   chronological
chronic, -ally
   chronical   chronicle
chronicle, -cled, -cling
chronicler
chronologer
chronological, -ly
chronology, -gies
chronometer
chrysalis, chrysalises
chrysanthemum
chubbily
chubbiness
chubby, -bier, -biest
   chubier   chubbier
   chuby   chubby
chuck, -ed, -ing
   chuckel   chuckle
chuckle, chuckled, chuckling
chuckler
chuff, -ed, -ing
chug, chugged, chugging

chum, chummed, chumming
chummy, -mier, -miest
chump
chunk
chunkiness
chunky, -kier, -kiest
church, -es
churinga
churl
churlish, -ly
churn, -ed, -ing
  churp   chirp
chute (drop)
  chute   shoot (gun)
chutney, -neys
  chutny   chutney
chutzpah
  cianide   cyanide
  cibernetics   cybernetics
cicada, -dae, -das
  cicatriss   cicatrix
cicatrix, cicatrices, cicatrixes

> For all other **cic-** words,
> look under **cyc-**.

cider
  cifer   cipher
cigar
  cigaret   cigarette
cigarette
  cignet   cygnet (swan)
  cignet   signet (ring)
  cilestial   celestial
cilium, cilia
  cilinder   cylinder
  cilindrical   cylindrical
  cimbal   cymbal(music)
  cimbal   symbol (sign)
  ciment   cement
  cinamon   cinnamon
cinch, -ches
cincture
cinder
cinderella
cinema
cinemascope
cinematic, -ally

cinematograph
cineraria
  cinic   cynic
  cinical   cynical
  cinicul   cynical
  cinima   cinema
  cinimatograf   cinematograph
  cinimatograph   cinematograph
  cinimon   cinnamon
cinnamon
  cinosure   cynosure
cipher
  cipress   cypress
circa
  circel   circle
  circit   circuit
circle, -cled, -cling
circlet
circuit, -ed, -ing
circuit-breaker
circuitous, -ly
circuitry
  circul   circle
circular, -ly
circularise, -rised, -rising
circularity
circulate, -lated, -lating
circulation
circulator
circulatory
circumcise, -cised, -cising
circumcision
circumference
  circumferense   circumference
circumnavigate, -gated, -gating
circumnavigation
circumnavigator
circumscribe, -ribed, -ribing
circumscription
circumspect
circumspection
circumstance
  circumstanse   circumstance
  circumstanshul   circumstantial
circumstantial, -ly
circumvent, -ed, -ing
circumvention

circus, circuses
cirrhosis
  cirriculum — curriculum
  cirrosis — cirrhosis
cirrus
cissy, cissies
  cist — cyst
cistern
  cistitis — cystitis
citadel
citation
cite, cited, citing (quote)
  cite — sight (see)
  cite — site (place)
  citie — city
citizen
citric acid
  citris — citrus
citron
citronella
  citros — citrus
citrous
citrus
city, cities
civet
civic
  civies — civvies
  civik — civic
civil, -ly
civilian
civilisation
civilise, -lised, -lising
civility, -ties
  civit — civet
civvies
clad
cladding
claim, -ed, -ing
claimable
  claimabul — claimable
claimant
claimer
clairvoyance
clairvoyant
clam, clammed, clamming
clamber, -ed, -ing
  clame — claim

  clamer — clamour
  clamerus — clamorous
clammily
clamminess
clammy, -mier, -miest
clamorous, -ly
clamour, -ed, -ing
clamp, -ed, -ing
  clamy — clammy
clan
clandestine, -ly
clang, -ed, -ing
clanger (error)
clangour (loud sound)
clangourous, -ly
clank, -ed, -ing
clannish, -ly
clap, clapped, clapping
clapper
clapperboard
claptrap
claret
clarify, -fied, -fying
clarification
clarifier
clarinet
clarinettist
clarion
clarionet
clarity
  clark — clerk
  claryon — clarion
clash, -ed, -ing
  clasify — classify
clasp, -ed, -ing
  clasroom — classroom
class, classes
classable
  classabul — classable
classer
classic
classical, -ly
classicism
classicist
classifiable
  classifiabul — classifiable
classification

classify, -fied, -fying
classroom
classy, classier, classiest
clatter, -ed, -ing
clause (grammar)
   clause — claws (animal)
   claustrofobia — claustrophobia
claustrophobia
claves
   clavicel — clavicle
clavichord
   clavicord — clavichord
clavier
claw, -ed, -ing
claws (animal)
   claws — clause (grammar)
clay
clayey
   clayie — clayey
clayish
   claym — claim
clean, -ed, -ing
cleanliness
cleanse, cleansed, cleansing
cleanskin
clear, -ed, -ing
clearance
clearly
clearness
clearway
cleat
cleavage
cleave, cleaved, cleaving
cleaver
   cleavidge — cleavage
   cleek — clique
   cleeshay — cliché
   cleet — cleat
   cleeve — cleave
   cleevage — cleavage
   cleever — cleaver
   cleevidge — cleavage
clef
cleft
clematis
clemency

   clemensy — clemency
clement
clench, -ed, -ing
   clenliness — cleanliness
   clense — cleanse
cleptomania
clergy, -gies
clergyman, -men
cleric
clerical, -ly
clerk
clever, cleverer, cleverest
cleverly
cleverness
clew (ball)
   clew — clue (hint)
clianthus
   clichay — cliché
cliché, -chés
click, -ed, -ing (sound)
   click — clique (group)
clicker
   clidesdale — clydesdale
client
clientele
   clientell — clientele
cliff
cliff-hanger
climacteric (crucial)
climactic (climax)
   climaks — climax
climate (weather)
climatic, -ally
climatology
climax, -maxes
climb, -ed, -ing (upward)
clime (region)
clinch, -ed, -ing
clincher
cling, clung, clinging
clinger
clinic
clinical, -ly
clink, -ed, -ing
clinker, -ed, -ing
clip, clipped, clipping
clipper

clique (group)
  clique   click (sound)
clitoris
  clitris   clitoris
cloak
cloak-and-dagger
cloakroom
clobber, -ed, -ing
clock, -ed, -ing
clockwise
clockwork
clod
cloddish
clodhopper
clog, clogged, clogging
cloggy
cloister, -ed, -ing
cloistral
  cloke   cloak
clone, cloned, cloning
  cloride   chloride
  clorinate   chlorinate
  clorine   chlorine
  clorofil   chlorophyll
  cloroform   chloroform
  clorophyll   chlorophyll
close, closed, closing
close, closer, closest
closed-circuit
closeness
closet, -ed, -ing
closure
clot, clotted, clotting
cloth, cloths (fabric)
clothe, clothed, clothing
clothes (garments)
clothier
cloud, -ed, -ing
cloudbank
cloudburst
cloudless, -ly
cloudy, cloudier, cloudiest
clout, -ed, -ing
clove
cloven
cloven-hoofed
clover

cloverleaf, -leaves
  clowd   cloud
  clowdless   cloudless
  clowdy   cloudy
clown, -ed, -ing
clownery
clownish, -ly
  clowt   clout
cloy, -ed, -ing
  cloyster   cloister
club, clubbed, clubbing
clubhouse
  cluch   clutch
cluck, -ed, -ing
clucky
clue, clued, cluing (hint)
  clue   clew (ball)
clump, -ed, -ing
clumpish
clumpy
clumsily
clumsiness
clumsy, -sier, -siest
clung
  clurgy   clergy
cluster, -ed, -ing
clutch, -ed, -ing
clutch-start
clutter, -ed, -ing
Clydesdale
coach, -ed, -ing
coachman, -men
  coacksial   coaxial
coagulate, -lated, -lating
coagulation
coagulator
  coaks   coax
coal
coaldust
coalesce, -lesced, -lescing
coalescence
coalescent
  coaless   coalesce
  coalessence   coalescence
  coalessent   coalescent
coalface
coalfield

coalishun	coalition	cockatrice	
coalition		cockatriss	cockatrice
coalitionist		cockcrow	
coalmine		cockelshell	cockleshell
coalminer		cockerel	
coalmining		cocker spaniel	
coarse, coarser, coarsest (rough)		cocket	coquette
coarse	course (path)	cocketry	coquetry
coarsen, -ed, -ing		cockeyed	
coast, -ed, -ing		cockfight	
coastal		cockily	
coaster		cockiness	
coastgard	coastguard	cockle	
coastguard		cockleshell	
coastline		cockney, -neys	
coat, -ed, -ing		cockpit	
coat-hanger		cockroach, -es	
coatless		cockroch	cockroach
coax, -ed, -ing		cockscomb	
coaxial		cockshure	cocksure
coaxingly		cocksure	
coaxiul	coaxial	cocktail	
cobalt		cocktale	cocktail
cobber		cockul	cockle
cobble, -bled, -bling		cocky, cockier, cockiest	
cobbler		coco, -cos (palm tree)	
cobblestone		cocoa (drink)	
cober	cobber	coconut	
coble	cobble	cocoon	
cobler	cobbler	coddle, -dled, -dling	
coblestone	cobblestone	code, coded, coding	
cobulstone	cobblestone	codecks	codex
cobra		codeen	codeine
cobweb		codeine	
cocain		codex, codices	
cocaine		codger	
cocane	cocaine	codicil	
cocanut	coconut	codiene	codeine
cocatoo	cockatoo	codification	
coccix	coccyx	codifier	
coccyx, -coccyges		codify, -fied, -fying	
coch	coach	codisil	codicil
cochineal		codle	coddle
cochineel	cochineal	codswallop	
cock, -ed, -ing		codul	coddle
cockade		co-ed	
cockatoo		coeducashun	coeducation

coeducation
coeducational
coefficient
  coefishent   coefficient
  coegsist   coexist
coequal, -ly
coequality
coerce, -erced, -ercing
coercible
  coercibul   coercible
coercion
coercive, -ly
  coerse   coerce
  coershun   coercion
  coersible   coercible
  coersive   coercive
coeval, -ly
  coevil   coeval
  coevul   coeval
coexist, -ed, -ing
coexistence
  coexistense   coexistence
coexistent
  cofee   coffee
  cofer   coffer
  cofey   coffee
  coff   cough
coffee
coffer
coffin
  cofin   coffin
cog
cogency
  cogenital   congenital
cogent, -ly
  coger   codger
cogitate, -tated, -tating
cogitation
cogitative
cognac
cognate
cognisance
  cognisanse   cognisance
cognisant
  cognishun   cognition
cognition
cognitive

cohabit, -ed, -ing
cohabitation
  cohearent   coherent
cohere, -hered, -hering
coherence
  coherense   coherence
coherent, -ly
  coheshun   cohesion
cohesion
cohesive, -ly
cohort
coiffure
  coifur   coiffure
coil, -ed, -ing
coin, -ed, -ing
coinage
coincide, -cided, -ciding
coincidence
coincident, -ly
  coinidge   coinage
  coinsidence   coincidence
  coinsident   coincident
coir
  coishun   coition
coition
coitus
coke, coked, coking
  coket   coquette
  cokoon   cocoon
col
cola
colander
  colapse   collapse
cold, -er, -est
  cole   coal
  colender   colander
  coler   choler (anger)
  colera   cholera
  coleric   choleric
  colesterol   cholesterol
coleus
colic
colicky
colitis
collaborate, -rated, -rating
collaboration
collaborator

collage
collapsable
collapse, -lapsed, -lapsing
collapsible
collar, -ed, -ing (neck)
   collar   choler (anger)
collarbone
collate, -lated, -lating
collateral
collation
collator
colleague
collect, -ed, -ing
collectable
collection
collective, -ly
collectivism
collector
college
collegian
collegiate
   coller   choler (anger)
   coller   collar (neck)
collide, -lided, -liding
collie
collier
colliery, -ries
collinear, -ly
collision
collocate, -cated, -cating
collocation
   collonial   colonial
colloquial, -ally
colloquialism
colloquy, -quies
collusion
collusive, -ly
cologne
colon
   colonade   colonnade

> For other **col-** words,
> look under **coll-**.

colonel
colonial, -ly
colonisation
colonise, -nised, -nising

coloniser
colonnade
colony, -nies
   color   colour
coloratura
   colorful   colourful
colossal, -ly
colossus, -lossuses
colour, -ed, -ing
colour-bar
colour-blindness
colourful, -fully
colt
coltish, -ly
   colum   column
columbine
column

> For other **col-** words,
> look under **coll-**.

columnist
coma (sleep)
   coma   comma (mark)
comatose, -ly
comb, -ed, -ing
combat, -bated, -bating
combatant
combative, -ly
comber
combination
combine, -bined, -bining
combustible
combustibility
   combustibul   combustible
combustion
come, came, come, coming
comeback
comedian
comedienne
comedy, -dies
comeliness
comely, -lier, -liest
   comend   commend
comestible
   comestibul   comestible
comet
comeuppance

comfert	comfort
comfertable	comfortable
comferter	comforter
comfort, -ed, -ing	
comfortable, -bly	
comforter	
comfortless, -ly	
comfy	
comic	
comical, -ly	
comicality	

> Look under **comm-** if the
> word is not under **com-**.

comma (mark)	
comma	coma (sleep)
command, -ed, -ing	
commandant	
commander	
commandment	
commando, -dos, -does	
commemorate, -rated, -rating	
commemoration	
commemorative, -ly	
commence, -menced, -mencing	
commencement	
commend, -ed, -ing	
commendable, -bly	
commendabul	commendable
commendation	
commendatory	
commense	commence
commensurable, -bly	
commensurabul	commensurable
commensurate	
comment, -ed, -ing	
commentary, -aries	
commentater	commentator
commentator	
commentry	commentary
commer	comma
commerce	
commercial, -ly	
commercialisation	
commercialise, -lised, -lising	
commercialism	
commershal	commercial

commershalise	commercialise
commisar	commissar
commisariat	commissariat
commisary	commissary
commiserate, -rated, -rating	
commiseration	
commishun	commission
commision	commission
commisionaire	commissionaire
commisioner	commissioner
commissar	
commissariat	
commissary, -saries	
commission	
commissionaire	
commissioner	
commit, -mitted, -mitting	
commitment	
committal	
committee	
commitul	committal
commo	
commodaty	commodity
commode	
commodious, -ly	
commodity, -ties	
commodius	commodious
commodoor	commodore
commodore	
common, -ly	
commonality, -ties	
commoner	
commonplace	
Commons	
commonsense	
commonsensical	
Commonwealth	
Commonwelth	Commonwealth
commoshun	commotion
commotion	
communal, -ly	
commune, -muned, -muning	
communicable	
communicabul	communicable
communicate, -cated, -cating	
communication	
communicative	

communicator
  communikay   communique
communion
communique
communism
communist
communistic
community, -ties
commutation
commute, -muted, -muting
commuter

> Look under **comm-** if the
> word is not under **com-**.

compact
  compair   compare (liken)
  compair   compere (stage)
companion
companionable, -bly
companionship
company, -nies
  companyun   companion
comparable, -bly
  comparabul   comparable
comparative, -ly
compare, -pared, -paring (liken)
  compare   compere (stage)
comparison
compartment
compartmentalise, -ised, -ising
  compas   compass
  compashun   compassion
  compashunate   compassionate
compass, -es
compass, -ed, -ing
compassion
compassionate, -nated, -nating
compatibility
compatible, -bly
  compatibul   compatible
  compatition   competition
compatriot
compel, -pelled, -pelling
compendium, -diums, -dia
compensate, -sated, -sating
compensation
compensator

compensatory
  compensatry   compensatory
  compeny   company
compere, -pered, -pering (stage)
  compere   compare (liken)
  competant   competent
  competative   competitive
compete, -peted, -peting
competency
  competense   competence
competent, -ly
  competishun   competition
competition
competitive, -ly
competitor
compilation
compile, -piled, -piling
compiler
  compinsation   compensation
complacency, -cies
complacent, -ly (smug)
complain, -ed, -ing
complainant
complaint
complaisant (obliging)
  complanant   complainant
  complane   complain
  complant   complaint
  complasense   complacence
  complasent   complacent
complement, -ed, -ing (complete)
  complement   compliment
                   (praise)
complementary (completing)
  complementary   complimentary
                   (free)
complete, -pleted, -pleting
completion
complex, -ly
complexion
complexity, -ties
compliable
  compliabul   compliable
compliance
compliant, -ly
complicate, -cated, -cating
complication

complicity
   complient   compliant
compliment, -ed, -ing (praise)
   compliment   complement
               (completely)
complimentary (free)
   complimentary   complementary
   complissity   complicity
comply, -plied, -plying
compo
component
comport
comportment
compose, -posed, -posing
composedly
   composhure   composure
   composishun   composition
composite, -ly
composition
compositor
compost
composure
   compot   compote
compote
compound, -ed, -ing
compoundable
   compoundabul   compoundable
comprehend, -ed, -ing
comprehendingly
   comprehenshun comprehension
comprehensible, -bly
comprehension
comprehensive, -ly
comprehensiveness
compress, -ed, -ing
compressibility
compressible
   compressibul   compressible
compression
compressor
comprisal
comprise, -prised, -prising
compromise, -mised, -mising
comptroller
   compulsery   compulsory
   compulshun   compulsion
compulsion

compulsive, -ly
compulsorily
compulsory
   compulsrey   compulsory
compunction
computability
computation
compute, -puted, -puting
computer
computerisation
computer program
computer terminal
   comrad   comrade
comrade
comradeship

> Look under **comm-** if the
> word is not under **com-**.

con, conned, conning
   conbine   combine
concave, -ly
concavity, -ties
conceal, -ed, -ing
concealable
   concealabul   concealable
concealment
concede, -ceded, -ceding
conceit
conceited, -ly
conceivable
conceivably
   conceivabul   conceivable
conceive, -ceived, -ceiving
   concensus   consensus
concentrate, -trated, -trating
concentration
concentric
concentricity
   concepshun   conception
concept
conception
conceptual, -ly
conceptualise, -lised, -lising
concern, -ed, -ing
concert, -ed, -ing
concertina
concertmaster

concerto, -tos, -ti
concession
conch, conchs, conches
  concherto   concerto
  conciet   conceit
  concieted   conceited
  concievable   conceivable
  concieve   conceive
conciliate, -ated, -ating
conciliation
conciliator
conciliatory
concise, -ly

> Look under **cons-** if the
> word is not under **conc-**.

conciseness
conclave
conclude, -cluded, -cluding
  conclushun   conclusion
conclusion
conclusive, -ly
concoct, -ed, -ing
concoction
concomitance
concomitancy
concomitant, -ly
concord
concordance
  concordanse   concordance
concordant
  concorse   concourse
concourse
  concreet   concrete
concrete, -creted, -creting
concretely
concreteness
concubinage
concubine
concupiscence
concupiscent
  concupissense concupiscence
  concupissent   concupiscent
concur, -curred, -curring
  concurence   concurrence
  concurent   concurrent
concurrence

concurrent, -ly
  concus   concuss
  concushun   concussion
concuss, -ed, -ing
concussion
concussive
  condament   condiment
  condaminium condominium
  condansation condensation
  condem   condemn
condemn, -ed, -ing
condemnation
condemnatory
  condence   condense
  condencer   condenser
condensation
condense, -densed, -densing
condenser
  condensor   condenser
condescend, -ed, -ing
condescension
condiment
  condisend   condescend
  condisension condescension
  condishun   condition
  condishunal   conditional
condition, -ed, -ing
conditional, -ly
condolatory
condole, -doled, -doling
condolence
  condolense   condolence
condolingly
condominium
condonation
condone, -doned, -doning
condor
conducive
  conducshun   conduction
conduct, -ed, -ing
  conducter   conductor
conductible
conductibility
  conductibul   conductible
conduction
conductivity, -ties
conductor

conductress
conduit
   condusive   conducive
cone
   conecshun   connection
   conect   connect
   conective   connective
confection
confectionary, -aries (factory)
confectionery, -eries (sweets)
   confedence   confidence
confederacy, -cies
   confederasy   confederacy
confederate, -rated, -rating
confederation
confer, -ferred, -ferring
conference
   conferm   confirm
confess, -ed, -ing
confesser
confession
confessional
confessor
confetti
confidant (trusted man)
   confidant   confident (sure)
confidante (trusted woman)
confide, -fided, -fiding
confidence
   confidenshul   confidential
confident (sure)
   confident   confidant
                 (trusted man)
confidential, -ly
confidentiality
   configeration   configuration
configuration
confine, -fined, -fining
confinement
confirm, -ed, -ing
confirmable
confirmation
confiscate, -cated, -cating
confiscation
conflagration
conflict, -ed, -ing
confluence

confluent
conform, -ed, -ing
conformable, -bly
   conformabul   conformable
conformist
conformity, -ties
confound, -ed, -ing
   confownd   confound
   confrence   conference
confront, -ed, -ing
confrontation
   confurm   confirm
confuse, -fused, -fusing
confusion
confutation
confute, -futed, -futing
conga (dance)
   conga   conger (eel)
congeal, -ed, -ing
   congeel   congeal
   congeneal   congenial
congenial, -ly
congeniality
congenital, -ly
conger (eel)
   conger   conga (dance)
congest, -ed, -ing
congestion
congestive
conglomerate, -rated, -rating
conglomeration
   congradulation   congratulation
   congragation   congregation
congratulate, -lated, -lating
congratulation
congratulatory
congregate, -gated, -gating
congregation
congregational
congress
congressional
   congrewent   congruent
   congrewus   congruous
congruence
congruent
congruity, -ties
congruous, -ly

conic
conical, -ly
conifer
coniferous
  conjeckture   conjecture
conjecturable, -bly
conjecture, -tured, -turing
  conjenial   congenial
  conjestion   congestion
conjoin, -ed, -ing
conjoint, -ly
  conjuce   conduce
conjugal, -ly
conjugality
conjugate, -gated, -gating
conjugation
  conjugel   conjugal
  conjuice   conduce
  conjuncshun   conjunction
conjunct, -ly
conjunction
conjunctional, -ly
conjunctive, -ly
conjunctivitis
conjuncture
conjuration
conjure, -jured, -juring
conjurer
conjuror
conk, -ed, -ing
conker (nut)
  conker   conquer (win)
  conkwest   conquest
con man, -men
connect, -ed, -ing
connectedly
connecter
connection
connective, -ly
connector
  connesser   connoisseur
  connewbial   connubial
conning tower
connivance
  connivanse   connivance
connive, -nived, -niving
connoisseur

connotation
connote, -noted, -noting
connubial, -ly
  connubiul   connubial
  conosseur   connoisseur
  conote   connote
conquer, -ed, -ing
conquerable
  conquerabul   conquerable
  conquerer   conqueror
conqueror
conquest
conquistador
consanguine
consanguineous, -ly
consanguinity
  consceintious conscientious
conscience
  conscienshus conscientious
conscientious, -ly
conscious, -ly
consciousness
  conscripshun conscription
conscript, -ed, -ing
conscription
  conseal   conceal
  conseat   conceit
consecrate, -crated, -crating
consecration
consecutive
  consede   concede
  consekwence consequence
consensus
consent, -ed, -ing
consequence
consequent
consequential, -ly
  conservatery conservatory
conservation
conservational
conservationist
conservative, -ly
conservatism
conservatoire
conservatorium
conservatory, -tries
  conservatry   conservatory

conserve, -served, -serving
conserver
  consession   concession
  consicrate   consecrate
consider, -ed, -ing
considerable, -ably
  considerabul   considerable
considerate, -ly
consideration
consign, -ed, -ing
consignable
  consignabul   consignable
consignee
consigner
  consignible   consignable
consignment
consignor
  consiliate   conciliate
  consine   consign
  consinee   consignee
  consinement   consignment
  consinor   consignor
  consise   concise
consist, -ed, -ing
consistence
consistency, -cies
  consistense   consistence
  consistensy   consistency
consistent, -ly
consolable
  consolabul   consolable
consolation
console, -soled, -soling
consoler
consolingly
consolidate, -dated, -dating
consolidated revenue
consolidation
consolidator
consommé
consonance
consonant, -ly
consort, -ed, -ing
consortium, -tia
conspicuous, -ly
conspicuousness
conspiracy, -cies

  conspirasy   conspiracy
  conspirater   conspirator
conspirator
conspiratory
  conspiratry   conspiratory
conspire, -spired, -spiring
constable
  constabul   constable
constabulary, -ries
constancy
  constansy   constancy
constant, -ly
  constapation   constipation
constellation
consternation
constipate, -pated, -pating
constipation
constituency, -cies
  constituensy   constituency
constituent
constitute, -tuted, -tuting
constitution
constitutional, -ly
constrain, -ed, -ing
constraint
  constrickshun   constriction
constrict, -ed, -ing
constriction
construct, -ed, -ing
construction
constructive, -ly
constructor
construe, -strued, -struing
consul
consular
consulate
  consuler   consular
consult, -ed, -ing
consultant
consultation
consultative
  consultent   consultant
consulter
consumable
  consumabul   consumable
consume, -sumed, -suming
consumer

consumerism	contiguity
consummate, -mated, -mating	contiguous, -ly
consummation	continence
consummative	continense continence
consummé consommé	continent
consumpshun consumption	continental
consumption	contingency, -cies
consumptive, -ly	contingensy contingency
contact, -ed, -ing	contingent, -ly
contact lenses	continnuation continuation
contageous contagious	continual, -ly
contagion	continuance
contagious, -ly	continuanse continuance
contagus contagious	continuation
contajus contagious	continue, -ued, -uing
contain, -ed, -ing	continuity, -ties
container	continuous, -ly
containment	continuum, -tinuums, -tinua
contaminate, -nated, -nating	contorshun contortion
contamination	contort, -ed, -ing
contane contain	contortion
contanement containment	contortionist
contaner container	contour
contemplate, -plated, -plating	contraband
contemplation	contraception
contemplative, -ly	contraceptive, -ly
contemporaneous, -ly	contrackshun contraction
contemporary, -raries	contract, -ed, -ing
contempt	contraction
contemptable contemptible	contractor
contemptible, -bly	contractual
contemptibul contemptible	contradickshun contradiction
contemptuous, -ly	contradict, -ed, -ing
contend, -ed, -ing	contradiction
contender	contradictory, -ries
contenshun contention	contralto, -ti
contenshus contentious	contrapshun contraption
content	contraption
contented, -ly	contrarily
contention	contrariness
contentious, -ly	contrariwise
contentment	contrary, -ries
contest, -ed, -ing	contrasepshun contraception
contestant	contraseptive contraceptive
contestent contestant	contrast, -ed, -ing
context	contravene, -vened, -vening
contextual, -ly	contravenshun contravention

contribushun   contribution
contribute, -buted, -buting
contribution
contributor
contributory
    contributry   contributory
    contrishun   contrition
contrite, -ly
contrition
contrivance
    contrivanse   contrivance
contrive, -trived, -triving
control, -trolled, -trolling
controllable
    controllabul   controllable
controller
    controvershal   controversial
controversial, -ly
controversy, -sies
contumely, -lies
contuse, -tused, -tusing
    contushun   contusion
contusion
contusive
conurbation
convalesce, -lesced, -lescing
convalescence
    convalescense   convalescent
convalescent
    convaless   convalesce
    convalessence   convalescence
convection
convective, -ly
convector
convene, -vened, -vening
convenience
    conveniense   convenience
convenient, -ly
convenor
    convenshun   convention
    convenshunal   conventional
convent
convention
conventional, -ly
conventionalism
converge, -verged, -verging
conversant, -ly

conversation
conversational, -ly
conversationalist
converse, -versed, -versing
conversely
    conversent   conversant
    convershun   conversion
conversion
convert, -ed, -ing
    convertabul   convertible
converter
convertible, -ly
    convertibul   convertible
convex, -ly
convexity, -ties
convey, -ed, -ing
conveyance
conveyancer
conveyancing
    conveyanse   conveyance
conveyor belt
    convickshun   conviction
convict, -ed, -ing
conviction
    convienence   convenience
convince, -vinced, -vincing
convincible
    convincibul   convincible
convincingly
convivial, -ly
convivialty
convocation
convoke, -voked, -voking
    convolushun   convolution
convolute, -luted, -luting
convolution
convoy, -ed, -ing
convulse, -vulsed, -vulsing
    convulshun   convulsion
convulsion
convulsive, -ly
    conyac   cognac
coo, cooed, cooing
cooee, cooeed, cooeeing
    cooger   cougar
cook, -ed, -ing
cookery, -eries

cookhouse

cookie, cookies

cookoo   cuckoo

cool, -ed, -ing

coolabah

coolabar   coolabah

coolamon

coolant

coolie (labourer)

coolly (calmly)

coop, -ed, -ing

co-op

cooper

cooperage

cooperate, -rated, -rating

cooperation

cooperative, -ly

coopon   coupon

co-opt, -ed, -ing

coordinate, -nated, -nating

coordination

coordinator

cop, copped, copping (accept)

coparison   comparison

cope, coped, coping (put up with)

coper   copper

copha

copier

co-pilot

copious, -ly

cop-out

copper

copperhead

copperplate

coppy   copy

copra

cops   copse

copse

cop shop

copula, -lae

copulate, -lated, -lating

copulation

copulative, -ly

copy, copies

copy, copied, copying

copybook

copycat, -catted, -catting

copyer   copier

copyist

copyright, -ed, -ing (licence)

copyrite   copyright

copywriter

coquet, -quetted, -quetting

coquetry

coquette

coquettish, -ly

coral (reef)

coral   choral (sing)

coral   corral (yard)

coralfish

corcus   caucus

cord (rope)

cord   chord (music)

cordage

corded

cordial, -ly

cordiality

cordige   cordage

cordon, -ed, -ing

cordon bleu

cords (trousers)

corduroy

core, cored, coring (centre)

core   caw (cry)

core   corps (group)

corecshun   correction

corect   correct

corection   correction

corective   corrective

corelate   correlate

corella

coreografy   choreography

corespond   correspond

corespondence   correspondence

corespondense   correspondence

co-respondent (divorce)

corespondent   correspondent

coriander

coridoor   corridor

coridor   corridor

Corinthian

coriografy   choreography

corispond   correspond

corispondence   correspondence

corispondent	correspondent	corpse (body)	
corister	chorister	corpse	corps (group)
cork, -ed, -ing		corpulence	
corkage		corpulense	corpulence
corker		corpulent, -ly	
corkscrew, -ed, -ing		corpus, -pora	
corm		corpuscle	
cormorant		corpuscular	
corn		corpusle	corpuscle
corncob		corpussel	corpuscle
cornea, -neas, -neae		corral, -ralled, -ralling (yard)	
corneal		corral	choral (sing)
corned beef		correckshun	correction
corneel	corneal	correct, -ed, -ing	
corner, -ed, -ing		correction	
cornerstone		correctional	
cornet		corrective, -ly	
cornflour		correlate, -lated, -lating	
cornia	cornea	correlation	
cornice, -niced, -nicing		correlative, -ly	
cornstalk		correlativity	
cornucopia		correspond, -ed, -ing	
corny, -nier, -niest		correspondence	
coroborate	corroborate	correspondent	
coroborator	corroborator	corridor	
coroboree	corroboree	Corriedale	
corode	corrode	corroborate, -rated, -rating	
corola	corolla	corroboration	
corolary	corollary	corroborative, -ly	
corolla		corroborator	
corollary, -ries		corroboree	
corona, -nas, -nae		corrode, -roded, -roding	
coronary		corrodible	
coronary thrombosis		corrodibul	corrodible
coronation		corrollary	corollary
coroner		corroshun	corrosion
coronet		corrosion	
coroshun	corrosion	corrosive, -ly	
corosive	corrosive	corrugate, -gated, -gating	
corparation	corporation	corrugated iron	
corperal	corporal	corrugation	
corporal, -ly		corrupshun	corruption
corporate, -ly		corrupt, -ed, -ing	
corporation		corruptabul	corruptible
corporeal, -ly		corruptible, -bly	
corps (group)		corruptibility	
corps	corpse (body)	corruptibul	corruptible

corruption		cost, cost, costed, costing	
corsage		cost	coast
corsair		co-star, -starred, -starring	
corsashun	causation	coster	
corse	coarse (rough)	costguard	coastguard
corse	course (path)	costliness	
corsen	coarsen	costly, -lier, -liest	
corset		costume, -tumed, -tuming	
corsetry		costume jewellery	
corshun	caution	cosy, -sies	
corshus	cautious	cosy, -sier, -siest	
corsit	corset	cot	
cort	caught (held)	cotage	cottage
cort	court (law)	cotchineal	cochineal
cort marshal	court martial	cote (shelter)	
cortage	cortege	cote	coat (garment)
cortege		coterie	
corterise	cauterise	cotige	cottage
cortex, -tices		coton	cotton
cortier	courtier	cotoneaster	
cortion	caution	cotonwool	cottonwool
cortious	cautious	cottage	
cortisan	courtesan	cotter pin	
cortisone		cotton	
cortly	courtly	cottonbush	
cortroom	courtroom	cottonwood	
cortship	courtship	cottonwool	
cortyard	courtyard	cottony	
corugate	corrugate	cou daytar	coup d'état
corupt	corrupt	couch	
coruptible	corruptible	cougar	
coruption	corruption	cough, -ed, -ing	
corus	chorus	could	
corvet	corvette	couldn't (could not)	
corvette		couldnt	couldn't
cos		coulter	
cosh		councel	council (meeting)
cosmetic			
cosmetically		councel	counsel (advice)
cosmografy	cosmography		
cosmography, -phies		council (meeting)	
cosmology		council	counsel (advice)
cosmonaut			
cosmonort	cosmonaut	counciller	councillor
cosmopolitan		councillor (member)	
cosmos		councillor	counsellor (adviser)
Cossack			

counsel, -selled, -selling (advice)

| counsel | council (meeting) |
| counseller | counsellor |

counsellor (adviser)

| counsellor | councillor (member) |

count, -ed, -ing
countdown
countenance, -nanced, -nancing

| countenanse | countenance |

counter
counteract, -ed, -ing
counteraction
counteractive, -ly
counterattack, -ed, -ing
counterbalance, -anced, -ancing
counter culture
counterespionage

| counterfeet | counterfeit |

counterfeit, -ed, -ing
counterfeiter
counterintelligence
countermand, -ed, -ing
counterpane
counterpart
counterpoint
counterproductive
counter-revolution
counter-revolutionary, -aries
countersign, -ed, -ing
countersignature

| countersine | countersign |
| counterwait | counterweight |

counterweight
countess

| countie | county |

countless
country, -tries
countryman, -men
countryside
county, -ties
coup, -coups

| coupay | coupé |

coup de grace
coup d'état
coupé

couple, -led, -ling
couplet
coupon
courage
courageous, -ly
courier
course (path)

| course | coarse (rough) |
| coursen | coarsen |

court, -ed, -ing (law)

| court | caught (held) |

courtesan
courtesy, -sies
courthouse
courtier
courtly, -lier, -liest

| court marshal | court martial |

court martial
courtroom
courtyard
cousin
couture
couturier
covenant
cover, -ed, -ing
coverage
covert, -ly
cover-up
covet, -ed, -ing
covetous, -ly
covey, -eys
coward (scared)

| coward | cowered (cringed) |

cowardice

| cowardiss | cowardice |

cowardly
cowboy
cower, -ed, -ing (cringe)

| cowerd | coward |
| cowered | coward (scared) |

cowl, -ed, -ing
cowlick
cowling

For **cown-** words,
look under **coun-**.

cowslip
cox
coxcomb
  coxe   coax
coxswain
coy, -ly
  coyn   coin
coyote
crab, crabbed, crabbing
crab-apple
crabby, -bier, -biest
crablouse
crack, -ed, -ing
crackdown
cracker
crackle, -led, -ling
crackpot
  crackul   crackle
cradle, -dled, -dling
cradle-snatcher
  cradul   cradle
craft
craftily
craftiness
craftsman, -men
craftsmanship
crafty, -tier, -tiest
crag
cragged
craggy, -gier, -giest
  crain   crane
crake
cram, crammed, cramming
cramp, -ed, -ing
cranberry, -ries
crane, craned, craning
cranial, -ly
cranium, -nia
crank, -ed, -ing
crankcase
crankiness
crankshaft
cranky, -kier, -kiest
cranny, -nies
craps
crapulous
crash, -ed, -ing

crasher
crass
crate, crated, crating
crater
cravat
crave, craved, craving
craven, -ly
craw
crawl, -ed, -ing
crawler
crayfish, -fishes, -fish
crayon, -ed, -ing
  craype   crepe
craypot
  craysh   crèche
craze, crazed, crazing
crazily
craziness
crazy, -zier, -ziest
  creacher   creature
creak, -ed, -ing (squeak)
  creak   creek (stream)
cream, -ed, -ing
creaminess
creamy, -mier, -miest
  creap   creep
crease, creased, creasing
create, -ated, -ating
  creater   creator
creation
creative, -ly
creativeness
creativity
creator
creature
crèche
  creecher   creature
credence
  credense   credence
  credenshul   credential
credential
credibility
credible
credibly
  credibul   credible
credit, -ed, -ing
creditable, -bly

creditabul — creditable
credit card
crediter — creditor
creditor
credo, -dos
credulity
credulous, -ly
credulousness
creed
creek (stream)
creek — creak (squeak)
creel
creem — cream
creep, crept, creeping
creeper
creepiness
creeps
creepy, -pier, -piest
cremate, -mated, -mating
cremation
crematorium
creme
crenellate, -lated, -lating
creole
creosote, -soted, -soting
crepe, creped, creping
crept
crepuscular
crescendo, -dos
crescent
cresh — crèche
creshendo — crescendo
cress
cressent — crescent
crest, -ed, -ing
crestfallen, -ly
cretin
cretinism
cretinous
creture — creature
crevase — crevasse
crevase — crevice
crevasse, -vassed, -vassing
crevice
creviss — crevice
crew, -ed, -ing
crewel (yarn)

crewel — cruel (harsh)
crewl — cruel
crew neck
crews (sailors)
crews — cruise (ship)
crib, cribbed, cribbing
cribage — cribbage
cribbage
cribbidge — cribbage
crick
cricket
cricketer
crier
crime
criminal, -ly
criminality, -ties
criminologist
criminology
crimp, -ed, -ing
crimpy, -pier, -piest
crimson
cringe, cringed, cringing
crinkle, -kled, -kling
crinkul — crinkle
crinkly
crinoline
cripple, -pled, -pling
cript — crypt
criptic — cryptic
criptograf — cryptograph
criptogram — cryptogram
criptograph — cryptograph
cripul — cripple
crisalis — chrysalis
crisalus — chrysalis
criscros — crisscross
crisen — christen
Crisendom — Christendom
crisis, -ses
crisp, -ed, -ing
crispness
crispy
crisscross
Crist — Christ
cristal — crystal
cristaline — crystalline
cristalise — crystallise

Cristian — Christian
Cristianity — Christianity
criteek — critique
criterion, -teria
critic
critical, -ly
criticise, -cised, -cising
criticism
critique
critisise — criticise
croak, -ed, -ing
croaky
crochet, -ed, -ing
crock
crockadile — crocodile
crockery
crocodile
crocus, crocuses
croft
crofter
croissant
crokay — croquet
cromatic — chromatic
crome — chrome
cromosome — chromosome
crone
crony, -nies
crood — crude
crook
crooked, -ly
crookedness
croon, -ed, -ing
crooner
crop, cropped, cropping
crop-dust, -ed, -ing
crop-duster
cropper
croquet (sport)
croquette (food)
crosier
cross, -ed, -ing
crossbar
crossbench
crossbencher
crossbones
crossbow
crossbreed, -bred, -breeding

crosscheck
cross-country
crosscut, -cut, -cutting
cross-examination
cross-examine, -ined, -ining
cross-examiner
cross-eyed
cross-fertilisation
cross-fertilise, -lised, -lising
crossover
cross-pollinate, -nated, -nating
cross-purpose
cross-reference, -renced, -rencing
crossroad
cross-section
cross-stitch, -ed, -ing
crosswise
crossword puzzle
crotch
crotchet
crotchetiness
crotchety
crouch, -ed, -ing
croup
croupier
crouton
crow, crowed, crowing
crowbar
crowd, -ed, -ing
croweater
crown, -ed, -ing
crown-of-thorns
crow's-foot, -feet
crow's-nest
crucial, -ly
crucibel — crucible
crucible
crucibul — crucible
crucifix
crucifixion
cruciform, -ly
crucify, -fied, -fying
crude, cruder, crudest
crudeness
crudity, -ties
cruel, cruelled, cruelling
cruelty, -ties

cruet
cruise, cruised, cruising (ship)
   cruise   crews (sailors)
cruiser
   crum   crumb
crumb, -ed, -ing
crumble, -bled, -bling
crumbly, -blier, -bliest
   crumbul   crumble
crummy, -mier, -miest
crumpet
crumple, -pled, -pling
   crumpul   crumple
   crumy   crummy
crunch, -ed, -ing
crunchy, -chier, -chiest
crusade, -saded, -sading
crusader
crush, -ed, -ing
   crushal   crucial
crusher
   crusibul   crucible
crust
crustacean
   crustashun   crustacean
crustiness
crusty, crustier, crustiest
crutch, -ed, -ing
crux, cruxes, cruces
   cruze   cruise
cry, cries
cry, cried, crying
crypt
cryptic, -ally
cryptogram
cryptograph
cryptographer
cryptographic
cryptography
   crysalis   chrysalis
crystal
crystalline
crystallisation
crystallise, -lised, -lising
cub
cubby, -bies
cubbyhole

cubbyhouse
cube, cubed, cubing
cubic
cubical, -ly (cube-shaped)
cubicle (room)
cubism
cubist
cubmaster
   cuboard   cupboard
   cuby   cubby
   cubyhole   cubbyhole
   cubyhouse   cubbyhouse
cuckold, -ed, -ing
cuckoldry
cuckoo
cucumber
cud
   cuddel   cuddle
cuddle, -dled, -dling
cuddlesome
cuddly
cuddy, -dies
cudgel, -elled, -elling
cudgerie
   cudly   cuddly
   cudos   kudos
cue, cued, cuing (billiards)
   cue   queue (line)
cuff, -ed, -ing
cuisine
   culcher   culture
cul-de-sac
   culer   colour
culinary
cull, -ed, -ing
culminate, -nated, -nating
culmination
   culots   culottes
culottes
culpability
culpable, -bly
   culpabul   culpable
culprit
cult
cultism
cultist
cultivate, -vated, -vating

cultivater	cultivator	cure, cured, curing	
cultivation		curency	currency
cultivator		curent	current (flow)
cultural, -ly		curette, -retted, -retting	
culture, -tured, -turing		curfew	
cultured pearl		curiculum	curriculum
culture shock		curio, curios	
culvert		curiosity, -ties	
cumbasome	cumbersome	curious, -ly	
cumbersome, -ly		curiousness	
cumbersum	cumbersome	curius	curious
cumfurt	comfort	curl, -ed, -ing	
cumin		curler	
cummerbund		curlew	
cumpass	compass	curly, -lier, -liest	
cumquat		curnel	colonel
cumulative, -ly		currage	courage
cumulus		curragus	courageous
cuning	cunning	currajong	
cunning, -ly		currant (fruit)	
cuntry	country	currant	current (flow)
cup, cupped, cupping		currawong	
cupboard		currency, -cies	
cupbord	cupboard	currensy	currency
cupful, cupfuls		current (flow)	
cupid		current	currant (fruit)
cupidity		current account	
cupola		currently	
cuppa		curriculum, -lums, -la	
cur		curriculum vitae	
curable, -bly		curry, -ries	
curacao		curry, -ried, -rying	
curacy, -cies		curse, cursed, cursing	
curage	courage	cursive, -ly	
curant	currant (fruit)	cursor	
curare		curt, -ly	
curate		curtail, -ed, -ing	
curater	curator	curtailment	
curative, -ly		curtain, -ed, -ing	
curator		curtale	curtail
curatorial		curtsy, -sies	
curb, -ed, -ing (control)		curtsy, -sied, -sying	
curb	kerb (gutter)	curvaceous	
curcuit	circuit	curvachure	curvature
curd		curvashus	curvaceous
curdle, -dled, -dling		curvature	
curdul	curdle	curve, curved, curving	

curvilinear
cushion, -ed, -ing
  cushon   cushion
cushy, cushier, cushiest
cusp
cuspid
cuss
cussed, -ly
custard
custard-apple
custodial
custodian
  custodiul   custodial
  custodiun   custodian
custom
customarily
customary, -aries
custom-built
customer
custom-made
cut, cut, cutting
cutback
cute, cuter, cutest
cuteness
  cutical   cuticle
cuticle
  cuticul   cuticle
cutlass
cutlery
cutlet
cut-off
cut-out
cut-price
cutter
cutthroat
cuttlebone
cuttlefish, -fishes, -fish
  cuttulbone   cuttlebone
cutworm
  cuvenant   covenant
  cuver   cover
  cuvet   covet
  cuvey   covey
cyanide
cybernetics
cyclamate
cyclamen

cycle, cycled, cycling
cyclic
cyclist
cycloid
cyclone
cyclonic
cyclostyle, -led, -ling
cyder
cygnet (swan)
  cygnet   signet (ring)
cylinder
cymbal (instrument)
  cymbal   symbol (sign)
cymbalist
cymbidium
cynic
cynical, -ly
cynicism
  cynoshure   cynosure
cynosure
cypher
cypress
cyst
cystitis
cytology
czar
czarina
czarist
Czech
Czechoslovak
Czechoslovakia

Dd

dab, dabbed, dabbing
dabble, -bled, -bling

dabed	dabbed
dabing	dabbing
dable	dabble
dabul	dabble

dachshund

dacks	daks
dacor	decor

dad
daddy-long-legs
daemon
daffodil

daffodill	daffodil

daffy, daffier, daffiest

dafny	daphne
dafodil	daffodil

daft

dager	dagger

dagger
dahlia

dail	dale

daily

daim	dame
daintie	dainty

daintily
dainty, -tier, -tiest

dair	dare

dairy, -ries (milk)

dairy	diary (book)

dais

daisie	daisy

daisy
daks

dalee	dally
dalia	dahlia

dally,-lied, -lying
Dalmatian

daly	daily

dam, dammed, damming (water)

dam	damn (swear)

damage, -aged, -aging
damageable
damask
dame

damedge	damage
damestic	domestic

damn, -ed, -ing (swear)

damn	dam (water)

damnable, -bly

damnabul	damnable

damnation
damp
dampcourse
dampen, -ed, -ing
damper
damsel

damsil	damsel
damsul	damsel

dance, danced, dancing
dancer
dandelion

dandilion	dandelion

dandle, -dled, -dling
dandruff

dane	deign
dangel	dangle

danger
dangerous, -ly

dangerus	dangerous

dangle, -gled, -gling

dangul	dangle
danjer	danger
danjerus	dangerous
daper	dapper
dappel	dapple

dapper, -ly
dapple, -pled, -pling

darby	derby

dare, dared, daring
daredevil

darey	dairy

dark, -ly
darken, -ed, -ing

darkin	darken

darkness
darkroom
  darlin   darling
darling
darn, -ed, -ing
dart, -ed, -ing
  darta   data
  dartabase   database
darter
dash, -ed, -ing
dashboard
  dashbord   dashboard
  dashound   dachshund
dastard, -ly
  dastid   dastard
  dastud   dastard
data
database
date, dated, dating
  dater   data
  datim   datum
datum
daub
  daufin   dauphin
daughter
daunt, -ed, -ing
dauphin
  dauter   daughter
  dawb   daub
dawdle, -dled, -dling
  dawdul   dawdle
dawn, -ed, -ing
  dawnt   daunt
  dawter   daughter
day
  daybrake   daybreak
daybreak
daydream
  daycor   decor
  dayify   deify
  dayis   dais
  dayity   deity
  daylia   dahlia
daylight
  daylite   daylight
  dayly   daily
  dayn   deign

  daysy   daisy
daze, dazed, dazing (stun)
  daze   days (time)
dazzle, -zled, -zling
dazzler
deacon
deactivate, -ated, -ating
dead, -ly
dead centre
deaden, -ed, -ing
dead heart
dead heat
deadline
deadlock
deadly, -lier, -liest
deadpan
dead reckoning
dead weight
deadwood
deaf
deafen, -ed, -ing
  deaft   deft
deal, dealt, dealing
dealer
  deam   deem
dean
deanery
dear, -ly (loved)
  dear   deer (animal)
dearth
death
death adder
deathly
death-wish

> Look under **di-** if the
> word is not under **de-**.

debacle
  debacul   debacle
debar, -barred, -barring
debase, -based, -basing
debasement
debatable, -bly
  debatabul   debatable
debate, -bated, -bating
  debatible   debatable
debauch, -ed, -ing

debauchery, -ries
  debbit — debit
  debensher — debenture
  debenshure — debenture
debenture
debilitate, -tated, -tating
debilitation
debility, -ties
debit, -ed, -ing
debonair
  deboo — debut
  debree — debris
debrief, -ed, -ing
debris
debt
  debter — debtor
debtor
debug, -bugged, -bugging
debunk, -ed, -ing
debut
debutante
decade
decadence
  decadense — decadence
decadent, -ly
decamp, -ed, -ing
decant, -ed, -ing
decanter
decapitate, -tated, -tating
decapitation
  decathalon — decathlon
decathlon
decay, -ed, -ing
decease, -ceased, -ceasing
deceit
deceitful, -ly
deceive, deceived, deceiving
decelerate, -rated, -rating
December
decency, -cies
decent, -ly
decentralisation
decentralise, -lised, -lising
  decepshun — deception
deception
deceptive, -ly
decibel

  decibell — decibel
decide, -cided, -ciding
decidedly
deciduous
  decieve — deceive
  decifer — decipher
decimal
decimate, -mated, -mating
decipher, -ed, -ing
  decishun — decision
decision
decisive, -ly
deck, -ed, -ing
  deckade — decade
deckchair
  deckchare — deckchair
  deckerate — decorate
deckhand
deckle
  deckul — deckle
declaim, -ed, -ing
declamation
declarable
  declarabul — declarable
declaratory
  declaratry — declaratory
declare, -clared, -claring
declassify, -fied, -fying
decline, -clined, -clining
decode, -coded, -coding
decompose, -posed, -posing
  decomposishun — decomposition
decomposition
  decompreshun — decompression
decompress, -ed, -ing
decompression
decongestant
decor
decorate, -rated, -rating
decoration
decorative, -ly
decorous, -ly
decorum
  decorus — decorous
decoy, -ed, -ing
decrease, -creased, -creasing
decree, -creed, -creeing

decreese	decrease		defector	
decrepit			defeet	defeat
decrepitude			defen	deafen
decrese	decrease		defence	

decry, -cried, -crying

ded	dead
deden	deaden

defend, -ed, -ing
defendant

defendent	defendant
defensable	defensible

> Look under **di-** if the word
> is not under **de-**.

defensible

defensibul	defensible

dedicate, -cated, -cating
dedication

defensive, -ly
defer, -ferred, -ferring

dedly	deadly

deferance	deference

deduce, -duced, -ducing
deduct, -ed, -ing
deductible

deference

deferense	deference
deferenshul	deferential

deductibul	deductible

deferential, -ly

deduction
deed

> For **deff-** words,
> look under **def-**.

deel	deal

deem, -ed, -ing

defiance

deen	dean

defianse	defiance

deep, -ly
deepen, -ed, -ing
deep freeze, -frozen, -freezing
deepwater
deer (animal)

defiant, -ly
deficiency, -cies
deficit

defience	defiance

deer	dear (loved)

defile, -filed, -filing

de-escalate, -lated, -lating

definate	definite

def	deaf

define, -fined, -fining

deface, -faced, -facing

definishun	definition
definit	definite

defacit	deficit

definite, -ly

de facto
defamation
defamatory

definition
definitive, -ly

defamatry	defamatory

defishency	deficiency
defishent	deficient
defisit	deficit

defame, -famed, -faming
default, -ed, -ing
defaulter
defeat, -ed, -ing
defeatism
defeatist
defecate, -cated, -cating

deflate, -flated, -flating
deflation
deflationary

defleckshun	deflection

defeckshun	defection

deflect, -ed, -ing
deflection

defect, -ed, -ing
defection
defective, -ly

defnite	definite

defoliant
defoliate, -ated, -ating
defoliation

deform, -ed, -ing
deformity, -ies
defraud, -ed, -ing
defrauder
defray, -ed, -ing
defreeze, -frozen, -freezing
  defrord   defraud
defrost, -ed, -ing
deft, -ly
deftness
defunct
defuse, -fused, -fusing
defy, -fied, -fying
  defyance   defiance
  defyant   defiant

> Look under **di-** if the word is
> not under **de-**.

degeneracy
  degenerasy   degeneracy
degenerate, -rated, -rating
degeneration
degradation
degrade, -graded, -grading
degree
  degridation   degradation
  dehidrate   dehydrate
dehydrate, -drated, -drating
dehydration
  deifie   deify
deify, -fied, -fying
deign
  deisel   diesel
  deitee   deity
deity, -ties
  dejeckshun   dejection
dejection
  dekay   decay
delay, -ed, -ing
  delecate   delicate
delectable, -bly
  delectabul   delectable
delegate, -gated, -gating
delegation
  delerious   delirious
  deleshun   deletion
delete, -leted, -leting

deleterious, -ly
deletion
  delfinium   delphinium
deli
deliberate, -rated, -rating
deliberately
deliberation
deliberative, -ly
delicacy, -cies
delicate, -ly
delicatessen
delicious, -ly
  delicous   delicious
  deligate   delegate
delight, -ed, -ing
delightful, -ly
delineate, -ed, -ing
delineation
  deliniate   delineate
  delinkwency   delinquency
  delinkwent   delinquent
  delinquancy   delinquency
delinquency
delinquent
delirious, -ly
delirium
  delirius   delirious
  delishus   delicious
  delite   delight
  deliteful   delightful
deliver, -ed, -ing
deliverance
  deliverence   deliverance
delivery, -eries
dell
dellie

> For other **dell-** words, look
> under **del-**.

  delood   delude
delphinium
  delt   dealt
delta
delude, -luded, -luding
deluge, -uged, -uging
  deluks   de luxe
  delushun   delusion

delusion
delusive, -ly
delusory
delve, delved, delving
demagogue
demagogy
demand, -ed, -ing
demarcate, -cated, -cating
demarcation
demean, -ed, -ing
  demeaner   demeanour
demeanour
  demensha   dementia
demented, -ly
dementia
demerara
demerit
demigod
demilitarised zone
demise
demister
demo
demob
demobilisation
demobilise, -lised, -lising
democracy, -cies
  democrasy   democracy
democrat
democratic, -ally
democratisation
  demografy   demography
demographic, -ally
demography
demolish, -ed, -ing
  demolishun   demolition
demolition
demolitionist
demon
demonic
demonology
demonstrable, -bly
  demonstrabul   demonstrable
demonstrate, -strated, -strating
  demonstrater   demonstrator
demonstration
demonstrator
demoralise, -lised, -lising

demote, -moted, -moting
demur, -murred, -murring (object)
  demur   demure (coy)
demure, -murer, -murest (coy)
  demure   demur (object)
den
  dence   dense
  dencher   denture
  dencity   density
  denem   denim
dengue
  deni   deny
denial
denigrate, -grated, -grating
denigration
denim
denizen

> For **denn-** words, look under
> **den-**.

denominate, -nated, -nating
denomination
denominational, -ly
denominator
denotable
  denotabul   denotable
denote, -noted, -noting
denounce, -nounced, -nouncing
denouncement
  denownse   denounce
dense, denser, densest
densely
  densitee   density
density
dent, -ed, -ing
dental
dentist
dentistry
denture
denude, -nuded, -nuding
denunciate, -ated, -ating
deny, denied, denying
  deoderant   deodorant
  deoderise   deodorise
deodorant
deodorise, -rised, -rising
  deparcher   departure

depart, -ed, -ing
department
departmental, -ly
departure
  depen   deepen
depend, -ed, -ing
dependable, -bly
  dependabul   dependable
dependant (noun)
dependence
dependency, -cies
  dependensy   dependency
dependent, -ly (adjective)
  dependible   dependable
  depickshun   depiction
depict, -ed, -ing
depiction
  depilatery   depilatory
depilatory, -ries
  depilatry   depilatory
  depleshun   depletion
deplete, -pleted, -pleting
depletion
  deploi   deploy
deplorable, -bly
  deplorabul   deplorable
deplore, -plored, -ploring
deploy, -ed, -ing
deployment
  depo   depot
deport, -ed, -ing
deportation
deportee
depose, -posed, -posing
deposit, -ed, -ing
  deposishun   deposition
  depositer   depositor
deposition
depositor
depository, -ries
  depositry   depository
depot

> For **depp-** words, look under
> **dep-**.

depraved
depravity, -ties

deprecate, -cated, -cating
deprecation
depreciate, -ated, -ating
depreciation
depredation
  depresherise   depressurise
  depreshiate   depreciate
  depreshun   depression
  depresive   depressive
  depresor   depressor
depress, -ed, -ing
depressant
  depressent   depressant
  depresshun   depression
depression
depressive, -ly
depressor
depressurise, -ised, -ising
  depricate   deprecate
deprive, -prived, -priving
depth
deputation
depute, -puted, -puting
  deputey   deputy
deputise, -tised, -tising
deputy, -ties

> Look under **di-** if the word is
> not under **de-**.

derail, -ed, -ing
derailment
  derale   derail
derange, -ranged, -ranging
derby, -bies
deregister, -ed, -ing
  derelickshun   dereliction
derelict
dereliction
  derick   derrick
deride, -rided, -riding
  derigible   dirigible
  derishun   derision
derision
derisive, -ly
derivation
derivative
derive, -rived, -riving

dermatitis
dermatologist
dermatology
  derogatery   derogatory
derogatory
  derogatry   derogatory
derrick

> For other **derr-** words, look
> under **der-**.

  dert   dirt
  derth   dearth
  derty   dirty
dervish
desalination
  desastrous   disastrous
descant
descend, -ed, -ing
descendant (noun)
descendent (adjective)
descent (down)
  descent   dissent (differ)
  desciple   disciple
describe, -scribed, -scribing
  descripshun   description
description
descriptive, -ly
descry, -cried, -crying
  desease   disease
  deseat   deceit
  deseave   deceive
desecrate, -crated, -crating
desecration
desegregate, -gated, -gating
desegregation
  desel   diesel
  deselerate   decelerate
  Desember   December
  desency   decency
  desend   descend
desensitise, -tised, -tising
  desent   decent
  desent   descent
  desentralise   decentralise
  desershun   desertion
desert, deserts
desert, -ed, -ing (leave)

  desert   dessert (food)
deserter
desertion
deserve, -served, -serving
  desese   disease
  desibel   decibel
de-sex, -sexed, -sexing
  desicate   desiccate
  desication   desiccation
desiccate, -cated, -cating
desiccation
  deside   decide
  desiduous   deciduous
design, -ed, -ing
designate, -nated, -nating
designation
  desimal   decimal
  desimate   decimate
  desimul   decimal
  desine   design
  desipher   decipher
desirability
desirable, -bly
  desirabul   desirable
desire, -sired, -siring
desirous
  desirus   desirous
desist, -ed, -ing
desk
  deskant   descant

> Look under **di-** if the word is
> not under **de-**.

desolate, -lated, -lating
desolation
  despach   despatch
despair, -ed, -ing
  despare   despair
despatch, -ed, -ing
  despensable   dispensable
desperado, -does, -dos
desperate, -ly
desperation
despicable, -bly
  despicabul   despicable
despise, -spised, -spising
despite

despoil, -ed, -ing
despoliation
despondency
  despondensy   despondency
despondent, -ly
despot
despotic
despotism
  desprate   desperate
dessert (food)
  dessert   desert (leave)
dessertspoon
destination
destine, -tined, -tining
destiny, -nies
  destitushen   destitution
destitute
destitution
destroy, -ed, -ing
destroyer
  destruckshun   destruction
destruct, -ed, -ing
destructible
  destructibul   destructible
destruction
destructive, -ly
desultory
  det   debt
detach, -ed, -ing
detachable
  detachabul   detachable
detail, -ed, -ing
detain, -ed, -ing
detainee
detainment
  detale   detail
  detane   detain
  deteckshun   detection
detect, -ed, -ing
detectable
  detectabul   detectable
detection
detective
detector
  detektive   detective
  detenshun   detention
detention

deter, -terred, -terring
  deter   debtor
  deterent   deterrent
detergent
  deterjent   detergent
deteriorate, -rated, -rating
deterioration
determinant
determination
determine, -mined, -mining
determinism
deterrence
deterrent
detest, -ed, -ing
detestable, -bly
  detestabul   detestable
detestation
  deth   death
detonate, -nated, -nating
detonation
detonator
detour, -ed, -ing
  detrackshun   detraction
detract, -ed, -ing
detraction
detractor
  detramental   detrimental
detriment
detrimental, -ly
  detterent   deterrent
  dettor   debtor
deuce
deutschmark
devaluation
devalue, -valued, -valuing
devastate, -tated, -tating
devastation
  devel   devil
develop, -ed, -ing
  develope   develop
  developement development
developer
development
developmental, -ly
deviance
deviancy
  devianse   deviance

deviansy — deviancy
deviant, -ly
deviate, -ated, -ating
deviation
device (thing)
  device — devise (plan)
  devide — divide
devil
devilish, -ly
devilment
devilry
devil's advocate
devious, -ly
devise, -vised, -vising (plan)
  devise — device (thing)
  devius — devious
devoid
  devolushun — devolution
devolution
devolutionary
devolve, -volved, -volving
Devonshire tea
  devoshun — devotion
devote, -voted, -voting
devotee
devotion
devour, -ed, -ing
devout, -ly
dew (water)
  dew — due (payable)
dewdrop
  dewey — dewy
dewy, dewier, dewiest
dexterity
dexterous, -ly
  dexterus — dexterous

Look under **de-** if the word is not under **di-**.

  diabeetes — diabetes
diabetes
diabetic
diabolic
diabolical, -ly
diadem
  diafanus — diaphanous
  diafram — diaphragm

diagnose, -nosed, -nosing
diagnosis, -ses
diagnostic
diagnostician
  diagnostishun — diagnostician
diagonal, -ly
diagram
diagrammatic, -ally
dial, dialled, dialling
dialect
dialectic
dialectician
  dialectishun — dialectician
  dialise — dialyse
  dialisis — dialysis
  dialog — dialogue
dialogue
dialyse, -lysed, -lysing
dialysis, -ses
diamante
diameter
diametrical, -ly
diamond
diaper
diaphanous, -ly
  diaphanus — diaphanous
diaphragm
  diarea — diarrhoea
diarist
diarrhoea
diary, -ries (book)
  diary — dairy (milk)
diatonic, -ally
diatribe
  dibase — debase
  dibate — debate
dibs
dice, diced, dicing
dicey
dichotomy, -mies
  dicipul — disciple
dick
dickens
dicky
  dicotomy — dichotomy
  dicshun — diction
  dicshunry — dictionary

dictate, -tated, -tating
dictation
dictator
dictatorial, -ly
  dictatoriul   dictatorial
  dictayshun   dictation
diction
dictionary, -aries
dictum, -ta, -tums
did
didactic, -ally
  diddel   diddle
diddle, -dled, -dling
diddler
  didel   diddle
didgeridoo
  didgit   digit
  didgitalis   digitalis
didn't (did not)
  didnt   didn't
  didul   diddle
die (singular of dice)
die, dies (tool)
die, died, dying (death)
  die   dye (colour)
dieback
die-casting
diehard
  dieing   dying (death)
  dieing   dyeing (colour)
  diernal   diurnal
diesel
diet, dieted, dieting
dietary
dietician
  dietishen   dietician

> For **dif-** words, look under **diff-**.

differ, -ed, -ing
difference
  differense   difference
  differenshul   differential
different, -ly
differential, -ly
differentiate, -ated, -ating
differentiation

difficult
difficulty, -ties
diffidence
diffident, -ly
diffuse, -fused, -fusing
  diffushun   diffusion
diffusion
  diflect   deflect
dig, dug, digging
  diger   digger
digest, -ed, -ing
digestible
  digestibul   digestible
digestion
digger
diggings
digit
digital
digital computer
digitalis
dignify, -fied, -fying
dignitary, -taries
  dignitry   dignitary
dignity, -ties
digress, -ed, -ing
  digresshun   digression
digression
digs
dike
  dil   dill
dilapidated
dilapidation
dilate, -lated, -lating
dilation
dilatory
  dilatry   dilatory
  dilema   dilemma
dilemma
  dilatent   dilettante
dilettante, -ti
  dilibag   dillybag
  dilidali   dilly dally
diligence
  diligense   diligence
diligent, -ly
dill
dillybag

dilly dally
dilushen — dilution
dilution
diluvial
diluvian

> Look under **de-** if the word is
> not under **di-**.

dim, dimmed, dimming
dim, dimmer, dimmest
dime
dimenshun — dimension
dimension
dimensional,-ly
dimer — dimmer
diminish, -ed, -ing
diminishing returns
diminushen — diminution
diminution
diminutive, -ly
dimmer
dimple, -pled, -pling
dimpul — dimple
dim sim
dimwit
dimwitted, -ly
dinamic — dynamic
dinamite — dynamite
dinamo — dynamo
dinasty — dynasty
dine, dined, dining (eat)
dine — dyne (unit)
diner (eating)
diner — dinner (food)
ding
dingbats
ding-dong
dinghy, -ghies (boat)
dingie — dinghy
dingo, -goes, -gos
dingy, -gier, -giest (dull)
dingy — dinghy (boat)
dink, -ed, -ing
dinkum
dinky, dinkier, dinkiest
dinky-di
dinner (food)

dinner — diner (eating)
dinosaur
dinosoar — dinosaur
dinosore — dinosaur
dint, -ed, -ing
diocese
diode
diokside — dioxide
dioxide
dip, dipped, dipping
diper — diaper
diper — dipper
diphtheria
diphthong
diploma
diplomacy, -cies
diplomasy — diplomacy
diplomat
diplomatic, -ally
dipper
dipsomania
dipsomaniac
diptych
dire, direr, direst
direckshun — direction
direct, -ed, -ing
direct current
directer — director
direct evidence
direction
directional
direction-finder
directive
directly
director
directory, -ries
directry — directory
direct tax
dirge
dirigible
dirigibul — dirigible
dirk
dirt
dirtily
dirty, dirtied, dirtying
dirty, dirtier, dirtiest
disable, -bled, -bling

disabul   disable
disabuse, -bused, -busing
disadvantage, -taged, -taging
disadvantageous, -ly
  disadvantige   disadvantage
  disadvantij   disadvantage
  disafect   disaffect
disaffect, -ed, -ing
disaffection
disagree, -greed, -greeing
disagreeable, -bly
disagreeableness
  disagreeabul   disagreeable
disagreement
disallow,-ed, -ing
  disalow   disallow
  disapear   disappear
  disapoint   disappoint
disappear, -ed, -ing
disappearance
  disappearanse   disappearance
disappoint, -ed, -ing
disappointment
disapproval
disapprove, -proved, -proving
  disaprove   disapprove
  disaray   disarray
disarray
  disasociate   disassociate
disassociate, -ated, -ating
disassociation
disaster
disastrous, -ly
  disastrus   disastrous
  disatisfy   dissatisfy
disavow, -ed, -ing
disavowal
disband, -ed, -ing
disbandment
  disbeleif   disbelief
  disbeleive   disbelieve
disbelief
disbelieve, -lieved, -lieving
disc
discard, -ed, -ing
disc brake
discern, -ed, -ing

discernible, -bly
  discernibul   discernible
discernment
discharge, -charged, -charging
disciple
disciplinarian
disciplinary
discipline, -plined, -plining
  discipul   disciple
disc jockey
disclaim, -ed, -ing
disclaimer
  disclaym   disclaim
disclose, -closed, -closing
disclosure
disco
  discolor   discolour
discolour, -ed, -ing
discolouration
  discomfert   discomfort
discomfit, -ed, -ing (thwart)
  discomfit   discomfort
discomfort, -ed, -ing (pain)

> Look under **de-** if the word is
> not under **di-**.

discompose, -posed, -posing
  discomposhur   discomposure
discomposure
disconcert, -ed, -ing
  disconneckshun   disconnection
disconnection
  disconsert   disconcert
disconsolate, -ly
discontent
discontinue, -tinued, -tinuing
discontinuity
discontinuous, -ly
discord
discordance
  discordanse   discordance
discordant, -ly
discotheque
discount, -ed, -ing
discourage, -raged, -raging
discouragement
discourse, -coursed, -coursing

discourteous, -ly
discourtesy
  discourtius   discourteous
discover, -ed, -ing
discoverer
discovery, -eries
  discownt   discount
discredit, -ed, -ing
discreditable, -bly
  discreditabul   discreditable
discreet (prudent)
  discreet   discrete (apart)
discrepancy
  discrepansy   discrepancy
  discreshun   discretion
  discreshunry   discretionary
discrete (apart)
discretion
discretionary
  discribe   describe
discriminate, -nated, -nating
discrimination
discriminator
discriminatory
  discriminatry   discriminatory
  discripshun   description
  discriptive   descriptive
  discuridge   discourage
discursive, -ly
  discurtious   discourteous
discus (sport)
  discushun   discussion
discuss, -ed, -ing (talk)
discussion
disdain, -ed, -ing
disdainful, -ly
  dise   dice
disease
diseased
  diseave   deceive
  diseckshun   dissection
  disect   dissect
disembark, -ed, -ing
disembarkation
  disemble   disembowel
disembodied
disembowel, -elled, -elling

  diseminate   disseminate
disenchant, -ed, -ing
disenchantment
  disenshun   dissension
disentangle, -gled, -gling
disentanglement
  disentry   dysentery
  disern   discern
  disernibul   discernible
  disertation   dissertation
  diservise   disservice
  disesed   diseased
  disfaver   disfavour
disfavour, -ed, -ing
  disfiger   disfigure
disfigure, -ed, -ing
disfranchise, -chised, -chising
disfranchisement
  disgise   disguise
disgorge, -gorged, -gorging
disgrace, -graced, -gracing
disgraceful, -ly
  disgracefull   disgraceful
disgruntled
disguise, -guised, -guising
disgust, -ed, -ing
disgustedly
dish, -ed, -ing
  disharmoney   disharmony
disharmony
  disharten   dishearten
dishcloth
dishearten, -ed, -ing
dishevelled
dishonest, -ly
dishonesty
  dishonor   dishonour
dishonour, -ed, -ing
  dishonourabel   dishonourable
dishonourable, -bly
  dishonourabul   dishonourable
  disidence   dissidence
  disident   dissident
  disign   design
disillusion, -ed, -ing
disillusionment
  disilushun   disillusion

disimilar — dissimilar
disimulate — dissimulate
disinclination
disincline, -clined, -clining
disinfect, -ed, -ing
disinfectant
disinfectent — disinfectant
disinherit, -ed, -ing
disinheritance
disintegrate, -grated, -grating
disintegration
disinter, -terred, -terring
disinterment
disinterested, -ly
disintigrate — disintegrate
disipate — dissipate
disipation — dissipation
disiple — disciple
disiplinary — disciplinary
disipline — discipline
disjoint, -ed, -ing
disk
diskwalify — disqualify
diskwiet — disquiet
diskwolify — disqualify
dislexia — dyslexia
dislike, -liked, -liking
dislocate, -cated, -cating
dislocation
dislodge, -lodged, -lodging
disloge — dislodge
disloyal, -ly
disloyalty, -ties
dismal, -ly
dismantel — dismantle
dismantle, -tled, -tling
dismantul — dismantle
dismay, -ed, -ing
dismember, -ed, -ing
dismemberment
dismisal — dismissal
dismiss, -ed, -ing
dismissal
dismount, -ed, -ing
dismownt — dismount
disobay — disobey
disobedience

disobediense — disobedience
disobedient, -ly
disobey, -ed, -ing
disoblige, -bliged, -bliging
disoloot — dissolute
disoluble — dissoluble
disolute — dissolute
disolution — dissolution
disolve — dissolve
disonance — dissonance
disonanse — dissonance
disonant — dissonant
disone — disown
disoner — dishonour
disonerable — dishonourable
disonest — dishonest

> Look under **de-** if the word is
> not under **di-**.

disorder
disorderliness
disorderly
disorganisation
disorganise, -nised, -nising
disorientate, -tated, -tating
disown, -ed, -ing
dispair — despair
disparage, -raged, -raging
disparagement
disparagingly
disparate, -ly
disparidge — disparage
disparige — disparage
disparity, -ties
dispashonate — dispassionate
dispashunate — dispassionate
dispassionate, -ly
dispatch, -ed, -ing
dispel, -pelled, -pelling
dispencable — dispensable
dispencary — dispensary
dispence — dispense
dispensable
dispensabul — dispensable
dispensary, -saries
dispensry — dispensary
dispensation

dispenser	
dispepsia	dyspepsia
dispersal	
disperse, -persed, -persing	
dispershun	dispersion
dispersion	
dispicable	despicable
dispirit, -ed, -ing	
dispite	despite
displace, -placed, -placing	
displaceable	
displaceabul	displaceable
displacement	
displacment	displacement
displase	displace
display, -ed, -ing	
displease, -pleased, -pleasing	
displeasure	
displese	displease
displeshur	displeasure
displesure	displeasure
disport, -ed, -ing	
disposable	
disposable income	
disposabul	disposable
dispose, -posed, -posing	
disposeshun	dispossession
disposess	dispossess
disposishun	disposition
disposition	
dispossess, -ed, -ing	
dispossession	
disprin	
disproporshun	disproportion
disproportion	
disproportionate, -ly	
disprove, -proved, -proving	
dispursal	dispersal
dispurse	dispurse
dispurshun	dispersion
disputable, -bly	
disputabul	disputable
disputation	
disputatious	
dispute, -puted, -puting	
disqualification	
disqualify, -fied, -fying	

disquiet, -ed, -ing	
disquietude	
disquite	disquiet
disregard, -ed, -ing	
disreguard	disregard
disrepair	
disrepare	disrepair
disreputable, -bly	
disreputible	disreputable
disrespect	
disrespectful, -ly	
disrespectfull	disrespectful
disrigard	disregard
disrispect	disrespect
disrobe, -robed, -robing	
disrupshun	disruption
disrupt, -ed, -ing	
disruption	
disruptive, -ly	
dissapate	dissipate
dissapear	disappear
dissapoint	disappoint
dissaprove	disapprove
dissatisfaction	
dissatisfy, -fied, -fying	
disscord	discord
dissect, -ed, -ing	
dissemble, -bled, -bling	
disseminate, -nated, -nating	
dissemination	
dissenshun	dissension
dissension	
dissent, -ed, -ing	
dissenter	
dissertation	
disservicabul	disserviceable
disservice	
disserviceable	
dissidence	
dissidense	dissidence
dissident, -ly	
dissimilar, -ly	
dissimilarity	
dissimulate, -lated, -lating	
dissimulation	
dissipate, -pated, -pating	
dissipation	

dissociate, -ated, -ating
dissociation
   disoloot   dissolute
dissoluble
   dissolubul   dissoluble
   dissolushun   dissolution
dissolute, -ly
dissolution
dissolvable
   dissolvabul   dissolvable
dissolve, -solved, -solving
dissonance
   dissonanse   dissonance
dissonant, -ly
   disstil   distil
dissuade, -suaded, -suading
distaff
distance, distanced, distancing
   distanse   distance
distant, -ly
distaste
distasteful, -ly
   distastefull   distasteful
distemper, -ed, -ing
distend, -ed, -ing
   distenshun   distention
   distent   distant
distention
   disterb   disturb
   disterbance   disturbance
distil, -tilled, -tilling
distillate
distillation
distillery, -eries
   distillry   distillery
   distincshun   distinction
distinct, -ly
distinction
distinctive, -ly
distinguish, -ed, -ing
distinguishable, -bly
   distingwish   distinguish
   distink   distinct
   distorshun   distortion
distort, -ed, -ing
distortion
   distrackshun   distraction

distract, -ed, -ing
distraction
distraught, -ly
   distrawt   distraught
distress, -ed, -ing
distressful, -ly
   distressfull   distressful
distressingly
distress signal
   distribushun   distribution
distribution
distributive, -ly
distributor
district
distrust, -ed, -ing
disturb, -ed, -ing
disturbance
   disturbanse   disturbance
disunion
disunite, -nited, -niting
disunity, -ties
   disurn   discern
   disurnible   discernible
disuse, -used, -using
   diswade   dissuade
   diswashun   dissuasion
   diswasive   dissuasive
ditch, -ed, -ing
ditch, -ditches
dither
dithering
dithery
   dito   ditto
ditto
ditty, -ties
   dity   ditty
divan
dive, dived, diving
dive-bomb
diver
diverge, -verged, -verging
divergence
   divergense   divergence
divergent, -ly
diverse, -ly
   divershun   diversion
diversification

diversify, -fied, -fying

| Look under **de-** if the word is not under **di-**. |

diversion
diversionary
  diversionry   diversionary
diversity, -ties
divert, -ed, -ing
divest, -ed, -ing
divestible
divide, -vided, -viding
dividend
divider
divination
divinatory
divine, -vined, -vining
divinely
diviner
  divinitey   divinity
divinity, -ties
  diviser   divisor
  divishun   division
divisible, -bly
  divisibul   divisible
  divisif   divisive
division
divisional, -ly
divisive, -ly
divisor
divorce, -vorced, -vorcing
divorcee
  divorse   divorce
  divorsee   divorcee
divulge, -vulged, -vulging
divulgence
  divulgense   divulgence
divvy, -vies
divvy, -vied, -vying
dixie
  dizier   dizzier
  diziest   dizziest
  dizmal   dismal
  dizolve   dissolve
  dizy   dizzy
dizzily
dizziness

dizzy, dizzied, dizzying
dizzy, dizzier, dizziest
do, did, done, doing
  do   doe (animal)
dob, dobbed, dobbing
dobbin
docile, -ly
docility
dock, -ed, -ing
docker
docket
  dockit   docket
dockyard
  docter   doctor
doctor, -ed, -ing
doctoral
doctorate
  doctrin   doctrine
  doctrinair   doctrinaire
doctrinaire
doctrinal, -ly
doctrine
  doctrinul   doctrinal
  doctrut   doctorate
document, -ed, -ing
documentary, -ries
documentation
  documentry   documentary
dodder, -ed, -ing
doddery
doddle
  doder   dodder
dodge, dodged, dodging
dodgem
dodger
dodgy, dodgier, dodgiest
  dodje   dodge
  dodjy   dodgy
dodo, -does, -dos
doe (animal)
  doe   dough (bread)
doer
does
doesn't (does not)
  doesnt   doesn't
  dof   doff
doff, -ed, -ing

doffin	dauphin	domane	domain
dog, dogged, dogging		dome	
dogbox		domed	
dogerul	doggerel	domestic, -ally	
dogfight		domesticate, -cated, -cating	
dogfish		domestication	
dogfite	dogfight	domesticity	
doggerel		domestisity	domesticity
doggo		domicile, -ciled, -ciling	
doghouse		domiciliary	
dogleg		dominance	
doglegged		dominanse	dominance
dogma, -mas, -mata		dominant, -ly	
dogmatic		dominate, -nated, -nating	
dogmatical, -ly		dominater	dominator
dogmatism		domination	
dogmatist		dominative	
dog paddle		dominator	
dog paddul	dog paddle	dominear	domineer
dog watch		domineer, -ed, -ing	
doilie	doily	dominent	dominant
doily, -lies		dominion	
doings		domino, -noes	
dol	dole (pay)	domino theory	
dol	doll (toy)	dominyun	dominion
dolar	dollar	domisile	domicile
Dolby system		domminate	dominate
doldrums		don, donned, donning	
dole, doled, doling (pay)		donate, -nated, -nating	
dole	doll (toy)	donater	donator
doler	dollar	donation	
dolerus	dolorous	donator	
dolfin	dolphin	done	
doll, -ed, -ing (toy)		doner	donor
doll	dole (pay)	dong, -ed, -ing	
dollar		donkey, -keys	
doller	dollar	donkey vote	
dollop		donkey's years	
dolly, dollies		donky	donkey
dolomite		donnybrook	
dolorous, -ly		donor	
dolorus	dolorous	don't (do not)	
dolour		dont	don't
dolphin		donut	
dolt		dooch	douche
doltish, -ly		doodad	
domain		doodah	

doodle, -dled, -dling
  doodul   doodle
doom, -ed, -ing
doomsday
door
  door   dour
doorjamb
doorknock, -ed, -ing
  doornock   doorknock
  doosh   douche
dope, doped, doping
dopey, dopier, dopiest
  dophin   dauphin
  dore   door
dormancy
  dormansy   dormancy
dormant
  dormitery   dormitory
  dormitry   dormitory
  dorn   dawn
dorsal
  dorsul   dorsal
  dorter   daughter
dory, -ries
dosage
dose, dosed, dosing
  dosier   dossier
  dosige   dosage
  dosije   dosage
  dosile   docile
  dosility   docility
doss, -ed, -ing
dossier
dot, dotted, dotting
dotage
dote, doted, doting
  dotidge   dotage
  dotije   dotage
dotterel
dottle
dotty, dottier, dottiest
  doubel   double
double, -led, -ling
double agent
double-barrelled
double bass
double-breasted

doublecross, -ed, -ing
double-dealing
double dissolution
double-dutch
double exposure
double-jointed
double standard
doublet
doublethink
double time
doubloon
doubt, -ed, -ing
doubtful, -ly
  doubtfull   doubtful
doubtingly
doubtless, -ly
douche, douched, douching
  douel   dowel
dough
doughnut
doughty, -tier, -tiest
dour, -ly
dourness
douse, doused, dousing
  dout   doubt
  doutful   doubtful
  doutless   doubtless
  douty   doughty
dove
dover
dovetail
  dovetale   dovetail
  dow   dhow (boat)
  dow   doe (animal)
  dow   dough (bread)
dowager
  dowdie   dowdy
dowdily
dowdiness
dowdy, -dier, -diest
  dowery   dowry
  dowey   doughy
down, -ed, -ing
down-and-out
downcast
  downey   downy
downfall

downfallen
downgrade, -graded, -grading
downhearted, -ly
downhill
down payment
downpipe
  downpore   downpour
downpour
downright, -ly
  downrite   downright
downstairs
downstream
down-to-earth
downtown
downtrodden
down-under
downward, -ly
downwards
  downwerds   downwards
downwind
downy, downier, downiest
  dowrie   dowry
dowry, -ries
dowse, dowsed, dowsing
  dowt   doubt
  dowtey   doughty
  dowtful   doubtful
  dowtless   doubtless
doxology, -gies
doyen
doze, dozed, dozing (sleep)
  doze   does
dozen, dozen, dozens
dozily
doziness
drab, drabber, drabbest
  draconean   draconian
draconian
draft, -ed, -ing (plan)
  draft   draught (air)
draft dodger
  draftey   draughty
  draftiness   draughtiness
  drafts   draughts
draftsman, -men
  drafty   draughty
drag, dragged, dragging

dragnet
dragonfly, -flies
dragoon, -ed, -ing
drag race
dragster
drain, -ed, -ing
drainage
  drainige   drainage
drainpipe
drake
dram
drama
dramatic, -ally
dramatics
dramatisation
dramatise, -tised, -tising
dramatist
drank
drape, draped, draping
draper
drapery, -eries
drastic, -ally
draught (air)
  draught   draft (plan)
draughtboard
draughthorse
draughts
draughtsman, -men
draughty, -tier, -tiest
draw, drew, drawn, drawing
drawback
drawbridge
  drawbrije   drawbridge
drawcard
drawer
drawing-pin
drawl, -ed, -ing
drawn
dray
dread, -ed, -ing
dreadful, -ly
  dreadfull   dreadful
  dreadnort   dreadnought
dreadnought
dream, dreamed, dreamt, dreaming
dreamer
dreamily

dreamless, -ly
dreamy, dreamier, dreamiest
drearily
dreariness
dreary, drearier, dreariest
dred   dread
dredful   dreadful
dredger
drednort   dreadnought
dreem   dream
drege   dredge
dregs
dreje   dredge
dremt   dreamt
drench, -ed, -ing
drerie   dreary
drery   dreary
dres   dress
dresie   dressy
dresige   dressage
dresmaker   dressmaker
dress, -ed, -ing
dressage
dress circle
dress down
dresser
dressmaker
dressmaking
dressy
drew
dri   dry
dribble, -bled, -bling
dribbler
dribbul   dribble
dribs and drabs
dribul   dribble
dried
drier
driest
drift, -ed, -ing
drifter
driftwood
drill, -ed, -ing
drily
drink, drunk, drinking
drinkable
drinkabul   drinkable

drink-driving
drive-in
drivel, -elled, -elling
driver
driveway
drizzle, -zled, -zling
drizzly
drizzul   drizzle
droll
drollery, -eries
drolly
dromedary, -daries
drone, droned, droning
drongo, -gos
drool, -ed, -ing
droop, -ed, -ing
droopy, -ier, -iest
drop, dropped, dropping
droplet
drop-out
dropper
dropsey   dropsy
dropsy
dross
drought
drousy   drowsy
drout   drought
drove, droved, droving
drover
drown, -ed, -ing
drowse, drowsed, drowsing
drowsey   drowsy
drowsily
drowsy, drowsier, drowsiest
drowt   drought
drub, drubbed, drubbing
drudge, drudged, drudging
drudgery, -eries
drug, drugged, drugging
druge   drudge
drugery   drudgery
drugstore
drum, drummed, drumming
drummer
drumstick
drunk
drunkard

drunken, -ly
drunkenness
dry, dried, drying
dry, drier, driest
dry cell
dry-clean
dryer
dryly
dryness
dual, -ly (two)
   dual   duel (fight)
dualism
duality
dub, dubbed, dubbing
   dubel   double
dubious, -ly
   dubius   dubious
   duble   double
   dubly   doubly
ducal, -ly
   duce   deuce
duck, -ed, -ing
duckbill
duckling
   ducktile   ductile
duco
duct
ductile
dud
dudgeon
due (owing)
   due   dew (water)
   duedrop   dewdrop
duel, -ed, -ing (fight)
   duel   dual (two)
   duelist   duellist
duellist
duet
duettist
   dufel   duffle
duffer
duffle
   dufful   duffle
dugong
dugout
duke
   dul   dull

dulcet
   duler   duller
   dulie   duly
dull
dullard
dullness
dully
   dulset   dulcet
duly
   dum   dumb
dumb, -ly
dumbbell
   dumbell   dumbbell
dumbfound, -ed, -ing
dumbness
   dumfound   dumbfound
dummy, -mies
dummy, -mied, -mying
   dumness   dumbness
dump, -ed, -ing
dumper
dumpling
   dumy   dummy
dun, dunned, dunning (demand)
   dun   done
dunce
dunderhead
dune
dung
dungaree
   dungen   dungeon
dungeon
   dunjun   dungeon
dunk, -ed, -ing
dunny
   dunse   dunce
duodenal
duodenum
dupe, duped, duping
   duplacate   duplicate
   duplecks   duplex
duplex
duplicate, -cated, -cating
duplication
duplicity, -ties
   duplisity   duplicity
durable, -bly

durability
  durabul   durable
duration
duress
  durge   dirge
  durible   durable
during
  durt   dirt
  durtie   dirty
  durty   dirty
dusk
duskiness
dusky, duskier, duskiest
dust, -ed, -ing
dustbin
duster
dustman, -men
dustpan
dust-up
dusty, dustier, dustiest
Dutch courage
  Dutch curije   Dutch courage
duteous, -ly
dutiable
  dutiabul   dutiable
  dutifree   duty-free
dutiful, -ly
duty, -ties
duty-free
  duv   dove
duvet
  duvtail   dovetail
  duvtale   dovetail
dux
  duzen   dozen
dwarf, dwarfs, dwarves
dwarf, -ed, -ing
dwarfish, -ly
dwell, dwelt, dwelled, dwelling
dwindle, -dled, -dling
  dworf   dwarf
  dworves   dwarfs
dye, dyed, dyeing (colour)
  dye   die (dead)
  dyed   died (dead)
  dyehard   diehard
  dyeing   dying (death)

dyer
dyke, dyked, dyking
dynamic, -ally
dynamics
dynamism
dynamite, -mited, -miting
dynamo, -mos
dynasty, -ties
dyne (unit)
  dyne   dine (eat)
dysentery
  dysentry   dysentery
dysfunction
dyslectic
dyslexia
dyslexic
dyspepsia
dyspeptic
dystrophy

Ee

each
eagel — eagle
eager
eagle
eaglehawk
eaglet
eal — eel
ear
earache
eardrum
earfone — earphone
earie — eerie (weird)
earie — eyrie (nest)
earing — earring
early, -lier, -liest
earmark, -ed, -ing
earmuf — earmuff
earmuff
earn, -ed, -ing
earner
earnest, -ly
earnestness
earnings
earphone
earring
earshot
earth, -ed, -ing
earthbound
earthen
earthenware
earthiness
earthling
earthly, -lier, -liest
earthquake
earthworm
earthy, earthier, earthiest
earwig
ease, eased, easing

easel
easement
easily
east
easten — eastern
East End
Easter
easterly
eastern
eastward, -ly
eastwards
easiness
easy, easier, easiest
eat, ate, eaten, eating
eatable
eatabul — eatable
eater
eau-de-Cologne
eaves
eavesdrop, -dropped, -dropping
eavesdropper
ebb, -ed, -ing
ebbony — ebony
ebonie — ebony
ebony, -onies
ebuliense — ebullience
ebulient — ebullient
ebullience
ebullient, -ly
eccentric, -ally
eccentricity, -ties
ecclesiastic
ecclesiastical, -ly
ecentric — eccentric
ech — each
echelon
echidna
echo, echoes
echo, echoed, echoing
eclair
eclare — eclair
eclectic, -ally
eclesiastic — ecclesiastic
eclipse, eclipsed, eclipsing
ecliptical, -ly
ecologey — ecology
ecological, -ly

ecologist
ecology
economic
economical, -ly
economics
economise, -mised, -mising
economist
economy, -mies
ecosphere
ecosystem

| ecsema | eczema |
| ecsentric | eccentric |

ecstasy, -sies
ecstatic, -ally
ecumenical, -ly
ecumenism
eczema
edam

| edem | edam |

eddy, eddies
eddy, eddied, eddying
edelweiss
edge, edged, edging
edger
edgeways

| edgey | edgy |

edginess
edgy, -ier, -iest
edible
edibility

| edibul | edible |

edict

| edie | eddy |

edify, -fied, -fying
edit, -ed, -ing

| editer | editor |

edition (book)

| edition | addition (add) |

editor
editorial, -ly
educable

| educabul | educable |

educate, -cated, -cating
education
educational, -ly
educationalist
educative

educator
Edwardian

edy	eddy
eeger	eager
eegle	eagle

eel

| eenin | oenin |
| eer | ear |

eerie, eerier, eeriest (weird)

| eerie | eyrie (nest) |

eerily
eeriness

| eermark | earmark |

> For **ef-** words,
> look under **eff-**.

efface, -faced, -facing
effect, -ed, -ing
effective, -ly
effectual, -ly
effeminacy

| effeminasy | effeminacy |

effeminate, -ly
effervesce, -vesced, -vescing
effervescence
effervescent, -ly

effervesent	effervescent
effervess	effervesce
effervessence	effervescence

efficacious, -ly
efficacy, -cies

| efficayshus | efficacious |

efficiency, -cies

| efficiensy | efficiency |

efficient, -ly
effigy, -gies
effloresce, -resced, -rescing
efflorescence
efflorescent
effluent
effluvium, -via, -viums
effort
effortless, -ly
effrontery, -teries

| effrontrey | effrontery |
| effushun | effusion |

effusion

effusive, -ly

efigy	effigy
eg	egg

egalitarian
egalitarianism
egg, -ed, -ing
eggcup
egghead
eggplant
eggshell
eggwhite

eggwite	eggwhite
Egipshun	Egyptian
Egipt	Egypt
egis	aegis

ego, egos
egocentric
egocentricity
egoism
egoist
egoistical, -ly

egosentric	egocentric

egotism
egotist
egotistical, -ly
egress
egret

> For **egs-** words,
> look under **ex-**.

Egypt
Egyptian
eiderdown
eight
eighteen
eighth
eightieth
eighty, eighties
eisteddfod
either
ejaculate, -lated, -lating
ejaculation

ejeckshun	ejection

eject, -ed, -ing
ejection
ejector
eke, eked, eking

eklipse	eclipse
eko	echo

> For **eks-** words,
> look under **ex-**.

ekumenical	ecumenical

> For **ekw-** words,
> look under **eq-**.

elaborate, -rated, -rating
elaborately
elaboration
elan
eland
elapse, elapsed, elapsing
elastic, -ally
elasticity

elastisitey	elasticity

elate, elated, elating
elbow, -ed, -ing
elbowroom
elder, -ly
elderberry, -ries
eldest

elecshun	election

elect, -ed, -ing
election
electioneer, -ed, -ing
elective
elector
electoral, -ly
electorate
electric
electrical, -ly
electrician
electricity
electrification

electrishun	electrician
electrisity	electricity

electrocardiogram
electrocardiograph

electrocushun	electrocution

electrocute, -cuted, -cuting
electrode
electrolysis
electromagnet
electromagnetic

electromotive
electron
electronic
electronic data processing
electronics
electroplate, -plated, -plating
electrostatic
elegance
| eleganse | elegance |
elegant, -ly
| elegey | elegy |
elegy, -gies
element
elemental, -ly
elementary
| elementery | elementary |
| elementul | elemental |
elephant
elephantine
| elevan | eleven |
elevate, -vated, -vating
| elevater | elevator |
elevation
elevator
eleven
eleventh
elf, elves
elfin
elfish
| elfs | elves |
elicit, -ed, -ing (draw)
elicit	illicit (wrong)
elifant	elephant
eliganse	elegance
eligant	elegant
eligible, -bly
eligibility
eligibul	eligible
elikser	elixir
eliment	element
elimentry	elementary
eliminate, -nated, -nating
eliminator
elipse	ellipse
elipsis	ellipsis
elishun	elision
elision

elite
elitism
elitist
| elivate | elevate |
elixir
Elizabethan
elk
ellipse
ellipsis, -ses
elliptical, -ly
| ellite | elite |
elm
| elocushun | elocution |
elocution
elocutionist
| elokwence | eloquence |
elongate, -gated, -gating
elongation
elope, eloped, eloping
elopement
eloper
| eloquant | eloquent |
eloquence
| eloquense | eloquence |
eloquent, -ly
else
| elsewere | elsewhere |
elsewhere
| elswhere | elsewhere |
elucidate, -dated, -dating
elucidation
elucidatory
elude, eluded, eluding (evade)
| elude | allude (say) |
| elusidate | elucidate |
elusive, -ly
elves
emaciate, -ated, -ating
emaciation
emanate, -nated, -nating
emanation
emancipate, -pated, -pating
emancipation
emancipator
emancipist
| emanent | eminent |
| emansipate | emancipate |

emasculate, -lated, -lating
emasculation
  emasiate   emaciate
embalm, -ed, -ing
embankment
  embarass   embarrass
embargo, -goes
embargo, -goed, -going
embark, -ed, -ing
embarkation
embarrass, -ed, -ing
embarrassment
embassy, -sies
embed, -bedded, -bedding
embellish, -ed, -ing
embellishment
ember
  embezel   embezzle
embezzle, -zled, -zling
embezzlement
embitter, -ed, -ing
emblazon, -ed, -ing
emblem
emblematic, -ally
  embodie   embody
embodiment
embody, -bodied, -bodying
embolism
  embos   emboss
emboss, -ed, -ing
embrace, -braced, -bracing
embraceable
  embrase   embrace
  embrio   embryo
embroider, -ed, -ing
embroidery, -deries
embroil, -ed, -ing
embryo, -os
embryonic
emend, -ed, -ing
emerald
  emerey   emery
emerge, emerged, emerging
emergence
emergency
  emergense   emergence
  emergensy   emergency

emergent
  emerie   emery
emeritus
emery
emetic
  emfasema   emphysema
  emfasise   emphasise
  emfatic   emphatic
emigrant
emigrate, -grated, -grating
eminence (high)
  eminense   eminence
eminent, -ly (known)
  eminent   imminent
                (near)
  emisary   emissary
  emishun   emission
emissary, -saries
emission
emit, emitted, emitting
emitter
emollient
emolument
  emoshun   emotion
emotion
emotional, -ly
emotionalism
emotionless, -ly
emotive, -ly
empanel, -elled, -elling
empathy
  emperer   emperor
emperor
emphasis, -ses
emphasise, -sised, -sising
emphatic, -ally
emphysema
empire
empirical, -ly
empiricism
empiricist
  empirisism   empiricism
employ, -ed, -ing
employable
  employabul   employable
employee
employer

employment
emporium, -poriums, -poria
empower, -ed, -ing
empress
   emptie   empty
emptiness
empty, -tied, -tying
empty, -tier, -tiest
   emrald   emerald
emu
emulate, -lated, -lating
emulation
   emulshun   emulsion
emulsion
enable, -bled, -bling
   enabul   enable
enact, -ed, -ing
enactment
enamel, -elled, -elling
enameller
   enamer   enamour
enamour, -ed, -ing
encapsulate, -lated, -lating
encephalitis
encephalogram
enchant, -ed, -ing
enchantment
   enciclical   encyclical
   enciclopedia   encyclopaedia
encircle, -cled, -cling
encirclement
   encircul   encircle
enclave
enclose, -closed, -closing
   encloshur   enclosure
enclosure
encode, -coded, -coding
encompass, -ed, -ing
encore, -cored, -coring
encounter
   encownter   encounter
encourage, -raged, -raging
encouragement
encroach, -ed, -ing
encumber, -ed, -ing
encumbrance
   encumbranse encumbrance

encyclical
encyclopaedia
encyclopaedic
end, -ed, -ing
endanger, -ed, -ing
endear, -ed, -ing
endearment
endeavour, -ed, -ing
   endeer   endear
endemic, -ally
   endever   endeavour
endive
endless, -ly
endorse, -dorsed, -dorsing
endorsement
endow, -ed, -ing
endowment
endurable, -bly
endurance
   enduranse   endurance
endure, -dured, -during
   endurible   endurable
endways
enema
enemy, -mies
energetic, -ally
energy, -gies
enervate, -vated, -vating
enervative
enfeeble, -bled, -bling
   enfeebul   enfeeble
enfold, -ed, -ing
enforce, -forced, -forcing
enforceable
   enforceabul   enforceable
enforcement
enforcer
   enforse   enforce
   enforsibul   enforceable
enfranchise, -chised, -chising
engage, -gaged, -gaging
engagement
   engajment   engagement
engender, -ed, -ing
engine
   enginear   engineer
engineer, -ed, -ing

English

engrave, -graved, -graving

engraver

engross, -ed, -ing

engulf, -ed, -ing

enhance, -hanced, -hancing

enhancement

   enhanse   enhance

enigma

enigmatic, -ally

   enima   enema

   enimy   enemy

   enithing   anything

   eniwhere   anywhere

   enjender   engender

   enjin   engine

   enjineer   engineer

   enjoi   enjoy

   enjoiabul   enjoyable

   enjoiment   enjoyment

enjoin, -ed, -ing

enjoy, -ed, -ing

enjoyable, -bly

   enjoyabul   enjoyable

enjoyment

enlarge, -larged, -larging

enlargement

enlarger

enlighten, -ed, -ing

enlightenment

enlist, -ed, -ing

enlistment

   enliten   enlighten

enliven, -ed, -ing

en masse

enmity, -ties

ennoble, -bled, -bling

enoblement

ennui

   enobul   ennoble

enormity, -ties

enormous, -ly

   enormus   enormous

enough

enquire, -quired, -quiring

enquirer

enquiry, -ries

enrage, -raged, -raging

   enrap   enwrap

   enrapcher   enrapture

enrich, -ed, -ing

enrichment

enrol, -rolled, -rolling

enrolment

en route

ensconce, -ed, -ing

   ensconse   ensconce

ensemble

   ensembul   ensemble

   ensercul   encircle

   enshure   ensure

ensign

   ensine   ensign

ensue, -sued, -suing

en suite

ensure, -sured, -suring

   ensweet   en suite

entail, -ed, -ing

   entale   entail

entangle, -gled, -gling

entanglement

   entangul   entangle

entente

enter, -ed, -ing

enteritis

enterprise

enterprising, -ly

entertain, -ed, -ing

entertainer

entertainment

   entertane   entertain

enthral, -led, -ling

enthuse, -thused, -thusing

enthusiasm

enthusiast

enthusiastic, -ally

entice, -ticed, -ticing

entire, -ly

entirety

   entise   entice

   entitel   entitle

   entitey   entity

entitle, -tled, -tling

entitlement

entity, -ties
entourage
  entouraje   entourage
entrails
entrance
  entranse   entrance
entrant
  entre   entree
entreat, -ed, -ing
entreaty, -treaties
entree
  entreet   entreat
  entreprener   entrepreneur
entrepreneur
entrepreneurial
entrust, -ed, -ing
entry, -tries
  enuff   enough
enumerable
  enumerabul   enumerable
enumerate, -rated, -rating
enumeration
enunciate, -ated, -ating
enunciation
  enunsiate   enunciate
enuresis
envelop, -ed, -ing (wrap up)
envelope (letter)
enviable, -bly
  enviabul   enviable
  envie   envy
envious, -ly
  envirament   environment
environment
environmental, -ly
environmentalism
environmentalist
environs
envisage, -aged, -aging
  envisidge   envisage
  envius   envious
  envoi   envoy
envoy
envy, -vies
envy, envied, envying
enwrap, enwrapped, enwrapping
  enzime   enzyme

enzyme
epaulet
  epawlet   epaulet
ephemeral, -ly
epic
epical, -ly
  epicenter   epicentre
epicentre
epicure
epicurean
epidemic
epidemical, -ly
epidermal
epidermis
  epigraf   epigraph
epigram
epigrammatic, -ally
epigraph
epilepsy
epileptic
  epilog   epilogue
epilogue
episcopacy, -cies
episcopal
Episcopalian
episode
episodic, -ally
  epissel   epistle
epitaph
  epitarf   epitaph
epithet
epitome
epitomise, -mised, -mising
epoch
epochal
  epok   epoch
  eppigram   epigram
equable, -bly
equal, equalled, equalling
equalise, -lised, -lising
equality, -ties
equanimity, -ties
equate, equated, equating
  equater   equator
equation
equator
equatorial

equestrian
equidistant, -ly
equilateral
equilibrium
equine
  equinocks   equinox
equinoctial
equinox
equip, equipped, equipping
equipment
equitable, -bly
  equitabul   equitable
equity, -ties
equivalence
  equivalense   equivalence
equivocal, -ly
equivocate, -cated, -cating
equivocation
era
eradicable, -bly
eradicate, -cated, -cating
eradication
  erand   errand
  erant   errant
erase, erased, erasing
eraser
erasion
  erata   errata
  eratic   erratic
  erayshure   erasure
  erban   urban
  erbane   urbane
  erbanise   urbanise
  erbanity   urbanity
  erchun   urchin
  erecshun   erection
erect, -ed, -ing
erection
  erer   error
  erge   urge
  ergent   urgent
ergonomics
  erie   eerie (weird)
  erie   eyrie (nest)
erk (rank)
  erk   irk (bore)
  erksome   irksome

  erl   earl
  erly   early
ermine
  ern   earn (money)
  ern   urn (vessel)
  ernest   earnest
erode, eroded, eroding
erogenous
  eroneous   erroneous
  eror   error
Eros
  eroshun   erosion
erosion
erotic, -ally
erotica
eroticism
  erotisism   eroticism
err, -ed, -ing
errand
erratic, -ally
erratum, -ta
erroneous, -ly
  erronius   erroneous
error
  errupt   erupt
ersatz
erstwhile
  erth   earth
  erthen   earthen
  erthly   earthly
  erudishun   erudition
erudition
erupt, -ed, -ing
eruption
  erwig   earwig
  esay   essay
escalate, -lated, -lating
  escalater   escalator
escalation
escalator
escapade
escape, -caped, -caping
escapee
escaper
escapement
escapism
escapist

escarpment
eschew, -ed, -ing
   eschue   eschew
escort, -ed, -ing
escutcheon
   escutshun   escutcheon
   esel   easel
   esence   essence
   esenshul   essential
Eskimo, -mos
   eskwire   esquire
esky
   esophagus   oesophagus
esoteric, -ally
especial, -ly
   espeshul   especial
espionage
esplanade
   esplanaid   esplanade
espousal
espouse, -poused, -pousing
   espowse   espouse
espresso
esprit
espy, -pied, -pying
esquire
essay, -ed, -ing (try)
   essay   assay (analyse)
essayist
essence
   essense   essence
   essenshul   essential
essential, -ly
establish, -ed, -ing
establishment
estate
esteem, -ed, -ing
   Ester   Easter
   estern   eastern
estimable, -bly
   estimabul   estimable
estimate, -mated, -mating
estimation
estimator
estrange, estranged, estranging
   estrogen   oestrogen
estuary, -aries

et cetera
etch, -ed, -ing
etcher
eternal, -ly
eternity, -ties
ether
   ether   either
ethereal, -ly
ethic
ethical, -ly
ethics
ethnic, -ally
ethnology
ethos
   etiket   etiquette
   etimology   etymology
   etiquet   etiquette
etymology, -gies
eucalyptus, -tuses, -ti
euchre, -chred, -chring
Euclid

> For **euf-** words, look under **euph-**.

eugenics
   Euklid   Euclid
eulogise, -gised, -gising
eulogy, -gies
eunuch
euphemism
euphemistic, -ally
euphony, -nies
euphoria
euphoric
   Eurapean   European
   Eurashun   Eurasian
Eurasian
eureka flag
eurhythmics
   eurithmics   eurhythmics
European
euthanasia
evacuate, -uated, -uating
evacuation
evacuee
evade, evaded, evading
evaluate, -ated, -ating

evaluation

   evangalist   evangelist

evangelical, -ly

   envangelicul   evangelical

evangelism

evangelist

   evaperate   evaporate

evaporate, -rated, -rating

evaporation

evasion

evasive, -ly

eve

   evedence   evidence

even, -ed, -ing

evenly

evenness

event

eventual, -ly

eventuality, -ties

eventuate, -ated, -ating

ever

evergreen

everlasting, -ly

every

everybody

everyday

everyone

everything

everywhere

   eves   eaves

evict, -ed, -ing

eviction

evictor

   evictshun   eviction

evidence, -denced, -dencing

evident, -ly

evil, -ly

evince, evinced, evincing

   evinse   evince

eviscerate, -rated, -rating

evocative

evoke, evoked, evoking

   evolushun   evolution

evolution

evolve, evolved, evolving

evolvement

   evry   every

ewe (sheep)

   ewe   yew (tree)

exacerbate, -bated, -bating

exacerbation

   exackly   exactly

exact, -ed, -ing

exactitude

exactly

exactness

   exagerate   exaggerate

exaggerate, -rated, -rating

exaggeration

exalt, -ed, -ing

exaltation

examination

examine, -ined, -ining

examiner

example

   exampul   example

   exaserbate   exacerbate

exasperate, -rated, -rating

exasperation

excavate, -vated, -vating

excavation

excavator

exceed, -ed, -ing (surpass)

   exceed   accede (agree)

exceedingly

excel, -celled, -celling

   excell   excel

excellence

excellency, -cies

   excellense   excellence

excellent, -ly

   excepshun   exception

except, -ed, -ing

exception

exceptional, -ly

excerpt

excess

excessive, -ly

exchange, -changed, -changing

exchangeable

exchequer

excise, -cised, -cising

   excishun   excision

excision

excitable, -bly
   excitabul   excitable
excite, -cited, -citing
excitement
exclaim, -ed, -ing
exclamation
exclamatory
   exclamatry   exclamatory
exclude, -luded, -luding
   exclushun   exclusion
exclusion
exclusive, -ly
excommunicate, -cated, -cating
excommunication
excrement
excrescence
   excreshun   excretion
   excressense   excrescence
excreta
excrete, -creted, -creting
excretion
excretory
excruciating, -ly
excursion
excusable, -bly
excuse, -cused, -cusing
execrable, -bly
execrate, -crated, -crating
   execushun   execution
execute, -cuted, -cuting
execution
executioner
executive
executor
exemplary
exemplify, -fied, -fying
   exempshun   exemption
exempt
exemptible
   exemptibul   exemptible
exemption
exercise, -cised, -cising
   exershun   exertion
exert, -ed, -ing
exertion
ex gratia
exhalation

exhale, -haled, -haling
exhaust, -ed, -ing
exhaustion
exhaustive, -ly
   exhibishun   exhibition
exhibit, -ed, -ing
exhibition
exhibitionism
exhibitionist
exhibitor
exhilarate, -rated, -rating
exhilaration
exhort, -ed, -ing
exhortation
exhume, -humed, -huming
exhumation
   exibit   exhibit
exigency, -cies
   exigensy   exigency
exile, -iled, -iling
exist, -ed, -ing
existence
   existense   existence
   existenshul   existential
existent
existential, -ly
existentialism
existentialist
exit
exodus
exonerate, -rated, -rating
exorbitant, -ly
exorcise, -cised, -cising
exorcism
exorcist
   exorsism   exorcism
   exorst   exhaust
   exort   exhort
   exortashun   exhortation
exoteric, -ally
exotic, -ally
expand, -ed, -ing
expanse
   expanshun   expansion
expansion
expansive, -ly
expansiveness

expatiate, -ated, -ating
expatriate, -ated, -ating
expatriation
expect, -ed, -ing
expectancy, -cies
expectant, -ly
expectation
expectorant
expectorate, -rated, -rating
expediency
  expediensy   expediency
expedient, -ly
  expedishun   expedition
expedite, -dited, -diting
expedition
expeditionary
expeditious, -ly
expeditiousness
expel, -pelled, -pelling
expend, -ed, -ing
expendable
  expendicher   expenditure
expenditure
expense
expensive, -ly
experience, -enced, -encing
experiment, -ed, -ing
experimental, -ly
experimentation
expert, -ly
expertise
expiate, -ated, -ating
expiation
expiration
expire, -pired, -piring
expiry, -ries
explain, -ed, -ing
explanation
explanatory
  explane   explain
  explanetry   explanatory
expletive
explicable, -bly
  explicabul   explicable
explicate, -cated, -cating
explicit, -ly
  explisit   explicit

explode, -ploded, -ploding
exploit, -ed, -ing
exploitation
exploration
exploratory
explore, -plored, -ploring
explorer
explosion
explosive, -ly
exponent
exponential, -ly
export, -ed, -ing
exporter
  exposay   exposé
expose, -posed, -posing
exposé
  exposhur   exposure
expostulate, -lated, -lating
exposure
expound, -ed, -ing
  expreshun   expression
  expresive   expressive
express, -ly
express, -ed, -ing
expression
expressionism
expressionist
expressive, -ly
  expresso   espresso
expressway
expropriate, -ated, -ating
expropriation
expulsion
expunction
expunge, -punged, -punging
expurgate, -gated, -gating
expurgation
exquisite, -ly
exquisiteness
  exseed   exceed
  exsel   excel
  exselence   excellence
  exserpt   excerpt
ex-serviceman, -men
extant
  extasy   ecstasy
  extatic   ecstatic

extemporaneous, -ly
extempore
extend, -ed, -ing
extendible
  extendibul   extendible
  extenshun   extension
extension
extensive, -ly
extent
extenuate, -ated, -ating
extenuation
  exterier   exterior
exterior
exterminate, -nated, -nating
extermination
exterminator
external, -ly
extinct
extinction
  extingshun   extinction
extinguish, -ed, -ing
extinguisher
extol, -tolled, -tolling
  extorshun   extortion
extort, -ed, -ing
extortion
extortionate, -ly
extortioner
extortionist
extra
  extracshun   extraction
extract, -ed, -ing
extractable
extraction
extracurricular
  extradishun   extradition
extradite, -dited, -diting
extradition
extramarital
extraneous, -ly
extraordinary
extrapolate, -ated, -ating
extrapolation
extrasensory
extraterrestrial
extravagance
extravagancy

extravagant, -ly
extravaganza
  extravert   extrovert
  extremast   extremist
extreme, -tremer, -tremest
extremely
extremism
extremist
extremity, -ties
extricate, -cated, -cating
extrication
extrovert
extrude, -truded, -truding
extrusion
exuberance
  exuberanse   exuberance
exuberant, -ly
exude, -uded, -uding
exult, -ed, -ing
exultant, -ly
exultation
  exume   exhume
eye, eyed, eyeing
eyeball
eyebrow
eyelash
eyelet
eyelid
eyesight
eyesore
eyetooth, -teeth
eyewash
eyewitness, -nesses
eyrie (nest)
  eyrie   eerie (weird)
  eze   ease
  ezel   easel
  ezy   easy

Ff

fable, -bled, -bling
fabric
fabricate, -cated -cating
fabrication
fabulous, -ly
   fabulus   fabulous
facade
face, faced, facing
faceless
facelift
   faceshus   facetious
facet, -eted, -eting
facetious, -ly
facia (panel)
   facia   fascia (band)
facial, -ly
facile, -ly
facilitate, -tated, -tating
facility, -ties
   facist   fascist
facsimile, -led, -leing
fact
faction
factionalism
factor
factory, -ries
factotum
factual, -ly
faculty, -ties
fad
faddish, -ly
fade, faded, fading
faeces
fag, fagged, fagging
faggot
   fagot   faggot
Fahrenheit
fail, -ed, -ing

fail-safe
failure
   failyer   failure
   faim   fame
   faimus   famous
fain (gladly)
   fain   feign (pretend)
faint, -ed, -ing (weak)
   faint   feint (pretend)
fair, -ly (honest)
   fair   fare (price)
fair game
fairway
fair-weather
   fairwell   farewell
fairy, -ries
fairytale
   fait   fate
   faitful   fateful
fait accompli
faith
faithful, -ly
faith-healing
fake, faked, faking
faker (fraud)
fakir (holy)
   falacy   fallacy
   falanx   phalanx
   falasius   fallacious
   falasy   fallacy
falcon
falconry
   fale   fail
   falesy   fallacy
   falible   fallible
   falic   phallic
fall, fell, fallen, falling
fallacious, -ly
fallacy, -cies
fallible, -bly
   fallibul   fallible
fallout
fallow
   fallus   phallus
   falow   fallow
false, falser, falsest
falsehood

falsetto, -tos		faranyx	pharynx
falsification		faraway	
falsify, -fied, -fying		farce	
falt	fault	fare, fared, faring (get on)	
falter, -ed, -ing		fare	fair (honest)
falteringly		farenhite	Fahrenheit
falure	failure	farewell	
falus	phallus	far-fetched	
fame, famed, faming		farm, -ed, -ing	
familial		farmacist	pharmacist
familiar, -ly		farmacy	pharmacy
familiarisation		farmasist	pharmacist
familiarise, -rised, -rising		farmer	
familiarity, -ties		farmstead	
familier	familiar	farrago, -goes	
family, -lies		farrier	
famine		farrow, -ed, -ing	
famished		far-sighted	
famous, -ly		farther (away)	
famus	famous	farther	father (parent)
fan, fanned, fanning		farthing	
fanatic		faryngitis	pharyngitis
fanatical, -ly		farytale	fairytale
fanaticism		fascia, fasciae (band)	
fancier		fascia	facia (panel)
fanciful, -ly		fascinate, -nated, -nating	
fancy, -cies		fascination	
fancy, -cied, -cying		fascism	
fancy, -cier, -ciest		fascist	
fane	fain (glad)	fase	face
fane	feign (pretend)	fase	phase
fanfair	fanfare	fasen	fasten
fanfare		faset	facet
fang		fasetious	facetious
fanlight		fasha	facia (panel)
fansie	fancy	fasha	fascia (band)
fansiful	fanciful	fashal	facial
fansy	fancy	fashion, -ed, -ing	
fantam	phantom	fashionable, -bly	
fantasey	fantasy	fashism	fascism
fantasia		fashist	fascist
fantasise, -sised, -sising		fashon	fashion
fantastic, -ally		fashonabul	fashionable
fantasy, -ies		fasilitate	facilitate
fantom	phantom	fasility	facility
far, farther, farthest		fasinate	fascinate
far, further, furthest	-	fasination	fascination

fast, -ed, -ing
fasten, -ed, -ing
fastener
fastidious, -ly
fastidiousness
   fastidius   fastidious
fat, fatted, fatting
fat, fatter, fattest
fatal, -ly
fatalism
fatalist
fatalistic, -ally
fatality, -ties
fate (destiny)
   fate   fete (fair)
fated
fateful, -ly
   faten   fatten
father, -ed, -ing (parent)
   father   farther (away)
Father Christmas
fatherhood
father-in-law, fathers-in-law
fatherland
fatherly
fathom, -ed, -ing
fathomable
fatigue, -tigued, -tiguing
fatten, -ed, -ing
fattener
fatty, -tier, -tiest
fatuous, -ly
faucet
fault, -ed, -ing
faultless, -ly
faulty, faultier, faultiest
faun (god)
   faun   fawn (deer)
fauna
faux pas
   faver   favour
   faverite   favourite
   faveritism   favouritism
   favorite   favourite
favour, -ed, -ing
favourable, -bly
favourite

favouritism
fawn, -ed, -ing (deer)
   fawn   faun (god)
   fawna   fauna
   faysha   facia (panel)
   faysha   fascia (band)
   fayshal   facial
faze, fazed, fazing
   feacher   feature
fealty, -ties
fear, -ed, -ing
fearful, -ly
   fearfull   fearful
fearless, -ly
fearsome, -ly
feasible, -bly
feasibility
   feasibul   feasible
feast, -ed, -ing
feat (act)
   feat   feet (body)
feather, -ed, -ing
featherbed, -bedded, -bedding
featherweight
feathery
feature, -tured, -turing
febrile
February
   Febuary   February
   feces   faeces
   fech   fetch
feckless, -ly
fecund
fecundity
   fedaration   federation
federal, -ly
federalism
federalist
federate, -rated, -rating
federation
fee
feeble, -bler, -blest
   feebul   feeble
feebleness
feebly
feed, fed, feeding
feedback

feeder
feel, felt, feeling
  feeld   field
feeler
  feend   fiend
  feest   feast
feet (body)
  feet   feat (act)
  feetul   foetal
  feetus   foetus
feign, -ed, -ing (pretend)
  feign   fain (glad)
  feild   field
  feind   fiend
feint, -ed, -ing (pretend)
  feint   faint (weak)
  fekund   fecund
  fekundity   fecundity
felicitate, -tated, -tating
felicitation
felicitous, -ly
felicity, -ties
feline, -ly
  felisitous   felicitous
  felisity   felicity
fell
fellow
fellowship
felon
felonious, -ly
felony, -nies
  felow   fellow
felt
female
feminine, -ly
femininity
feminism
femme fatale
femur
fence, fenced, fencing
fend, -ed, -ing
fender
  fenix   phoenix
fennel
  fenomenon   phenomenon
  fenominal   phenomenal
  fense   fence

  fer   fir (tree)
  fer   fur (pelt)
feral
  feret   ferret
  ferie   ferry
  ferl   furl
  ferlong   furlong
ferment, -ed, -ing
fermentation
fern
fernery, -ries
ferny
  fernice   furnace
  fernish   furnish
  ferniture   furniture
ferocious, -ly
ferocity
  feroshus   ferocious
ferret, -ed, -ing
ferrous
ferrule , -ruled, -ruling (tip)
  ferrule   ferule (rod)
ferry, -ries
ferry, -ried, -rying
ferryboat
  ferther   further
  ferthest   furthest
fertile, -ly
fertilisation
fertilise, -lised, -lising
fertiliser
fertility
ferule, -ruled, -ruling (rod)
  ferule   ferrule (tip)
fervency
fervent, -ly
  ferver   fervour
fervid, -ly
fervour
  fery   ferry
  fesant   pheasant
  fesible   feasible
festal, -ly
fester, -ed, -ing
festival
festive, -ly
festivity, -ties

festoon, -ed, -ing
   feta   fetta (cheese)
fetch, -ed, -ing
fete, feted, feting (fair)
   fete   fate (destiny)
   feter   fetter (chain)
   fether   feather
fetid, -ly
fetish
fetishism
fetlock
fetta (cheese)
fetter, -ed, -ing (chain)
fettle
fettler
feud, -ed, -ing
feudal, -ly
feudalism
fever
fevered
feverish, -ly
few
   fewd   feud
   fewdal   feudal
fey, -ly
fez, fezzes
   fezant   pheasant
   fial   file (papers)
   fial   phial (tube)
fiance (man)
fiancee (woman)
   fiansey   fiancee
fiasco, -cos
fib, fibbed, fibbing
fibber
   fiber   fibber
   fiber   fibre
fibre
fibreglass
fibro
fibrositis
fibrous, -ly
   fibrus   fibrous
fibula
fickle, -kly
fickleness
   ficshun   fiction

fiction
fictional, -ly
   fictishus   fictitious
fictitious, -ly
fiddle, -dled, -dling
fiddler
fiddlesticks
fiddly
fidelity, -ties
fidget, -ed, -ing
fidgety
   fidle   fiddle
field, -ed, -ing
fielder
fieldsman, -men
fiend
fiendish, -ly
fierce, fiercer, fiercest
fiercely
fierceness
   fierey   fiery
   fierse   fierce
fiery, fierier, fieriest
fiesta
fife
fifteen
fifteenth
fifth
fiftieth
fifty
fifty-fifty
fig
   figer   figure
   figerative   figurative
   figet   fidget
fight, fought, fighting
fighter
figment
figuration
figurative, -ly
figure, -ured, -uring
figurehead
figurine
Fiji
Fijian
   fiksation   fixation
   fiksative   fixative

fikscher fixture

> For other fila- words,
> look under **phila-**.

filch, -ed, -ing
filcher
file, filed, filing (paper)
 file phial (tube)
 filet fillet
filial, -ly
filibuster
 filie filly
filigree
 filip fillip
Filipino
 Filippines Philippines
 filistine philistine
fill, -ed, -ing
filler
fillet
fillip
filly, -lies
film, -ed, -ing
filmy, filmier, filmiest

> For filo- words,
> look under **philo-**.

filter, -ed, -ing
filth
filthily
filthiness
filthy, filthier, filthiest
filtrate, -trated, -trating
filtration
 fily filly
fin, finned, finning
final, -ly (end)
finale (last part)
finalisation
finalise, -lised, -lising
finalist
finality, -ties
finance, -nanced, -nancing
financial, -ly
financier
 finanse finance
finch, -ches

find, found, finding
finder
fine, fined, fining
fine, finer, finest
finely
fineness
finery, -ries
finesse, -nessed, -nessing
finetuner
finger
fingernail
fingerprint
fingertip
finical, -ly
finicky
finis (conclusion)
finish, -ed, -ing
finisher
finite, -ly
fiord
fir (tree)
 fir fur (pelt)
fire, fired, firing
firearm
firebreak
fire-escape
fire-extinguisher
firefly, -flies
fireman, -men
fireplace
fireproof
firescreen
fireworks
firm, -ed, -ing
firmament
first, -ly
first-hand
first-past-the-post
fiscal, -ly
fish, fishes, fish
fisherman, -men
fishery, -ries
fish-eye lens
fishmonger
fish-net
fishplate
 fishun fission

fishy, fishier, fishiest
   fisile   fissile
   fision   fission

> For other **fisi-** words,
> look under **physi-**.

   fiskle   fiscal
fissile
fission
fissure, -sured, -suring
fist
fisticuff
fistula, -las, -lae
fit, fitted, fitting
fit, fitter, fittest
   fite   fight
fitful, -ly
   fitfull   fitful
fitness
fitter
five
fiver
fix, fixed, fixing
fixated
fixation
fixative
   fixcher   fixture
fixity, -ties
fixture
fizz, -ed, -ing
fizzer
fizzle, -zled, -zling
   fizzul   fizzle
fizzy, -zier, -ziest
fjord
flabbergast, -ed, -ing
flabbily
flabbiness
flabby, -bier, -biest
   flabergast   flabbergast
   flaby   flabby
flaccid, -ly
flaccidity
flag, flagged, flagging
flagellate, -lated, -lating
flagon
flagrant, -ly

flagship
flagstone
flail, -ed, -ing
flair (talent)
   flair   flare (blaze)
flak
flake, flaked, flaking
flakily
flaky, flakier, flakiest
flamboyance
flamboyancy
flamboyant, -ly
flame, flamed, flaming
flamenco, -cos
flamethrower
flame-tree
flamingo, -gos, -goes
flammable
   flammabul   flammable
flan
   flanel   flannel
flange, flanged, flanging
   flanje   flange
flank, -ed, -ing
flannel, -elled, -elling
flannelette
   flanul   flannel
flap, flapped, flapping
flapjack
flapper
flare, flared, flaring (blaze)
   flare   flair (talent)
flash, -ed, -ing
flashback
flashbulb
flashgun
flashlight
flashpoint
flashy, flashier, flashiest
flask
flat, flatted, flatting
flat, flatter, flattest
   flaten   flatten
   flater   flatter
flatette
flatfoot, -feet
flat-footed, -ly

flathead
flatten, -ed, -ing
flatter, -ed, -ing
flatterer
flattery, -teries
flatulence
  flatulense   flatulence
flatulent, -ly
flaunt, -ed, -ing
flautist
  flaver   flavour
flavour, -ed, -ing
flaw, -ed, -ing (fault)
  flaw   floor (room)
flax
flaxen
flay, -ed, -ing
flea (insect)
  flea   flee (escape)
flea-bitten
  fleat   fleet
fleck, -ed, -ing
flecks (spots)
  flecks   flex (bend)
fledge, fledged, fledging
flee, fled, fleeing (escape)
  flee   flea (insect)
fleece, fleeced, fleecing
fleeciness
fleecy, fleecier, fleeciest
  fleese   fleece
fleet, -ly
fleeting, -ly
fleetness
  flegling   fledgling
  flegmatic   phlegmatic
  fleks   flecks (spots)
  fleksible   flexible
  flem   phlegm
  flert   flirt
flesh
fleshy, fleshier, fleshiest
fleur-de-lis, fleurs-de-lis
flew (fly)
  flew   flu (ill)
  flew   flue (passage)
flex, -ed, -ing (bend)

  flex   flecks (spots)
flexible, -bly
flexitime
  fli   fly
flibbertigibbet
flick, -ed, -ing
flicker, -ed, -ing
flick-knife, flick-knives
flier
flight
flightiness
flighty, -tier, -tiest
flimsily
flimsiness
flimsy, -sies
flimsy, -sier, -siest
flinch, -ed, -ing
flinchingly
fling, flung, flinging
flint
flinty, flintier, flintiest
flip, flipped, flipping
  flipansy   flippancy
  flipant   flippant
  fliper   flipper
flippancy
flippant, -ly
flipper
flirt, -ed, -ing
flirtation
flirtatious, -ly
flit, flitted, flitting
  flite   flight
  flo   floe (ice)
  flo   flow (pour)
float, -ed, -ing
floatation
floater
flock, -ed, -ing
flocks (groups)
  flocks   phlox (plant)
floe (ice)
  floe   flow (pour)
flog, flogged, flogging
flood, -ed, -ing
floodgate
floodlight, -lit, -lighting

floor, -ed, -ing (room)
   floor   flaw (fault)
floorboard
   flooride   fluoride
   floot   flute
flop, flopped, flopping
floppily
floppy, -pier, -piest
floppy disc
flora, floras, florae
floral, -ly
florescence (flowering)
   florescence   fluorescence
                (giving light)
florescent
   florescent   fluorescent
florid, -ly
   floridate   fluoridate
florin
   florish   flourish
florist
floss
flossy, flossier, flossiest
flotation
   flote   float
flotilla
flotsam and jetsam
flounce, flounced, flouncing
flounder, -ed, -ing
   flounse   flounce
flour (grain)
   flour   flower (plant)
flourish, -ed, -ing
floury
flout, -ed, -ing
flow, -ed, -ing
flower, -ed, -ing (plant)
   flower   flour (grain)
flowerbed
flowery, -rier, -riest
flown
   flownder   flounder
   flownse   flounce
flow-on
   flowt   flout
   flox   phlox
flu (ill)

   flu   flew (fly)
   flu   flue (passage)
fluctuate, -ated, -ating
fluctuation
flue (passage)
   flue   flew (fly)
   flue   flu (ill)
fluency
   fluensy   fluency
fluent, -ly
fluff, -ed, -ing
fluffily
fluffiness
fluffy, fluffier, fluffiest
fluid, -ly
fluidity
fluke, fluked, fluking
   fluks   flux
fluky, flukier, flukiest
flunk, -ed, -ing
fluoresce, -resced, -rescing
fluorescence (giving light)
fluoridate, -dated, -dating
fluoridation
   flurish   flourish
flurry, -ries
flurry, -ried, -rying
   flurt   flirt
   flurtation   flirtation
   flury   flurry
flush, -ed, -ing
fluster, -ed, -ing
flute, fluted, fluting
flutter, -ed, -ing
fluvial
flux
fly, flies
fly, flew, flown, flying
flyblown
flycatcher
flyleaf, -leaves
flyover
flytrap
flyweight
flywheel
foal, -ed, -ing
foam, -ed, -ing

fob, fobbed, fobbing
    fobia   phobia
focal, -ly
focus, -ci or -cuses
focus, -cused, -cusing or -cussed,
  -cussing
focuser
fodder
foe
    foe pas   faux pas
foetal
foetus
fog, fogged, fogging
fogey, fogeys
fogginess
foggy, -gier, -giest
foghorn
fogy, -gies
foible
    foier   foyer
foil, -ed, -ing
foist, -ed, -ing
    foks   fox
fold, -ed, -ing
folder
    fole   foal
foliage
foliaged
    foliaje   foliage
foliation
    folie   folly
folio, -lios
folk
folk dance
    folklaw   folklore
folklore
follicle
    follicul   follicle
follow, -ed, -ing
follower
folly, -lies
    folow   follow
    foly   folly
    fome   foam
foment, -ed, -ing
fond, -ly
fondant

fondle, -dled, -dling
fondness
fondue
    fondul   fondle
    fone   phone
    fonetic   phonetic
    fonograf   phonograph
font
    fony   phony
food
foodstuff
fool, -ed, -ing
foolery, -eries
foolhardiness
foolhardy, -dier, -diest
foolish, -ly
foolishness
foolproof
foolscap
foot, feet
football
footballer
foothill
foothold
footie
footing
footlights
footloose
footman, -men
footnote
footpath
footprint
footsore
footstep
footwork
fop
foppish, -ly
for (with the purpose of)
    for   fore (front)
    for   four (number)
forage, -raged, -raging
foray
    forbarance   forbearance
forbear, -bore, -borne, -bearing
forbearance
forbid, -bad, -bidden, -bidding
    forbode   forebode

forcasle	forecastle
forcast	forecast
forcastle	forecastle

force, forced, forcing
forceful, -ly
forceps, -ceps, -cipes
forcible, -bly

forcibul	forcible
forclose	foreclose

ford, -ed, -ing
fordable
fore (front)

fore	four (number)

forearm
forebear
forebode, -boded, -boding
forecast, -ed, -ing
forecaster
forecastle
foreclose, -closed, -closing
forefather
forefinger
forego, -gone, -going (go before)

forego	forgo (give up)

foreground
forehand
forehead
foreign
foreigner
foreknow, -knew, -knowing
foreknowledge
foreman, -men

foren	foreign
forener	foreigner

forerunner
foresee, -saw, -seeing
foreshadow, -ed, -ing
foreshore
foresight
foreskin
forest, -ed, -ing
forestall, -ed, -ing
forester
forestry
foretaste, -tasted, -tasting
foretell, -told, -telling
forethought

forever
forewarn, -ed, -ing
foreword (book)

foreword	forward (ahead)

forfeit, -ed, -ing
forfeiture

forfit	forfeit
forfiture	forfeiture
forgary	forgery

forge, forged, forging
forgery, -eries
forget, -got, -gotten, -getting
forgetful, -ly
forget-me-not
forgettable
forgive, -gave, -given, -giving
forgiveness
forgo, -went, -gone, -going (give up)

forgo	forego (go before)

For **for-** words, also
look under **fore-**.

forige	forage
forin	foreign

fork, -ed, -ing
fork-lift
forlorn, -ly
form, -ed, -ing
formal, -ly
formalise, -lised, -lising
formality, -ties
format
formation
formative, -ly
former, -ly
formica
formidable, -bly

formidabul	formidable

formula, -las, -lae
formulate, -lated, -lating
formulation
formulator

forn	faun (god)
forn	fawn (deer)

fornicate, -cated, -cating

fornication
  forsable   forcible
forsake, -sook, -saken, -saking
  forse   force
  forseps   forceps
  forsful   forceful
  forsible   forcible
  forsight   foresight
fort (soldiers)
  fort   fought (fight)
forte (strong)
forth (away)
  forth   fourth
                (number)
forthcoming
forthright
forthwith
fortieth
fortification
fortify, -fied, -fying
fortitude
fortnight
fortnightly
  fortnite   fortnight
fortress
fortuitous, -ly
  fortuitus   fortuitous
fortunate, -ly
fortune
fortune-teller
forty, -ties
forum, forums, fora
forward (ahead)
  forward   foreword
                (book)
forwards
  fosfate   phosphate
  fosforesent   phosphorescent
  fosforus   phosphorus
  fosil   fossil
fossick, -ed, -ing
fossil
foster, -ed, -ing

> For foto- words,
> look under **photo-**.

foul, -ed, -ing (dirt)

  foul   fowl (bird)
found, -ed, -ing
foundation
founder, -ed, -ing
foundling
foundry, -dries
fount
fountain
four (number)
  four   fore (ahead)
four-stroke
  fourt   fort (soldiers)
  fourt   fought (fight)
fourteen
fourteenth
fourth, -ly
  fourty   forty
fowl (bird)
  fowl   foul (dirt)
  fownd   found
  fowndation   foundation
  fowndry   foundry
  fownt   fount
  fowntain   fountain
fox, foxes
foxhole
fox-hunting
foxtrot
foxy, foxier, foxiest
  foyble   foible
foyer
fracas
  fracshun   fraction
  fracshus   fractious
fraction
fractional, -ly
fractious, -ly
fracture, -tured, -turing
fragile, -ly
fragility, -ties
fragment, -ed, -ing
fragmentary
fragmentation
fragmented
  fragmentry   fragmentary
fragrance
  fragranse   fragrance

fragrant, -ly
frail, -ly
frailty, -ties
frame, framed, framing
frame-up
framework
franc (money)

   franc   frank (mark)
franchise
frangipanni, -nies
frank, -ed, -ing (mark)

   frank   franc (money)
frankfurt
frankincense
frantic, -ally

   frase   phrase
   frate   freight
fraternal, -ly
fraternisation
fraternise, -nised, -nising
fraternity, -ties
fraud
fraudulence

   fraudulense   fraudulence
fraudulent, -ly
fraught

   fraut   fraught
   frawd   fraud
   frawdulence   fraudulence
   frawdulent   fraudulent
   frawt   fraught
fray, -ed, -ing
frazzle, -zled, -zling

   frazzul   frazzle
freak
freakish, -ly
freckle, -led, -ling
free, freed, freeing
free, freer, freest
freeborn
freedom
freehand
freehold
freelance, -lanced, -lancing
freelancer
freeload, -ed, -ing
freeloader

freely
freeman, -men
Freemason
Freemasonry
free-range
freesia
freestanding
freestyle
freeway
freewheel, -ed, -ing
freeze, froze, frozen, freezing (cold)

   freeze   frieze (band)
freezer
freight, -ed, -ing
freighter

   freind   friend
   frekwency   frequency
   frekwent   frequent
French

   frend   friend
   frendly   friendly
   frendship   friendship
frenetic, -ally

   frenzie   frenzy
frenzied
frenzy, -zies
frenzy, -zied, -zying
frequency, -cies

   frequensy   frequency
frequent, -ly
fresco, -coes
fresco, -coed, -coing
fresh, -ly
freshen, -ed, -ing
freshener
fresher
freshness
freshwater

   fresko   fresco
fret, fretted, fretting
fretful, -ly
fretwork
Freudian

   fri   fry
friable

   friabul   friable
friar

fricassee, -seed, -seeing
  fricshun   friction
friction
frictional, -ly
Friday
fridge
friend
friendliness
friendly, -lier, -liest
friendship
  frier   friar
Friesian
frieze (band)
  frieze   freeze (cold)
frigate
fright
frighten, -ed, -ing
frightener
frightful, -ly
  frightfull   frightful
frigid, -ly
frigidity, -ties
frigidness
frill, -ed, -ing
frill-necked lizard
fringe, fringed, fringing
frippery, -ries
frisk, -ed, -ing
friskily
frisky, friskier, friskiest
  frite   fright
  friteful   frightful
  friten   frighten
  friter   fritter
fritter, -ed, -ing
frivolity, -ties
frivolous, -ly
  frivolus   frivolous
frizz, frizzes
frizz, frizzed, frizzing
frizzle, -zled, -zling
frizzy
  frizzul   frizzle
fro
frock, -ed, -ing
frog
frogman, -men

frogmarch, -ed, -ing
frogmouth
  Froidian   Freudian
frolic, -icked, -icking
frolicsome, -ly
frond
front, -ed, -ing
frontage
frontal, -ly
frontbencher
frontier
  frontige   frontage
  froogal   frugal
  frooishun   fruition
  froot   fruit
  frootful   fruitful
frost, -ed, -ing
frostbite, -bit, -bitten, -biting
frostily
frosty, -tier, -tiest
froth, -ed, -ing
frothiness
frothy, frothier, frothiest
frown, -ed, -ing
frowzy, -zier, -ziest
froze
frozen, -ly
fructose
frugal, -ly
frugality, -ties
  fruishun   fruition
fruit, -ed, -ing
fruiterer
fruit-fly
fruitful, -ly
fruition
fruitless, -ly
fruity, -tier, -tiest
frump
frumpish, -ly
  frunt   front
  fruntal   frontal
  fruntier   frontier
frustrate, -trated, -trating
frustration
  frut   fruit
  fruterer   fruiterer

frutful	fruitful
frutie	fruity
fry, fried, frying	
fry, fries	
fucher	future
fucheristic	futuristic
fuchsia	
fudal	feudal
fudalism	feudalism
fuddle, -dled, -dling	
fuddul	fuddle
fude	feud
fudge, fudged, fudging	
fuel, fuelled, fuelling	
fuel-injection	
fuel-injector	
fugitive	
fugue	
ful	full
fulcrum, -crums, -cra	
fulfil, -filled, -filling	
fulfilment	
full	
full-back	
full-blooded	
fullfil	fulfil
fully	
fully-fledged	
fulminate, -ated, -ating	
fulscap	foolscap
fulsome, -ly	
fulsomeness	
fumble, -bled, -bling	
fumbler	
fumbul	fumble
fume, fumed, fuming	
fumigant	
fumigate, -gated, -gating	
fumigation	
fumigator	
fun	
funcshun	function
function	
functional, -ly	
functionalism	
functionary, -ries	
fund, -ed, -ing	

fundamental, -ly	
funel	funnel
funeral	
funereal, -ly	
funfair	
fungicide	
fungus, fungi	
funicular	
funily	funnily
funk, -ed, -ing	
funnel, -nelled, -nelling	
funnel-web	
funnily	
funny, -nier, -niest	
fur, furred, furring (pelt)	
fur	fir (tree)
furbish, -ed, -ing	
furie	furry (fur)
furie	fury (anger)
furier	furrier
furious, -ly	
furius	furious
furl, -ed, -ing	
furlong	
furlough	
furm	firm
furmament	firmament
furment	ferment
furmentation	fermentation
furn	fern
furnace	
furnish, -ed, -ing	
furnisher	
furnishings	
furniture	
furore	
furphy,-phies	
furrier	
furrow, -ed, -ing	
furry, -rier, -riest (fur)	
furst	first
further	
furtherance	
furthest	
furtive, -ly	
fury, -ries (anger)	
fus	fuss

fuse, fused, fusing
fuselage

fusha	fuchsia
fusier	fussier
fusiest	fussiest
fusilade	fusillade
fusilage	fuselage

fusilier
fusillade
fusion
fuss, -ed, -ing
fusspot
fussy, -sier, -siest
futile, -ly
futility, -ties
future
futurism
futuristic
futurology
fuzz
fuzzily
fuzziness
fuzzy, -zier, -ziest

fyord	fiord
fyord	fjord

For fysi- words, look
under **physi-**.

Gg

gab, gabbed, gabbing
gabardine
gabble, -bled, -bling (talk)
gable (roof)

| gabul | gabble (talk) |
| gabul | gable (roof) |

gadget
Gaelic

| gaf | gaff (hook) |
| gaf | gaffe (mistake) |

gaff (hook)
gaffe (mistake)
gag, gagged, gagging
gaga

| gage | gauge |
| gaget | gadget |

gaggle

| gagit | gadget |
| gagul | gaggle |

gaiety, -ties

| gail | gale |

gaily
gain, -ed, -ing
gainful, -ly
gainsay, -said, -saying
gait (walk)

| gait | gate (opening) |

gaiter

| gaitey | gaiety |

gala (festival)

| gala | galah (bird) |

galah (bird)

galaksey	galaxy
galant	gallant
galantry	gallantry
galaw	galore

galaxy, -axies
gale

galery	gallery
galey	galley
galivant	gallivant

gall, -ed, -ing
gallant, -ly
gallantry, -tries
galleon
gallery, -leries
galley, -leys
gallivant, -vanted, -vanting
gallon
gallop, galloped, galloping (pace)
gallows
gallstone
gallup poll (survey)

| galon | gallon |
| galop | gallop (pace) |

galore
galoshes

| galows | gallows |
| galup poll | gallup poll |

galvanise, -nised, -nising
galvanised iron

| galy | galley |

gambit
gamble, -bled, -bling (chance)
gambol, -bolled, -bolling (frolic)
game, gamed, gaming
gamesmanship
gamin (urchin)
gamma
gammon (bacon)
gammy, -mier, -miest
gamut
gander
gang
gangling
ganglion, -glia, -glions
gangplank

| gangreen | gangrene |

gangrene
gangrenous

| gangrenus | gangrenous |

gangster
gangway
gannet
gantry, -tries

gaol (prison)
  gaol   goal (aim)
gaolbird
gaoler
gap
gape, -ed, -ing
garage, -raged, -raging
  garantee   guarantee
  garantee   guaranty
  garantor   guarantor
garb, -ed, -ing
garbage
  garbige   garbage
garble, -bled, -bling
  garbul   garble
  gard   guard
garden, -ed, -ing
gardener
gardenia
  gardian   guardian
garfish, -fish, -fishes
gargle, -gled, -gling
  gargoil   gargoyle
gargoyle
  gargul   gargle
garish, -ly
  garison   garrison
garland, -landed, -landing
garlic
garment
garner, -ed, -ing
garnet
garnish, -ed, -ing
garnishee, -sheed, -sheeing
  garnit   garnet
garrison, -ed, -ing
  garrot   garrotte
garrotte, -rotted, -rotting
garrulity
garrulous, -ly
garter
  garulus   garrulous
gas, gases
gas, gassed, gassing
gasbag, -bagged, -bagging
  gasebo   gazebo
  gaselene   gasoline

gaseous
gash, gashed, gashing
  gasious   gaseous
gasket
gasmask
gasolene
gasoline
gasometer
gasp, -ed, -ing
  gassey   gassy
gassy, -sier, -siest
  gastley   ghastly
gastric
gastritis
gastroenteritis
gastronome
gastronomy
gate (opening)
  gate   gait (walk)
gateau, -teaux
gatecrash, -crashed, -crashing
  gater   gaiter
gateway
gather, -ed, -ing
gauche
  gaudie   gaudy
gauge, gauged, gauging
gaunt, -ly
gauntlet
gauze
gave
gavel
  gavot   gavotte
gavotte
  gawdie   gaudy
gawk, -ed, -ing
gawky, -kier, -kiest
  gawl   gall
  gawnt   gaunt
  gawntlet   gauntlet
  gawse   gauze
gay, gayer, gayest
  Gaylic   Gaelic
  gayn   gain
  gaysha   geisha
gaze, -ed, -ing
gazebo, -bos, -boes

gazel   gazelle
gazelle
gazette, -etted, -etting
gazump, -ed, -ing
gear, -ed, -ing
gearbox, -boxes
gear-ratio
gearstick
gearwheel
gecko, -os, -oes
geebung
geek
gees   geese
geese
geezer
Geiger counter
geisha, -shas
gel, gelled, gelling
gelatin   gelatine
gelatine
gelatinous, -ly
gelatinus   gelatinous
gelato
geld, gelded, gelding
gelignite
gem, gemmed, gemming
gemfish, -fish, -fishes
Gemini
gen, genned, genning
gendarme, -darmes
gender
gene
genealogist
genealogy, -gies
genee   genie
general, -ly
generalise, -ised, -ising
generality, -ties
generate, -ed, -ing
generation
generation-gap
generator
generic
generical, -ly
generosity, -ties
generous, -ly
generus   generous

genesis, -ses
genetic
genetical, -ly
genetics
geney   genie
genial, -ly
genie
geniology   genealogy
genital
genius, geniuses
genocide
genoside   genocide
genre
gent
genteel, -ly (proper)
genteel   gentle
gentile (Christian)
gentility, -ties
gentle, -tler, -tlest
gentleman, -men
gentlewoman, -women
gentrey   gentry
gentrification
gentry
gentul   gentle
gentulman   gentleman
genuflect, -ed, -ing
genuin   genuine
genuine, -ly
genuineness
genus, genera
geny   genie
geofysics   geophysics
geografey   geography
geography, -phies
geologist
geology, -gies
geometrey   geometry
geometric
geometrical, -ly
geometry, -tries
geophysicist
geophysics
georgette
geranium
gerd   gird
gerder   girder

gerdle	girdle	giddy, -dier, -diest	
gerdul	girdle	gide	guide
geriatric		gidgee	
gerilla	gorilla	gidgie	gidgee
gerilla	guerilla	gidie	giddy
gerkin	gherkin	gidy	giddy
gerl	girl	gift	
germ		gig, gigged, gigging	
German		gigantic, -ally	
germane		giggle, -gled, -gling	
germinal		gigolo, -los	
germinate, -nated, -nating		gigul	giggle
gerontology		gil	gill
gerth	girth	gild, gilded, gilding (gold)	
gerund		gild	guild (union)
gerymander	gerrymander	gile	guile
gescha	gesture	gilgai	
geser	geyser	gilgy	gilgai
gess	guess	gill	
gest	guest	giloteen	guillotine
gestate, -tated, -tating		gilotine	guillotine
gestation		gilt (gold)	
gesticulate, -lated, -lating		gilt	guilt
gesture, -tured, -turing		giltey	guilty
get, got, getting		gilty	guilty
getaway		gim	gym
getto	ghetto	gimick	gimmick
geyser		gimkana	gymkhana
ghastly, -lier, -liest		gimlet	
gherkin		gimmick	
ghetto, ghettos, ghettoes		gimnasium	gymnasium
ghost, -ly		gimnastics	gymnastics
ghoul		gin, ginned, ginning	
ghoulish, -ly		ginecology	gynaecology
ghoulishness		giney	guinea
giant		gineypig	guineapig
gibber		gingam	gingham
gibberish		ginger	
gibbet, -beted, -beting		gingerley	gingerly
gibe, gibed, gibing (mock)		gingerly	
gibe	jibe (sail)	gingham	
giber	gibber	gingivitis	
giberish	gibberish	ginie	guinea
gibet	gibbet	giniepig	guineapig
giblet		ginjer	ginger
gidance	guidance	ginjivitis	gingivitis
gidanse	guidance	ginseng	

gip — gyp
gipsey — gipsy
gipsie — gipsy
gipsum — gypsum
gipsy, -sies
giraf — giraffe
gird, -ed, -ing
girder
girdle, -dled, -dling
girdul — girdle
girl
girocompass — gyrocompass
giroscope — gyroscope
girth
gise — guise
gismo
gist
gitar — guitar
give, gave, given, giving
giy — guy
gizerd — gizzard
gizzard
glacial, -ly
glacier
glad, gladded, gladding
glad, gladder, gladdest
glade
gladen — gladden
gladiater — gladiator
gladiator
glamer — glamour
glamorous, -ly
glamour
glance, -ed, -ing
gland
glandular
glanduler — glandular
glanse — glance
glare, glared, glaring
glas — glass
glashal — glacial
glasier — glacier
glass, glasses
glasshouse
glassy, -sier, -siest
glaucoma
glawcoma — glaucoma

glaze, glazed, glazing
glazier
glea — glee
gleam, -ed, -ing
glean, -ed, -ing
glee
gleem — gleam
gleen — glean
glib, glibber, glibbest
glicerine — glycerine
glide, glided, gliding
glider
glimmer, -ered, -ering
glimpse, glimpsed, glimpsing
glimse — glimpse
glint, -ed, -ing
glisen — glisten
gliserin — glycerine
glisten, -ed, -ing
glitter, -ed, -ing
glo — glow
gloat, -ed, -ing
glob
global, -ly
globe, globed, globing
globule
gloo — glue
gloocose — glucose
gloom
gloomily
gloomy, -mier, -miest
glooten — gluten
glorie — glory
glorify, -fied, -fying
glorious, -ly
glorius — glorious
glory, glories
glory, gloried, glorying
glos — gloss
glosary — glossary
gloss, glossed, glossing
glossary, -ries
glossie — glossy
glossy, glossier, glossiest
glote — gloat
glove
glow, -ed, -ing

glower, -ered, -ering
glucose
glue, glued, gluing
glum, -ly
glut, glutted, glutting
gluten (glue)
  glutten   glutton
glutton (eat)
  gluv   glove
glycerine
gnarled
gnash, -ed, -ing
gnat
gnaw, gnawed, gnawing
gnome
gnu, gnus
go, gone, going
goad, -ed, -ing
goal (aim)
  goal   gaol (prison)
goalkeeper
goanna
goat
goatee
gob
  gobbel   gobble
gobble, -bled, -bling
gobbledegook
gobbler
go-between
goblet
goblin
  gobul   gobble
go-cart
God
godchild, -children
goddess
godforsaken
godly, -lier, -liest
godparent
godsend, -sent, -sending
godspeed
goer
goes
goggle, -gled, -gling
  gogul   goggle
  goiter   goitre

goitre
go-kart
gold
golden, -ly
goldfield
goldfish
goldmine
  gole   goal (aim)
golf (game)
  golf   gulf (bay)
golliwog
gollywog
  gon   gone
gondola
gondolier
gone
goner
gong
goo
good, better, best
  gooda   gouda
goodbye, -byes
goodnight
goodwill
gooey, gooier, gooiest
goof, goofed, goofing
googly
  gool   ghoul
  goolash   goulash
  goormand   gourmand
  goormay   gourmet
goose, geese
  gooseberie   gooseberry
gooseberry, -ries
goosestep, -stepped, -stepping
gopher
gore, gored, goring
gorge, gorged, gorging
gorgeous, -ly
  gorgus   gorgeous
gorilla (ape)
  gorilla   guerilla
                     (soldier)
gormandise, -dised, -dising
gorse
gory, gorier, goriest
  gosamer   gossamer

goshawk

gosip   gossip

gosling

go-slow

gospel

gospeller

gossamer

gossip, -ed, -ing

gost   ghost

gote   goat

Gothic

gouda

gouge, gouged, gouging

goul   ghoul

goulash

gourd

gourmand

gourmet

gout

goven   govern

govern, -ed, -ing

governer   governor

governess

government

governmental, -ly

governor

governor-general, governors-general

govner   governor

gowge   gouge

gawt   gout

grab, grabbed, grabbing

grace, graced, gracing

graceful, -ly

gracious, -ly

gradation

grade, graded, grading

grader

gradient

gradual, -ly

graduate, -ated, -ating

graduation

graf   graph

graffiti

grafic   graphic

grafics   graphics

grafite   graphite

grafiti   graffiti

graft, grafted, grafting

grail

grain

graling   grayling

gram

gramar   grammar

gramarian   grammarian

gramatical   grammatical

gramer   grammar

gramerfone   gramophone

grammar

grammarian

grammatical, -ly

gramophone

grampus

gran

granary, -ries

grand

grandeur

grandiloquent, -ly

grandiose, -ly

grandiosity

grandparent

grandstand

grane   grain

grange

granie   granny

granit   granite

granite

granny, grannies

grant,-ed, -ing

granular

granulate, -lated, -lating

granule

grany   granny

grape

grapefruit, grapefruit

grapevine

graph, -ed, -ing

graphic

graphical, -ly

graphics

graphite

graple   grapple

grapnel

grapple, -pled, -pling

grappul   grapple

gras — grass
grase — grace
grashoper — grasshopper
grashus — gracious
grasp, -ed, -ing
grass
grasshopper
glassland
grassroots
grassy, -sier, -siest
grate (fireplace)
grate, grated, grating (rub)
grate — great (large)
grateful, -ly
gratification
gratify, -fied, -fying
gratingly
gratis
gratitude
gratuitey — gratuity
gratuitous, -ly
gratuitousness
gratuitus — gratuitous
gratuity
grave
gravel, gravelled, gravelling
gravelly
gravie — gravy
gravitashun — gravitation
gravitate, -tated, -tating
gravitation
gravity, -ties
gravure
gravvity — gravity
gravy, -vies
grayhownd — greyhound
grayl — grail
grayling
grayn — grain
graze, grazed, grazing
grazier
grease, greased, greasing
greasepaint
great (large)
great — grate (rub)
greatful — grateful
grede — greed

greed
greedily
greedy, greedier, greediest
greef — grief
green
greenery, -eries
greengrocer
greenhorn
greenhouse
greese — grease
greet, -ed, -ing
gregarious, -ly
gregarius — gregarious
greif — grief
greive — grieve
greivus — grievous
gremlin
grenade
grenadier
grene — green
grenery — greenery
grengroser — greengrocer
grenhorn — greenhorn
grenhous — greenhouse
grese — grease
grete — greet
grevance — grievance
grevanse — grievance
greve — grieve
grevillea
grevus — grievous
grew
grey
greyhound
greyness
grid
griddle, -dled, -dling
griddul — griddle
gridiron
grief
grief-stricken
grievance
grievanse — grievance
grieve, -ed, -ing
griever
grievous, -ly
griffin

grill, -ed, -ing (cook)
grille (screen)
griller (barbeque)
  griller   gorilla
  griller   guerilla
grim, grimmer, grimmest
grimace, -maced, -macing
  grimase   grimace
grime, grimed, griming
grimy, grimier, grimiest
grin, grinned, grinning
grind, ground, grinding
grinder
grindstone
  grined   grind
grip, gripped, gripping (hold)
gripe, griped, griping (pain)
grippe (flu)
  grisel   gristle (fibre)
  grisel   grizzle (whine)
grisly, -lier, -liest
  grissle   gristle (fibre)
  grissle   grizzle (whine)
grist
gristle (fibre)
grit, gritted, gritting
grizzle, -zled, -zling (whine)
  grizzle   gristle (fibre)
grizzleguts
  gro   grow
groan, groaned, groaning (moan)
  groan   grown (mature)
grocer
grocery, -ceries
grog
groggy, -gier, -giest
groin (body)
  groin   groyne (jetty)
  grone   groan
  grone   grown
  groo   grew
  grool   gruel
  groop   group
  groosum   gruesome
groove, grooved, grooving
  groovey   groovy
groovy, -vier, -viest

  grooyere   gruyere
grope, groped, groping
groper
  gros   gross
  groser   grocer
gross, grosses
  grotesk   grotesque
grotesque, -ly
  groto   grotto
grotto, -toes, -tos
grotty, -tier, -tiest
  groty   grotty
grouch, -ed, -ing
  groun   grown
ground, -ed, -ing
  groundsheat groundsheet
groundsheet
groundsman, -men
group, -ed, -ing
grouse, groused, grousing
grout, -ed, -ing
grove
grovel, -elled, -elling
  grovle   grovel
grow, grew, grown, growing
grower
growl, -ed, -ing
grown (mature)
  grown   groan (moan)
  grownd   ground
  growse   grouse
growth
groyne (jetty)
  groyne   groin (body)
grub, grubbed, grubbing
grubber
grubby, -bier, -biest
grudge, -ed, -ing
gruel, gruelled, gruelling
gruesome, -ly
gruesomeness
  gruf   gruff
gruff, -ly
  gruge   grudge
grumble, -led, -ling
  grumbul   grumble
grummet

grumpie   grumpy
grumpy, -pier, -piest
grunt, -ed, -ing
grunter

grusome   gruesome
grusum   gruesome
gruyaire   gruyère
gruyare   gruyère
gruyère
G-string
guano, -nos
guarantee, -teed, -teeing
guarantor
guaranty, -tied, -tying
guaranty, -ties
guard, -ed, -ing
guardian
guava
gudgeon
guerilla (soldier)

guerilla   gorilla (ape)
guernsey, -seys
guess, -ed, -ing
guest
guesthouse, -houses

gufaw   guffaw
guffaw, -awed, -awing
guidance
guide, guided, guiding
guideline
guild (union)

guild   gild (gold)
guile
guileless, -ly
guillotine, -tined, -tining

guiloteen   guillotine
guilotine   guillotine
guilt
guiltily
guilty, -tier, -tiest
guinea
guineapig
guise, guised, guising
guitar

gul   gull
gulash   goulash
gulch

gulet   gullet
guley   gully
gulf (bay)

gulf   golf (game)
gulible   gullible
gulie   gully
gull, -ed, -ing
gullet
gullible, -bly
gullibility

gullibul   gullible
gully, gullies
gulp, -ed, -ing

guly   gully
gum, gummed, gumming
gumboil
gumboot
gummy, -mier, -miest
gumnut
gumption

gumshun   gumption
gun, gunned, gunning
gung ho
gunk

gunl   gunwale
gunman, -men
gunmetal

gunnel   gunwale
gunner
gunnery, -eries
gunny, -nies
gunnysack
gunpowder
gunsmith
gunwale
guppy, -pies

gurdle   girdle
gurgle, -gled, -gling

gurgul   gurgle
gurnard, -nards

gurnerd   gurnard
gurth   girth
guru, gurus
gush, gushed, gushing
gusset

gussit   gusset
gust, -ed, -ing

gusto
gut, gutted, gutting
  guter   gutter
  guteral   guttural
  gutersnipe   guttersnipe
gutless, -ly
  gutsa   gutser
gutser
  gutsie   gutsy
gutsy
gutter
guttersnipe
guttural, -ly
  guvern   govern
  guverness   governess
  guvernment   government
  guvner   governor
guy
  guzul   guzzle
guzzle, guzzled, guzzling
  gwano   guano
  gwava   guava
  gybe   gibe
gym
  gymkana   gymkhana
gymkhana
gymnasium, -nasiums, -nasia
gymnastics
gynaecological
gynaecologist
gynaecology
gyp, gypped, gypping
gypsum
gypsy, -sies
gyrate, -ed, -ing
gyrocompass
gyroscope

Hh

habeas corpus	
haberdasher	
haberdashery, -ries	
habet	habit
habias corpus	habeas corpus
habichual	habitual
habichuate	habituate
habit	
habitable, -bly	
habitabul	habitable
habitat	
habitation	
habitual, -ly	
habituate, -ated, -ating	
hach	hatch
hachery	hatchery
hachett	hatchet
hacienda	
hack, -ed, -ing	
hackle, -led, -ling	
hackney, -neyed, -neying	
hacksaw	
hackul	hackle
hackwork	
haddock	
hades	
hadn't (had not)	
hadnt	hadn't
haematology	
haemefilia	haemophilia
haemoglobin	
haemophilia	
haemorage	haemorrhage
haemorrhage, -haged, -haging	
haemorrhoid	
haemorroid	haemorrhoid
haft, -ed, -ing	
hag	

hagard	haggard
hagerd	haggard
haggard, -ly	
haggis	
haggle, -gled, -gling	
hagiography, -phies	
hagis	haggis
hagul	haggle
haiku	
hail (ice)	
hail	hale (robust)
hailstone	
hailstorm	
hair (head)	
hair	hare (animal)
hair	heir (inherit)
hairdo, -dos	
hairdresser	
hairline	
hairpiece	
hairpin	
hairspring	
hair-trigger	
hairy, -rier, -riest	
haka	
hake, hake, hakes	
hakea	
halcion	halcyon
halcyon	
hale, haler, halest (robust)	
hale	hail (ice)
haleluya	hallelujah
halestone	hailstone
halestorm	hailstorm
half	
half-back	
half-baked	
half-blood	
half-breed	
half-brother	
half-caste	
half-cock	
half-forward	
half-hearted, -ly	
half-life	
half-mast	
half-measure	

half-mesure	half-measure	hand, handed, handing	
half-moon		handbag	
half-sister		handball	
half-time		handbill	
half-truth		handbook	
halfway		handbrake	
halfway house		handclap, -clapped, -clapping	
halfwit		handcuff, -cuffed, -cuffing	
halibut, -buts		handey	handy
halilooya	hallelujah	handeywork	handiwork
halitosis		handicap, -capped, -capping	
hall (room)		handicraft	
hall	haul (carry)	handie	handy
hallelujah		handiwork	
halleluyah	hallelujah	handkerchief, -chiefs, -chieves	
hallmark		handle, -dled, -dling	
hallo (greet)		handlebar	
hallow, -ed, -ing (holy)		handler	
Halloween		handmade (article)	
hallucinate, -nated, -nating		handmaid (servant)	
hallucination		hand-me-down	
hallucinogen		handout	
halmark	hallmark	hand-pick, -picked, -picking	
halo, -loes, -los (light)		handpiece	
halo	hallo (greet)	handrail	
halo	hallow (holy)	handriting	handwriting
halogen		handset	
Haloween	Halloween	handshake	
halsiun	halcyon	handsome, -somer, -somest (fine)	
halt, -ed, -ing		handspring	
halter		handstand	
halusinate	hallucinate	hand-to-mouth	
halusinogen	hallucinogen	handul	handle
halve, -ed, -ing		handwriting	
halyard		handy, -dier, -diest	
halyerd	halyard	handyman	
ham, hammed, hamming		hang, hung or hanged, hanging	
hamburger		hangar (shed)	
hamer	hammer	hangar	hanger (clothes)
ham-fisted			
hamlet		hangdog	
hammer, -ed, -ing		hanger (clothes)	
hammerhead		hanger	hangar (shed)
hammock		hanger-on, hangers-on	
hamper, -ered, -ering		hang-glider	
hamster		hangi	
hamstring, -strung, -stringing		hangkerchief	handkerchief

hangman		hardnose	
hangover		hard-pressed	
hang-up		hardship	
hank		hardtop	
hanker, -ed, -ing		hardware	
hankerchief	handkerchief	hardwear	hardware
hankie		hardwood	
hankuff	handcuff	hardy, hardier, hardiest	
hanky, hankies		hare (animal)	
hanky-panky		hare	hair (head)
Hansard		hare	heir (inherit)
hansom (cab)		harebrained	
hansom	handsome (fine)	harelip	
		harem	
hansum	handsome	harico	haricot
hapen	happen	haricot	
haphazard, -ly		hark, -ed, -ing	
hapie	happy	harlot	
hapless, -ly		harm, -ed, -ing	
happen, -ened, -ening		harmonic	
happily		harmonica	
happy, happier, happiest		harmonious, -ly	
happy-go-lucky		harmonise, -nised, -nising	
hapy	happy	harmonium	
harang	harangue	harmonius	harmonious
harangue, -rangued, -ranguing		harmony, -nies	
haras	harass	harness,-ed, -ing	
harass, -ed, -ing		harow	harrow
harassment		harp, -ed, -ing	
harber	harbour	harpoon	
harbinger		harpsichord	
harbour, -ed, -ing		harpsicord	harpsichord
hard, -ly		harpy	
hardback		harrier	
hard-bitten		harrow, -ed, -ing	
hardboard		harry, -ried, -rying	
hard-core		harsh, -ly	
hard-court		hart (deer)	
harden, -ed, -ing		hart	heart (body)
hard-hearted, -ly			
hardie	hardy		
hard-hit			
hardihood			
hardiness			
hardlie	hardly		
hardline			
hardness			

For all other **hart-** words, look under **heart-**.

harum-scarum	
harve	halve
harvest, -ed, -ing	
harvester	
harvist	harvest

hary	hairy	hawlidge	haulage
has-been		hawlige	haulage
hasen	hasten	hawlier	haulier
hash, -ed, -ing		hawnch	haunch
hashish		hawnet	hornet
hasn't (has not)		hawnt	haunt
hasnt	hasn't	hawse (ship)	
hasock	hassock	hawse	horse (animal)
hasp		hawser	
hassel	hassle	hawthorn	
hassle, -led, -ling		hawticulcher	horticulture
hassock		hawticulture	horticulture
haste, -tily		hawtie	haughty
hasten, -ed, -ing		hawty	haughty
hasty, hastier, hastiest		hay (grass)	
hatch, -ed, -ing		hay	hey (cry)
hatchback		hayday	heyday
hatcherey	hatchery	hayfever	
hatchery, -eries		haystack	
hatchet		haywire	
hatchway		hazard	
hate, -ed, -ing		hazardous, -ly	
hateful, -ly		haze, hazed, hazing	
hatred		hazel	
hatrid	hatred	hazerd	hazard
hatstand		head, -ed, -ing	
hatter		headache	
hat-trick		headcount, -ed, -ing	
haughty, -tier, -tiest		headdress	
haul, -ed, -ing (carry)		header	
haul	hall (room)	headfirst	
haulage		headfone	headphone
haulier		head-hunting	
haulige	haulage	headlamp	
haunch		headland	
haunt, -ed, -ing		headlight	
haute cuisine		headline, -lined, -lining	
hav	have	headlite	headlight
have		headlong	
haven		headman	
haven't (have not)		headmaster	
havent	haven't	headmistress	
haversack		head-on	
havoc, -ocked, -ocking		headphone	
hawk, -ed, -ing		headquarters	
hawker		headset	
hawl	haul	headshrinker	

headspring
headstand
head start
headstone
headstream
headstrong
headwaters
headway
headwind
headword
heady, -dier, -diest
heal (health)
   heal   heel (shoe)
health
healthy, -thier, -thiest
heap, -ed, -ing
hear, heard, hearing (listen)
   hear   here (place)
heard (listen)
   heard   herd (animals)
hearer
hearing aid
hearsay
hearse
heart (body)
heartache
heart attack
heartbeat
heartbreak
heartbroken, -ly
heartburn
hearten, -ed, -ing
heartfelt
hearth
heartless, -ly
heart-rending, -ly
heartstring
heart-throb
hearty, -tily
heat, -ed, -ing
heater
heath
heathen, -then, -thens
heather
heatwave
heave, -ed, -ing
heave-ho

heaven, -ly
heavy, -ily
heavy-duty
heavy-handed, -ly
heavy-hearted, -ly
heavy-laden
heavyweight
Hebrew
   Hebroo   Hebrew
heck
heckle, -led, -ling
hectare
hectic, -ally
hector, -ed, -ing
he'd (he would)
   hed   head (body)
   hed   he'd (he would)
hedge, hedged, hedging
hedgehog
hedonism
heed, -ed, -ing
heedless, -ly
heehaw
heel (shoe)
   heel   heal (health)
heeler
   heematology   haematology
   heemoglobin   haemoglobin
   heemophilia   haemophilia
   heep   heap
   heer   hear (listen)
   heer   here (place)
   heet   heat
   heeth   heath
   hefer   heifer
   heftie   hefty
heft, -ed, -ing
hefty, -tier, -tiest
   hege   hedge
hegemony, -nies
heifer
height
heighten, -ed, -ing
   heighth   height
heinous, -ly
   heinus   heinous
heir (inherit)

heir	hair (head)	hena	henna
heir	here (place)	hence	
heir apparent, heirs apparent		henchman, -men	
heiress		henge	
heirloom		henna	
heist, -ed, -ing		henpeck, -pecked, -pecking	
heith	height	hens	hence
hel	hell	henus	heinous
held		hepatic	
helicopter		hepatitis	
heliograf	heliograph	heptagon	
heliograph		herald, -ed, -ing	
heliotrope		heraldic, -ally	
helipad		heraldrey	heraldry
heliport		heraldry, -dries	
helium		herb	
hell		herbaceous	
he'll (he will)		herbage	
hell	he'll	herbalist	
hell-bent		herbashus	herbaceous
hellcat		herbicide	
Hellenic		herbiside	herbicide
hellfire		herbivore	
hello, -los		herbivorous	
hello, -loed, -loing		herbivorus	herbivorous
hell's angel		herculean	
helm		herd (animals)	
helmet		herd	heard (listen)
helmsman, -men		herdsman, -men	
helo	hello	here (place)	
helot		here	hear (listen)
help, -ed, -ing		hereafter	
helpless, -ly		hereby	
helpmate		hereditary	
helter-skelter		hereditey	heredity
helth	health	hereditrey	hereditary
helthy	healthy	heredity, -ties	
hemerige	haemorrhage	Hereford	
hemeroid	haemorrhoid	herein	
hem, hemmed, hemming		hereof	
hemisfare	hemisphere	heresay	hearsay
hemisfear	hemisphere	heresie	heresy
hemisphere		heresy, -sies	
hemlock		heretic	
hemp		hereto	
hemstitch, -stitched, -stitching		hereunder	
hen		hereupon	

herewith
  hering → herring
heritable, -ly
heritage
  heritige → heritage
  herl → hurl
  hermafrodite → hermaphrodite
hermaphrodite
hermaphroditism
  hermatage → hermitage
hermetic
hermetical, -ly
hermit
hermitage
  hermitige → hermitage
hernia, -nias
hero, -roes
heroic
heroical, -ly
  heroicle → heroical
heroin (drug)
heroine (female hero)
heroism
heron
hero-worship, -shipped, -shipping
  herpeas → herpes
herpes
herring, -rings, -ring
herringbone
hers
  herse → hearse
herself
  hert → hurt
  hertle → hurtle
  hertul → hurtle
hertz
he's (he is, or he has)
  hes → he's
  hesian → hessian
hesitancy
  hesitansey → hesitancy
hesitant, -ly
hesitate, -tated, -tating
hesitation
hessian
heterogeneity
heterogeneous, -ly

  heterogenius → heterogeneous
heterosexual,-ly
  hethen → heathen
  hether → heather
het-up
heuristic, -ally
  heve → heave
  heven → heaven
  hevenly → heavenly
  hevie → heavy
  hevily → heavily
  heviwait → heavyweight
  hevy → heavy
hew, hewed, hewn, hewing (cut)
  hew → hue (colour)
hex
hexagon
hexagonal, -ly
hexameter
hey (cry)
  hey → hay (grass)
heyday

For other **hi-** words, look under **hy-**.

hi (cry)
  hi → high (up)
  hiasinth → hyacinth
hiatus, -tuses
hiatus hernia
hibernate, -nated, -nating
hibiscus
  hibrid → hybrid
hiccup, -ed, -ing
  hich → hitch
  hichhike → hitchhike
hick
hickory, -ries
  hicup → hiccup
hidden
hide, hid, hiding
hideaway
hidebound
hideous, -ly
hide-out
  hidius → hideous
hidy-hole

hier	hire	hind	
hierarchy, -chies		hinder, -ed, -ing	
hierarkey	hierarchy	hinderanse	hindrance
hieroglific	hieroglyphic	Hindoo, -doos	
hieroglyphic, -ally		Hindooism	
hi-fi		hindquarter	
high, -ly		hindrance	
highborn		hindranse	hindrance
highbrow		hindsight	
high-class		hindsite	hindsight
higher (up)		Hindu	
higher	hire (rent)	Hinduism	
highfalutin		hiness	highness
high-fidelity		hinge, -ed, -ing	
high-grade		hint, -ed, -ing	
high-handed, -ly		hinterland	
highland		hip, hipped, hipping	
highlight		hipbath	
highly-wrought		hipie	hippie
high-minded, -ly		hipopotamus	hippopotamus
highness		hippie, -ies	
high-pitched		Hippocratic oath	
high-powered		hippopotamus, -muses, -mi	
high-pressure		hipster	
high-rise		hipy	hippie
high-speed		hire, hired, hiring (rent)	
high-spirited		hire	higher (up)
hight	height	hireling	
high-tension		hire-purchase	
highway		hiroglific	hieroglyphic
highwayman, -men		hiss, -ed, -ing	
hijack, -ed, -ing		histerey	history
hike, -ed, -ing		histeria	hysteria
hil	hill	histogram	
hiland	highland	historian	
hilarious, -ly		historic	
hilarius	hilarious	historiography	
hilight	highlight	history, -ries	
hilite	highlight	histrey	history
hill		histrionic, -ally	
hillbilly, -lies		hit, hit, hitting	
hillock		hitch, -ed, -ing	
hilly, hillier, hilliest		hitchhike, -hiked, -hiking	
hilt		hite	height
him (he)		hither	
him	hymn (song)	hitherto	
himself		hive, -ed, -ing	

hiway	highway

> For other **hi-** words,
> look under **hy-**.

ho	hoe
hoaks	hoax
hoard, -ed, -ing (gather)	
hoard	horde (mob)
hoarding	
hoare	whore
hoarse, hoarser, hoarsest (voice)	
hoarse	hawse (ship)
hoarse	horse (animal)
hoary, hoarier, hoariest (old)	
hoax, -ed, -ing	
hob	
hobbel	hobble
hobble, -bled, -bling	
hobby, -bies	
hobbyhorse	
hobie	hobby
hobnail	
hobnob, -nobbed, -nobbing	
hobo, -bos, -boes	
hochpoch	hotchpotch
hock, -ed, -ing	
hockey	
hockie	hockey
hocus-pocus, -cussed, -cussing	
hod	
hoe, hoed, hoeing (tool)	
hoes	hose (water)
hog, hogged, hogging	
hogget	
hogshead	
hogshed	hogshead
hogwash	
hoi polloi	
hoist, -ed, -ing	
hokem	hokum
hokey pokey	
hokum	
hold, held, holding	
holdfast	
hold-up	
hole, holed, holing (opening)	
hole	whole (all)

holey	wholly
holiday	
holie	holly (plant)
holie	holy (saint)
holie	wholly (all)
holihock	hollyhock
holiness	
holland	
holler, -ed, -ing (shout)	
hollow, -ly (hole)	
holly, -lies (plant)	
holly	holy (saint)
holly	wholly (all)
hollyhock	
holocaust	
holocost	holocaust
holow	hollow
holster	
holus-bolus	
holy, -lier, -liest (saint)	
holy	holly (plant)
holy	wholly (all)
homage	
homburg	
home, -ed, -ing	
home-brew	
homeland	
homely, -lier, -liest	
homeopathy	
homesick	
homespun	
homestead	
homeward	
homework	
homicide	
homige	homage
homiley	homily
homily, -lies	
homiopathy	homeopathy
homiside	homicide
homogeneous, -ly	
homogenise, -nised, -nising	
homogenius	homogeneous
homonim	homonym
homonym	
homophone	
Homo sapiens	

homoseksual	homosexual	hope, hoped, hoping	
homoseksuality	homosexuality	hopeful	
homosexual		hopefull	hopeful
homosexuality		hopeless, -ly	
hone, honed, honing		hopper	
honest, -ly		hopping-mouse	
honesty		hopsack	
honey, honeys		hopscotch	
honeybee		horde, horded, hording (animals)	
honeycomb		horde	hoard (gather)
honeydew		hore	whore
honeyeater		horendus	horrendous
honeymoon		horer	horror
honeysuckle		horible	horrible
hongi		horid	horrid
honie	honey	horific	horrific
honk,-ed, -ing		horify	horrify
honky-tonk		horizon	
honorarium, -rariums, -raria		horizontal, -ly	
honorary		hormone	
honorific, -ally		horn, -ed, -ing	
honour, -ed, -ing		hornbill	
honourable, -bly		hornpipe	
hony	honey	horn-rimmed	
hood, -ed, -ing		horny, -nier, -niest	
hoodlum		horology	
hoodwink, -ed, -ing		horor	horror
hoof, hoofs, hooves		horoscope	
hook, -ed, -ing		horrendous, -ly	
hookah		horrible, -bly	
hooker		horribul	horrible
hookie	hooky	horrid, -ly	
hook-up		horrific	
hookworm		horrify, -fied, -fying	
hooky		horror	
hoola-hoola	hula-hula	hors d'oeuvre	
hooligan		horse, horses (animal)	
hoop		horse, horsed, horsing	
hooping coff	whooping	horse	hawse (ship)
	cough	horse	hoarse (voice)
hoopla		horseflesh	
hooray		horseplay	
hooroo		horsepower	
hoot, -ed, -ing		horserace	
hooter		horseradish	
hoover		horseshoe, -shoed, -shoeing	
hop, hopped, hopping		horsy, -sier, -siest	

hortative, -ly
hortatory
  horthorn   hawthorn
  horticulcher   horticulture
horticulture
  hortie   haughty
hose, hosed, hosing (water)
  hose   hoes (tools)
hosiery
hospice
hospitable, -bly
  hospitabul   hospitable
hospital
hospitality, -ties
host, -ed, -ing
hostage
  hostaple   hospital
hostel
hostess
  hostige   hostage
hostile, -ly
hostility, -ties
hot, hotted, hotting
hot, hotter, hottest
hot-blooded
hotchpotch
hotel
hotelier
  hoter   hotter
  hotest   hottest
hotfoot
hothead
hot-headed, -ly
  hothed   hothead
  hotheded   hotheaded
hothouse
hotplate
hotpot
hot rod
hot seat
hot-shot
hot-water bottle
hound, -ed, -ing
hound's-tooth
hour (time)
  hour   our
hourglass

houri, -ris
hourly
house, houses
house, housed, housing
houseboat
housebreaker
housebroken
housecoat
housefly, -flies
household
housekeeper
housemaid
House of Commons
houseproud
house-train
house-warming
housewife, -wives
housey-housey
housie-housie
housing
hovel, -elled, -elling
hover, -ed, -ing
hovercraft
how
however
howl, -ed, -ing
howler
  hownd   hound
  howse   house
howsoever
hoy
hoyden
  hu   hew (cut)
  hu   hue (colour)
hubbub
  huch   hutch
huckster
huddle, -dled, -dling
hue (colour)
  hue   hew (cut)
  huf   huff
huff, -ed, -ing
hug, hugged, hugging
huge, huger, hugest
  hul   hull
hula-hula
  hulabaloo   hullabaloo

hulk

hull,-ed, -ing

hullabaloo

hullo

hum, hummed, humming

human

humane, -ly

humanism

humanist

humanitarian

humanity, -ties

humanly

humanoid

humble, -bled, -bling

humble, -bler, -blest

humble pie

humbug, -bugged, -bugging

humbul   humble

humdinger

humdrum

humer   humour

humerist   humorist

humerus, -meri (bone)

humerus   humorous (funny)

humid, -ly

humidifier

humidity

humiliate, -ated, -ating

humiliation

humility, -ties

hummingbird

hummock

humock   hummock

humorist

humorous, -ly (funny)

humorous   humerus (bone)

humour, -ed, -ing

hump, -ed, -ing

humpback

humpy, -pier, -piest

humus

hunch, -ed, -ing

hunchback

hundred, -dreds

hundredfold

hundredth

huney   honey

hunger

hungrie   hungry

hungry, -grier, -griest

hunie   honey

hunk

hunt, -ed, -ing

hunter

huntress

huntsman, -men

Huon pine

huray   hurray

hurd   heard (listen)

hurd   herd (animals)

hurdiegurdie   hurdy-gurdy

hurdle, -dled, -dling

hurdul   hurdle

hurdy-gurdy, -dies

huricane   hurricane

hurie   hurry

hurl, -ed, -ing

hurlie-burlie   hurly-burly

hurly-burly, -burlies

hurmit   hermit

hurnia   hernia

hurray

hurricane

hurry, -ried, -rying

hurse   hearse

hurt, hurt, hurting

hurtel   hurtle

hurtle, -tled, -tling

hurtul   hurtle

hurtz   hertz

hury   hurry

husband

husbandry

hush, -ed, -ing

husie   hussy

husk

huskie   husky

husky, -kier, -kiest (hoarse)

husky, -kies (dog)

hussar

hussel   hustle

hussey   hussy

hussul   hustle

hussy, -sies
hustings
hustle, -tled, -tling
hut, hutted, hutting
hutch
hutkeeper
hyacinth
hybrid
hydatids
hydra, -dras, -drae
hydrangea
   hydranja   hydrangea
hydrant
hydrate, -drated, -drating
hydration
hydraulic, -ally
hydrocarbon
hydrochloric acid
hydro-electric
   hydrofobia   hydrophobia
hydrofoil
hydrogen
hydrologist
hydrology
   hydrolic   hydraulic
hydrolysis, -ses
hydrometer
hydroplane, -planed, -planing
hydroponics
hydrous
hydroxide
hyena
   hygene   hygiene
hygiene
hygienic, -ally
hygroscopic
   hym   hymn
hymen
hymn (song)
hymnal
hype, hyped, hyping
hyperactive
hyperbola, -las (curve)
hyperbole (overstatement)
hypersensitive
hypertension
hyphen

hyphenate, -nated, -nating
hypnosis, -ses
hypnotherapy
hypnotise, -tised, -tising
hypnotism
hypo
hypochondria
hypocrisy, -sies
hypocrite
hypodermic
hypodermic syringe
hypotenuse
hypothesis, -ses
hypothesise, -sised, -sising
hypothetical, -ly
hysterectomy, -mies
hysteria
hysteric
hysterical, -ly

Ii

ibis
ice, iced, icing
iceberg
icebound
icebox
icebreaker
ice-cream
icepack
icepick

ich	itch

icicle

iclesiastic	ecclesiastic
iclipse	eclipse

icon, icons
iconoclast

iconomey	economy
iconomist	economist

icy, icier, iciest
idea
ideal, -ly
idealise, -ised, -ising
idealism
idem
identical, -ly

identicul	identical

identification
identify, -fied, -fying
identikit
identity, -ties
ideology, -gies

iderdown	eiderdown

ides

idilic	idyllic
idill	idyll

idiocy, -cies

idiologey	ideology

idiom
idiomatic, -ally

idiosincrasy	idiosyncrasy

idiosyncrasy, -sies
idiot

idium	idiom

idle, idled, idling (not busy)

idle	idol (statue)

idler
idol (statue)

idol	idle (not busy)

idolatry, -tries
idolise, -lised, -lising

idyl	idyll

idyll
idyllic, -ally

iface	efface
ifect	effect
ifel	Eiffel
ifeminite	effeminate
ificiency	efficiency
igalitarian	egalitarian

igloo, -loos
igneous

ignishun	ignition

ignite, -nited, -niting
ignition
ignition coil

ignius	igneous

ignoble, -bly
ignominy, -minies

ignor	ignore

ignoramus, -muses
ignorant, -ly
ignore, -nored, -noring
iguana

iguarna	iguana
ijaculation	ejaculation
ijection	ejection

ikon, ikons

ikuip	equip
ikwivocal	equivocal
ikwivocate	equivocate
il	I'll (I will)
il	ill (sick)
ilaberate	elaborate
iland	island
ilapse	elapse
ilation	elation

ilastic	elastic
ilate	elate
ile	aisle (passage)
Ile	I'll (I will)
ile	isle (island)
ilect	elect
ilection	election
ilectorate	electorate
ilectrocute	electrocute
ilectronic	electronic
ilegal	illegal
ilegibul	illegible
ilegitimate	illegitimate
ileven	eleven
ilicit	elicit
ilicit	illicit
ilikser	elixir
iliminate	eliminate
ilimination	elimination
ilipse	ellipse
iliptic	elliptic
ilisit	elicit
ilisit	illicit
iliteracy	illiteracy
iliterate	illiterate
ilixir	elixir

ilk
I'll (I will)
ill, worse, worst (sick)
ill-advised, -ly
ill-assorted
ill-bred
ill-defined
illegal, -ly
illegible, -bly

illegibul	illegible

illegitimate, -ly
ill-fated
ill-gotten
ill health
illiberal, -ly
illicit, -ly (unlawful)

illicit	elicit (evoke)

illiteracy
illiterate
ill-mannered, -ly
ill-natured, -ly

illness
illogical, -ly
ill-treat, -ed, -ing
illuminate, -nated, -nating
illumination
illumine, -mined, -mining
ill-use, -used, -using
illusion (deception)

illusion	allusion (brief reference)
illusion	elusion (evade)

illusive (deceptive)

illusive	allusive
illusive	elusive

illusory
illustrate, -strated, -strating
illustration
illustrative, -ly
illustrator
illustrious, -ly
ill will

ilogical	illogical
ilope	elope
ilucidate	elucidate
ilude	elude
iluminate	illuminate
ilumination	illumination
ilusidate	elucidate
ilusion	allusion
ilusion	elusion
ilusion	illusion
ilusive	allusive
ilusive	elusive
ilusive	illusive
ilustrate	illustrate
ilustration	illustration
ilustrator	illustrator
ilustrius	illustrious

I'm (I am)

Im	I'm
imaciate	emaciate
imaculate	immaculate

image, -aged, -aging
imagery, -ries

imagin	imagine

imaginary, -ries
imagination

imaginative
imagine, -ined, -ining

imancipate	emancipate
imansipation	emancipation
imashiate	emaciate
imaterial	immaterial
imature	immature
imaturity	immaturity

imbalance

imbalanse	imbalance
imbarrass	embarrass

imbecile, -ly

imbeseal	imbecile

imbibe, -bibed, -bibing
imbroglio, -os
imbue, -bued, -buing

imerge	emerge
imergence	emergence
imergency	emergency
imergent	emergent
imetic	emetic
imission	emission
imit	emit

For other **im-** words, look
under **imm-**.

imitate, -tated, -tating
imitation
immaculate, -ly
immanent (inherent)

immanent	eminent (known)
immanent	imminent (near)

immaterial, -ly
immature, -ly
immeasurable, -bly
immediate, -ly
immemorial, -ly
immense, -ly
immerse, -mersed, -mersing

immershun	immersion

immersion

immesurable	immeasurable

immigrant
immigrate, -grated, -grating
imminent (near)

imminent	eminent (known)
imminent	immanent (inherent)

immobile
immobility
immoderate, -ly
immodest, -ly
immolate, -lated, -lating
immoral, -ly
immortal, -ly
immortalise, -lised, -lising
immortality, -ties
immovable, -bly
immune, -ly
immunise, -nised, -nising
immunology
immure, -mured, -muring
immutable, -bly

imolient	emollient
imolument	emolument
imoshen	emotion
imoshun	emotion
imoshunal	emotional
imotion	emotion
imotive	emotive

imp
impact, -ed, -ing
impair, -ed, -ing
impale, -paled, -paling
impalpable, -bly

impare	impair
imparshal	impartial

impart, -ed, -ing
impartial, -ly

impasable	impassable
impashent	impatient
impasioned	impassioned
impasive	impassive

impassable, -bly
impasse
impassioned, -ly
impassive, -ly
impatient, -ly
impeach, -ed, -ing

impecabul	impeccable

impeccable, -bly

impecunious, -ly
  impecunius   impecunious
impede, -peded, -peding
impediment, -ary
  impeech   impeach
impel, -pelled, -pelling
impenetrable, -bly
  impenge   impinge
imperative, -ly
  imperceptibel   imperceptible
imperceptible, -bly
imperfect, -ly
imperial, -ly
imperialism
imperil, -rilled, -rilling
imperious, -ly
  imperius   imperious
impermeable, -bly
  impermeabul   impermeable
  imperseptibul   imperceptible
impersonal, -ly
impersonate, -nated, -nating
impertinence
  impertinense   impertinence
imperturbable, -bly
impervious, -ly
  impervius   impervious
impetuous, -ly
impetus, -tuses
impiety, -ties
impinge, -pinged, -pinging
impious, -ly
impish, -ly
  impius   impious
implacable, -bly
  implacabul   implacable
implant, -ed, -ing
implausible, -bly
  implausibul   implausible
implement, -ed, -ing
implicate, -cated, -cating
implication
implicit, -ly
  implie   imply
implied
  implisit   implicit
implode, -ploded, -ploding

implore, -plored, -ploring
imply, -plied, -plying
impolite, -ly
impolitic, -ly
import, -ed, -ing
importance
  importanse   importance
important, -ly
importunate, -ly
importune, -tuned, -tuning
  imposcher   imposture
impose, -posed, -posing
  imposibul   impossible
  imposishun   imposition
imposition
impossible, -bly
  imposter   impostor
impostor
imposture
impotence
impotent, -ly
impound, -ed, -ing
impoverish, -ed, -ing
impracticability
impracticable, -bly
  impracticabul   impracticable
impractical, -ly
imprecate, -cated, -cating
imprecise, -ly
impregnable, -bly
  impregnabul   impregnable
impregnate, -nated, -nating
  impres   impress
impresario, -os
  impreshun   impression
  impreshunable   impressionable
  impreshunism   impressionism
  impresise   imprecise
  impresive   impressive
impress, -pressed, -pressing
impression
impressionable, -bly
impressionism
impressive, -ly
imprimatur
imprint, -ed, -ing
imprison, -ed, -ing

improbable, -bly
impromptu
improper, -ly
impropriety, -ties
improve, -proved, -proving
improvement
improvident, -ly
improvise, -vised, -vising
imprudent, -ly
  impruve — improve
impudent, -ly
impugn, -ed, -ing
impulse
  impune — impugn
impunity
impure, impurer, impurist
impute, -puted, -puting
  imulshun — emulsion
  imune — immune
  imunologey — immunology
  imurge — emerge
in
  in — inn (hotel)
inability
  in absenshia — in absentia
in absentia
  inaccessabul — inaccessible
inaccessible, -bly
inaccuracy, -cies
inactive, -ly
  inacuracy — inaccuracy
  inacurasey — inaccuracy
  inadekwat — inadequate
inadequate, -ly
inadvertent, -ly
inalienable, -bly
  inalienabul — inalienable
inane, -ly
inanimate, -ly
inappreciable, -bly
  inappreciabul — inappreciable
inappropriate, -ly
  inapropriate — inappropriate
inapt, -ly
inaptitude
inarticulate, -ly
inasmuch as

  inate — innate
  inatentive — inattentive
inattentive, -ly
inaugural
inaugurate, -rated, -rating
inauspicious, -ly
  inawmus — enormous
  inawspishus — inauspicious
inborn
inbreed, -bred, -breeding
incalculable, -bly
in camera
incandescence
incandescent, -ly
  incandesence — incandescence
incantation
incapable, -bly
  incapabul — incapable
incapacitate, -tated, -tating
incapacity, -ties
  incapasitate — incapacitate
  incapasitey — incapacity
incarcerate, -rated, -rating
incarnate, -nated, -nating
  incarserate — incarcerate
incendiary, -aries
incense (perfume)
incense, -censed, -censing (angry)
incentive
inception
incessant, -ly
  incessent — incessant
incest
incestuous, -ly
inch, -ed, -ing
incidence
incident
incidental, -ly
incinerate, -rated, -rating
incinerator
incipient, -ly
incise, -cised, -cising
incision
incisive, -ly
incisor
incite, -cited, -citing (urge)
  incite — insight (see)

incivility, -ties
inclement, -ly
inclination
incline, -clined, -clining
   inclose   enclose
include, -cluded, -cluding
inclusion
inclusive, -ly
incognito, -tos
incoherent, -ly
income
incommensurable, -bly
incommensurate, -ly
incommode, -moded, -moding
incommodity, -ties
incommunicability
incommunicable, -bly
incommunicado
incommunicative, -ly
incomparable, -bly
incompatible, -bly
   incompatibul   incompatible
incompetent, -ly
incomplete, -ly
incomprehensible, -bly
incomprehension
   incomunicado   incommunicado
inconceivable, -bly
   inconcievable   inconceivable
inconclusive, -ly
incongruous, -ly
   incongruus   incongruous
   inconseavable   inconceivable
inconsequent, -ly
inconsequential, -ly
inconsiderate, -ly
   inconsistant   inconsistent
inconsistent,-ly
inconsolable, -bly
   inconsolabul   inconsolable
inconspicuous, -ly
inconstant, -ly
incontestable, -bly
   incontestabul   incontestable
incontinent, -ly
incontrovertible, -bly
inconvenience, -ienced, -iencing

inconvenient, -ly
   incorect   incorrect
   incorigibul   incorrigible
incorporate, -rated, -rating
incorporation
incorrect, -ly
incorrigible, -bly
incorrupt, -ly
incorruptible, -bly
increase, -creased, -creasing
incredible, -bly
   incredibul   incredible
incredulity
incredulous, -ly
   incredulus   incredulous
increment
incremental
   increse   increase
incriminate, -nated, -nating
incubate, -bated, -bating
incubator
inculcate, -cated, -cating
   incum   income
incumbent, -ly
incumbrance
incur, -curred, -curring
incurable, -bly
   incurabul   incurable
   incurshun   incursion
incursion
indebted
indecent, -ly
indecipherable
   indecishun   indecision
indecision
indecisive, -ly
indeclinable
   indeclinabul   indeclinable
indecorous, -ly
   indecorus   indecorous
indeed
indefatigable, -bly
   indefatigabul   indefatigable
indefeasible, -bly
   indefeasibul   indefeasible
indefensible, -bly
   indefensibul   indefensible

indefinable, -bly
  indefinabul   indefinable
indefinite, -ly
  indeks   index
indelible, -bly
  indelibul   indelible
indelicate, -ly
  indemnifie   indemnify
indemnify, -fied, -fying
indemnity, -ties
  indencher   indenture
indent, -ed, -ing
indenture, -tured, -turing
independent, -ly
in-depth
indescribable, -bly
  indescribabul   indescribable
  indesent   indecent
  indesiferable   indecipherable
  indespensable   indispensable
indestructible, -bly
  indestructibul   indestructible
  indeted   indebted
indeterminate, -ly
index, -dexes, -dices
indexation
Indian
indiarubber
indicate, -cated, -cating
indicative, -ly
indicator
indices
indict, -ed, -ing
indictment
  indiferent   indifferent
indifferent, -ly
indigenous, -ly
indigent, -ly
indigestible, -bly
  indigestibul   indigestible
indigestion
indignant, -ly
indignation
indignity, -ties
indigo, -gos
  indipendent   independent
indirect, -ly

indiscreet, -ly
  indiscreshun   indiscretion
  indiscrete   indiscreet
indiscretion
indiscriminate, -ly
  indisishun   indecision
  indisisive   indecisive
  indisoluble   indissoluble
indispensable, -bly
  indispensabul   indispensable
indisposed
indisposition
indisputable, -bly
  indisputabul   indisputable
indissoluble, -bly
indistinct, -ly
indistinguishable, -bly
indite, -dited, -diting (write)
  indite   indict (accuse)
individual, -ly
individualism
individualist
individuality, -ties
indivisible, -bly
  indivisibul   indivisible
indoctrinate, -nated, -nating
indolent, -ly
indomitable, -bly
  indomitabul   indomitable
indoor
indubitable, -bly
  indubitabul   indubitable
induce, -duced, -ducing
  inducshion   induction
  inducshun   induction
induct, -ed, -ing
induction
inductive, -ly
inductor
indulge, -dulged, -dulging
indulgence
  indulgense   indulgence
indulgent, -ly
  industrey   industry
industrial, -ly
industrialise, -lised, -lising
industrialism

industrialist
industrious, -ly
  industrius — industrious
industry, -tries
inebriate, -ated, -ating
inebriation
inedible
  inedibul — inedible
  inefable — ineffable
  inefective — ineffective
  inefectual — ineffectual
ineffable, -bly
ineffective, -ly
ineffectual, -ly
inefficient, -ly

> For **ineks-** words, look
> under **inex-**.

inelegant, -ly
ineligible, -bly
  ineligibul — ineligible
inept, -ly
inequality, -ties
inequitable, -bly
  inequitabul — inequitable
inequity, -ties
ineradicable, -bly
  ineradicabul — ineradicable
  inersha — inertia
inert, -ly
inertia
inescapable, -bly
  inescapabul — inescapable
  inesenshul — inessential
inessential, -ly
inestimable, -bly
  inestimabul — inestimable
inevitable, -bly
  inevitabul — inevitable
inexact, -ly
inexcusable, -bly
inexhaustible, -bly
inexorable, -bly
  inexorabul — inexorable
inexpedient, -ly
inexpensive, -ly
inexperienced

  inexperiense — inexperience
inexpert, -ly
inexplicable, -bly
inexplicit, -ly
inexpressible, -bly
in extremis
inextricable, -bly
  infalible — infallible
  infalibul — infallible
infallible, -bly
  infamey — infamy
infamous, -ly
  infamus — infamous
infamy, -mies
infancy, -cies
  infansey — infancy
infant
infanticide
  infantiside — infanticide
infantile
  infantrey — infantry
infantry
infatuate, -ated, -ating
infatuation
  infecshun — infection
infect, -ed, -ing
infection
infectious, -ly
infelicity, -ties
infer, -ferred, -ferring
inference
  inferense — inference
  inferier — inferior
inferior
inferiority complex
  inferm — infirm
  infermarey — infirmary
infernal, -ly
inferno, -nos
infertile
infest, -ed, -ing
infidel
infidelity, -ties
infighting
infiltrate, -trated, -trating
infinite, -ly
infinitesimal, -ly

infinitey   infinity
infinitive, -ly
infinity, -ties
   infirior   inferior
infirm, -ly
infirmary, -ries
   inflamabul   inflammable
   inflamatry   inflammatory
inflame, -flamed, -flaming
inflammable, -bly
inflammation
inflammatory
inflatable
inflate, -flated, -flating
inflation
inflect, -ed, -ing
inflection
inflexible, -bly
inflict, -ed, -ing
infliction
inflow
influence, -enced, -encing
   influense   influence
   influenshul   influential
influential, -ly
influenza
   influks   influx
inform, -ed, -ing
informal, -ly
informant
information
informer
   infracshun   infraction
infraction
infra-red
infrastructure
   infrekwency   infrequency
   infrekwent   infrequent
infrequency
infrequent, -ly
infringe, -fringed, -fringing
infuriate, -ated, -ating
   infurnal   infernal
infuse, -fused, -fusing
infusion
   infusun   infusion
ingenious, -ly (clever)

   ingenius   ingenious
ingenue
ingenuity, -ties
ingenuous, -ly (innocent)
   ingenuus   ingenuous
ingest, -ed, -ing
ingestion
   Inglish   English
ingot
ingrain, -ed, -ing
   ingrashiate   ingratiate
ingrate
ingratiate, -ated, -ating
ingratitude
   ingrave   engrave
ingredient
ingress
   in-groop   in-group
in-group
ingrown
inhabit, -ed, -ing
inhalant
inhalation
inhale, -haled, -haling
   inhear   inhere
inhere, -hered, -hering
inherent, -ly
inherit, -ed, -ing
inheritance
   inheritanse   inheritance
   inhibishun   inhibition
inhibit, -ed, -ing
inhospitable, -bly
   inhospitabul   inhospitable
inhospitality
inhuman, -ly
inhumane, -ly
inhumanity, -ties
   inikwality   inequality
   inikwity   iniquity
   inikwitus   iniquitous
inimical, -ly
inimitable, -bly
inimitability
   inimitabul   inimitable
   inings   innings
   iniquitey   iniquity

iniquitous, -ly
  iniquitus — iniquitous
iniquity, -ties (sin)
  iniquity — inequity (unfair)
  inishal — initial
  inishative — initiative
  inishiate — initiate
initial, -ialled, -ialling
initiate, -ated, -ating
initiation
initiative
inject, -ed, -ing
injection
  injenue — ingenue
  injere — injure
in-joke
injudicious, -ly
  injudishus — injudicious
injunction
  injunkshun — injunction
injure, -jured, -juring
  injurey — injury
  injurius — injurious
injury, -ries
injustice
  injustise — injustice
ink
  inkeeper — innkeeper
inkling
  inkwest — inquest
  inkwire — enquire
  inkwisitive — inquisitive
  inkwisitor — inquisitor

> For other **ink-** words,
> look under **inc-**.

  inlade — inlaid
inland
in-law
inlay, -laid, -laying
inlet
in loco parentis
inmate
in memoriam
inmost
inn (hotel)

innards
innate, -ly
inner
  innerject — interject
innermost
innings
innkeeper
innocence
innocent, -ly
innocuous, -ly
innovate, -vated, -vating
innovation
innovative, -ly
innovatory
innuendo, -dos
innumerable, -bly
innumerate
  inocent — innocent
inoculate, -lated, -lating
inoculation
  inocuus — innocuous
  inofensive — inoffensive
inoffensive, -ly
inoperable, -bly
inoperative, -ly
  inoportune — inopportune
inopportune, -ly
  inordible — inaudible
  inordibul — inaudible
inordinate, -ly
inorganic, -ally
  inorgural — inaugural
  inorgurate — inaugurate
  inormity — enormity
  inormous — enormous
  inorspishus — inauspicious
  inosence — innocence
  inosent — innocent
  inough — enough
  inovate — innovate
in-patient
  in-payshent — in-patient
input
inquest
inquietude
inquire, -quired, -quiring
inquiry, -ries

inquisitive, -ly
  inrage — enrage
inroad
  inrode — inroad
insalubrious, -ly
  insalubrius — insalubrious
  insaine — insane
insane, -ly
insanitary
  insanitey — insanity
  insanitry — insanitary
insanity, -ties
insatiable, -bly
  insayshabul — insatiable
inscribe, -scribed, -scribing
inscription
inscrutable, -bly
inscrutability
insect
insecticide
  insectiside — insecticide
insecure, -ly
insecurity, -ties
inseminate, -nated, -nating
insemination
  insendiary — incendiary
insensate, -ly
  insense — incense
insensible, -bly
insensibility, -ties
  insensibul — insensible
insensitive, -ly
insensitivity
  insentive — incentive
inseparable, -bly
  inseperabul — inseparable
  inseprabul — inseparable
  insepshun — inception
insert, -ed, -ing
insertion
  insertitude — incertitude
in-service
  insesent — incessant
  insest — incest
  insestuous — incestuous
inset, -set, -setting
  inshoranse — insurance

  inshore — ensure (certain)
  inshore — insure (protect)
  inshorense — insurance
inside
  insidense — incidence
  insident — incident
  insidentul — incidental
insidious, -ly
  insidius — insidious
insight, (see)
  insight — incite (urge)
insignia
insignificance
insignificant, -ly
insincere, -ly
insincerity, -ties
  insinerate — incinerate
  insinerater — incinerator
  insinsere — insincere
  insinserity — insincerity
insinuate, -ated, -ating
insipid, -ly
  insipient — incipient
  insiser — inciser
  insision — incision
  insisive — incisive
insist, -ed, -ing
insistence
insistent, -ly
  insite — incite (urge)
  insite — insight (see)
  insivility — incivility
insobriety
insofar
insolence
  insolense — insolence
insolent, -ly
insolubility
insoluble, -bly
  insolubul — insoluble
insolvency
  insolvensy — insolvency
insolvent
insomnia
  inspechun — inspection
inspect, -ed, -ing
  inspecter — inspector

inspection
inspector
inspiration
inspire, -spired, -spiring
instability
  instagate   instigate
  instal   install
install, -ed, -ing
  installment   instalment
instalment
instance, -stanced, -stancing
  instanse   instance
instant, -ly
instantaneous, -ly
  instantanius   instantaneous
  instatution   institution
instead
  insted   instead
instep
instigate, -gated, -gating
  instigater   instigator
instigation
instigator
  instil   instill
  instilashun   instillation
instill, -stilled, -stilling
instillation
instinct
instinctive, -ly
  institushen   institution
institute, -tuted, -tuting
institution
institutional, -ly
institutionalise, -lised, -lising
  instremunt   instrument
instruct, -ed, -ing
instruction
instructive, -ly
instrument
instrumental, -ly
instrumentalist
instrumentation
instrument panel
insubordinate, -ly
insubordination
  insubstanshul   insubstantial
insubstantial, -ly

  insue   ensue
insufferable, -bly
insufficiency
insufficient, -ly
  insuffishency   insufficiency
  insufrabul   insufferable
insular, -ly
insularity
insulate, -lated, -lating
insulation
insulin
insult, -ed, -ing
insuperable, -bly
  insuperabul   insuperable
insurance
  insuranse   insurance
insure, -sured, -suring
  insurecshun   insurrection
insurgence
insurgency
  insurgense   insurgence
insurgent
insurmountable, -bly
insurrection
  insurshun   insertion
  insurt   insert
intact
intaglio, intaglios, intagli
  intail   entail
intake
intangible, -bly
  intangibul   intangible
integer
integral, -ly
integrate, -grated, -grating
integrated circuit
integration
integrity
  intelect   intellect
  intelectual   intellectual
  inteligense   intelligence
  inteligensia   intelligentsia
  inteligent   intelligent
  inteligibul   intelligible
intellect
intellectual, -ly
intelligence

intelligent, -ly
intelligentsia
intemperance
   intemperanse   intemperance
intemperate, -ly
intend, -ed, -ing
intense, -ly
   intenshun   intention
intensify, -fied, -fying
intensive, -ly
intent, -ly
intention
intentional, -ly
inter, -terred, -terring
interact, -ed, -ing
interaction
inter alia
intercede, -ceded, -ceding
intercept, -ed, -ing
interception
interceptor
   interceshun   intercession
intercession
intercessor
interchange, -changed, -changing
interchangeable, -bly
intercom
intercontinental
   intercorse   intercourse
intercourse
interdependence
interdependency
interdependent, -ly
interdict
interdisciplinary
   interelate   interrelate
interest, -ed, -ing
interface, -faced, -facing
   interfear   interfere
interfere, -fered, -fering
interference
interfuse, -fused, -fusing
intergalactic
   interier   interior
interim
interior
interject, -ed, -ing

interjection
injector
interlace, -laced, -lacing
interline, -lined, -lining
interlock, -ed, -ing
   interloap   interlope
   interlood   interlude
interlope, -loped, -loping
interloper
interlude
   intermarie   intermarry
intermarry, -ried, -rying
intermediary, -aries
intermediate, -ly
interment
intermesh, -ed, -ing
intermezzo, -zos, -zi
interminable, -bly
   interminabul   interminable
   intermishun   intermission
intermission
intermittent, -ly
intern
internal, -ly
internal-combustion engine
internalise, -lised, -lising
   internashunal   international
international, -ly
internationale
internationalism
internecine
internee
   internisine   internecine
   interogate   interrogate
interpersonal, -ly
interplay, -ed, -ing
interpolate, -lated, -lating
interpose, -posed, -posing
interpret, -ed, -ing
interpretation
interpreter
interracial, -ly
interregnum, -nums
interrelate, -lated, -lating
interrogate, -gated, -gating
interrogation
interrogative, -ly

interrogator	
interrupt, -ed, -ing	
interruption	
intersect, -ed, -ing	
intersection	
intersede	intercede
intersepshun	interception
intersept	intercept
interseshun	intercession
intersperse, -spersed, -spersing	
interspurse	intersperse
interstate	
interstice, -tices	
intertwine, -twined, -twining	
interupshun	interruption
interurban	
interval	
interveiw	interview
intervene, -vened, -vening	
intervener	
intervenor	intervener
intervenshun	intervention
intervention	
interview, -ed, -ing	
interviewer	
intervue	interview
interweave, -woven, -weaving	
interweaver	
intestate	
intestine	
intice	entice
intiger	integer
intigral	integral
intigrate	integrate
intimacy, -cies	
intimasy	intimacy
intimate, -ly	
intimate, -mated, -mating	
intimation	
intimidate, -dated, -dating	
intimidation	
intimidator	
intoksicate	intoxicate
intolerable, -bly	
intolerabul	intolerable
intolerance	
intoleranse	intolerance

intolerant, -ly	
intonation	
intone, -toned, -toning	
in toto	
intoxicant	
intoxicate, -cated, -cating	
intoxication	
intractable, -bly	
intractabul	intractable
intransigence	
intransigency	
intransigense	intransigence
intransigensy	intransigency
intransigent, -ly	
intransitive, -ly	
intrastate	
intra-uterine device	
intravenous, -ly	
intravenus	intravenous
in-tray	
intreege	intrigue
intrepid, -ly	
intricacy, -cies	
intricasey	intricacy
intricate, -ly	
intrigue, -trigued, -triguing	
intriguer	
intrinsic, -ally	
introduce, -duced, -ducing	
introducshun	introduction
introduction	
introductory	
introduse	introduce
introode	intrude
introosive	intrusive
introspection	
introvert, -ly	
intrude, -truded, -truding	
intruder	
intrushun	intrusion
intrusion	
intrusive, -ly	
intrust	entrust
intuishun	intuition
intuition	
intuitive, -ly	
inturn	intern

inturnal	internal
inuendo	innuendo
inumerabul	innumerable
inumerate	enumerate
inumeration	enumeration
inunciate	enunciate
inundate, -dated, -dating	
inundation	
inunsiate	enunciate
inure, inured, inuring	
inursha	inertia
inurt	inert
invade, -vaded, -vading	
invalid, -ly	
invalidate, -dated, -dating	
invalidation	
invaluable, -bly	
invaluabul	invaluable
invaluble	invaluable
invariability	
invariable, -bly	
invariabul	invariable
invasion	
invatation	invitation
invay	inveigh
invaygul	inveigle
invective, -ly	
inveigh, -ed, -ing	
inveigle, -gled, -gling	
inveigul	inveigle
invenshun	invention
invent, -ed, -ing	
invention	
inventive, -ly	
inventor	
inventory, -tories	
inventry	inventory
inverse, -ly	
invershun	inversion
inversion	
invert, -ed, -ing	
invertebrate	
invest, -ed, -ing	
investagation	investigation
investichure	investiture
investigate, -gated, -gating	
investigation	

investigator	
investiture	
investment	
inveterate	
invidios	invidious
invidious, -ly	
invidiousness	
inviegh	inveigh
inviegle	inveigle
invigorate, -rated, -rating	
invincible, -bly	
invinsibul	invincible
inviolable, -bly	
inviolabul	inviolable
inviolate, -ly	
invisibility	
invisible, -bly	
invisibul	invisible
invitation	
invite, -vited, -viting	
in vitro	
invocation	
invoice, -voiced, -voicing	
invoise	invoice
invoke, -voked, -voking	
involuntary, -tarily	
involuntrey	involuntary
involushun	involution
involution	
involve, -volved, -volving	
involvement	
invulnerable, -bly	
invulnerabul	invulnerable
inverce	inverse
invirt	invert
inward, -ly	
inwardness	
inwards	
inwood	inward
inyure	inure
iodene	iodine
iodine	
ion (atom)	
ion	iron (metal)
ionesfere	ionosphere
ionise, -nised, -nising	
ionosphere	

iony	irony	irreducibility	
iota		irreducible, -bly	
IOU		irreducibul	irreducible
iradiate	irradiate	irrefutable, -bly	
iradicate	eradicate	irrefutabul	irrefutable
irascibility		irregardless	
irascible, -bly		irregular, -ly	
irascibleness		irregularity, -ties	
irascibul	irascible	irrelevance	
irase	erase	irrelevancy	
irate, -ly		irrelevansey	irrelevancy
irational	irrational	irrelevant, -ly	
ire		irreligious, -ly	
		irreligus	irreligious

> For other ir- words,
> look under **irr-**.

		irreparable, -bly	
iridesense	iridescence	irreparabul	irreparable
iridesent	iridescent	irreplacabul	irreplaceable
iridescence		irreplaceable, -bly	
iris, irises		irrepresibul	irrepressible
Irish		irrepressible, -bly	
irk (bore)		irreproachable, -bly	
irk	erk (rank)	irreprochabul	irreproachable
irksome, -ly		irresistabul	irresistible
irksum	irksome	irresistible, -bly	
iron, -ed, -ing (metal)		irresolute, -ly	
iron	ion (atom)	irrespective, -ly	
ironbark		irresponsibility	
ironeus	erroneous	irresponsible, -bly	
ironic, -ally		irresponsibul	irresponsible
ironmonger		irretraceable, -bly	
ironmongery		irretraseabul	irretraceable
ironware		irretrievable, -bly	
irony, -nies		irretrievabul	irretrievable
iroshun	erosion	irreverant	irreverent
irosion	erosion	irreverence	
irotic	erotic	irreverent, -ly	
irradiashun	irradiation	irreverint	irreverent
irradiate, -ated, -ating		irreversibility	
irradiation		irreversible, -bly	
irrashionul	irrational	irreversibul	irreversible
irrational, -ly		irrevocable, -bly	
irreconcilable, -bly		irrevocabul	irrevocable
irrecoverable, -bly		irridescent	iridescent
irrecoverabul	irrecoverable	irrigate, -gated, -gating	
irredeemable, -bly		irrigation	
irredeemabul	irredeemable	irrisistabel	irresistible
		irrisistabul	irresistible

irritability
irritable, -bly
  irritabul   irritable
irritancy
  irritansey   irritancy
irritant
irritate, -tated, -tating
irritation
  irrupshun   irruption
irrupt, -ed, -ing
irruption
irruptive, -ly
  isalate   isolate
  isatope   isotope
  ise   ice
  ishue   issue
  isicul   icicle
  isight   eyesight
Islam
Islamic
island
islander
isle (island)
  isle   aisle (passage)
isn't (is not)
  isnt   isn't
isobar
isolate, -lated, -lating
isolation
isolationism
isolationist
isosceles
  isosilese   isosceles
isotope
Israeli
  Isralie   Israeli
issue, issued, issuing
isthmus, -muses
  istmus   isthmus
italic
itch, -ed, -ing
item
itemise, -mised, -mising
iterate, -rated, -rating
iteration
  iternal   eternal
  iternally   eternally

  iternity   eternity
itinerant, -ly
itinerary, -ries
it'll (it will)
  itll   it'll
it's (it is)
its (possessive)
  its   it's (it is)
itself
  ivacuate   evacuate
  ivacuation   evacuation
  ivade   evade
  ivaluate   evaluate
  ivaluation   evaluation
  ivaporate   evaporate
  ivaporation   evaporation
  ivasion   evasion
  ivasive   evasive
I've (I have)
  Ive   I've
  ivent   event
  iventual   eventual
  ivery   ivory
  ivey   ivy
  ivict   evict
  iviction   eviction
  ivoke   evoke
  ivolve   evolve
ivory, -ries
ivory tower
  ivry   ivory
ivy, ivies
Ivy League

Jj

jab, jabbed, jabbing
jabber
jabiru
jacana
jacaranda
jack
jackal
jackass
jackdaw
   jackdoor   jackdaw
jackeroo
jacket
jackhammer
jack-in-the-box
jackknife, -knives
jack-of-all-trades
jackpot, -potted, -potting
Jacobean
jade, jaded, jading
jaffle
   jafful   jaffle
jag, jagged, jagging
jaguar
jail
jake
jalopy, -lopies
jam, jammed, jamming
jam (food)
   jam   jamb (door)
jamb (door)
jamboree
   jamborie   jamboree
jangle, -gled, -gling
   jangul   jangle
   janiter   janitor
janitor
January
   Janurey   January

Japanese, -nese
japonica
jar, jarred, jarring
jargon
jarrah
   jarrar   jarrah
   jasmin   jasmine
jasper
jaundice, -diced, -dicing
   jaundise   jaundice
jaunt, -ed, -ing
   jauntie   jaunty
jaunty, -tier, -tiest
javelin
   javlin   javelin
jaw
   jawndise   jaundice
   jawnt   jaunt
jay
jaywalk, -ed, -ing
jaywalker
   jaz   jazz
jazz
jazzy, -zier, -ziest
jealous, -ly
jealousy, -ousies
   jealus   jealous
jeans
jeep
jeer, -ed, -ing
Jehovah
Jehovah's Witness
jejune
   jelie   jelly
jelly, -lies
jelly, -lied, -lying
jellyfish, -fish, -fishes
   jelous   jealous
   jelus   jealous
   jely   jelly
   jemey   jemmy
   jemie   jemmy
jemmy, -mies
jemmy, -mied, -mying
   jemy   jemmy
jeopardise, -dised, -dising
jeopardy

jepardise — jeopardise
jepardy — jeopardy
jerboa
jeribilt — jerry-built
jerk, -ed, -ing
jerkin
jerky, -kily
jerry, -ries
jerry-build, -built, -building
jerry can
jersey
jersie — jersey
jest, -ed, -ing
jester
Jesuit
Jesus
jet, jetted, jetting
jetie — jetty
jetison — jettison
jet lag
jettison, -ed, -ing
jetty, -ties
jety — jetty
Jew
Jewish
jewel, -elled, -elling (cut gem)
jewel — dual (two)
jewel — duel (fight)
jewel — joule (unit)
jeweler — jeweller
jeweller
jewellery
jewelrey — jewellery
jewfish
Jewry (Jewish people)
jewry — jury (court)
jew's harp
jib, jibbed, jibbing
jibe, jibed, jibing (sail)
jibe — gibe (scoff)
jiffy, -fies
jifie — jiffy
jify — jiffy
jig, jigged, jigging
jigger
jiggle, -gled, -gling
jiggul — jiggle

jigsaw
jillaroo
jilt, -ed, -ing
jim — gym
jimkana — gymkhana
jin — gin
jingel — jingle
jingle, -gled, -gling
jingoism
jingul — jingle
jinks — jinx
jinx, -es
jirashun — gyration
jiration — gyration
jiro — gyro
jiroscope — gyroscope
jist — gist
jiter — jitter
jitter, -ed, -ing
jittery
jive, jived, jiving
job, jobbed, jobbing
jobber
jockey, -eys
jockey, -eyed, -eying
jockie — jockey
jockstrap
jocky — jockey
jocose, -ly
jocosity, -ties
jocular, -ly
jocularity, -ties
jocund, -ly
jocundity, -ties
jodhpurs
jodpurs — jodhpurs
joey, -eys
jog, jogged, jogging
jogger
jogtrot, -trotted, -trotting
johnnycake
joi — joy
join, joined, joining
joiner
joinery
joint, -ly
joist

joke, joked, joking
joker
   jollitey   jollity
jollity, -ties
jolly, -lier, -liest
jolt, -ed, -ing
   joly   jolly
jonah
jonathan
jonquil
   Joo   Jew
   Jooish   Jewish
   jool   joule (unit)
   Joone   June
   joopiter   Jupiter
   joose   deuce (two)
   joose   juice (liquid)
   joote   jute
jostle, -tled, -tling
   josul   jostle
jot, jotted, jotting
jotter
joule (unit)
   joule   dual (two)
   joule   duel (fight)
   joule   jewel (gem)
journal
journalese
journalism
journalist
   journel   journal
journey, -neys
journey, -neyed, -neying
joust, -ed, -ing
Jove
jovial, -ly
joviality
jowl
joy
joyful, -ly
joyous, -ly
joy-ride, -rode, -riding
joystick
   joyus   joyous
   ju   Jew
jube
jubilant, -ly

jubilate, -lated, -lating
jubilation
jubilee
   jubilie   jubilee
   juce   deuce (two)
   juce   juice (liquid)
Judaism
judas
judge, judged, judging
judgement
judgment
   judicacher   judicature
   judicachur   judicature
judicature
judicial, -ly
judiciary, -aries
judicious, -ly
   judishul   judicial
   judisharey   judiciary
   judishous   judicious
   judishus   judicious
judo
   juel   dual (two)
   juel   duel (fight)
   juel   jewel (gem)
   juel   joule (unit)
jug, jugged, jugging
   juge   judge
   juggement   judgement
juggernaut
juggle, -gled, -gling
juggler
   jugul   juggle
jugular
juice (liquid)
   juice   deuce (two)
juiciness
juicy, -cier, -ciest
   Juish   Jewish
jujitsu
jukebox
   jukstapose   juxtapose
julep
   Juli   July
July
jumble, -bled, -bling
jumbo, -bos

jumbuck
  jumbul   jumble
jump, -ed, -ing
jumper
jump-start
jump suit
jumpy, jumpier, jumpiest
junction
juncture
June
jungle
  jungul   jungle
  junier   junior
junior
juniper
junk
  junkcher   juncture
junket
junkie
  junkshere   juncture
  junkshun   junction
  junkshure   juncture
junta
Jupiter
  jurer   juror
  juri   jury
juridical, -ly
  jurisdickshion jurisdiction
  jurisdickshun jurisdiction
jurisdiction
jurisprudence
  jurisprudense jurisprudence
  jurisprudunse jurisprudence
jurist
  jurnal   journal
  jurney   journey
juror
jury, -ries
  juse   juice
  jusie   juicy
jussive
just, -ly
justice
justice of the peace
  justifiabel   justifiable
justifiable, -bly
justification

justify, -fied, -fying
  justise   justice
jut, jutted, jutting
jute
juvenile, -ly
  juwel   dual (two)
  juwel   duel (fight)
  juwel   jewel (gem)
  juwel   joule (unit)
  juxapose   juxtapose
  juxaposition juxtaposition
juxtapose, -posed, -posing
juxtaposition
  jym   gym
  jyroscope   gyroscope

Kk

Look under **c** if the word is not under **k**

kadaicha man
kaleidoscope
  kalidascope   kaleidoscope
  kalidescope   kaleidoscope
kalsomine, -mined, -mining
kamikaze
kampong
kanaka
kangaroo
kaolin
ka pai
kapok
kaput
karate
  karkey   khaki
  karki   khaki
karma
karri, -ris (tree)
  karri   carry (bring)
kauri, -ris
kayak
kebab
kedgeree
keel, -ed, -ing
keen, -ly
keenness
keep, kept, keeping
keeper
keg
kelp
  kelpey   kelpie
kelpie
  kelt   Celt
  keltic   Celtic
ken, kenned, kenning

  kenel   kennel
kennel, -nelled, -nelling
kept
keratin
kerb (gutter)
  kerb   curb (check)
kerchief
kerfuffle
kernel (core)
  kernel   colonel (army)
kero
  keropody   chiropody
  keroseen   kerosene
kerosene
kerosine
kestrel
ketch
ketchup
  ketle   kettle
kettle
kettledrum
  kettul   kettle
  kew   cue
  kew   queue (line)
kewpie
key, keys (lock)
key, keyed, keying
  key   quay (wharf)
keyboard
keystone
khaki, -kis
kibble, -bled, -bling
  kibbul   kibble
  kiak   kayak
kibbutz
kick, kicked, kicking
kick-off
kid, kidded, kidding
kidnap, -napped, -napping
kidney, -neys
kikuyu
kill, killed, killing
killer
killjoy
kiln
kilo
kilogram

kilojoule

kilometer   kilometre
kilometre
kilowatt
kilowatt-hour
kilt
kilter
kimono, -nos
kin
kina
kind, -ly
kindness
kindergarten
kindle, -dled, -dling
kindly, -lier, -liest
kindred

kindrid   kindred
kindrud   kindred
kindul   kindle

kinetics
king
kingdom
kingly
kingfish
kingfisher
kingpin
kink, kinked, kinking
kinkiness
kinky, -kier, -kiest
kinsfolk
kinship
kinsman, -men
kiosk
kip, kipped, kipping
kipper
kirk

kiropody   chiropody

kismet
kiss, kissed, kissing
kissable
kit, kitted, kitting
kitbag
kitchen
kite

kiten   kitten

kith

kitie   kitty

kitsch
kitten
kittenish, -ly
kitty, -ties

kity   kitty

kiwi

kiyak   kayak

klaxon
kleptomania
knack
knacker
knapsack
knave (rogue)

knave   nave (church)

knead, -ed, -ing, (dough)

knead   need (want)

knee, kneed, kneeing
kneecap
kneel, knelt, kneeling
knell, -ed, -ing
knew

knew   gnu (animal)
knew   new

knickerbockers
knick-knack
knife, knives
knife, knifed, knifing
knight (lord)

knight   night (time)

knighthood
knit, knitted, knitting
knitwear
knob, knobbed, knobbing (handle)
knobbly
knobby, -bier, -biest
knock, -ed, -ing
knockabout
knock-back
knockdown
knocker
knock-knee
knockout
knoll
knot, knotted, knotting (tie)

knot   not (denial)

knothole
knotty, -tier, -tiest

know, knew, known, knowing
know-all
know how
knowledge
knowledgeable, -bly
knuckle, -led, -ling
knuckle-duster
koala
   kola   koala
kookaburra
koori
korodji
Koran
korowai
   koroway   korowai
kosher
kowtow, -ed, -ing
Kremlin
kris
Krishna
kudos
kumquat
kung-fu
kurrajong

> For kw- words, look under
> **qu-**.

kylie

LI

label, -belled, -belling
 laber   labour
labial, -ly
labiate
 labirinth   labyrinth
labium, -bia
 lable   label
 labor   labour
laboratory, -ries
 laboratrey   laboratory
laborious, -ly
 laborius   laborious
labour, -ed, -ing
labourer
labour-intensive
Labrador
 labratory   laboratory
 labrinth   labyrinth
 laburnem   laburnum
laburnum
labyrinth
labyrinthine
lace, laced, lacing
lacebark
lacerate, -rated, -rating
laceration
 lach   latch
lack, -ed, -ing
lackadaisical, -ly
 lacker   lacquer
lackey, -eys
lackey, -eyed, -eying
 lacky   lackey
laconic, -ally
lacquer, -ed, -ing
 lacross   lacrosse
lacrosse
lactate, -tated, -tating

lactation
lacteal, -ly
lactic
lactose
lad
ladder
lade, laded, laden, lading (load)
 lade   laid (placed)
 ladel   ladle
 lader   ladder
 ladie   lady
ladle, -dled, -dling
 ladul   ladle
lady, -dies
ladybird
lag, lagged, lagging
 lagard   laggard
lager
laggard, -ly
 laghable   laughable
lagoon
laid (placed)
 laid   lade (load)
laid-back
 laim   lame
lain (did lie)
 lain   lane (passage)
lair (den)
 lair   layer
 laissay fair   laissez faire
laissez faire
 laitie   laity
laity
lake
 lakross   lacrosse
 laks   lax
 laksative   laxative
lam, lammed, lamming (spike)
 lam   lamb (sheep)
lama
lamb (sheep)
 lamb   lam (spike)
lambaste, -basted, -basting
lame, lamed, laming
lame, lamer, lamest
lament, -ed, -ing
lamentable, -bly

lamentation
laminate, -nated, -nating
lamington
lamp
lampoon, -ed, -ing
lampoonist
lamp-post
   lampray   lamprey
lamprey, -reys
lance, lanced, lancing
lancet
land, -ed, -ing
landfall
landform
landlady, -dies
landlocked
landlord
landlubber
landmark
landmass
landmine
land rights
landscape, -scaped, -scaping
landslide
lane (passage)
   lane   lain (did lie)
language
languid, -ly
languish, -ed, -ing
   languer   languor
languorous, -ly
   langwid   languid
   langwidge   language
   langwish   languish
lank, -ly
   landladie   landlady
   lanladie   landlady
   lanlady   landlady
   lanlord   landlord
lanolin
lanoline
   lanse   lance
   lanser   lancer
   lanset   lancet
lantana
lantern
lanyard

lap, lapped, lapping
lapel
lapelled
lapidary, -ries
lapis lazuli
lap-lap
lapse, lapsed, lapsing
larceny, -nies
larcenous, -ly
   larconic   laconic
lard
larder
large, -ly
largess
lariat
   laringitis   laryngitis
   larinx   larynx
lark
larrikin
   larseny   larceny
larva, -vae (insect)
   larva   lava (rock)
laryngitis
larynx, larynxes
lascivious, -ly
   lase   lace
laser
   laserate   lacerate
lash, -ed, -ing
   lasitude   lassitude
   lasivious   lascivious
   lasivius   lascivious
   lasoo   lasso
   lasor   laser
lass
lassitude
lasso, -sos, -soes
lasso, -soed, -soing
last, lasted, lasting
last-ditch
lastly
latch, -ed, -ing
latchkey
late, later, latest
lately
latency
   latensey   latency

latent, -ly
lateral, -ly
latex, latexes
lath (strip)
lathe (machine)
lather, -ed, -ing
lathery
Latin
latise — lattice
latitude
latrine
latter
lattice
laud, lauded, lauding (praise)
laud — lord (ruler)
laudable, -bly
laudanum
laudation
laudatory
laugh, laughed, laughing
laughable, -bly
laughter
laun — lawn
launch, launched, launching
launder, -ed, -ing
laundrey — laundry
laundromat
laundry, -dries
laureate
laurel, -relled, -relling
lauyer — lawyer
lava (rock)
lava — larva (insect)
lavatory, -ries
lavatree — lavatory
lavatrey — lavatory
lave, laved, laving
lavender
lavish, lavished, lavishing
law (rule)
law — lore (learn)
lawd — laud (praise)
lawd — lord (ruler)
lawdabul — laudable
lawful, -ly
lawless, -ly
lawn

lawnch — launch
lawnder — launder
lawndrey — laundry
lawndromat — laundromat
lawndry — laundry
lawsuit
lawsute — lawsuit
lawyer
lax, -ly
lax — lacks
laxadasical — lackadaisical
laxative
laxity
lay, laid, laying (rest)
lay — lei (flowers)
laybie — lay-by
lay-by
layer
layette
layman, -men
layout
laze, lazed, lazing
lazily
lazy, -zier, -ziest
lea (meadow)
lea — lee (shelter)
leach, -ed, -ing (filter)
leach — leech (worm)
lead, led, leading (show)
lead (metal)
lead — led (shown)
leaden, -ly
leader
leadership
leaf, leaves
leaflet
league
leak (hole)
leak — leek (food)
leakage
lean, leant or leaned, leaning (bend)
leant — Lent (season)
leant — lent (did lend)
lean-to
leap, leapt or leaped, leaping
leapfrog, -frogged, -frogging
learn, learnt or learned, learning

learner		leesiun	lesion
lease, leased, leasing		leeward	
leasehold		leeway	
leash, -ed, -ing		leewood	leeward
leashur	leisure	left	
leason	liaison	leftenant	lieutenant
least		leftenent	lieutenant
leasure	leisure	left-footer	
leasurely	leisurely	left-handed	
leather		leftist	
leatherjacket		leftward	
leave, left, leaving		left-winger	
leaven, -ed, -ing		leg, legged, legging	
leaver	lever	legacy, -cies	
lecher (man)		legal, -ly	
lecher	lecture (talk)	legalese (language)	
lecherous, -ly		legalisation	
lecherus	lecherous	legalise, -lised, -lising (authorise)	
lechery		legalism	
lectern		legality, -ties	
lector		legand	legend
lecture, -tured, -turing		legasey	legacy
lecturer		legashen	legation
led (shown)		legate	
led	lead (metal)	legation	
ledge		legend	
ledger (book)		legendary, -ries	
ledger	leger (stand)	legendrey	legendary
lee (shelter)		leger (stand)	
lee	lea (meadow)	leger	ledger (book)
leeason	liaison	leghorn	
leech (worm)		legibel	legible
leech	leach (filter)	legibility	
leed	lead	legible, -bly	
leef	leaf	legion	
leeflet	leaflet	legionary, -ries	
leege	liege	legionnaire	
leegue	league	legislachur	legislature
leek (food)		legislate, -lated, -lating	
leek	leak (hole)	legislation	
leen	lean	legislative, -ly	
leep	leap	legislator	
leer, -ed, -ing		legislature	
lees		legitimacy	
leese	lease	legitimasey	legitimacy
leesh	leash	legitimate, -mated, -mating	
leesion	lesion	legume	

lei, leis (flowers)		lerch	lurch
lei	lay (rest)	lerk	lurk
leisure		lern	learn
leisurely		lesen	lessen (reduce)
lejun	legion	lesen	lesson (study)
lejunry	legionary	lesbian	
leksicografer	lexicographer	lesbianism	
leksicografey	lexicography	leishur	leisure
leksicographer	lexicographer	lesion	
leksicon	lexicon	leson	lessen (reduce)
leming	lemming	leson	lesson (study)
lemming		less	
lemon		lessee	
lemonade		lessen (reduce)	
lemur		lesson (study)	
lend, lent, lending		lessor	
lender		lest	
length		lesure	leisure
lengthen, -ed, -ing		let, let, letting	
lengthily		letdown	
lengthways		leter	letter
lengthwise		leter	litre
lengthy, -thier, -thiest		lethal, -ly	
lenience		lethargey	lethargy
leniency		lethargic, -ally	
leniense	lenience	lethargy, -gies	
leniensy	leniency	lether	leather
lenient, -ly		letice	lettuce
lenity, -ties		letise	lettuce
lens, lenses		letre	litre
lense	lens	letter	
Lent (season)		lettered	
lent	leant (bent)	letterhead	
lenth	length	letterpress	
lentil (pea)		lettuce	
lentil	lintel (beam)	let-up	
Leo		letuse	lettuce
leonine		leucosis	
leopard		leukaemia	
leotard		leve	leave
lepard	leopard	levee (bank)	
leper		levee	levy (tax)
leperd	leopard	level, -elled, -elling	
leprechaun		leveller	
leprechorn	leprechaun	level-headed	
leprosy		levelheded	level-headed
lept	leapt	leven	leaven

lever, -ed, -ing
leverage
leviathan
  levie   levee (bank)
  levie   levy (tax)
levitate, -tated, -tating
levitation
levity, -ties
  levrage   leverage
levy, levies (tax)
levy, levied, levying (tax)
  levy   levee (bank)
lewd, -ly
  lexicografer   lexicographer
  lexicografey   lexicography
lexicographer
lexicography
lexicon
  lezbian   lesbian
  li   lie
liability, -ties
liable (legal)
  liabul   libel (crime)
  liabul   liable (legal)
liaise, -aised, -aising
liaison
liana
liar (tell lies)
  liar   lyre (music)
  liason   liaison
  libarian   librarian
  libary   library
libel, -belled, -belling (crime)
  libel   liable (legal)
  libelus   libellous
  libul   liable
libellous, -ly
liberal, -ly
liberalism
liberate, -rated, -rating
liberation
liberator
  libertey   liberty
libertine
liberty, -ties
libidinal
libidinous, -ly

libido
Libra
  libralism   liberalism
librarian
library, -ries
libretto, -tos, -ti
  librian   librarian
lice
  licee   lychee
licence (noun)
license, -censed, -censing
licensee
  licenshiate   licentiate
  licenshius   licentious
  licenshus   licentious
licentiate
licentious, -ly
  lichee   lychee
lichen
  lichenis   lichenous
lichenous
  lichenus   lichenous
lick, -ed, -ing
  licker   liqueur
  licker   liquor
licorice
  licorish   licorice
  licoriss   licorice
  lickrish   licorice
lid
lie, lied, lying (untruth)
lie, lay, lain, lying (recline)
  lie   lye (solution)
liege
lien
  liesure   leisure
lieu (instead)
  lieu   loo (toilet)
lieutenant
life, lives
lifebelt
lifeboat
  lifeboy   lifebuoy
lifebuoy
lifeguard
lifeless, -ly
lifelike

lifelong
lifesaver
lifestyle
lifetime
lift, -ed, -ing
lift-off
  ligacher   ligature
  ligachur   ligature
ligament
light, lighted, lighting
lighten, -ed, -ing
light-fingered
light-headed
light-hearted, -ly
lighthouse
lightly
lightning
lightweight
ligneous
lignite
like, liked, liking
likeable
likelihood
likely, -lier, -liest
  likelyhood   likelihood
liken, likened, likening
likeness
likewise
  likorish   licorice
  likoriss   licorice
  likrish   licorice

> For likw- words, look
> under **liqu-**.

lilac
  lilak   lilac
  lile   lisle
  lilie   lily
Lilliputian
lilly pilly
lilt, -ed, -ing
lily, -ies
lily-livered
limb
limber, limbered, limbering
limbo, -bos
lime, limed, liming

limelight
  limelite   limelight
limerick
  limersene   limousine
limestone
limey, -meys
  limf   lymph
  limfatic   lymphatic
limit, -ed, -ing
limitation
limousine
limp, -ed, -ing
limpet
  limph   lymph
  limphatic   lymphatic
limpid, -ly
linchpin
  linch   lynch
linctus
line, lined, lining (mark)
  line   lion (cat)
lineage
lineal, -ly
lineament (detail)
linear, -ly
  lineige   lineage
linen
liner
linesman, -men
line-up
ling, lings
linger, -ed, -ing
lingerie
lingo, -goes
lingual, -ly
linguist
linguistic, -ally
  lingwal   lingual
  lingwist   linguist
  linier   linear
liniment (oil)
  liniment   lineament
                (detail)
link, linked, linking
linkage
linnet
linocut

linoleum
  linolium   linoleum
linotype, -typed, -typing
linseed
lint
lintel (beam)
  lintel   lentil (pea)
  linx   lynx
lion (cat)
  lion   line (mark)
lioness
lion-hearted, -ly
lionisation
lionise, -nised, -nising
  liotard   leotard
lip
lip-read, -read, -reading
lip-salve
lip-service
lipstick
liquefier
liquefy, -fied, -fying
  liquer   liqueur
  liquer   liquor
liqueur (drink)
  liqueur   liquor (spirits)
liquid
liquidambar
liquidate, -dated, -dating
liquidation
liquidator
liquidity
liquor (spirits)
  liquor   liqueur (drink)
liquorice
  liquoris   liquorice
  liquorish   liquorice
  lire   lyre
  lirebird   lyrebird
  liric   lyric
  lirical   lyrical
  lise   lice
  lisen   listen
  lisence   licence (noun)
  lisence   license (verb)
  lisen   listen
  lisensee   licensee

  lisentiate   licentiate
  lisentius   licentious
lisle
lisp, -ed, -ing
lissom
  lissum   lissom
list, -ed, -ing
listen, -ed, -ing
listless, -ly
lit
litany, -nies
  lite   light
  litel   little
  liter   litre
  liter   litter
  literacher   literature
  literachur   literature
literacy
literal, -ly
literary, -ily
  literasy   literacy
  literat   literate
literate
literati
literature
  litergy   liturgy
  litewait   light-weight
lithe, -ly
lithesome
lithium
  lithograf   lithograph
lithograph
lithographic, -ally
lithography
litigant
litigation
litigator
  litle   little
litmus
  litening   lightning
  litracher   literature
  litrachur   literature
litre
litter, -ed, -ing
litterbug
little, less, least
  litul   little

liturgey	liturgy	loch (lake)	
liturgical, -ly		lock (door)	
liturgy, -gies		locker	
liv	live	locket	
livary	livery	lockjaw	
live, lived, living		locksmith	
livelihood		lockup	
lively, -lier, -liest		locomoshun	locomotion
livelyhood	livelihood	locomotion	
liven, -ed, -ing		locomotive	
liver		locum	
liverish		locust	
liverwurst		lode (ore)	
livery, -ries		lode	load (burden)
livestock		lodestar	
livewire		lodestone	
livid, -ly		lodge, lodged, lodging	
livlie	lively	lodger	
livrey	livery	lofe	loaf
liying	lying	loft, lofted, lofting	
lizard		loftily	
lizerd	lizard	lofty, -tier, -tiest	
llama		log, logged, logging	
lo	low	loganberie	loganberry
load, -ed, -ing (burden)		loganberry, -ries	
load	lode (ore)	logarithm	
loaf, loaves		logbook	
loam, -ed, -ing		loge	lodge
loan (lend)		loger	logger
loan	lone (alone)	logerithm	logarithm
loath (unwilling)		loggerhead	
loathe, loathed, loathing (hate)		logic	
loathsome, -ly		logical, -ly	
lob, lobbed, lobbing		logicality	
lobby, -bies		logistics	
lobby, -bied, -bying		loier	lawyer
lobe		loin	
lobie	lobby	loincloth	
lobotomy		loiter, -ed, -ing	
lobster		loiterer	
loby	lobby	lol	loll
local, -ly		lolipop	lollipop
locale		loll, -ed, -ing	
localise, -lised, -lising		lollipop	
locality, -ties		lolly, -lies	
locate, -cated, -cating		lome	loam
location		lone (alone)	

lone   loan (lend)
loneliness
lonely, -lier, -liest
loner
lonesome, -ly
lonesum   lonesome
long, -ed, -ing
longevity
longhand
longing, -ly
longitude
longitudinal, -ly
long-playing
long-sighted
longstanding
long-suffering
long-term
longwinded, -ly
loo (toilet)
loo   lieu (instead)
loobricant   lubricant
loobricate   lubricate
loocid   lucid
loocrative   lucrative
loodicrous   ludicrous
loodicrus   ludicrous
loofah
look, -ed, -ing
lookemia   leukaemia
looker   lucre
lookout
lookwarm   lukewarm
loom, -ed, -ing
loominus   luminous
loon
loona   luna
loonatic   lunatic
loony, loonier, looniest
loop, -ed, -ing
loophole
loose, loosed, loosing (free)
loose, looser, loosest
loose   lose (fail)
loose-leaf
loosen, -ed, -ing
loosing   losing
loot (booty)

loot   lute (music)
lop, lopped, lopping (cut)
lope, loped, loping (run)
lopsided, -ly
loquacious, -ly
loquacity
loquashius   loquacious
loquashus   loquacious
loquat
lord (ruler)
lord   laud (praise)
lordly, -lier, -liest
lord mayor
lore (learn)
lore   law (rule)
lorel   laurel
lorgnette
loriat   laureate
lorie   lorry
lorikeet
lornch   launch
lornyet   lorgnette
lorry, lorries (truck)
lory, lories (bird)
los   loss
lose, lost, losing (fail)
lose   loose (free)
loser
loshion   lotion
loshun   lotion
loss
lot, lotted, lotting
lotery   lottery
lothe   loathe
lothsum   loathsome
lotion
lotry   lottery
lots
lottery, -teries
lotto
lotus
loud, -ly
loudhailer
loudspeaker
lounge, lounged, lounging
louse, lice
louse, loused, lousing

lousy, lousier, lousiest
lout
  louver   louvre
louvre
love, loved, loving
loveliness
lovelorn
lovely, -lier, -liest
lover
  loves   loaves
low, lower, lowest
lowboy
lowbrow
  lowd   loud
low-down (mean)
lowdown (truth)
lower, -ed, -ing
low-key
lowland
lowly, -lier, -liest
  lownge   lounge
low-pressure
  lowse   louse
  lowt   lout
low-voltage
loyal, -ly
loyalty, -ties
  loyle   loyal
lozenge
  lozinge   lozenge
  lu   lieu (instead)
  lu   loo (toilet)
lubber, -ly
  luber   lubber
lubricant
lubricate, -cated, -cating
lubrication
  lucer   lucre
lucerne
lucid, -ly
Lucifer
luck, -ily
lucky, -ier, -iest
lucky dip
lucrative, -ly
lucre
  lude   lewd

ludicrous, -ly
ludo
luff, -ed, -ing
lug, lugged, lugging
  lugage   luggage
luggage
lugger
  lugige   luggage
  lugsuriant   luxuriant
lugubrious, -ly
  lukemia   leukaemia
lukewarm
  luksuriant   luxuriant
  luksuriate   luxuriate
  luksurius   luxurious
  luksury   luxury
  lul   lull
  lulabie   lullaby
lull, -ed, -ing
lullaby, -bies
lullaby, -bied, -bying
lumbago
lumbar (back)
lumber (timber)
lumberjack
luminance
luminary, -naries
luminescence
luminescent
  luminessence   luminescence
  luminessent   luminescent
luminosity, -ties
luminous, -ly
  luminus   luminous
lump, -ed, -ing
lunacy, -cies
lunar
  lunasey   lunacy
lunatic
lunch, -ed, -ing
luncheon
lung
lunge, lunged, lunging
lungfish
lupin
lupus
lurch, lurched, lurching

lure, lured, luring
lurex
lurid, -ly
lurk, lurked, lurking
  lurn   learn
luscious, -ly
lush, -ly
  lushes   luscious
  lushious   luscious
  lushus   luscious
  lused   lucid
  lusid   lucid
lust, lusted, lusting
  luster   lustre
lustful, -ly
  lustie   lusty
lustre
lustrous, -ly
lusty, -tier, -tiest
lute, luted, luting (music)
  lute   loot (booty)
Lutheran
  luv   love
  luve   love
  luver   lover
  luvley   lovely
  luvlier   lovelier
lux
  luxery   luxury
luxuriance
luxuriant, -ly
luxuriate, -ated, -ating
luxurious, -ly
luxury, -ries
lyceum
lychee
lye (solution)
  lye   lie (untruth)
  lye   lie (recline)
lying-in
lymph
lymphatic
lynch, -ed, -ing
lynx, lynxes (wildcat)
  lynx   links
lyre (musical instrument)
  lyre   liar (tell lies)

lyrebird
lyric
lyrical, -ly
lyricist

Mm

macabre
macadam
macadamia nut
macaroni, -nis, -nies
macaw
mace
  mach   match
machete
machinate, -nated, -nating
machination
machine, -chined, -chining
machinery, -ries
mackerel
mackintosh, mackintoshes
macramé
mad, madder, maddest
mad, madded, madding
madam
madcap
made (produced)
  made   maid (girl)
madeira
mademoiselle
  maden   madden
  madera   madeira
madness
madonna
madrigal
maelstrom
maestro
mafia
magazine
maggot
magic
magical, -ly
magician
  magishion   magician
  magishun   magician

magisterial, -ly
magistrate
  magizine   magazine
  magnanimis   magnanimous
magnanimity
magnanimous, -ly
  magnanimus   magnanimous
  magnat   magnate
  magnat   magnet
magnate (wealth)
magnesium
magnet (attract)
magnetic, -ally
magnetisation
magnetise, -tised, -tising
magnetism
magnetite
magneto, -tos
magnification
magnificence
magnificent, -ly
magnifier
  magnifisense   magnificence
  magnifisent   magnificent
  magnifisunt   magnificent
magnify, -fied, -fying
magnitude
magnolia
magnum, -nums
  magot   maggot
magpie
  mahem   mayhem
mah-jong
mahogany, -nies
maid (girl)
  maid   made
maiden
mail (letters)
  mail   male (man)
mailbox, mailboxes
maim, -ed, -ing
main (chief)
  main   mane (hair)
mainland
mainline, -lined, -lining
mainliner
mainstay

mainstream
maintain, -ed, -ing
maintenance

  maintenanse   maintenance
maisonette
maize (corn)

  maize   maze (puzzle)
  majer   major
  majestey   majesty
majestic, -ally
majesty, -ties

  majong   mah-jong
major
majority, -ties

  makaber   macabre
  makadam   macadam
make, made, making
makeshift
make-up
mako

  maladey   malady
maladjusted
maladjustment
malady, -dies
malaise
malapropism

  malard   mallard
malaria

  malase   malaise
male (man)

  male   mail (letters)
  maleable   malleable
  malefacshun   malefaction
malefaction
malefactor

  malet   mallet
malevolence

  malevolense   malevolence
malevolent, -ly
malformation
malformed

  malfuncshion   malfunction
  malfuncshun   malfunction
malfunction, -ed, -ing

  maliable   malleable
malice
malicious, -ly

malign, -ed, -ing
malignance
malignancy

  malignansey   malignancy
malignant, -ly

  maline   malign
malinger, -ed, -ing
malingerer

  malise   malice
  malishus   malicious
mall
mallard, -lards, -lard
malleability
malleable

  malleabul   malleable
mallee
mallet

  mallow   mellow
  malnutrishun   malnutrition
malnutrition
malpractice

  malpractise   malpractice
  malstrom   maelstrom
malt (liquor)

  malt   moult (lose)
Malthusian
maltreat, -ed, -ing

  maltreet   maltreat
maluka

  mamal   mammal
  mamarey   mammary
  mame   maim
mamilla, -millae
mamma, mammae
mammal
mammary
mammon
mammoth

  mamon   mammon
  mamoth   mammoth
man, men
man, manned, manning
manacle, -cled, -cling

  manacul   manacle
manage, -aged, -aging
manageability
manageable, -bly

management
manager
manageress
managerial, -ly
manana
manchester
mandarin (bureaucrat)
mandarine (fruit)
mandate, -dated, -dating
mandatory, -ries

mandatry   mandatory
mandolin
mandrax
mane (hair)

mane   main (chief)
maner   manner (way)
maner   manor (house)
mange

mangel   mangle
manger
mangle, -gled, -gling
mango, -goes, -gos
mangrove

mangul   mangle
mangy, -gier, -giest
manhandel   manhandle
manhandle, -dled, -dling
manhandul   manhandle
manhole
manhood
mania
maniacal, -ly
manic
manic-depression
manic-depressive
manicure, -cured, -curing
manidge   manage
manifest, -ed, -ing
manifestation
manifesto, -tos
manifold

manige   manage
manikin (dwarf)

manikin   mannequin
                (model)
manila

manipulashun   manipulation

manipulate, -lated, -lating
manipulation
manipulative
manipulator
manipulatory

manje   mange
manjer   manger
manjy   mangy
mankind
manly, -lier, -liest
manna (food)

manna   manner (way)
manna   manor (house)
mannequin
manner (way)

manner   manna (food)
manner   manor (house)
mannered
mannerism
manoeuvrability
manoeuvrable
manoeuvre, -vred, -vring

manoover   manoeuvre
manoovrabul   manoeuvrable
manor (house)

manor   manna (food)
manor   manner (way)
manpower
manse

manshun   mansion
mansion
manslaughter

manslorter   manslaughter
mantel (shelf)

mantel   mantle (cloak)
mantelpiece
mantilla
mantis, -tises
mantissa
mantle (cloak)

mantle   mantel (shelf)
mantul   mantel (shelf)
mantul   mantle (cloak)
manual, -ly

manufacsher   manufacture
manufacture, -tured, -turing
manure, -nured, -nuring

manuscript
many, more, most
   maonaise   mayonnaise
Maori, -ris
map, mapped, mapping
   mapel   maple
maple
mar, marred, marring
marathon
maraud, -ed, -ing
   marawed   maraud
marble, -bled, -bling
   marbul   marble
marcasite
March
march, -ed, -ing
marcher
marchioness
mare (horse)
   mare   mayor (chief)
   mareene   marine
margarine
margin
marginal, -ly
   mariage   marriage
   marie   marry
marijuana
marina
marinade, -naded, -nading
marinate, -nated, -nating
marine
mariner
   marionet   marionette
marionette
marital, -ly
maritime
   maritul   marital
   mariwana   marijuana
marjoram
mark, marked, marking
marker
market, -ed, -ing
marketeer
   markey   marquee
   markey   marquis
marksman, -men
marksmanship

   markuis   marquis
marlin
marlock
marmalade
   marone   maroon
maroon
   marow   marrow
marquee (tent)
marquis (nobleman)
marri (tree)
   marri   marry (unite)
marriage
marrow
marry, -ried, -rying (unite)
   marry   marri (tree)
Mars
marsh
marshal, -shalled, -shalling (officer)
   marshal   martial (brave)
marshland
marshmallow
   marshul   marshal
   marshul   martial
marshy, -shier, -shiest
marsupial
mart
   marter   martyr
martial (brave)
   martial   marshal
             (officer)
martinet
martini
martyr
martyrdom
marvel, -velled, -velling
marvellous, -ly
Marxism
Marxist
   mary   marry
marzipan
   mas   mass
   masacer   massacre
   masacre   massacre
   masage   massage
mascara
mascot
masculine, -ly

masculinity

mase   mace

mash, -ed, -ing

   mashene   machine

   mashine   machine

   mashinry   machinery

   masive   massive

mask, -ed, -ing

   maskerade   masquerade

masochism

masochist

   masocism   masochism

mason

masonic

masonite

masonry, -ries

masquerade, -raded, -rading

mass, -ed, -ing

   massacer   massacre

massacre, -cred, -cring

massage, -saged, -saging

masseur

massif (mountain)

massive, -ly (large)

mass media

mass-produce, -duced, -ducing

   massur   masseur

mast

mastectomy, -mies

master

   masterbate   masturbate

masterful, -ly

mastermind

   masterpeace   masterpiece

masterpiece

masthead

mastiff

masturbate, -bated, -bating

masturbation

mat, matted, matting (rug)

   mat   matt (dull)

matador

match, -ed, -ing

matchmaker

mate, mated, mating

   mater   matter

material, -ly

materialisation

materialise, -lised, -lising

materialism

materialist

maternal, -ly

maternity

mateship

matey

mathematical, -ly

mathematician

mathematics

   mathematisian   mathematician

maths

matilda

   matinay   matinee

matinee

   mating   matting

   matress   mattress

matriarch

matriarchal

matriarchic

matriarchy, -chies

matriculant

matriculate, -lated, -lating

matriculation

matrimony, -nies

matrix, matrices

matron, -ly

matt (dull)

matter

matting

mattock

mattress

maturation

mature, -tured, -turing

maturity

maudlin, -ly

maul, -ed, -ing

mausoleum, -leums, -lea

mauve

maverick

   mawgage   mortgage

mawkish, -ly

   mawl   maul

   mawsoleum   mausoleum

maxi

maxim

maximisation
maximise, -mised, -mising
maximum, -ma, -mums
maybe
May Day
mayhem
mayonnaise
mayor (chief)

   mayor   mare (horse)
mayoralty, -ties
mayoress
maypole
maze (puzzle)

   maze   maize (corn)
mazurka
mead
meadow

   meager   meagre
meagre, -ly

   meak   meek
meal
mean, meant, meaning (intend)

   mean   mien (show)
meander, -ed, -ing
meantime
meanwhile

   measels   measles
measles
measure, -ured, -uring
measurement
meat (flesh)

   meat   meet (contact)
   meat   mete (measure)
   mecanic   mechanic
   mecanise   mechanise
   mecanism   mechanism
mechanic
mechanical, -ly
mechanisation
mechanise, -nised, -nising
mechanism
medal, -alled, -alling (award)
medallion

   medcine   medicine
meddle, -dled, -dling (interfere)
meddler

   medeval   mediaeval

media
mediaeval
median

   mediashun   mediation
mediate, -ated, -ating
mediation
meditator
medic
medical, -ly
medicate, -cated, -cating
medication
medicinal, -ly
medicine
medieval, -ly

   mediocer   mediocre
mediocre
mediocrity, -ties

   medisinal   medicinal
   medisine   medicine
meditate, -tated, -tating
meditation
meditator
medium, -dia, -diums

   medle   meddle
   medler   meddler
medley, -leys

   medly   medley
   medow   meadow
   medsine   medicine
   medul   meddle
   meed   mead
meek, -ly

   meel   meal
   meen   mean (intend)
   meen   mien (show)
   meening   meaning
meerschaum

   meershum   meerschaum
   meesels   measles
meet, met, meeting (contact)

   meet   meat (flesh)
   meet   mete (measure)
   megafone   megaphone
megalomania
megalomaniac
megaphone

   meger   meagre

mekanic	mechanic
mekanical	mechanical
mekanise	mechanise
mekanism	mechanism

melaleuca
melancholia
melancholic, -ally
melancholy, -cholies
Melanesian
melee

meliflous	mellifluous

meliorate, -rated, -rating
melioration
meliorator
mellifluous, -ly
mellow, -ly

melodey	melody

melodic, -ally
melodious, -ly

melodius	melodious

melodrama
melodramatic, -ally
melody, -dies
melon

melow	mellow

melt, melted, melting
member
membership

membrain	membrane

memento, -tos
memo, memos
memoir

memorabel	memorable

memorabilia
memorable,-bly

memorabul	memorable

memorandum, -dums

memorey	memory

memorial, -ly
memorise, -rised, -rising
memory, -ries

memrable	memorable

menace, -aced, -acing
menagerie

menajery	menagerie
menase	menace

mend, -ed, -ing

mendacious, -ly
mendacity, -ties

mendashus	mendacious
mendasity	mendacity

mendicant
menial, -ly
meningitis

meninjitis	meningitis

meniscus, -nisci
menopause

menopaws	menopause
menshion	mention
menshun	mention

menstruate, -ated, -ating
menstruation
mensuration

ment	meant

mental, -ly

mentalitey	mentality

mentality, -ties
menthol
mentholated
mention, -ed, -ing
mentor
menu

merang	meringue

mercantile
mercenary, -naries

mercenrey	mercenary

mercer
mercerise, -rised, -rising
mercery, -ries
merchandise, -dised, -dising
merchant
merchantman, -men
merciful, -ly
merciless, -ly
mercurial, -ly
mercury, -ries
mercy, -cies
mere, -ly
meretricious, -ly

meretrishious	meretricious
meretrishus	meretricious

merge, merged, merging
merger
meridian

merie	merry
meringue	
merino, -nos	
merit, -ed, -ing	
meritories	meritorious
meritorious, -ly	
meritorius	meritorious
mermade	mermaid
mermaid	
merriment	
merry, -rier, -riest	
merry-go-round	
merrymaker	
mersenry	mercenary
mersy	mercy
mery	merry
mesa	
mescalin	
mesenger	messenger
mesh, -ed, -ing	
mesige	message
mesmerise, -rised, -rising	
mesmerism	
mess, -ed, -ing	
message	
messenger	
Messiah	
Messianic	
messmate	
Messrs	
mesure	measure
metabolic	
metabolise, -lised, -lising	
metabolism	
metafisicul	metaphysical
metafisics	metaphysics
metafor	metaphor
metaforic	metaphoric
metaforicul	metaphorical
metal, -alled, -alling (element)	
metal	mettle (energy)
metalic	metallic
metallic	
metallurgic	
metallurgical, -ly	
metallurgist	
metallurgy	

metalurgey	metallurgy
metamorfic	metamorphic
metamorfosus	metamorphosis
metamorphic	
metamorphosis, -ses	
metaphor	
metaphoric	
metamorphical, -ly	
metaphrase, -phrased, -phrasing	
metaphysical, -ly	
metaphysics	
metastasise, -sised, -sising	
mete, meted, meting (measure)	
mete	meat (flesh)
mete	meet (contact)
meteor (streak)	
meteor	metier (trade)
meteoric, -ally	
meteorite	
meteorological, -ly	
meteorology	
meter (measure)	
meter	metre (distance)
methadone	
methane	
methed	method
methedrine	
methilate	methylate
metho	
method	
methodical, -ly	
Methodist	
methodology, -gies	
methylate, -lated, -lating	
meticulous, -ly	
meticulus	meticulous
metier (trade)	
metier	meteor (streak)
metiorology	meteorology
metre (distance)	
metre	meter (measure)
metric	
metricate, -cated, -cating	
metrication	
metric system	

metronome		middul	middle
metropolis, -lises		middy, -dies (beer)	
metropolitan		middy	midi (skirt)
mettle (energy)		midel	middle
mettle	metal (element)	midge	
metul	mettle (energy)	midget	
mew, -ed, -ing		midi (skirt)	
mews (stables)		midi	middy (beer)
mews	muse (think)	midil	middle
mezanine	mezzanine	midling	middling
mezzanine		midnight	
mi	my	midnite	midnight
mia-mia		mid-off	
miander	meander	mid-on	
miaow, -ed, -ing		midriff	
miasma, -mas, -mata		midshipman, -men	
miasmatical		midst	
miasmic		midul	middle
mica		mid wicket	
mice		midwife, -wives	
microbe		mien (show)	
microbial		mien	mean (intend)
microbic		miff	
microbiological		mige	midge
microbiologist		might (power)	
microbiology		might	mite (small)
micro-economics		mighty, -tier, -tiest	
microfiche		migit	midget
microfilm		migraine	
microfone	microphone	migrane	migraine
micrometer		migrant	
micron		migrate, -grated, -grating	
microphone		migration	
microprocessor		migratory	
microprosessor	microprocessor	migreat	migrate
microscope		mika	mica
microscopic, -ally		mikado, -dos	
microwave		miksamotosis	myxomatosis
midair		mikscher	mixture
midday		mikschur	mixture
middel	middle	mikser	mixer
middle, -led, -ling		miksture	mixture
middleman, -men		mil (millilitre)	
middle-of-the-road		mil	mill (grind)
middlewait	middleweight	mild, -ly	
middleweight		mildew, -ed, -ing	
middling		mildu	mildew

mile
mileage
milestone
mileniem	millennium
milenium	millennium
milet	millet
milibar	millibar
milieu
mililiter	millilitre
milimeter	millimetre
miliner	milliner
miling	milling
milinry	millinery
milion	million
milionair	millionaire
milipeed	millipede
milisha	militia
militancy
militansy	militancy
militant, -ly
militarism
militarist
militaristic, -ally
military
militia
milk, -ed, -ing
milksop
milky, -kier, -kiest
Milky Way
mill, milled, milling (grind)
millennial, -ly
millennium, -niums, -nia
miller
millet
millibar
millligram
millilitre
millimetre
milliner
millinery
million
millionaire
millipede
millpond
millstone
millwheel
milyou	milieu

mime, mimed, miming
mimic, -icked, -icking
mimicry, -ries
mimosa
minaret
mince, minced, mincing
mincemeat
mincer
mind, minded, minding
mindful, -ly
mine, mined, mining
minefield
miner (worker)
| miner | minor (less) |
| miner | myna (bird) |
mineral
mineralogical, -ly
mineralogist
mineralogy
minestrone
| minestroney | minestrone |
| minestrony | minestrone |
minesweeper
| mingel | mingle |
mingle, -led, -ling
| mingul | mingle |
mingy, -gier, -giest
mini
miniature
minibus
| minicher | miniature |
| minichur | miniature |
minim
minimal, -ly
minimise, -mised, -mising
minimiser
minimum, -mums, -ma
minion
| miniscule | minuscule |
miniskirt
minister
ministerial, -ly
ministration
ministrative, -ly
| ministrey | ministry |
ministry, -tries
| minit | minute |

mink, minks (animal)
  minks   minx (girl)
minnow, -nows
minor (lesser)
  minor   miner (worker)
  minor   myna (bird)
minority, -ties
  minow   minnow
  minse   mince
minstrel
mint, -ed, -ing
minuet
minus
minuscule
minute, -uted, -uting
minx (girl)
  minx   minks
               (animals)
  minyouet   minuet
  miopia   myopia
  miow   miaow
  miracel   miracle
miracle
  miracul   miracle
miraculous, -ly
  miraculus   miraculous
mirage
mire, mired, miring
  mirer   mirror
  miriad   myriad
mirrnyong
mirror, -ed, -ing
mirth
mirthful, -ly
  mis   miss
  misadvencher misadventure
  misadvenchur misadventure
misadventure
  misal   missal
misanthrope
misanthropic, -ally
misanthropist
misanthropy
misapprehension
misappropriate, -ated, -ating
misappropriation
  misapropriate misappropriate

misbehave, -haved, -having
miscarriage
miscarry, -ried, -rying
  miscariage   miscarriage
  miscarie   miscarry
  miscarige   miscarriage
miscast, -cast, -casting
miscellaneous, -ly
miscellany, -nies
mischance
  mischanse   mischance
mischief
  mischievious mischievous
mischievous, -ly
  mischif   mischief
  mischivus   mischievous
misconceive, -ceived, -ceiving
misconceiver
  misconcepshun misconception
misconception
  misconcieve misconceive
misconduct
  misconsepshun misconception
misconstrue, -strued, -struing
miscreant
misdeed
misdemeanour
  misdemener misdemeanour
misdo, -did, -done, -doing
  mise   mice
  miselanius   miscellaneous
  miselany   miscellany
  miself   myself
  miseltoe   mistletoe
miser
miserable, -ly
  miserabul   miserable
misere
miserly
misery, -ries
misfit, -fitted, -fitting
misfortune
misgiving
mishap
  mishapen   misshapen
  mishion   mission
mishmash

misile	missile
misiltoe	mistletoe
misis	misses
misive	missive
misus	missus
mislay, -laid, -laying	
misle	missal (book)
misle	missile (weapon)
mislead, -led, -leading	
misleader	
misleed	mislead
misnoma	misnomer
misnomer	
misogynist	
misogynous	
misogyny	
misojonist	misogynist
misojonous	misogynous
misojony	misogyny
mispell	misspell
misplace, -placed, -placing	
misplacement	
misplase	misplace
misprint, -ed, -ing	
misrabul	miserable
misrepresent, -ed, -ing	
miss, misses	
miss, missed, missing	
missal (book)	
missal	missile (weapon)
misselaney	miscellany
misselanius	miscellaneous
misselany	miscellany
misses (fail)	
misses	missus (wife)
misshape, -shaped, -shaping	
missile (weapon)	
missile	missal (book)
mission	
missionary, -ries	
missive	
misspell, misspelt, misspelling	
missus (wife)	
mist (cloud)	
mist	missed

mistake, -took, -taking	
mistaken	
misteltoe	mistletoe
mister	
misterey	mystery
misterius	mysterious
mistery	mystery
mistic	mystic
mistic	mystique
mistify	mystify
mistletoe	
mistreat, -ed, -ing	
mistress	
mistrial	
mistrust, -ed, -ing	
misty, -tier, -tiest	
misul	missal
misul	missile
misultoe	mistletoe
misunderstand, -stood, -standing	
misuse, -used, -using	
mite (small)	
mite	might (power)
miten	mitten
miter	mitre
mith	myth
mithical	mythical
mithology	mythology
mitie	mighty
mitigate, -gated, -gating	
mitre, -tred, -tring	
mitt	
mitten	
mix, mixed, mixing	
mixamotosis	myxomatosis
mixcher	mixture
mixchur	mixture
mixer	
mixture	
mix-up	
mizzenmast	
mnemonics	
mo	mow
moa (bird)	
moa	mower (lawn)
moan, moaned, moaning	
moaner	

moat
mob, mobbed, mobbing
mobile, -ly
   mobiliety   mobility
mobilisation
mobilise, -lised, -lising
mobility
moccasin
mock, mocked, mocking
mocker
mockery, -ries
mockingbird
   mockry   mockery
mock-up
modal (manner)
   modal   model
            (example)
   moddul   modal
   moddul   model
mode
model, -elled, -elling (example)
modeller
   moden   modern
moderate, -rated, -rating
moderation
moderator
modern, -ly
modernity, -ties
modest, -ly
modesty, -ties
modicum
   modifi   modify
modifiable
   modifiabul   modifiable
modification
modifier
modify, -fied, -fying
   modlin   maudlin
   modul   model
modular
modulate, -lated, -lating
modulation
modulator
module
   moduler   modular
   modulur   modular
mogo

mogul
mohair
Mohammedan
   mohare   mohair
moiety, -ties
   moischer   moisture
   moischur   moisture
   moisen   moisten
   moisun   moisten
moist, -ly
moisten, -ed, -ing
moisture
   mokasin   moccasin
moke
molar
   molases   molasses
molasses
   molasus   molasses
   mold   mould
mole
molecular, -ly
molecule
molest, -ed, -ing
molestation
   molicodle   mollycoddle
   molicodul   mollycoddle
moll
mollify, -fied, -fying
mollusc
mollycoddle, -dled, -dling
moloch
Molotov cocktail
   molt   malt (liquor)
   molt   moult (lose)
molten
   molusk   mollusc
molybdenum
moment
momentarily
momentary
momentous, -ly
momentum, -ta
   monakey   monarchy
monarch
monarchal, -ly
monarchic, -ally
monarchist

monarchy, -chies
monastery, -teries
monastic, -ally
monasticism
monastry   monastery
Monday
mone   moan
monetary, -rily
money, monies
moneychanger
money-grubber
money-grubbing
moneylender
money market
money order
monga   monger
mong
monger
Mongol
Mongolian
Mongolism
Mongoloid
mongoose, -gooses
mongrel
mongrul   mongrel
moniter   monitor
monitor, -ed, -ing
monk
monkey, -keys
monkey, -keyed, -keying
monkey-wrench
monochromatic, -ally
monochrome
monochromic
monocle
monocled
monocul   monocle
monogamist
monogamous
monogamus   monogamous
monogamy
monograf   monograph
monogram
monograph
monokrome   monochrome
monokside   monoxide
monolith

monolithic
monolog   monologue
monologue
monoplain   monoplane
monoplane
monopoley   monopoly
monopolisation
monopolise, -lised, -lising
monopoly, -lies
monorail
monosilabic   monosyllabic
monosilabul   monosyllable
monosyllabic, -ally
monosyllable
monotone
monotonous, -ly
monotonus   monotonous
monotony
monoxide
monsoon
monsoonal
monster
monstera deliciosa
monstrosity, -ties
monstrous, -ly
monstrus   monstrous
montage
month
monument
monumental, -ly
mooch, -ed, -ing
mood
moody, -dier, -diest
moon
moonlight
moonshine
moonstone
moony, -nier, -niest
moor, -ed, -ing (land)
moor   more (further)
Moor (Muslim)
moorhen
moose, moose (animal)
moose   mouse (rodent)
moose   mousse (food)
moosli   muesli
moot

moovabul   moveable
moove   move
mop, mopped, mopping
mope, moped, moping
moped
mopoke
moral, -ly
moralise, -lised, -lising
moralist
moralistic
moralitey   morality
morality, -ties
morass
moratorium, -toria, -toriums
moray, -rays (eel)
morays   mores (custom)
morbid, -ly
morbidity
mordant, -ly
mordern   modern
more, most (further)
more   moor (tie up)
moreover
mores (custom)
morfine   morphine
morg   morgue
morgage   mortgage
morganatic, -ally
morgige   mortgage
morgue
moribund, -ly
moribundity
Mormon
Mormonism
morn (morning)
morn   mourn (sorrow)
mornay
mornful   mournful
morning (day)
morning   mourning
                  (sorrowing)
moron
moronic
morose, -ly
morover   moreover
morow   morrow
morphine

morrow
morse code
morsel
mortafy   mortify
mortal, -ly
mortality, -ties
mortar
mortarboard
mortgage, -gaged, -gaging
mortgagee
mortgagor
mortice, -ticed, -ticing
mortifi   mortify
mortification
mortify, -fied, -fying
mortiss   mortice
mortuary, -ries
mos   moss
mosaic
moselle
moshun   motion
mosk   mosque
moskito   mosquito
mosque
mosquito, -toes
moss
most, -ly
mot
mote (dust)
mote   moat (ditch)
motel
moter   motor
motervate   motivate
motet
moth, moths
mothballs
mother
mother-in-law, mothers-in-law
motherland
mother-of-pearl
motif (figure)
motif   motive (reason)
motion, -ed, -ing
motivate, -vated, -vating
motivation
motivational
motive (reason)

motive | motif (figure)
motle | mottle
motley, -leys
motly | motley
moto | motto
motor, -ed, -ing
motorbike
motorcycle
motorcyclist
motorist
mottle, -tled, -tling
motto, -tos
mould, moulded, moulding
moulder, -ed, -ing
mouldy, -dier, -diest
moult, -ed, -ing (lose)
moult | malt (liquor)
mound
mount, mounted, mounting
mountain
mountaineer
mountainous, -ly
mountenus | mountainous
mountun | mountain
mourn, -ed, -ing (sorrow)
mourn | morn (morning)
mourner
mournful, -ly
mourning (sorrowing)
mourning | morning (day)
mouse, mice (rodent)
mouse, moused, mousing
mouse | moose (animal)
mouse | mousse (food)
moussaka
mousse (food)
moustache
mousy, -sier, -siest
mouth, mouths
mouthful, -fuls
mouthpeace | mouthpiece
mouthpiece
mouth-to-mouth
movabel | moveable
movabul | moveable
move, moved, moving

moveable, -ly
movement
movie
mow, mowed, mowing
mower
mownd | mound
mownt | mount
mowntain | mountain
mowntenus | mountainous
mowntun | mountain
mowse | mouse
mowth | mouth
mozzarella
Mr., Messrs.
Mrs.
Ms.
much, more, most
muchooal | mutual
mucilage
mucilaginous
muck, mucked, mucking
muckrake, -raked, -raking
muck-up
mucky, -ier, -iest
mucous (of mucus)
mucus
mud, mudded, mudding
muddie (crab)
muddie | muddy (dirty)
muddle, -dled, -dling
muddler
muddy, -died, -dying (dirty)
muddy, -dier, -diest (dirty)
muddy | muddie (crab)
mudel | muddle
mudflat
mudflow
mudguard
mudhopper
mudlark
mudle | muddle
mudrunner
mudskipper
mudslinger
muesli
muezzin
muff, -ed, -ing

muffin
muffle, -fled, -fling
muffler
  mufful — muffle
  mufin — muffin
mufti, -tis
mug, mugged, mugging
mugga
mugger
muggins
muggy, -gier, -giest
  mukus — mucous
  mukus — mucus
mulatto, -tos, -toes
  mulberie — mulberry
mulberry, -ries
mulch, -ed, -ing
mule
muleteer
mulga
mulgara
mulish, -ly
mull, -ed, -ing
mullet, -lets, -let
mulligatawny
mullion
mullock
mulloway
  multaple — multiple
  multch — mulch
multicultural
multifaceted
multifarious, -ly
  multifarius — multifarious
  multifaseted — multifaceted
multigrade
multilateral, -ly
multimillionaire
  multinashionul — multinational
multinational
multipartite
multiple
multiple sclerosis
  multipli — multiply
multiplication
multiplicative, -ly
multiplicity, -ties

multiplier
  multiplisity — multiplicity
multiply, -plied, -plying
  multipul — multiple
multitude
multitudinous, -ly
  multitudinus — multitudinous
  mulyun — mullion
mum
mumble, -bied, -bling
mumbo jumbo
  mumbul — mumble
  mumie — mummy
  mumifi — mummify
mummer
mummification
mummify, -fied, -fying
mummy, -mies
mummy, -mied, -mying
mumps
  mumy — mummy
munch, munched, munching
munchies
  mundain — mundane
mundane, -ly
  Munday — Monday
  munetry — monetary
  mungrel — mongrel
municipal, -ly
municipality, -ties
  munie — money
  munishun — munition
  munisipality — municipality
  munk — monk
  munky — monkey
  munth — month
  muny — money
  mur — myrrh
mural
murder, -ed, -ing
murderer
murderess
murderous, -ly
murk, -ily
murky, -kier, -kiest
  murmer — murmur
murmur, -ed, -ing

murrain
  murth   mirth
  murtle   myrtle
  mus   mews (stables)
  mus   muse(think)
muscat
muscatel
muscle, -cled, -cling (body)
  muscle   mussel (fish)
muscle-bound
Muscovy duck
muscular, -ly
muscularity
muse, mused, musing (think)
  muse   mews (stables)
  musel   muscle (body)
  musel   mussel (fish)
museum
mush, -ed, -ing
mushroom, -ed, -ing
mushy, -ier, -iest
music
musical, -ly
musician
  musishun   musician
musk
  muskatel   muscatel
musket
musketeer
musketry
muskrat, -rats
Muslim, -lims
muslin
mussel (fish)
  mussel   muscle (body)
must
  mustache   moustache
  mustash   moustache
mustang
mustard
muster, -ed, -ing
  musterd   mustard
  mustie   musty
mutant, -ly
mutate, -tated, -tating
mutation
mute, muted, muting

  muter   mutter
mutilate, -lated, -lating
mutilation
mutilator
  mutinear   mutineer
mutineer
mutinous, -ly
  mutinus   mutinous
mutiny, -nies
mutiny, -nied, -nying
  muton   mutton
mutt
mutter, -ed, -ing
mutton
mutton-bird
mutton-chops
mutual, -ly
mutuality
muu-muu
muzak
  muzul   muzzle
muzzle, -zled, -zling
myall
myna (bird)
  myna   miner (worker)
  myna   minor (less)
myopia
myopic
myriad
myrrh
myrtle
myself
mysterious, -ly
  mysterius   mysterious
mystery, -ries
mystic (symbol)
mystical, -ly
mysticism
mystification
mystify, -fied, -fying
mystique (secret)
  mystisism   mysticism
  mystry   mystery
myth
mythical, -ly
mythology, -gies
myxomatosis

Nn

nab, nabbed, nabbing
  nabor   neighbour
  nachur   nature
  nachurul   natural
  nack   knack
  nacker   knacker
  nacker   nacre
nacre (pearl)
nacreous
nadir
nag, nagged, nagging
nagger
nail, nailed, nailing
naive, -ly
naivety
naked, -ly
nakedness
  nakid   naked
  nale   nail
namby-pamby, -bies
name, named, naming
namely
namesake
  nanie   nanny
nankeen kestrel
nanny, -ies
nannygai
nanny-goat
  nany   nanny
nap, napped, napping
napalm
  naparm   napalm
nape
napery
naphtha
naphthalene
  napie   nappy
napkin

nappe (rock)
nappy, -pies (cloth)
  napsack   knapsack
  naptha   naphtha
  narate   narrate
  narative   narrative
narcissism
narcissistic
narcissus, -cissuses, -cissi
narcosis
narcotic
nark, -ed, -ing
  narl   gnarl
  narow   narrow
narrate, -rated, -rating
narration
narrative, -ly
narrator
narrow, -ly
  narsissism   narcissism
  narsissistic   narcissistic
  narsisus   narcissus
nasal, -ly
nasalisation
nasalise, -lised, -lising
nasality
nascence
nascency
nascent, -ly
  nasel   nasal
  nash   gnash
  nashun   nation
  nashunal   national
  nastie   nasty
nasty, -tier, -tiest
  nat   gnat
natal
natch
  natel   natal
  nater   natter
  nateral   natural
  naty   natty
nation
national, -ly
nationalism
nationalist
nationalistic, -ally

nationality, -ties		nayl	nail
nation-state		Nazi, -zis	
native		Nazism	
Nativity		nead	knead
Natsi	Nazi	nead	need
natter, -ed, -ing		neadel	needle
natty, -tier, -tiest		neadil	needle
natul	natal	neadle	needle
natur	nature	neadless	needless
natural, -ly		neap	
naturalisation		near, -ed, -ing	
naturalise, -lised, -lising		nearby	
naturalism		nearly	
naturalist		nearside	
naturalistic		neat, -ly	
nature		nebula, -lae, -las	
naturopathy		nebulous, -ly	
naty	natty	nebulus	nebulous
naught		necesarey	necessary
naughty, -tier, -tiest		necesitate	necessitate
nausea		necesitey	necessity
nauseate, -ated, -ating		necessarily	
nauseation		necessary, -saries	
nauseous, -ly		necessitate, -tated, -tating	
nautical, -ly		necessity, -ties	
nautilus, -luses		neck	
naval (ship)		neckerchief	
naval	navel (body)	neckliss	necklace
nave (church)		necklace	
nave	knave (rogue)	necksus	nexus
navel (body)		necktie	
navel orange		necromancer	
navie	navvy	necromancy	
navie	navy	necromanser	necromancer
navigabel	navigable	necromansey	necromancy
navigable, -bly		necrofilia	necrophilia
navigate, -gated, -gating		necrofiliac	necrophiliac
navigation		necrofilism	necrophilism
navigator		necrophilia	
navul	naval (ship)	necrophiliac	
navul	navel (body)	necrophilism	
navvy, -vies (worker)		necropolis, -lises	
navy, -vies (warships)		nectar	
naw	gnaw	nectarine	
nay (no)		nee (name)	
nay	neigh (horse)	nee	knee (limb)
naybour	neighbour	need, -ed, -ing (necessary)	

need	knead (dough)	neither (nor)	
need	kneed (use knee)	neither	nether (below)
needful, -ly		nek	neck
needle, -dled, -dling		neklace	necklace
needless, -ly		neklis	necklace
needlework		nekrofilia	necrophilia
needul	needle	nekropolis	necropolis
neel	kneel	nell	knell
neer	near	nemesis, -ses	
ne'er-do-well		nemisis	nemesis
neet	neat	nemonics	mnemonics
nefarious, -ly		neofite	neophyte
nefarius	nefarious	Neolithic	
nefew	nephew	neologise, -gised, -gising	
negate, -gated, -gating		neon	
negation		neophyte	
negative, -tived, -tiving		nephew	
negativity		nephrism	
negatory		nephritic	
neglect, -ed, -ing		nephritis	
neglectful, -ly		nepotism	
negligee		Neptune	
negligence		nerd	
negligense	negligence	nerve, nerved, nerving	
negligent, -ly		nerve centre	
negligibility		nerve-racking	
negligible, -bly		nerveous	nervous
negligibul	negligible	nerveus	nervous
neglijay	negligee	nervous, -ly	
negoshabul	negotiable	nervy, -vier, -viest	
negoshiate	negotiate	nesessary	necessary
negotiability		nesessitate	necessitate
negotiable, -bly		nesessitey	necessity
negotiant		nesessity	necessity
negotiate, -ated, -ating		nesle	nestle
negotiation		nest, -ed, -ing	
Negro, -groes		nestle, -tled, -tling	
Negroid		nesul	nestle
neice	niece	net, netted, netting	
neigh (horse)		netball	
neigh	nay (no)	netha	neither (nor)
neighbor	neighbour	netha	nether (below)
neighbour		nether (below)	
neighbourhood		nether	neither (nor)
neighbouring		nettle, -tled, -tling	
neighbourly		nettul	nettle
		network	

neumatic	pneumatic
neural, -ly	
neuralgia	
neuralgic	
neuritic	
neuritis	
neurological, -ly	
neurologist	
neurology	
neurone	
neurosis, -ses	
neurotic, -ally	
neuter	
neutral, -ly	
neutralisation	
neutralise, -lised, -lising	
neutrality	
neutron	
neva	never
never-never	
nevertheless	
new (novel)	
new	gnu (animal)
new	knew
newclear	nuclear
newcleus	nucleus
newcomer	
newfangled	
Newfoundland	
newmatic	pneumatic
newmonia	pneumonia
newral	neural
newrologist	neurologist
newrone	neurone
newrosis	neurosis
newrotic	neurotic
news	
newsagency	
newsagent	
newscast, -cast, -casting	
newscaster	
newsletter	
newsman, -men	
newspaper	
newspeak	
newsprint	
news reader	

newsreel	
newt	
newter	neuter
newtralise	neutralise
newtron	neutron
New Zealander	
next	
next of kin	
nexus, nexus	
ni	nigh
nib	
nibbel	nibble
nibble, -bled, -bling	
nibbler	
nibul	nibble
nice, nicer, nicest	
nicety, -ties	
niche	
nick, -ed, -ing	
nickel, -elled, -elling	
nickerbockers	knickerbockers
nickers	knickers
nickle	nickel
nicknack	knick-knack
nickname, -named, -naming	
nicks	nix
nicotine	
niece	
niether	neither
nifarius	nefarious
nife	knife
niftie	nifty
nifty, -tier, -tiest	
nigel	niggle
nigerd	niggard
niggard	
niggle, -gled, -gling	
nigh	
night, -ly (time)	
night	knight (lord)
nightcap	
nightclub	
nightdress	
nightingale	
nightjar	
nightmare	
nightmarish	

nightsoil		nitrify, -fied, -fying	
nightwatchman		nitrite	
nigle	niggle	nitrogen	
niglect	neglect	nitrogenous	
nigul	niggle	nitrogliserine	nitroglycerine
nihilism		nitroglycerine	
nil		nitrojen	nitrogen
nilon	nylon	nitting	knitting
nimble, -bler, -blest		nitty-gritty	
nimbul	nimble	nitwit	
nimbus, -bi, -buses		nives	knives
nimf	nymph	nix	
nimph	nymph	no (denial)	
nine		no	know
ninepins		nob (person)	
nineteen		nob	knob (handle)
nineteenth		no-ball	
ninety, -ties		nobble, -bled, -bling	
ninie	ninny	nobie	knobby
ninny, -nies		nobility, -ties	
ninth, -ly		noble, nobler, noblest	
nion	neon	nobleman, -men	
nip, nipped, nipping		nobody, -bodies	
nipie	nippy	nobul	noble
niple	nipple	nock	knock
nipper		nocker	knocker
nipple		nockneed	knock-kneed
nippy, -pier, -piest		nocturnal, -ly	
nipul	nipple	nocturne	
nipy	nippy	nod, nodded, nodding	
nirvana		nodal	
nise	nice	noddy, -dies	
nisitey	nicety	node	
nit (insect)		nodular	
nit	knit (stitch)	nodule	
nite	knight (lord)	Noel	
nite	night (time)	noes (denials)	
niter	nitre	noes	knows
nither	neither	noes	nose (on face)
nitpick, -ed, -ing		noggin (cup, head)	
nitpicker		nogging (timber)	
nitrate, -trated, -trating		no-go	
nitration		no-hoper	
nitre		noise, noised, noising	
nitric		noisily	
nitrifi	nitrify	noisiness	
nitrification		noisome, -ly	

noisy, noisier, noisiest
noisy miner
  noledge   knowledge
  noll   knoll
nomad
nomadic, -ally
nomadism
no-man's-land
nom de plume
  nome   gnome
nomenclature
nominal, -ly
nominate, -nated, -nating
nomination
nominative
nominator
nominee
  non   none
nonaggression
  nonagressiun   nonaggression
nonagon
nonce
nonchalance
non-combatant
non-commissioned
non-committal, -ly
non compos
  non compus   non compos
non-conducting
non-conformance
non-conformity
nondescript
none
nonentity, -ties
nonetheless
non-fiction
non-fictional
nonflammable
nong
  no-nonsence   no-nonsense
no-nonsense
nonpareil
nonplus, -plussed, -plussing
non-productive, -ly
non-proliferation
non-representational
non-sectarian

  nonsence   nonsense
nonsense
nonsensical, -ly
non-U
non-violence
non-violent, -ly
noodle
  noogar   nougat
nook
noon
noose, noosed, noosing
nope
nor
  nor   gnaw
Nordic
norm
normal, -ly
normalcy
normalisation
normalise, -lised, -lising
Norman
normative, -ly
  norsia   nausea
  norsiate   nauseate
  nort   naught (ruin)
  nort   nought (nil)
  nortey   naughty
north
northerly
northern
northerner
northward, -ly
  nortickel   nautical
  nortie   naughty
nose, nosed, nosing (on face)
  nose   knows
  nose   noes (denial)
nosebag
nosedive, -dived, -diving
nosegay
nosey, -sier, -siest
nosily
nosiness
nostalgia
nostalgic, -ally
  nostrem   nostrum
nostril

nostrim	nostrum	novitiate	
nostrum		now	
nosy, -sier, -siest		nowadays	
not (denial)		nowhere	
not	knot (tie)	nowing	knowing
nota bene		nowledge	knowledge
notability		noxious, -ly	
notable, -bly		noxius	noxious
notarial, -ly		nozzle	
notary, -ries		nozzul	nozzle
notation		nu	gnu (animal)
notch, -ed, -ing		nu	knew
note, noted, noting		nu	new (novel)
notefy	notify	nuance	
nothing		nuanse	nuance
notice, -ticed, -ticing		nub	
noticeable, -bly		nubile	
noticeabul	noticeable	nuckle	knuckle
notifiable		nuclear	
notification		nuclear bomb	
notifier		nuclear energy	
notify, -fied, -fying		nuclear family	
notion		nuclear fishun	nuclear fission
notional, -ly		nuclear fission	
not negotiable		nuclear fusion	
notories	notorious	nuclear power	
notoriety, -ties		nuclear reaction	
notorious, -ly		nuclear reactor	
notorius	notorious	nucleus, -clei, -cleuses	
notwithstanding		nude, -ly	
nougar	nougat	nudge, nudged, nudging	
nougat		nudism	
nought		nudist	
noughts-and-crosses		nudity	
noun		nuge	nudge
nourish, -ed, -ing		nugget	
nourishingly		nuisance	
nourishment		nulifi	nullify
nous		null	
nouveau riche, nouveaux riches		nulla-nulla	
novel		nullification	
novelette		nullify, -fied, -fying	
novelist		num	numb
novella, novellas, novelle		numatic	pneumatic
novelty, -ties		numb, numbed, numbing	
November		number, -ed, -ing	
novice		numberless	

numberplate
numbness
numbskull
numeracy
numeral
   numerasy   numeracy
numerate, -rated, -rating
numeration
numerator
numerical, -ly
   numericul   numerical
numerological
numerology
numerous, -ly
   numerus   numerous
numismatics
numismatist
   numonia   pneumonia
nun (woman)
   nun   none (no one)
nunnery, -neries
   nupshal   nuptial
nuptial
   nural   neural
   nuralgia   neuralgia
   nurcher   nurture
   nuritis   neuritis
   nurologist   neurologist
   nurone   neurone
   nurosis   neurosis
   nurotic   neurotic
nurse, nursed, nursing
nursery, -eries
   nursrey   nursery
nurture, -tured, -turing
   nurve   nerve
   nusance   nuisance
   nuse   news
   nuspaper   newspaper
nut, nutted, nutting
   nuter   neuter
nutcracker
nutmeg
   nutral   neutral
nutrient
nutriment
   nutrishun   nutrition

   nutrishus   nutritious
nutrition
nutritional, -ly
nutritionist
nutritious, -ly
   nutron   neutron
nuts
nutshell
nutty, -tier, -tiest
   nuty   nutty
   nuzul   nuzzle
nuzzle, -zled, -zling
nylon
   nymf   nymph
nymph
nymphomania
nymphomaniac

Oo

oaf
oak
oar (boat)
  oar awe (dread)
  oar or
  oar ore (rock)
oasis, oases
oat
oath, oaths
oatmeal
  obay obey
  obbese obese
obduracy
  obdurasey obduracy
obdurate, -ly
obedience
  obediense obedience
obedient, -ly
obeisance
  obeisanse obeisance
obelisk
obese, -ly
obesity
  obessence obeisance
obey, -ed, -ing
obituary, -aries
  objecshun objection
  objay dart objet d'art
object, -ed, -ing
objection
objectionable, -bly
  objectionabul objectionable
objective, -ly
objectivity
objector
objet d'art, objets d'art
oblation
  obleek oblique

obligate,-gated, -gating
obligation
obligatory
oblige, obliged, obliging
  oblik oblique
oblique, obliqued, obliquing
obliquity, -ties
obliterate, -rated, -rating
oblivion
oblivious, -ly
  oblivius oblivious
oblong
obloquy, -quies
  obnokshus obnoxious
obnoxious, -ly
  obo oboe
oboe
oboist
obscene, -ly
obscenity, -ties
obscure, -scured, -scuring
obscure, -scurer, -scurest
obscurity, -ties
obsecrate, -crated, -crating
  obseen obscene
  obsekwies obsequious
  obsekwius obsequious
obsequious, -ly
observance
observant, -ly
observation
observatory, -tories
  observatry observatory
observe, -served, -serving
  obseshun obsession
obsess, -ed, -ing
obsession
obsessive, -ly
obsolescence
obsolescent, -ly
  obsolesense obsolescence
  obsolesent obsolescent
obsolete, -ly
obstacle
  obstacul obstacle
  obstatrician obstetrician
obstetric, -ally

obstetrician
obstetrics
  obstetrishen   obstetrician
  obstetrishun   obstetrician
obstinacy, -cies
  obstinasey   obstinacy
obstinate, -ly
obstreperous, -ly
  obstreperus   obstreperous
  obstrucshun   obstruction
obstruct, -ed, -ing
obstruction
obstructive, -ly
obtain, -ed, -ing
  obtane   obtain
  obtroode   obtrude
  obtroosive   obtrusive
obtrude, -truded, -truding
obtrusive, -ly
obtuse, -ly
obverse, -ly
obviate, -ated, -ating
obviation
obvious, -ly
  obvius   obvious
  ocasion   occasion
  occashun   occasion
occasion, -ed, -ing
occasional, -ly
Occident
occidental
occlude, -cluded, -cluding
  occlushun   occlusion
occlusion
  occular   ocular
occult
occultism
occupancy
occupant
occupation
occupational
  occupent   occupant
  occupi   occupy
occupy, -pied, -pying
occur, -curred, -curring
  occurense   occurrence
occurrence

ocean
Oceania
oceanic
  oceanografey   oceanography
oceanographer
oceanography
ocelot
  ocher   ochre
ochre, ochred, ochring
ochrous
ocker
  Ocktober   October
o'clock
  oclood   occlude
  ocloosion   occlusion
  ocsident   Occident
octagon
octagonal, -ly
octane
octave
octavo
octet
October
octogenarian
octopus, -puses, -pi
ocular, -ly
  ocult   occult
  ocupancy   occupancy
  ocupant   occupant
  ocupi   occupy
  ocur   occur
  ocurence   occurrence
  ocurents   occurrence
  od   odd
odd, -ly
oddball
oddbod
oddity, ties
oddment
odds
odds-on
  odeclone   eau-de-Cologne
  oderus   odorous
  odiferus   odoriferous
odious, -ly
  odissey   odyssey
odium

odius — odious
odontology
odor — odour
odoriferous, -ly
odorous, -ly
odour
odyssey
Oedipus complex
oenin
oesofagus — oesophagus
oesophagus, -gi
oestrogen
of
  of — off (away)
  ofal — offal
  ofence — offence
  ofend — offend
  ofen — often
  ofense — offence
  ofensive — offensive
  ofer — offer
off (away)
  off — of
offal
off-beat
off-colour
offcourse
off-cut
offence
offend, -ed, -ing
offender
  offense — offence
offensive, -ly
offer, -ed, -ing
offering
offertory, -ries
offhand
offhanded, -ly
office
officer
official, -ly
officialdom
officiate, -ated, -ating
officiation
officious, -ly
offing
  offise — office

offishul — official
offishus — officious
off-limits
off-load, -loaded, -loading
off-peak
off-putting
off-season
offset, -set, -setting
offshoot
offshore
off side (cricket)
offside (rugby)
offsider
offspring
  oficial — official
  oficiate — officiate
  oficious — officious
  ofis — office
  ofiser — officer
  ofishal — official
  ofishiate — officiate
  ofishus — officious
  ofset — offset
  ofshoot — offshoot
  ofside — offside
  ofspring — offspring
oft
often
  ogel — ogle
  oger — ogre
ogle, ogled, ogling
ogre
oh
ohm
oil, oiled, oiling
oilcloth
oilfield
  oilly — oily
oil rig
oilskin
oily, oilier, oiliest
ointment
  oister — oyster
  ok — oak
okay
  oks — ox
  oksalic acid — oxalic acid

oksidate	oxidate	on	own
okside	oxide	once	
oksident	Occident	oncore	encore
oksidise	oxidise	oncourse	
oksyacetylene	oxyacetylene	one (number)	
oksygen	oxygen	one	won (win)
oksymoron	oxymoron	one-eyed	
old, older, oldest		one-off	
olden		oner	owner
oldish		oneres	onerous
old-timer		onerous, -ly	
oleaginous		onership	ownership
oleaginus	oleaginous	oneself	
oleander		one-sided, -ly	
olearia		onest	honest
olfachun	olfaction	one-upmanship	
olfaction		oniks	onyx
olfactory, -ries		onion	
olfactry	olfactory	onist	honest
oligarch		onor	honour
oligarchic		onistey	honesty
oligarchy, -chies		onley	only
oligarkey	oligarchy	only	
Olimpic	Olympic	onorarey	honorary
oliv	olive	onorarium	honorarium
olive		onrabul	honourable
omelette		onrush	
omen		onset	
ominous, -ly		on side (cricket)	
ominus	ominous	onside (rugby)	
omishun	omission	onslaught	
omission		onslawt	onslaught
omit, omitted, omitting		onslort	onslaught
omlet	omelette	onto	
omnibus, -buses		ontological	
omnipotence		ontology	
omnipotense	omnipotence	ontray	entree
omnipotent, -ly		ontreprener	entrepreneur
omnipresence		onus	
omnipresent		onward	
omniscience		onwards	
omniscient, -ly		onyx	
omnisiense	omniscience	oomph	
omnisient	omniscient	ooze, oozed, oozing	
omnivorous, -ly		opacity, -ties	
omnivorus	omnivorous	opake	opaque
on		opal	

opaline
opaque, opaqued, opaquing
  opasity   opacity
  opeate   opiate
open, -ed, -ing
openly
open-minded
open-range
open-verdict
opera
operable, -bly
  operabul   operable
operate, -rated, -rating
  operater   operator
operatic, -ally
operation
operational, -ly
operative, -ly
operator
operetta
ophthalmic
ophthalmologist
ophthalmology
opiate, -ated, -ating
opine, opined, opining
opinion
opinionated
  opinyun   opinion
opium
  oponent   opponent
  oportune   opportune
  oportunitey   opportunity
  opose   oppose
  oposishun   opposition
  oposite   opposite
  oposition   opposition
opossum
  oposum   opossum
opponency
opponent
opportune, -ly
opportunism
opportunist
opportunity, -ties
oppose, -posed, -posing
opposite
opposition

oppress, -ed, -ing
oppression
oppressive, -ly
oppressor
opprobrious, -ly
opprobrium
  oprabul   operable
  oprate   operate
  opreshun   oppression
  opresive   oppressive
  opress   oppress
  opshun   option
  opshunul   optional
opt, -ed, -ing
  opthalmic   ophthalmic
  opthalmology   ophthalmology
optic
optical, -ly
optician
optics
optimism
optimist
optimistic, -ally
optimum, -ma, -mums
option
optional, -ly
  optishun   optician
optometrist
optometry
opulence
  opulense   opulence
opulent, -ly
opus, opuses, opera
or
  or   awe (dread)
  or   oar (boat)
  or   ore (rock)
  ora   aura
oracle
  oracul   oracle
oracular, -ly
oral, -ly (spoken)
  oral   aural (hear)
  orangatang   orang-outang
orange
orang-outang
  orashun   oration

orater	orator	orfanaje	orphanage
oration		orful	awful
orator		orfun	orphan
oratorical, -ly		organ	
oratorio, -rios		organdie, -dies	
oratory, -ries		organic, -ally	
oratrey	oratory	organisation	
orb		organise, -nised, -nising	
orbit, -ed, -ing		organism	
orbital		organist	
orcestra	orchestra	organza	
orcestral	orchestral	orgasm	
orcestrate	orchestrate	orgenism	organism
orchard		orger	auger (tool)
orchardist		orger	augur (omen)
orchestra		orgey	orgy
orchestral, -ly		orgiastic	
orchestrate, -trated, -trating		orgy, -gies	
orchestration		orical	auricle (ear)
orchid		orical	oracle (seer)
orcid	orchid	oriel	
ordain, -ed, -ing		orient	
ordanal	ordinal	oriental	
ordane	ordain	orientate, -tated, -tating	
ordeal		orientation	
ordenrey	ordinary	orienteering	
order, -ed, -ing		orifice	
orderly, -lies		orifise	orifice
orderliness		origami	
ordinal		origin	
ordinance (law)		original, -ly	
ordinariness		originality, -ties	
ordinary, -ries		originate, -nated, -nating	
ordination		oringe	orange
ordinry	ordinary	oriole	
orditer	auditor	orjy	orgy
orditrey	auditory	orkestra	orchestra
ordnance (weapons)		orkestral	orchestral
ordnance	ordinance (law)	orkestrate	orchestrate
ordure		orkestration	orchestration
ore (rock)		orkid	orchid
ore	oar (boat)	ornament	
ore	or (either)	ornamental, -ly	
ore	awe (dread)	ornamentation	
oregano		ornate, -ly	
orfan	orphan	ornimant	ornament
orfanage	orphanage	orning	awning

ornithologist
ornithology
orotund
orphan
orphanage
Orphism
orris
  orspishus   auspicious
  orstruck   awestruck
  orsum   awesome
  ort   aught
  ort   ought
  orthedoks   orthodox
orthodontic
orthodontics
orthodontist
orthodox
orthodoxy, -doxies
  orthografey   orthography
orthography, -phies
orthopaedic
orthopaedics
orthopaedist
orthopaedy
  orthopeadic   orthopaedic
  orthority   authority
  oscilation   oscillation
oscillate, -lated, -lating (move)
  oscillate   osculate (kiss)
oscillation
oscillator
oscilloscope
osculate, -lated, -lating (kiss)
  osculate   oscillate (move)
  oseanic   oceanic
  oselot   ocelot
  oshun   ocean
osier
  osifi   ossify
  osler   ostler
osmosis
  ospray   osprey
osprey, -preys
  ossifi   ossify
ossification
ossify, -fied, -fying
  ossilate   oscillate

  ossilation   oscillation
  ossiloscope   oscilloscope
  osteapath   osteopath
ostensible, -bly
  ostensibul   ostensible
ostentation
ostentatious, -ly
osteoarthritis
osteomyelitis
osteopath
osteopathic
osteopathy
ostler
ostracise, -cised, -cising
ostracism
  ostrasise   ostracise
  ostrasism   ostracism
ostrich
  ote   oat
  oter   otter
  oth   oath
other
otherwise
otherworldly
otic
otiose, -ly
otiosity
  otoman   ottoman
otter
ottoman, -mans
ouch
ought (should)
  ought   aught (any part)
ouija
  oul   owl
ounce
  ounse   ounce
our (us)
  our   hour
  ourly   hourly
ours
ourself, -selves
oust, ousted, ousting
ouster
out, -ed, -ing
outback

outbilding / outbuilding
outboard
outbrake / outbreak
outbreak
outbuilding
outburst
outcast
outcome
outcri / outcry
outcrop, -cropped, -cropping
outcry, -cries
outdate, -dated, -dating
outdo, -done, -doing
outdoor
outdoors
outer
outfall
outfield
outfit, -fitted, -fitting
outflank, -ed, -ing
outfox, -ed, -ing
outgoing
outgrow, -grew, -grown, -growing
outgrowth
outhouse
outhowse / outhouse
outlandish, -ly
outlast, -ed, -ing
outlaw
outlawry
outlay, -laid, -laying
outlet
outline, -lined, -lining
outlive, -lived, -living
outlook
outlying
outmode, -moded, -moding
out-of-date
out-of-doors
out-of-pocket
out-of-the-way
outpatient
outpayshent / outpatient
outperform, -ed, -ing
outplay, -ed, -ing
outpoint, -ed, -ing
outpooring / outpouring

outpost
outpouring
output
outrage, -raged, -raging
outrageous, -ly
outraygus / outrageous
outrider
outrigger
outright
outrite / outright
outset
outside
outsider
outsize
outskirts
outspoken, -ly
outstanding, -ly
outstretch, -ed, -ing
outstrip, -stripped, -stripping
outward, -ly
outwards
outweigh
outwit, -witted, -witting
ouze / ooze
ov / of
oval, -ly
ovarey / ovary
ovary, -ries
ovate
ovation
oven
ovenproof
ovenware
ovenwear / ovenware
over, -ly
overall
overarm
overawe, -awed, -awing
overawl / overall
overbalance, -anced, -ancing
overbalanse / overbalance
overbare / overbear
overbear, -bore, -borne, -bearing
overbid, -bid, -bidding
overboard
overbord / overboard
overbridge

overcast, -cast, -casting
overcharge, -charged, -charging
overcoat
overcome, -came, -come, -coming
  overdew   overdue
overdo, -did, -done, -doing
overdose, -dosed, -dosing
overdraft
overdraw, -drew, -drawn, -drawing
overdress, -ed, -ing
overdrive, -drove, -driven, -driving
  overdu   overdue
overdue
overestimate, -mated, -mating
overestimation
overflow, -flowed, -flowing
overgrown
overhang, -hung, -hanging
overhaul, -ed, -ing
  overhawl   overhaul
overhead
overhear, -heard, -hearing
overhearer
  overhed   overhead
  overherd   overheard
  overhere   overhear
  overjoid   overjoyed
overjoyed
overkill
overland
overlander
overlap, -lapped, -lapping
overlay, -laid, -laying
overleaf
  overleef   overleaf
overlie, -lay, -lain, -lying (lie over)
  overlie   overly
overlook
overly (excessively)
  overly   overlie
overnight
  overnite   overnight
  overore   overawe
  overought   overwrought
overpass
overpower, -ed, -ing
  overeach   overreach

  overeech   overreach
  overiding   overriding
overreach, -ed, -ing
override, -rode, -ridden, -riding
  overrool   overrule
overrule, -ruled, -ruling
overrun, -ran, -run, -running
  overule   overrule
  overun   overrun
overseas (abroad)
oversee, -saw, -seen, -seeing
overseer
overshadow, -ed, -ing
overshoot, -shot, -shooting
oversight
  oversite   oversight
overstate, -stated, -stating
overstatement
overstay, -ed, -ing
overstep, -stepped, -stepping
overstock, -ed, -ing
oversubscribed
overt, -ly
overtake, -taken, -taking
  overtaks   overtax
overtax
overthrow, -thrown, -throwing
overtime, -timed, -timing
overtone
overture, -tured, -turing
overturn, -ed, -ing
overview
  overwait   overweight
  overwate   overweight
overweight
  overwelm   overwhelm
  overwerk   overwork
overwhelm, -ed, -ing
overwork, -worked, -working
overwrought
ovine
  ovipares   oviparous
  oviparis   oviparous
oviparous, -ly
  oviparus   oviparous
ovoid (egg)
  ovoid   avoid (evade)

ovulate, -lated, -lating
ovulation
ovule
ovum, ova
   owa   hour
   owa   our
owe, owed, owing (debt)
   owe   oh (cry)
owl
own, -ed, -ing
   ownce   ounce
owner
ownership
   ownly   only
   owst   oust
   owt   out
ox, oxen
oxalis
oxidate, -dated, -dating
oxidation
oxide
oxidisable
   oxidisabul   oxidisable
oxidisation
oxidise, -dised, -dising
oxidiser
   oxigenate   oxygenate
oxyacetylene
oxygen
oxygenate, -nated, -nating
oxygenation
oxygenise, -nised, -nising
oxymoron, -mora
oyster
Oz
ozone
ozonize, -ized, -izing
ozonosphere

Pp

pace, paced, pacing
pacemaker
pacer

pach	patch
pachwork	patchwork

pacific, -ally
pacification
pacifier
pacifism
pacifist
pacify, -fied, -fying
pack, -ed, -ing
package
packer
packet
packhorse

packije	package

pact
pad, padded, padding
paddle, -dled, -dling
paddler
paddle-steamer
paddock

paddul	paddle

paddy, -dies
paddy-wagon

pade	paddy
padie	paddy

padlock, -ed, -ing
padre

padrey	padre
pady	paddy

paediatrician
paediatrics
pagan
paganism
page, paged, paging
pageant

pageantry, -ries

pagentry	pageantry

pageboy
pager
pagoda
pail (bucket)

pail	pale (white)

pain (ache)

pain	pane (glass)

painful, -ly
pain-killer
painstaking, -ly
paint, -ed, -ing
painter
pair, -ed, -ing (two)

pair	pare (trim)
pair	pear (fruit)

pakeha
pal, palled, palling (friend)
palace

palase	palace

palatable, -bly
palatal, -ly (taste)
palate (mouth)

palate	palette (board)
palate	pallet (bed)
palate	pellet (ball)

palatial, -ly (palace)
pale, paled, paling (white)
pale, paler, palest

pale	pail (bucket)

palette (board)

palette	pallet (bed)
paliate	palliate
palid	pallid

palindrome
paling
palisade, -saded, -sading
pall, palled, palling (satiate)
pallbearer
pallet (bed)

pallet	palette (paint)
pallet	pellet (ball)

palliate, -ated, -ating
palliation
palliative, -ly
pallid, -ly

pall-mall (game)
pall-mall   pell-mell
           (haste)
pallor
palm, -ed, -ing
palmist
palmistry
palmy, -mier, -miest
palomino, -nos
palor   pallor
palpable, -bly
palpabul   palpable
palpitate, -tated, -tating
palpitation
palsie   palsy
palsied
palsy, -sies
paltrie   paltry
paltriness
paltry, -trier, -triest
pamplet   pamphlet
pampas
pamper, -ed, -ing
pamphlet
pamphleteer
pan, panned, panning
panacea
panache
Panama hat
panash   panache
pancake, -caked, -caking
pancreas
pancreatic
panda (animal)
pandemonium
pander, -ed, -ing (indulge)
pane (glass)
pane   pain (ache)
paneful   painful
panegyric, -ally
panel, -elled, -elling
panellist
panestaking   painstaking
pang
panic, -icked, -icking
paniced   panicked
panicky

panic-stricken
panigiric   panegyric
panik   panic
pannier
pannikin
panorama
panoramic, -ally
pansie   pansy
pansy, -sies
pant, -ed, -ing
pantaloon
pantechnicon
pantheism
pantheist
pantheistic, -ally
pantheon
panther
panthion   pantheon
panties
pantihose
pantingly
pantograf   pantograph
pantograph
pantomime
pantomine   pantomime
pantrey   pantry
pantry, -ries
pants
panza   panzer
panzer
pap
papa
papacy, -cies
papal
papasy   papacy
paper
paperback
paperbark
paperboy
paperclip
paper-mache   papier-mâché
paperwait   paperweight
paperweight
papier-mâché
papirus   papyrus
papism
papoose

papouse	papoose	parameter	
pappa	papa	paramiter	parameter
pappoose	papoose	paramoor	paramour
papprika	paprika	paramount	
pappyrus	papyrus	paramour	
paprica	paprika	paramownt	paramount
paprika		paranoia	
papul	papal	paranoiac	
papyrus, -ri		paranoid	
parable		parapet	
parabola		paraphernalia	
parabul	parable	paraphrase, -phrased, -phrasing	
parachute		paraplegic	
paracide	parricide	paraplijic	paraplegic
paracleet	paraclete	parashoot	parachute
paraclete		parashute	parachute
parade, -raded, -rading		parasite	
paradice	paradise	parasitic, -ally	
paradigm		parasitism	
paradime	paradigm	parasol	
paradise		parasoll	parasol
paradoks	paradox	paratrooper	
paradox		parboil, -ed, -ing	
parady	parody	parboyle	parboil
parafernalia	paraphernalia	parcel, -celled, -celling	
paraffin		parch, -ed, -ing	
parafin	paraffin	parchment	
parafrase	paraphrase	pardon, -ed, -ing	
paragon		pardonable	
paragraf	paragraph	pardonabul	pardonable
paragraph		pardoner	
parakeet		pare (trim)	
parakete	parakeet	pare	pair (two
paralax	parallax	pare	pear (fruit)
paralel	parallel	parent	
paralelagram	parallelogram	parentage	
paralise	paralyse	parental, -ly	
paralisis	paralysis	parenthesis, -ses	
paralitic	paralytic	parentige	parentage
parallax		parfait	
parallel, -leled, -leling or -lelled, -lelling		parfay	parfait
		pariah	
parallelogram		parie	parry
paralyse, -lysed, -lysing		parish, parishes	
paralysis		parishioner	
paralytic		parishoner	parishioner
paramedical		pariside	parricide

parisidul	parricidal	parsimony	
parity		parsley	
park, -ed, -ing		parslie	parsley
parka		parsly	parsley
parket	parquet	parsnip	
parking-meter		parson	
Parkinson's disease		parsonage	
parlament	parliament	parsonige	parsonage
parlance		parsul	parcel
parlans	parlance	part, -ed, -ing	
parlay	parley	partake, -took, -taken, -taking	
parlement	parliament	partial, -ly	
parlementarey	parliamentary	partiality, -ties	
parlementry	parliamentary	participant	
parler	parlour	participate, -pated, -pating	
parlermade	parlour-maid	participle	
parley, -leyed, -leying		participul	participle
parliament		particle	
parliamentarian		particul	particle
parliamentary		particular, -ly	
parlour		partie	party
parlour-maid		partime	part-time
parm	palm	partisan	
parmist	palmist	partishun	partition
parochial, -ly		partisipant	participant
parochialism		partisipate	participate
parody, -dies		partisipul	participle
parody, -died, -dying		partition, -ed, -ing	
parograf	paragraph	partly	
paragraph	paragraph	partner, -ed, -ing	
parokial	parochial	partridge	
paroksism	paroxysm	partrige	partridge
parole, -roled, -roling		part-time	
paroll	parole	party, -ties	
parot	parrot	pars	pass
paroxysm		pary	parry
parquet, -queted, -queting		pasabul	passable
parranoia	paranoia	pascal	paschal
parricide		paschal	
parrot		pascher	pasture
parry, parried, parrying		pase	pace
parse, parsed, parsing		pasemaker	pacemaker
parsel	parcel	paserby	passer-by
parshal	partial	pashonate	passionate
parshialitey	partiality	pashun	passion
parsimonious, -ly		pasific	pacific
parsimonius	parsimonious	pasify	pacify

pasige	passage	patchy, patchier, patchiest	
pasinger	passenger	pâté	
pasive	passive	patella, -tellae	
pasivitey	passivity	paten	pattern
Pasover	Passover	patent, -ed, -ing	
paspalum		patent-leather	
pasport	passport	pater	patter
pass, passed, passing		patern	pattern
passable, -bly		paternal, -ly	
passabul	passable	paternalism	
passage, -saged, -saging		paternity	
passbook		path	
passé		pathetic, -ally	
passenger		pathological, -ly	
passer-by, passers-by		pathology, -gies	
passige	passage	pathos	
passion		patie	patty
passionate, -ly		patience (calm)	
passionfruit		patient, patients (ill)	
passive, -ly		patient, -ly	
passivity		patina	
Passover		patio, patios	
passport		patiserey	patisserie
password		patisserie	
past		patois, patois	
pasta (dough)		patriarch	
pasta	pastor (priest)	patriarchal, -ly	
paste, pasted, pasting		patriarchy, -archies	
pasteboard		patriark	patriarch
pastel		patrician	
pasterise	pasteurise	patricide	
pasteurise, -ed, -ing		patrimony, -monies	
pastiche		patriot	
pastie	pasty	patriotic, -ally	
pastime		patriotism	
pastor (priest)		patrishun	patrician
pastoral, -ly		patriside	patricide
pastoralist		patrol, patrolled, patrolling	
pastrami		patron	
pastry, -tries		patronage	
pasture, -ed, -ing		patroness	
pasty, -ties		patronige	patronage
pasword	password	patronise, -ed, -ing	
pat, patter, patting		patter, -ed, -ing	
patay	pâté	pattern, -ed, -ing	
patch, -ed, -ing		patty, -ies	
patchwork		paturnal	paternal

paturnitey	paternity	paysnent	patient	
patwa	patois	paytent	patent	
paucity		pea		
paun	pawn	peace (calm)		
paunch, paunches		peace	piece (part)	
paunchy		peaceable, -bly		
pauper		peaceabul	peaceable	
pause, paused, pausing (stop)		peaceful, -ly		
pause	paws (feet)	peach, peaches		
pave, paved, paving		peacock		
pavement		peak, -ed, -ing (top)		
pavilion		peak	peek (look)	
pavlova		peak	pique (anger)	
paw (foot)		peal, -ed, -ing (ring)		
paw	poor (needy)	peal	peel (skin)	
paw	pore (skin)	peanut		
paw	pour (flow)	peap	peep	
pawcelain	porcelain	pear (fruit)		
pawch	porch	pear	pair (two)	
pawk	pork	pear	pare (trim)	
pawkupine	porcupine	pearage	peerage	
pawl	pall	pearce	pierce	
pawlbarer	pall-bearer	pearl (gem)		
pawlsied	palsied	pearl	purl (knit)	
pawlsy	palsy	pearly, -lies		
pawltrey	paltry	peasant		
pawn, -ed, -ing		peasantry		
pawnbroker		peashooter		
pawnbroking		peashuter	peashooter	
pawnch	paunch	peat		
pawnografey	pornography	pebble		
pawpaw		pecadillo, -loes, -los		
pawper	pauper	pecan		
pawpus	porpoise	peck, -ed, -ing		
pawse	pause (stop)	peckish, -ly		
pawselin	porcelain	pecock	peacock	
pawshun	portion	pectin		
pawsitey	paucity	pectoral		
pay, paid, paying		peculiar, -ly		
payable		peculiarity, -ties		
payabul	payable	pecuniary		
payload		pedagog	pedagogue	
payment		pedagogic, -ally		
paynt	paint	pedagogue		
payola		pedagogy		
payroll		pedal, -alled, -alling (bike)		
payshence	patience	pedant		

pedantic, -ally	pelt, -ed, -ing
pedantry, -ries	pelusid pellucid
peddle, -dled, -dling (sell)	pelvis, -ves
peddle pedal (bike)	pen, penned, penning
pederast	penal
pederastic, -ally	penalisation
pederasty	penalise, -lised, -lising
pedestal, -stalled, -stalling	penalty, -ties
pedestrian	penance
pedicure	penanse penance
pedigree	penant pennant
pedlar	pence
peek, -ed, -ing (look)	penchant
peek peak (top)	pencil, -cilled, -cilling
peek pique (anger)	pendant
peel, -ed, -ing (skin)	pendent
peel peal (ring)	pending
peep, -ed, -ing	pendulous, -ly
peepshow	pendulum
peer, -ed, -ing (look)	pendulus pendulous
peer pier (wharf)	penetrable, -bly
peerage	pentrabul penetrable
peeress	penetrate, -trated, -trating
peerige peerage	penetration
peerless, -ly	penfriend
peevish	penguin
peewee	pengwin penguin
peewit	penicillin
peg, pegged, pegging	peniless penniless
peice piece	peninsula
pejorative, -ly	penis, -nes, -nises
pek peck	penisilin penicillin
pekant piquant	penitenshary penitentiary
Pekinese	penitenshul penitential
Pekingese	penitent, -ly
pekish peckish	penitential, -ly
pelargonium	penitentiary, -ries
pelican	penknife, -knives
pellet (ball)	pen-name
pellet palate (mouth)	pennant
pellet palette (board)	penniless
pellet pallet (bed)	pennon
pell-mell (haste)	penny, pennies, pence
pell-mell pall-mall	penny-farthing
(game)	penny-pinching
pellucid, -ly	penological
pelmet	penologist

penology		percentile	
pen-pusher		percepshun	perception
pense	pence	perceptabul	perceptible
penshun	pension	perceptible, -bly	
penshuner	pensioner	perception	
pensil	pencil	perceptive, -ly	
pension		perceptual, -ly	
pensionable		percession	procession
pensionabul	pensionable	perch, perches	
pensioner		perch, -ed, -ing	
pensive, -ly		perchase	purchase
pentagon		percipience	
pentathalon	pentathlon	percipient	
pentathlon		percolate, -lated, -lating	
penthouse		percolater	percolator
penthowse	penthouse	percolation	
pent-up		percolator	
penultimate, -ly		percushun	percussion
penumbra, -brae, -bras		percussion	
penurious, -ly		percussionist	
penury		percussive	
penut	peanut	perdishun	perdition
peon		perdition	
peony, -nies		peregrinate, -nated, -nating	
people, -pled, -pling		peremptoriness	
pep, pepped, pepping		peremptory, -torily	
peper	pepper	perennial, -ly	
pepermint	peppermint	perfeckshun	perfection
pepery	peppery	perfect, -ed, -ing	
pepper		perfectible	
peppercorn		perfectibul	perfectible
peppermint		perfection	
peppery		perfectionism	
pep pill		perfectionist	
pep talk		perfidious, -ly	
peptic		perfidius	perfidious
perambulate, -lated, -lating		perfidy, -dies	
perambulation		perforate, -rated, -rating	
perambulator		perforation	
perambulatory		perforce	
per annum		perform, -ed, -ing	
per capita		performance	
perceivable, -bly		performanse	performance
perceive, -ceived, -ceiving		perfume, -fumed, -fuming	
per cent		perfumery, -ries	
percentage		perfunctory, -torily	
percentige	percentage	perfunctry	perfunctory

pergarey	perjury
pergative	purgative
pergatry	purgatory
perge	purge
pergola	
perhaps	
perhibit	prohibit
periferal	peripheral
perifery	periphery
peril, -rilled, -rilling	
perilous, -ly	
perilus	perilous
perimeter	
period	
periodic	
periodical, -ly	
peripatetic	
peripheral, -ly	
periphery, -ries	
periscope	
perish, -ed, -ing	
perishable	
perishabul	perishable
perisher	
peritonitis	
periwinkle	
perjure, -jured, -juring	
perjurer	
perjury, -ries	
perk, -ed, -ing	
perkushun	percussion
perky, -kier, -kiest	
perl	pearl (gem)
perl	purl (knit)
perloin	purloin
perloyn	purloin
perm, -ed, -ing	
permananse	permanence
permanence	
permanency, -cies	
permanent, -ly	
permanganate	
permeability	
permeable	
permeate, -ated, -ating	
permeation	
permiate	permeate

permisabul	permissible
permishun	permission
permissible, -bly	
permission	
permissive, -ly	
permissiveness	
permit, -mitted, -mitting	
permutation	
permute, -muted, -muting	
pernicious, -ly	
perniciousness	
pernickety	
pernishus	pernicious
perokside	peroxide
peroration	
peroxide, -ided, -iding	
perpechual	perpetual
perpechuate	perpetuate
perpendicular, -ly	
perpendicularity	
perpetrate, -trated, -trating	
perpetrater	perpetrator
perpetration	
perpetrator	
perpetual, -ly	
perpetuate, -ated, -ating	
perpetuation	
perpetuator	
perpetuity, -ties	
perport	purport
perpose	purpose
perquisite (profit)	
perquisite	prerequisite (necessary)
per say	per se
per se	
perse	purse
persecushun	persecution
persecute, -cuted, -cuting	
persecution	
persecutor	
persepshun	perception
perseptabul	perceptible
perseve	persevere
perseverance	
persevere, -vered, -vering	
Persian	

persimmon
persist, -ed, -ing
persistence
person
personable, -bly
personage
personal, -ly (private)
   personal — personnel
      (employees)
personalise, -lised, -lising
personality, -ties
persona non grata
personate, -ated, -ating
   personible — personable
personification
personify, -fied, -fying
personnel (employees)
   personnel — personal
      (private)
perspective, -ly
   perspeks — perspex
   perspektive — perspective
perspex
perspicacious, -ly
perspicacity
perspicuous, -ly
perspicuousness
perspiration
perspire, -spired, -spiring
persuade, -suaded, -suading
persuader
   persuashun — persuasion
persuasion
persuasive, -ly
   persuit — pursuit
   perswade — persuade
   perswasion — persuasion
pert, -ly
pertness
pertain, -ed, -ing
   pertane — pertain
pertinacious, -ly
pertinacity
pertinent, -ly
perturb, -ed, -ing
perturbable
peruse, -rused, -rusing

pervade, -vaded, -vading
pervasion
pervasive, -ly
perverse, -ly
   pervershun — perversion
perversion
perversity, -ties
pervert,-ed, -ing
perverter
   pervurse — perverse
   pervurshun — perversion
   pervurt — pervert
   pesabul — peaceable
   pesant — peasant
   pesary — pessary
   pese — peace
   pesimism — pessimism
   pesimist — pessimist
pessary, -ries
pessimism
pessimist
pest
pester, -ed, -ing
pesticide
pestilence
   pestilense — pestilence
pestilent, -ly
   pestiside — pesticide
pestle
   pesul — pestle
pet, petted, petting
petal
petard
   peteet — petite
peter, -ed, -ing
   peticoat — petticoat
   petie — petty
   petishun — petition
petite
petition, -ed, -ing
petrel (bird)
   petrel — petrol (fuel)
petrify, -fied, -fying
petrol (fuel)
   petrol — petrel (bird)
petroleum
   petrul — petrel (bird)

petrul   petrol (fuel)
petticoat
pettily
pettiness
petty, -tier, -tiest
petulance
petulant, -ly
petunia
pevish   peevish
pew
pewter
phalanger
phalanx, -anxes or -anges
phalus   phallus
phallic
phallus, phalluses, phalli
phantasm
phantasmagoria
phantom
Pharaoh
pharisaic
pharisee
pharmaceutical, -ly
pharmacist
pharmacy, -cies
pharyngitis
pharynx, pharynges, pharynxes
phase, phased, phasing
pheasant
phenacetin
phenix   phoenix
phenol
phenomenal, -ly
phenomenon, -mena
phesant   pheasant
phial (vessel)
philander, -ed, -ing
philanderer
philanthropic, -ally
philanthropist
philanthropy, -pies
philarmonic   philharmonic
philatelist
philately
philharmonic
Philippines
philosofer   philosopher

philosofical   philosophical
philosofy   philosophy
philosopher
philosophical, -ly
philosophise, -phised, -phising
philosophy, -phies
philter   philtre
philtre, -tred, -tring

> For **phis-** words, look
> under **phys-**.

phlegm
phlegmatic, -ally
phlem   phlegm
phlox
phobia
phobic
phoenix
phone
phonetic, -ally
phonograf   phonograph
phonogram
phonograph
phony, phonier, phoniest
phosfate   phosphate
phosforus   phosphorus
phosphate
phosphor
phosphorescent
phosphorus
photo, photos
photocopier
photocopy, -pies
photocopy, -copied, -copying
photoelectric
photo-finish
photogenic
photograf   photograph
photograph, -graph, -graphing
photographic, -ally
photography
photostat, -stated, -stating
photosynthesis
phrase, phrased, phrasing
phraseology
phrenetic, -ally
phylactery, -teries

physic (medicine)
physical, -ly
physician
physicist
physics
physiognomy, -mies
physiological, -ly
physiology
physiotherapist
physiotherapy
physique
pi (Greek letter)
  pi   pie (food)
pianist
piano, pianos
pianoforte
  piatsa   piazza
piazza
  pibald   piebald
picador
  picancy   piquancy
  picaniny   piccaninny
piccaninny, -nies
piccolo, -los
  pich   pitch
  picinic   picnic
pick, -ed, -ing
pickaxe, -axed, -axing
picket, -ed, -ing
pickle, -led, -ling
pickpocket
pick-up
picnic, -nicked, -nicking
picnicker
pictorial, -ly
picture, -tured, -turing
picturesque
pidgin (talk)
  pidgin   pigeon (bird)
pie (food)
  pie   pi (Greek
                     letter)
piebald
piece, pieced, piecing (part)
  piece   peace (calm)
piecemeal
piecework

pier (wharf)
  pier   peer (look)
pierce, pierced, piercing
  pierse   pierce
piety, -ties
pig, pigged, pigging
pigeon (bird)
  pigeon   pidgin (talk)
pigeonhole, -holed, -holing
pigeon-toed
  pigery   piggery
piggery, -geries
piggyback
pig-headed
  pigiback   piggyback
  pigin   pidgin (talk)
  pigin   pigeon (bird)
pig-iron
piglet
pigment
pigmentation
pigmy, -mies
pigskin
pigstick, -ed, -ing
pigsticker
pigsty, -sties
pigtail
  pigtale   pigtail
  pijamas   pyjamas
pikau
pike, piked, piking
pikelet
pilchard
pile, piled, piling
pile-up
pilfer, -ed, -ing
pilferage
pilferer
  pilferige   pilferage
pilgrim
pilgrimage
  pilgrimige   pilgrimage
  pilige   pillage
  pilion   pillion
pill
pillage, -laged, -laging
pillager

pillar
pillbox, -boxes
pillion
pillory, -ries
pillory, -ried, -rying
pillow, pillows
  pilon   pylon
  pilory   pillory
pilot, -ed, -ing
pilotage
  pilow   pillow
  pilyun   pillion
pilsener
pimp, -ed, -ing
pimple
pimply, -plier, -pliest
  pimpul   pimple
pin, pinned, pinning
  pinacle   pinnacle
pinafore
pinball
pince-nez
pincers
pinch, -ed, -ing
pincher
pincushion
pine, pined, pining
pineapple
  pineappul   pineapple
pin-feather
ping, -ed, -ing
ping-pong
pinion, -ed, -ing
pink, -ed, -ing
pinnacle, -cled, -cling
pinpoint, -ed, -ing
pinprick
  pinsers   pincers
pinstripe
pint
pintuck, -ed, -ing
pin-up
  pinyun   pinion
  pionear   pioneer
pioneer, -ed, -ing
pious, -ly
pip, pipped, pipping

pipe, piped, piping
pipedream
pipeline
pipi
pipit
pippin
pipsqueak
piquancy
piquant, -ly
pique, piqued, piquing
piracy
  piramid   pyramid
piranha
  pirasy   piracy
pirate, -rated, -rating
piratical, -ly
  pire   pyre
  pirooet   pirouette
pirouette, -etted, -etting
piscatorial
Pisces
pistachio, -chios
pistil (flower)
pistol (gun)
piston
pit, pitted, pitting
  pitanse   pittance
pitapat, -patted, -patting
pitch, -ed, -ing
pitch-black
pitchblende
pitcher (baseball)
  pitcher   picture (image)
pitchfork, -ed, -ing
pitchi
piteous, -ly
  piter-pater   pitter-patter
pitfall
pith
pithead
pithy, -ier, -iest
pitiable, -ly
  pitiabul   pitiable
pitiful, -fully
pitiless, -ly
pittance
  pittanse   pittance

pitter-patter
pittosporum
pituitary, -taries
pituri
pity, pities
pity, pitied, pitying
  pius   pious
pivot, -ed, -ing
pivotal, -ly
pixie, pixies
pixy, pixies
pizza
pizzicato
placability
placable, -bly
  placabul   placable
placard, -ed, -ing
placate, -cated, -cating
placatory
place, placed, placing (position)
  place   plaice (fish)
placebo, -bos, -boes
placement
placenta, -tas, -tae
placental
placid, -ly
placidity
placket
  plagarism   plagiarism
  plage   plague
plagiarise, -rised, -rising
plagiarism
plagiarist
plague, plagued, plaguing
plaice (fish)
plaid (cloth)
plain, -ly (clear)
  plain   plane (flat)
plain-clothes
plain-spoken
plains wanderer
plaint
plaintiff (sue)
plaintive, -ly (sad)
plait, -ed, -ing (braid)
  plait   plate (dish)
  plaket   placket

plan, planned, planning
plane, planed, planing (flat)
  plane   plain (clear)
planet
planetarium
planetary
plank
plankton
planner
plant, -ed, -ing
plantation
planter
  plantif   plaintiff (sue)
  plantive   plaintive (sad)
plaque
  plase   place (position)
  plase   plaice (fish)
  plasenta   placenta
  plasid   placid
plasma
plaster, -ed, -ing
plasterboard
plasterer
plastic, -ally
  plasticene   plasticine
plasticine
plasticity
  plastisene   plasticine
plate, plated, plating (dish)
  plate   plait (braid)
plateau, -eaus, -eaux
platelet
  plater   platter
platform
  platichude   platitude
platinum
  platipus   platypus
platitude
platitudinous
  plato   plateau
Platonic
platoon
platter
platypus, -puses, -pi
plaudit
plausible, -bly
  plausibul   plausible

play, -ed, -ing
playback
playboy
player
playful, -ly
playground
play-off
   playrite   playwright
playwright
plaza
plea, pleas (request)
plead, -ed, -ing
   pleas   please (satisfy)
pleasant, -ly
pleasantry, -tries
please, pleased, pleasing (satisfy)
pleasurable, -bly
   pleasurabul   pleasurable
pleat, -ed, -ing
   plebean   plebeian
plebeian
plebiscite
   plebisite   plebiscite
plectrum, -tra, -trums
pledge, pledged, pledging
   plee   plea
   pleed   plead
   pleet   pleat
   plege   pledge
plenary, -rily
plenipotentiary, -ries
plenitude
plenteous, -ly
plentiful, -ly
   plentius   plenteous
plenty
   plesant   pleasant
   plese   pleas (requests)
   plese   please (satisfy)
   plesurabul   pleasurable
   plesure   pleasure
plethora
pleurisy
   pli   ply
pliable, -bly
   pliabul   pliable
pliant, -ly

pliers
plight, -ed, -ing
Plimsoll line
plinth
   plite   plight
   pliwood   plywood
plod, plodded, plodding
plodder
   ploi   ploy
plonk, -ed, -ing
   ploomage   plumage
   plootocrasy   plutocracy
   plooviul   pluvial
plop, plopped, plopping
plot, plotted, plotting
plough, -ed, -ing
ploughshare
plover
   plow   plough
ploy
pluck, -ed, -ing
plucky, -ily
plug, plugged, plugging
plum (fruit)
   plum   plumb (test)
plumage
plumb, -ed, -ing (test)
plumber
plumbline
plume, plumed, pluming
   plumige   plumage
   plumline   plumbline
   plummer   plumber
plummet, -ed, -ing
plump, -ed, -ing
plunder, -ed, -ing
plunge, plunged, plunging
plural
pluralism
plurality, -ties
   plurasy   pleurisy
plus
plus-fours
plush
plutocracy, -cies
plutocrat
plutonium

pluvial
ply, plies
ply, plied, plying
plywood
pneumatic, -ally
pneumonia
poach, -ed, -ing
poacher
  poch   poach
pock
pocket, -ed, -ing
pocket-book
pocket-knife, -knives
pocket-money
pockmark
pod, podded, podding
poddy
podiatrist
podiatry
podium, -dia
poem
poet
poetess
poetic
poetical, -ly
poetry
pogrom
poignancy
poignant, -ly
  poinancy   poignancy
  poinant   poignant
poinsettia
point,-ed, -ing
point-blank
pointedly
pointer
pointillism
pointless, -ly
poise, poised, poising
poison, -ed, -ing
poisoner
poisonous, -ly
poke, poked, poking
poker
pokey, pokies (machine)
poky, -kier, -kiest (small)
polar (region)

  polar   poler (horse)
polarise, -rised, -rising
polarity
polaroid
pole, poled, poling (stick)
  pole   poll (vote)
polemic
polemical, -ly
  polen   pollen
poler (horse)
  poler   polar (region)
  polese   police
police, -liced, -licing
policeman, -men
policewoman, -women
policy, -cies
  poligamus   polygamous
  poligamy   polygamy
  poliglot   polyglot
  poligon   polygon
  polinate   pollinate
  Polineshun   Polynesian
poliomyelitis
  polip   polyp
polish, -ed, -ing
  polisy   policy
politburo
polite, -ly
politic
  polithene   polythene
political, -ly
politician
politicise, -cised, -cising
politicking
politics
  politishun   politician
polka, -kaed, -kaing
poll, -ed, -ing (vote)
  poll   pole (stick)
pollard
pollen
pollinate, -nated, -nating
pollination
pollster
pollutant
pollute, -luted, -luting
pollution

polo		pool, -ed, -ing	
polo-neck		poop, -ed, -ing	
poltegist	poltergeist	poor, -ly (needy)	
poltergeist		poor	paw (foot)
poltise	poultice	poor	pore (skin)
poltry	poultry	poor	pour (flow)
polushun	pollution	poorhouse	
polute	pollute	pop, popped, popping	
polyandrous		popcorn	
polyandry		pope	
polyanthus		popery	
polyester		popet	poppet
polygamist		popie	poppy
polygamous, -ly		popish, -ly	
polygamy		poplar (tree)	
polyglot		poplin	
polygon		popourri	potpourri
Polyneshun	Polynesian	poppet	
Polynesian		poppy, -pies	
polyp		poppycock	
polysaturated		populace	
polythene		popular, -ly (known)	
polyunsaturated		popularise, -rised, -rising	
pomander		popularitey	popularity
pomegranate		popularity	
pomel	pommel	populase	populace
Pomeranian		populate, -lated, -lating	
pommel, -melled, -melling		population	
pommy, -mies		populer	popular
pomp		populous, -ly	
pompom		populus	populous
pomposity		popy	poppy
pompous, -ly		por	paw (foot)
poncho, -chos		por	poor (needy)
ponder, -ed, -ing		por	pore (skin)
ponderous, -ly		por	pour (flow)
ponderus	ponderous	porcelain	
ponie	pony	porcelane	porcelain
pontiff		porch	
pontifical, -ly		porcupine	
pontificate, -cated, -cating		pore (skin)	
pontoon		pore	paw (foot)
pony, -nies		pore	poor (needy)
ponytail		pore	pour (flow)
pooch		porfrey	porphyry
poodle		poridge	porridge
poodul	poodle	porige	porridge

pork
   porkupine — porcupine
   pornografy — pornography
pornographer
pornographic
pornography
porosity
porous
porphyry, -ries
porpoise, -poises
   porpus — porpoise
porridge
   porselin — porcelain
   porshun — portion
   porslin — porcelain
port
portable
portal
portend, -ed, -ing
   portenshus — portentous
portent
portentous, -ly
porter
portfolio, -lios
porthole
portico, -coes, -cos
portion, -ed, -ing
portly, -lier, -liest
portmanteau, -teaus, -teaux
portrait
portraiture
portray, -ed, -ing
portrayal
   portret — portrait
   portul — portal
   porus — porous
   poschur — posture
pose, posed, posing
poser
   poseshun — possession
   posess — possess
   posessive — possessive
   posey — posy
posh, -ly
   poshun — potion
   posibility — possibility
   posibul — possible

   posishun — position
position
positive, -ly
posse
possess, -ed, -ing
possession
possessive, -ly
possessor
possible, -bly
possibility, -ties
   possibul — possible
possum
post, -ed, -ing
postage
postal
postcard
postcode
postdate, -dated, -dating
poster
   posterier — posterior
posterior, -ly
posterity
postern
postgraduate
posthaste
posthumous, -ly
   posthumus — posthumous
   postige — postage
post-mortem
post-office
postpone, -poned, -poning
postponement
postulant
postulate, -lated, -lating
   postumus — posthumous
posture, -tured, -turing
posy, -sies
pot, potted, potting
potable
potash
   potasium — potassium
potassium
potato, -toes
pot-bellied
pot-belly, -lies
potency
   potenshul — potential

potensy	potency
potent	
potentate	
potential, -ly	
potentiality, -ties	
poter	potter
potery	pottery
pothole	
potion	
potluck	
potpourri, -ris	
pottage	
potter, -ed, -ing	
pottery, -ries	
potty, -ties	
pouch, pouches	
poulterer	
poultice, -ticed, -ticing	
poultise	poultice
poultry	
pounce, pounced, pouncing	
pound, -ed, -ing	
pour, -ed, -ing	
pour	poor (needy)
pour	pore (skin)
pout, -ed, -ing	
poverty	
poverty-stricken	
powch	pouch
powder, -ed, -ing	
powdery	
power, -ed, -ing	
powerful, -ly	
powerhouse	
powerless, -ly	
pownce	pounce
pownd	pound
powt	pout
pow wow, -wowed, -wowing	
pox	
practicable, -bly	
practicabul	practicable
practical, -ly	
practicality	
practice, -ticed, -ticing	
practician	
practise, -tised, -tising	

practishun	practician
practishuner	practitioner
practitioner	
pragmatic, -ally	
pragmatism	
pragmatist	
prairey	prairie
prairie	
praise, praised, praising	
praiseworthy, -thily	
pram	
prance, pranced, prancing	
prandial, -ly	
prang, -ed, -ing	
prank	
pranse	prance
prarey	prairie
prase	praise
prate, prated, prating	
prattle, -tled, -tling	
pratul	prattle
prawn	
pray, -ed, -ing (beg)	
pray	prey (hunt)
prayer	
prayerbook	
preach, -ed, -ing	
preacher	
preamble	
preambul	preamble
prearrange, -ranged, -ranging	
precarious, -ly	
precaution	
precautionary	
precautionry	precautionary
precawshun	precaution
precede, -ceded, -ceding (before)	
precede	proceed (ahead)
precedence	
precedent (law)	
precedent	president (head)
precept	
preceptor	
prech	preach
precinct	

precious, -ly
  precipatation   precipitation
precipice
  precipise   precipice
precipitant, -ly
precipitate, -tated, -tating
precipitation
precipitous, -ly
  precipitus   precipitous
precis (summary)
precise, -ly (exact)
  precishun   precision
precision
preclude, -cluded, -cluding
precocious, -ly
precocity
preconceive, -ceived, -ceiving
  preconcieve   preconceive
  preconsepshun   preconception
preconception
  preconseve   preconceive
  precoshus   precocious
precursor
  predater   predator
predator
predatory
predecessor
  predesessor   predecessor
predestination
predestine, -tined, -tining
predetermination
predetermine, -mined, -mining
predicament
predicate, -cated, -cating
predicative, -ly
predict, -ed, -ing
predictable, -bly
  predictabul   predictable
prediction
predictor
  predilecshun   predilection
predilection
predispose, -posed, -posing
predisposition
predominance
predominant, -ly
predominate, -ated, -ating

pre-eminence
pre-eminent, -ly
pre-empt, -ed, -ing
pre-emptory
preen, -ed, -ing
prefabricate, -cated, -cating
prefabrication
preface, -faced, -facing
prefatory, -rily
prefect
prefecture
prefer, -ferred, -ferring
preferable, -bly
preference
  preferense   preference
  preferenshul   preferential
preferential, -ly
preferment
  prefice   preface
  prefiks   prefix
prefix
pregnancy, -cies
  pregnansy   pregnancy
pregnant, -ly
prehensile
prehistoric, -ally
prejudge, -judged, -judging
prejudgment
prejudice, -diced, -dicing
prejudicial, -ly
  prejudise   prejudice
  prejudishul   prejudicial
prelate
preliminary, -aries
prelude, -luded, -luding
premarital
premature, -ly
premenstrual tension
premier (chief)
premiere (first performance)
premise, -ised, -ising
premises
premium
  premonishun   premonition
premonition
premonitory
prenatal

prene   preen
preoccupation
preoccupy, -pied, -pying
preparation
preparatory, -rily
  preparatry   preparatory
prepare, -pared, -paring
preponderance
preponderant, -ly
preposition
preposterous, -ly
  prerekwisit   prerequisite
prerequisite (necessary)
  prerequisite   perquisite
                    (profit)
prerogative
  pres   press
presage, -saged, -saging
  prescripshun   prescription
prescription
prescriptive, -ly
  presede   precede
  presedence   precedence
  presedent   precedent
  presedent   president
  preseed   precede
  preseleckshun   preselection
preselect, -ed, -ing
preselection
presence
  presense   presence
present, -ed, -ing
presentable, -bly
presentation
presentiment
presently
  presept   precept
preservation
preservative
preserve, -served, -serving
  presher   pressure
  presherise   pressurise
  preshus   precious
preside, -sided, -siding
presidency
  presidenshul   presidential
  presidensy   presidency

president
presidential
  presige   presage
  presinct   precinct
  presipice   precipice
  presipis   precipice
  presipitate   precipitate
  presipitus   precipitous
  presise   precise
press, -ed, -ing
press-up
pressure, -sured, -suring
pressurisation
pressurise, -rised, -rising
  prest   priest
  prestege   prestige
  presthood   priesthood
prestige
prestigious, -ly
  prestigus   prestigious
presto
presume, -sumed, -suming
presumption
presumptuous, -ly
  presumshun   presumption
  presumtuus   presumptuous
presuppose, -posed, -posing
presupposition
pretence
pretend, -ed, -ing
pretender
  pretense   pretence
  pretenshun   pretension
  pretenshus   pretentious
pretension
pretentious, -ly
preternatural, -ly
pretext
  pretie   pretty
prettily
prettiness
pretty, -tier, -tiest
  prety   pretty
pretzel
prevail, -ed, -ing
  prevale   prevail
prevalence

prevalense   prevalence
prevalent, -ly
prevaricate, -cated, -cating
prevarication
    prevenshun   prevention
prevent, -ed, -ing
preventable, -bly
    preventabul   preventable
preventative, -ly
prevention
preventive, -ly
preview, -ed, -ing
previous, -ly
prey, -ed, -ing (hunt)
    prey   pray (beg)
    pri   pry
price, priced, pricing
priceless, -ly
prick, -ed, -ing
prickle, -led, -ling
prickly, -lier, -liest
    prickul   prickle
pride, prided, priding
    prie   pry
    prier   prior
    priery   priory
priest
priesthood
priestly, -lier, -liest
prig
priggish, -ly
prim, primmer, primmest
primacy
prima donna
prima-facie
primary, -ries
primer
primeval, -ly
primitive, -ly
primogenitor
primogeniture
primordial, -ly
    primrey   primary
primrose
primula
primus
prince

princedom
princely, -lier, -liest
princess
principal (head)
principality, -ties
principle (law)
    principul   principal (head)
    prinse   prince
    prinsess   princess
    prinsipal   principal
    prinsipality   principality
print, -ed, -ing
printer
printery, -ries
print-out
prion
prior
priority, -ties
priority-paid
priory, -ries
prise, prised, prising (move)
    prise   price (cost)
    prise   prize(award)
prism
prismatic, -ally
prison
prisoner
prissy, -ier, -iest
    pristeen   pristine
pristine
privacy, -cies
    privasy   privacy
    privisy   privacy
private, -ly
privateer
privation
    privelage   privilege
privet
    privie   privy
privilege, -leged, -leging
privy, -vies
prize, prized, prizing (award)
    prizm   prism
probability, -ties
probable, -ly
    probabul   probable

probate, -bated, -bating
probation
probationer
probe, probed, probing
  probible   probable
probity
problem
problematic, -ally
procedural, -ly
procedure
proceed, -ed, -ing
  proceshun   procession
process, -ed, -ing
procession
processional, -ly
processor
proclaim, -ed, -ing
proclamation
  proclaym   proclaim
procrastinate, -nated, -nating
procrastination
procrastinator
procreate, -ated, -ating
proctor
procurable
  procurabul   procurable
procure, -cured, -curing
procurer
prod, prodded, prodding
prodigal, -ly
prodigality, -ties
prodigious, -ly
  prodigus   prodigious
prodigy, -gies
  prodijus   prodigious
produce, -duced, -ducing
producer
producible
  producshun   production
product
production
productive, -ly
productivity
  produse   produce
  produser   producer
profane, -faned, -faning
profanely

profanity, -ties
  profecy   prophecy (noun)
  profecy   prophesy (verb)
  profer   proffer
  profeser   professor
  profeshunal   professional
  profesor   professor
profess, -ed, -ing
professional, -ly
professionalism
professor
professorial, -ly
  profet   profit (gain)
  profet   prophet (seer)
proffer, -ed, -ing
proficiency, -cies
proficient, -ly
profile, -filed, -filing
  profishency   proficiency
  profishent   proficient
profit, -ed, -ing
profitable, -bly
  profitabul   profitable
profiteer, -ed, -ing
profitless
profligacy
profligate, -ly
pro-forma
profound, -ly
  profownd   profound
profundity, -ties
profuse, -ly
  profushun   profusion
profusion
progenitor
progeny, -nies
prognosis, -noses
prognostic
prognosticate, -cated, -cating
prognostication
program, -grammed, -gramming
programmable
programme
programmer
  progreshun   progression
progress, -ed, -ing

progression

progressive, -ly

   prohibishun   prohibition

prohibit, -ed, -ing

prohibition

prohibitive, -ly

   projecshun   projection

project, -ed, -ing

projectile

projection

projectionist

projector

   proksimate   proximate

   proksy   proxy

prolapse, -lapsed, -lapsing

proletarian

proletariat

proliferate, -rated, -rating

prolific, -ally

   prolog   prologue

prologue

prolong, -ed, -ing

prolongation

prom

promenade, -naded, -nading

prominence

   prominense   prominence

prominent, -ly

promiscuity, -ties

promiscuous, -ly

   promiscuus   promiscuous

promise, -mised, -mising

promissory

promontory, -ries

   promontry   promontory

promoter

promotion

   promp   prompt

prompt, -ed, -ing

prompter

promulgate, -gated, -gating

promulgation

prone

prong, -ed, -ing

pronoun

pronounce, -nounced, -nouncing

pronouncement

   pronown   pronoun

   pronownse   pronounce

pronto

pronunciation

   prood   prude

proof, -ed, -ing

proofread, -read, -reading

proofreader

   proon   prune

   proove   prove

prop, propped, propping

propaganda

propagate, -gated, -gating

propagation

propagator

propane

propel, -pelled, -pelling

propellant (noun)

propellent (adjective)

propeller

propensity, -ties

proper, -ly

property, -ties

prophecy, cies

prophesy, -sied, -sying

prophet

prophetess

prophetical, -ly

   prophilactic   prophylactic

prophylactic

   propishiate   propitiate

   propishus   propitious

propitiate, -ated, -ating

propitious, -ly

proponent

   proporshunal   proportional

proportion

proportional, -ly

proportionate, -ly

proposal

propose, -posed, -posing

proposer

   proposishun   proposition

proposition

propound, -ed, -ing

   propownd   propound

proprietary

proprieter   proprietor
proprietor
proprietry   proprietary
propriety, -ties
propulsion
pro-rata
prorogue, -rogued, -roguing
prosaic, -ally
proscenium, -nia
proscribe, -scribed, -scribing
proscription
prose
    prosecushun   prosecution
prosecute, -cuted, -cuting
prosecution
prosecutor
    prosedure   procedure
    proseed   proceed
    proselite   proselyte
proselyte, -lyted, -lyting
proselytise, -tised, -tising
    prosess   process
    prosicute   prosecute
    prosilite   proselyte
    prosilitise   proselytise
prosody
prospect, -ed, -ing
prospective, -ly
prospector
prospectus
prosper, -ed, -ing
prosperity, -ties
prosperous, -ly
    prosperus   prosperous
prostate gland
prosthesis, -ses
    prostitushen   prostitution
prostitute, -tuted, -tuting
prostitution
prostrate, -trated, -trating
prostration
protagonist
protea
    protecshun   protection
protect, -ed, -ing
protection
protectionist

protective, -ly
protector
protectorate
    proteen   protein
protégé
protein
protest, -ed, -ing
Protestant
Protestantism
protestation
protocol
proton
    prototipe   prototype
prototype
protract, -ed, -ing
protractor
    protrood   protrude
    protrooshun   protrusion
protrude, -ruded, -ruding
protrusion
protruberance
protruberant, -ly
proud, -ly
provable
prove, proved, proven, proving
provender
proverb
proverbial, -ly
provide, -vided, -viding
providence
    providense   providence
provident, -ly
providential, -ly
provider
province
provincial, -ly
    provinshul   provincial
    provishun   provision
provision
provisional, -ly
proviso
provocation
provocative, -ly
provoke, -voked, -voking
provost
prow
    prowd   proud

prowess
prowl, -ed, -ing
proximate, -ly
proximity
proxy, proxies
  prozaic   prosaic
prude
prudence
  prudense   prudence
prudent, -ly
prudential, -ly
prudish, -ly
prune, pruned, pruning
prunus
prurience
prurient, -ly
  Prushan   Prussian
Prussian
pry, pried, prying
psalm
psalmist
psaltery, -teries
pseudo
pseudonym
psyche
psychedelic
psychiatric, -ally
psychiatrist
psychiatry
psychic, -ally
psychoanalyse, -lysed, -lysing
psychoanalysis
psychoanalyst
psychological, -ly
psychologist
psychology, -gies
psychopath
psychopathy
psychosis, -ses
psychosomatic
psychotherapist
pschotherapy
psychotic

> For psyco- words, look
> under **psycho-**.

  psykey   psyche

  psykic   psychic
ptomaine
puberty
pubes
pubescence
pubescent
pubic
  publesher   publisher
public, -ly
publican
publication
publicise, -cised, -cising
publicity
publish, -ed, -ing
publisher
  publisise   publicise
  publisity   publicity
puce
puck
pucka (genuine)
pucker, -ed, -ing (fold)
pudding
puddle, -dled, -dling
  puddul   puddle
  puding   pudding
puerile, -ly
puerility, -ties
puff, -ed, -ing
puffin
puffy, -fier, -fiest
  pufy   puffy
pugilism
pugilist
pugilistic, -ally
pugnacious, -ly
pugnacity
  pugnasity   pugnacity
pug-nosed
pukka
pulchritude
  pulie   pulley
  pulkritude   pulchritude
pull, -ed, -ing
pullet
pulley, -leys
pullover
pulmonary

pulmonry   pulmonary
pulp, -ed, -ing
pulpit
pulpwood
pulpy, -pier, -piest
pulsar
pulsate, -ated, -ating
pulsation
pulsator
pulse, pulsed, pulsing
     pulser   pulsar
pulverise, -rised, -rising
puma
pumice
     pumise   pumice
     pumkin   pumpkin
pummel, -melled, -melling
pump, -ed, -ing
pumpernickel
pumpkin
pun, punned, punning
     punative   punitive
punch, -ed, -ing
punch-drunk
punch-up
punctilious, -ly
     puntilius   punctilious
punctual, -ly
punctuality
punctuate, -ated, -ating
punctuation
puncture, -tured, -turing
pundit
pungency
pungent, -ly
     punie   puny
punish, -ed, -ing
punishable
punishment
punitive, -ly
     pungensy   pungency
     punjent   pungent
punk
punnet
punt, -ed, -ing
punter
puny, -nier, -niest

pup, pupped, pupping
     pupet   puppet
     pupie   puppy
pupil
puppet
puppeteer
puppetry
puppy, -pies
     pur annum   per annum
     puray   puree
     purceive   perceive
purchase, -chased, -chasing
purdah
pure, purer, purest
puree, -reed, -reeing
purgative, -ly
purgatory
     purgatry   purgatory
purge, purged, purging
     purifie   purify
purify, -fied, -fying
     purile   puerile
puritan
puritanical, -ly
puritanism
     puritie   purity
purity
     purje   purge
     purjery   perjury
purl, -ed, -ing (knit)
     purl   pearl (gem)
purloin, -ed, -ing
     puroolense   purulence
purple, -pled, -pling
purport, -ed, -ing
purpose
purposeful, -ly
     purpul   purple
purr, -ed, -ing
purser
pursuant, -ly
pursue, -sued, -suing
pursuit
     pursute   pursuit
purulence
purulent, -ly
     purvay   purvey

purvey, -ed, -ing
purveyor
pus
   puse   puce
push, -ed, -ing
pushbike
push-button
pushover
push-up
pushy
pusillanimous, -ly
pussyfoot
put, put, putting
putative, -ly
   puter   pewter
   putie   putty
putrefaction
putrefy, -fied, -fying
putrescent
putrid, -ly
   putrify   putrefy
putt, -ed, -ing
putter
putty, -ties
putty, puttied, puttying
put-upon
   puty   putty
   puzel   puzzle
puzzle, -zled, -zling
   pye   pi (Greek
                  letter)
   pye   pie (food)
pygmy, -mies
pyjamas
pylon
pyramid
pyramidal, -ly
pyre
pyrex
   pyric   pyrrhic
pyrotechnics
pyrrhic
pythagoras
python
pyx

Qq

qeue	queue
quack, -ed, -ing	
quackery, -eries	
quad (timber)	
quadrangle	
quadrangul	quadrangle
quadrant	
quadrafonic	quadraphonic
quadraphonic	
quadrasonic	
quadratic	
quadril	quadrille
quadrille	
quadrillion	
quadriplegia	
quadriplegic	
quadruped	
quadrupedal	
quadruple, -pled, -pling	
quadruplet	
quadrupul	quadruple
quaff, quaffed, quaffing	
quagmire	
quail	
quaint, -ly	
quaintness	
quake, quaked, quaking	
Quaker	
Quakerism	
qualification	
qualifi	qualify
qualified	
qualifier	
qualify, -fied, -fying	
qualitative, -ly	
quality, -ties	
qualm	
quandary, -ries	

quandong	
quandry	quandary
quango	
quantifi	quantify
quantifiable	
quantification	
quantify, -fied, -fying	
quantitative, -ly	
quantity, -ties	
quarantine, -tined, -tining	
quarel	quarrel
quarey	quarry
quark	
quarm	qualm
quarrel, -relled, -relling	
quarreller	
quarrelsome, -ly	
quarry, -ries	
quarry, -ried, -rying	
quart, quarts	
quarter	
quarterdeck	
quarterly	
quartermaster	
quartet	
quartile	
quarto, -tos	
quartz (rock)	
quartz	quarts (measures)
quash, -ed, -ing	
quasi	
quatrain	
quattrocento	
quaver, -ed, -ing	
quavery	
quay (wharf)	
que	cue (billiards)
que	queue (line)
queasy, -sier, -siest	
queasiness	
queen, -ly	
queer, -ly	
queerness	
quell, -ed, -ing	
queller	
quench, -ed, -ing	

quenchable
quenchless
  querie — query
querulous, -ly
querulousness
  querulus — querulous
query, -ries
query, -ried, -rying
  queschun — question
quest, -ed, -ing
quester
question, -ed, -ing
questionable, -bly
  questionair — questionnaire
questioner
questionnaire
  questyun — question
queue, queued, queuing
quibble, -bled, -bling
quibbler
  quibel — quibble
  quich — quiche
quiche
quick, -ly
quicken
quickie
quicklime
quickness
quicksand
quicksilver
quickstep
quick-tempered
quick-witted
quid, quid, quids
quid pro quo
quiescence
quiescent, -ly
  quiesense — quiescence
quiet, -ly (silent)
  quiet — quite (rather)
quieten, -ed, -ing
quietness
quill
quilt
quilted
quince
quinella

quinine
  quinse — quince
quinsy, -sies
  quintesense — quintessence
quintessence
quintessential
quintet
quintette
quintuple, -pled, -pling
quintuplet
  quintupul — quintuple
quip, quipped, quipping
quipster
quire (paper)
  quire — choir (sing)
quirk
  quish — quiche
  quisine — cuisine
quit, quitted or quit, quitting
quite (rather)
  quite — quiet (silent)
quits
quitter
quiver, -ed, -ing
quivery
quixotic
quixotism
quiz, quizzes
quiz, quizzed, quizzing
quizzical, -ly
quod (prison)
  quod — quad (timber)
quoit
quokka
quorum
  quoshent — quotient

> For other quo- words, look
> under **qua-**.

quota
quotation
quote, quoted, quoting
quotient

Rr

rabbi, -bis
rabbinical
rabbit, -bited, -biting
rabbiter
rabble, -bled, -bling
rabblerouser
   rabi   rabbi
rabid, -ly
rabies
   rabit   rabbit
   rabud   rabid
   rabul   rabble
raccoon
race, raced, racing
   racecorse   racecourse
racecourse
racegoer
racehorse
racer
racetrack
raceway
racial, -ly
racialism
racialist
racism
racist
rack, -ed, -ing
rack-and-pinion
racket, -ed, -ing
racketeer
   rackit   racket
   raconter   raconteur
raconteur
racquet
racy, -cier, -ciest
radar
raddle, -led, -ling
   rade   raid

   radeo   radio
radial, -ly
   radialogy   radiology
radial-ply
radian
radiance
   radianse   radiance
radiant, -ly
radiate, -ated, -ating
   radiater   radiator
radiation
radiator
radical, -ly
radicalism
   radicul   radical
radii
radio, -dioed, -dioing
radioactive
radioastronomy
   radiografy   radiography
radiogram
radiographer
radiography
radiologist
radiology
radiotelephone
radiotherapy
radish
   radiul   radial
radium
radius, radii, radiuses
raffia
raffish, -ly
raffle, -led, -ling
raft
rafter
rag, ragged, ragging
ragamuffin
rage, raged, raging
raglan
ragout, -gouted, -gouting
ragtime
raid, -ed, -ing
rail, -ed, -ing
raillery, -ries
railroad
railway

raiment
rain, -ed, -ing (water)
  rain — reign (rule)
  rain — rein (bridle)
rainbird
rainbow
raincoat
rainfall
rainforest
raise, raised, raising (lift)
  raise — rays (beams)
raisin
raison d' être
  raisun — raisin
  raje — rage
rake, raked, raking
rakish, -ly
  rakket — racket
  rale — rail
  ralie — rally
rally, -lies
rally, -lied, -lying
ram, rammed, ramming
ramble, -bled, -bling
rambler
  rambul — ramble
ramification
ramify, -fied, -fying
ramp
rampage, -paged, -paging
rampageous, -ly
  rampagius — rampageous
rampant, -ly
rampart
ramrod
ramshackle
  ramshackul — ramshackle
ranch
rancher
rancid
rancidity
rancorous, -ly
rancour
  rancur — rancour
  rancurus — rancorous
random, -ly
randy

rane — rain (water)
rane — reign (rule)
rane — rein (bridle)
range, ranged, ranging
rangefinder
ranger
  rangul — wrangle
rank, -ed, -ing
rankle, -kled, -kling
ransack, -ed, -ing
  ransid — rancid
ransom, -ed, -ing
  ransome — ransom
  ransum — ransom
rant, -ed, -ing
rap, rapped, rapping (strike)
  rap — wrap (cover)
rapacious, -ly
rapacity
  rapashus — rapacious
  rapasity — rapacity
  rapcher — rapture
rape, raped, raping
rapid, -ly
rapid-fire
rapier
rapine
rapist
rapport
rapprochement
  rapsody — rhapsody
rapt (engrossed)
  rapt — wrapped (cover)
rapture
rapturous, -ly
  rapturus — rapturous
rare, rarer, rarest
  rarefacshun — rarefaction
rarefaction
rarefy, -fied, -fying
rarely
raring
rarity, -ties
  rasbery — raspberry
rascal
rascality, -ties

rascally
rase, rased, rasing (destroy)
   rase   race (run)
   rase   raise (lift)
rash, -ly
   rashal   racial
   rashalist   racialist
rasher
   rashio   ratio
rashness
   rashul   racial
   rashun   ration
   rashunalise   rationalise
   rasin   raisin
   rasism   racism
   rasist   racist
   raskul   rascal
rasp, -ed, -ing
raspberry, -ries
rat, ratted, ratting
   ratabul   rateable
ratchet
rate, rated, rating
   rateo   ratio
ratepayer
   rath   wrath
rather
ratification
ratify, -fied, -fying
ratio, -tios
ration, -ed, -ing
rational, -ly (reasonable)
rationale (statement)
rationalise, -lised, -lising
rationalism
rationality, -ties
rat-race
rattan
rattle, -tled, -tling
rattlesnake
rattletrap
ratty, -tier, -tiest
   ratul   rattle
raucous, -ly
   raucus   raucous
ravage, -aged, -aging
ravager

rave, raved, raving
ravel, -elled, -elling
raven
   ravene   ravine
ravenous, -ly
   ravige   ravage
ravine
ravioli
ravish, -ed, -ing
raw (uncooked)
   raw   roar (noise)
   rawcus   raucous
rawhide
ray
rayon
rays (beams)
   rays   raise (lift)
   rays   raze (destroy)
raze, razed, razing (destroy)
   razer   razor
razoo
razor
reach, -ed, -ing
   reacktion   reaction
react, -ed, -ing
reaction
reactionary
reactive, -ly
reactor
read, read, reading (book)
   read   red (colour)
   read   reed (plant)
readable, -bly
   readabul   readable
reader
readership
readily
readiness
ready, readied, readying
ready, readier, readiest
ready-made
   reaf   reef
reafforest, -ed, -ing
reafforestation
reagent
   reak   reek (smell)
   reak   wreak (inflict)

real, -ly (true)
  real   reel (wind)
realign, -ed, -ing
realisation
realise, -lised, -lising
realism
realist
realistic, -ally
reality, -ties (fact)
realm
  realter   realtor
realtor
realty (real estate)
ream, reamed, reaming
reap, -ed, -ing
reaper
reappear, -ed, -ing
rear, -ed, -ing
  reargard   rearguard
rearguard
rearmament
reason, -ed, -ing
reasonable, -bly
  reasonabul   reasonable
reassemble, -bled, -bling
  reassembul   reassemble
reassert, -ed, -ing
reassertion
reassess, -ed, -ing
reassessment
reassurance
reassure, -sured, -suring
  reath   wreath
rebate, -bated, -bating
rebel, -belled, -belling
rebellion
rebellious, -ly
  rebelyun   rebellion
  rebild   rebuild
rebound, -ed, -ing
  rebownd   rebound
rebuff, -ed, -ing
rebuild, -built, -building
rebuke, -buked, -buking
rebut, -butted, -butting
  rebutal   rebuttal
rebuttal

recalcitrance
recalcitrant
recall, -ed, -ing
recant, -ed, -ing
recantation
recapitulate, -lated, -lating
recapitulation
recede, -ceded, -ceding
receipt
  receit   receipt
receive, -ceived, -ceiving
receiver
receivership
recent, -ly
  recepe   recipe
  recepshun   reception
  recepshunist   receptionist
receptacle
  receptacul   receptacle
reception
receptionist
receptive, -ly
  receshun   recession
recess, -ed, -ing
recessive, -ly
  rech   retch (vomit)
  rech   wretch (victim)
recidivism
recidivist
  reciept   receipt
  recieve   receive
recipe
recipient
reciprocal, -ly
reciprocate, -cated, -cating
reciprocation
reciprocity
  reciprosity   reciprocity
recital
recitation
recite, -cited, -citing
  reck   wreck
  reckage   wreckage
reckless, -ly
reckon, -ed, -ing
reclaim, -ed, -ing
reclamation

reclassify, -fied, -fying
recline, -clined, -clining
recluse
recognisable, -bly
   recognisabul   recognisable
recognise, -nised, -nising
   recognishun   recognition
recognition
recoil, -ed, -ing
   recolecshun   recollection
recollect, -ed, -ing
recollection
recommend, -ed, -ing
recommendation
reconcile, -ciled, -ciling
reconciliation
recondite
recondition, -ed, -ing
reconnaissance
   reconnoiter   reconnoitre
reconnoitre, -tred, -tring
reconsider, -ed, -ing
   reconsile   reconcile
   reconsiliation   reconciliation
reconstruct, -ed, -ing
reconstruction
   recoop   recoup
record, -ed, -ing
recorder
   recorse   recourse
recount, -ed, -ing
recoup, -ed, -ing
recourse
recover, -ed, -ing
recovery, -eries
   recownt   recount
recreant, -ly
recreation
recriminate, -nated, -nating
recrimination
recriminatory
recruit, -ed, -ing
recruitment
   recrute   recruit
rectangle
   rectangul   rectangle
rectangular, -ly

rectification
rectifier
rectify, -fied, -fying
rectilinear, -ly
   rectilinier   rectilinear
rectitude
rector
rectory, -ries
rectum
recumbency
   recumbensy   recumbency
recumbent, -ly
recuperate, -rated, -rating
recuperation
recuperative
recur, -curred, -curring
recurrence
   recurrense   recurrence
recurrent, -ly
recyclable
   recyclabul   recyclable
recycle, -cycled, -cycling
   recycul   recycle
red, redder, reddest (colour)
   red   read (book)
redbreast
   redbrest   redbreast
redden, -ed, -ing
reddish
   reddy   ready
redeem, -ed, -ing
redeemable, -ably
redeemer
   redempshun   redemption
redemption
redemptive
   reden   redden
   redeploi   redeploy
redeploy, -ed, -ing
redeployment
redevelop, -ed, -ing
redevelopment
red-handed
   redie   ready
redistribute, -buted, -buting
redistribution
redolence

redolent, -ly
redouble, -led, -ling
redoubtable, -bly
redound, -ed, -ing
   redoutabul   redoubtable
redress, -ed, -ing
redskin
reduce, -duced, -ducing
   reducksun   reduction
reduction
redundancy, -cies
   redundansy   redundancy
reduplicate, -cated, -cating
redwood
reed (plant)
   reed   read (book)
reedwarbler
reedy, reedier, reediest
reef, -ed, -ing
reefer
reek, -ed, -ing (smell)
   reek   wreak (inflict)
reel, -ed, -ing (wind)
   reel   real (true)
re-elect, -ed, -ing
re-election
re-entry, -tries
refer, -ferred, -ferring
referee, -reed, -reeing
reference
   referense   reference
referendum, -da, -dums
referent
referral
refill, -ed, -ing
refine, -fined, -fining
refinement
refinery, -ries
   refleckshun   reflection
reflect, -ed, -ing
reflection
reflector
   refleks   reflex
reflex
refloat, -ed, -ing
reform, -ed, -ing
reformation

reformatory, -ries
reformer
   refrackshun   refraction
refraction
refractive, -ly
refrain, -ed, -ing
   refrence   reference
refresh, -ed, -ing
refresher
refreshment
refrigerant
refrigerate, -rated, -rating
   refrigerater   refrigerator
refrigeration
refrigerator
refuel, -elled, -elling
refuge
refugee
refulgence
refulgent, -ly
refund, -ed, -ing
refurbish, -ed, -ing
refusal
refuse, -fused, -fusing
refutation
refute, -futed, -futing
regain, -ed, -ing
regal, -ly (royal)
regale, -galed, -galing (feast)
regalia
   regane   regain
regard, -ed, -ing
regardless, -ly
regatta
   regeme   regime
regency, -cies
regenerate, -rated, -rating
regeneration
regenerative, -ly
regent
regime
regimen
regiment
regimental
regimentation
region
regional, -ly

regionalism
register, -ed, -ing
registrar
registration
registry, -tries
  regon   region
  regreshun   regression
regress, -ed, -ing
regression
regressive, -ly
regret, -gretted, -gretting
  regretabul   regrettable
regretful, -ly
regrettable, -bly
  regualation   regulation
  reguard   regard
regular, -ly
regularity
regulate, -lated, -lating
regulation
regulator
regulatory
  reguler   regular
regurgitate, -tated, -tating
rehabilitate, -tated, -tating
rehabilitation
rehash, -ed, -ing
rehearsal
rehearse, -hearsed, -hearsing
  reherse   rehearse
reign, -ed, -ing (king)
  reign   rain (water)
  reign   rein (bridle)
reimburse, -bursed, -bursing
reimbursement
rein, -ed, -ing (bridle)
  rein   rain (water)
  rein   reign (rule)
reincarnation
reindeer, -deer
reinforce, -forced, -forcing
reinforcement
reinstate, -stated, -stating
reiterate, -rated, -rating
reiteration
reiterative, -ly
  rejeckshun   rejection

reject, -ed, -ing
rejection
  rejeme   regime
  rejister   register
rejoice, -joiced, -joicing
rejoin, -ed, -ing
rejoinder
  rejoise   rejoice
  rejoovenate   rejuvenate
rejuvenate, -nated, -nating
rejuvenation
  rekord   record

> For **rekw-** words, look
> under **requ-**.

  relaks   relax
relapse, -lapsed, -lapsing
relate, -lated, -lating
relation
relative, -ly
relativity
relax, -ed, -ing
relaxation
relay, -ed, -ing
release, -leased, -leasing
relegate, -gated, -gating
relegation
  releif   relief
relent, -ed, -ing
relentless, -ly
  relese   release
relevance
relevancy
  relevanse   relevance
relevant, -ly
  releve   relieve
  reli   rely
reliable, -bly
reliability
  reliabul   reliable
reliance
reliant
relic
relief
relieve, -lieved, -lieving
religion
religious, -ly

religun	religion
religus	religious
relinkwish	relinquish
relinquish, -ed, -ing	
relish, -ed, -ing	
relm	realm
reluctance	
reluctanse	reluctance
reluctant,-ly	
rely, relied, relying	
remain, -ed, -ing	
remainder	
remains	
remand, -ed, -ing	
remark, -ed, -ing	
remarkable, -bly	
remedial, -ly	
remedy, -dies	
remedy, -died, -dying	
remember, -ed, -ing	
remembrance	
remembranse	remembrance
remind, -ed, -ing	
reminder	
reminisce, -nisced, -niscing	
reminiscence	
reminiscent, -ly	
reminisense	reminiscence
reminisent	reminiscent
reminiss	reminisce
remishun	remission
remiss, -ly	
remission	
remit, -mitted, -mitting	
remittance	
remnant	
remonstrate, -trated, -trating	
remonstrative	
remooval	removal
remoove	remove
remorse	
remorseful, -ly	
remote, remoter, remotest	
remotely	
removable	
removalist	
remove, -moved, -moving	

remunerate, -rated, -rating	
remuneration	
remunerative, -ly	
ren	wren
Renaissance	
renal	
rench	wrench
rend, rent, rending	
render, -ed, -ing	
rendezvous, -voused, -vousing	
rendition	
renegade	
renege, reneged, reneging	
renew, -ed, -ing	
renounce, -nounced, -nouncing	
renovate, -vated, -vating	
renovater	renovator
renovation	
renovator	
renown	
renowned	
rent, -ed, -ing	
rental	
rentul	rental
renue	renew
renunciation	
reorganisation	
reorganise, -nised, -nising	
repair, -ed, -ing	
repairer	
reparable, -bly	
reparation	
repartee	
repast	
repatriate, -ated, -ating	
repatriation	
repay, -paid, -paying	
repeal, -ed, -ing	
repeat, -ed, -ing	
repeatedly	
repeater	
repel, -pelled, -pelling	
repellant	repellent
repellent, -ly	
repent, -ed, -ing	
repentance	
repentanse	repentance

repentant, -ly
  repercushun   repercussion
repertoire
repertory, -ries
  repetishus   repetitious
repetition
repetitious, -ly
  repetry   repertory
  repitition   repetition
replace, -placed, -placing
replacement
replay, -played, -playing
replenish, -ed, -ing
replenishment
replete
replica
reply, -plies
reply, -plied, -plying
report, -ed, -ing
reportable
reporter
repose, -posed, -posing
repository, -tories
  repositry   repository
  reposseshun   repossession
repossess, -ed, -ing
repossession
  reprehenshun   reprehension
reprehensible, -bly
reprehension
represent, -ed, -ing
representation
representational
representative, -ly
  represhun   repression
repress, -ed, -ing
  repressabul   repressible
repressible
repression
repressive, -ly
reprieve, -prieved, -prieving
reprimand, -ed, -ing
reprint, -ed, -ing
reprisal
  reprisul   reprisal
reproach, -ed, -ing
reproachable, -bly

reprobate, -bated, -bating
reprobation
  reproch   reproach
reproduce, -duced, -ducing
  reproducshun   reproduction
reproduction
reproof, -ed, -ing
reprove, -proved, -proving
reproval
reptile
reptilian
republic
republican
republicanism
repudiate, -ated, -ating
repudiation
repugnance
  repugnanse   repugnance
repugnant, -ly
repulse, -pulsed, -pulsing
repulsion
repulsive, -ly
reputable, -bly
  reputabul   reputable
reputation
repute, -puted, -puting
request, -ed, -ing
requiem
  requierment   requirement
require, -quired, -quiring
requirement
  requisishun   requisition
requisite
requisition
  rerite   rewrite
  reritten   rewritten
  rerote   rewrote
rescind, -ed, -ing
rescue, -cued, -cuing
rescuer
research, -ed, -ing
researcher
  reseat   receipt
  resede   recede
  reseipt   receipt
resemble, -bled, -bling
  resembul   resemble

resent, -ed, -ing (hurt)
   resent   recent (new)
resentful, -ly
resentment
   resepshun   reception
   reseptacul   receptacle
   reseptive   receptive
   reserch   research
reservation
reserve, -served, -serving
reservoir
   resess   recess
   resesshun   recession
   resession   recession
reset, -set, -setting
   reseve   receive
   resevoir   reservoir
reside, -sided, -siding
residence
   residenshul   residential
resident
residential
   residivision   recidivism
residual, -ly
residuary
residue
resign, -ed, -ing
resignation
resilience
resilient, -ly
resin
   resind   rescind
resinous
   resinus   resinous
   resipe   recipe
   resipient   recipient
   resiprocul   reciprocal
   resiprosity   reciprocity
resist, -ed, -ing
resistance
   resitation   recitation
resistor
   resite   recite
resolute, -ly
resolution
resolve, -solved, -solving
resonance

resonant, -ly
resonate, -nated, -nating
   resorce   resource
resort, -ed, -ing
resound, -ed, -ing
resource
resourceful, -ly
respect, -ed, -ing
respectability, -ties
respectable, -bly
   respectabul   respectable
respectful, -ly
respective, -ly
respiration
respirator
respiratory
   respiratry   respiratory
respite
resplendent, -ly
   responce   response
respond, -ed, -ing
respondent
response
responsibility, -ties
responsible, -bly
responsive, -ly
rest, -ed, -ing (sleep)
   rest   wrest (grab)
   restaration   restoration
restaurant
   resterant   restaurant
restful, -ly
   restitushion   restitution
restitution
restive, -ly
   restle   wrestle
   restler   wrestler
restless, -ly
restoration
restorative
restore, -stored, -storing
restrain, -ed, -ing
restraint
   restricshun   restriction
restrict, -ed, -ing
restriction
restrictive, -ly

restructure, -tured, -turing
result, -ed, -ing
resultant
resumay   résumé (review)
résumé (review)
resume, -sumed, -suming (take up)
resumption
resurgence
resurgent
resurrect, -ed, -ing
resurrection
resuscitate, -tated, -tating
resuscitation
resuscitator
resusitation   resuscitation
retail, -ed ,-ing
retain, -ed, -ing
retainer
retaliate, -ated, -ating
retaliation
retard, -ed, -ing
retardation
retch, -ed, -ing (vomit)
retch   wretch (victim)
retention
retentive, -ly
reticence
reticent, -ly
retina, -nas, -nae
retinew   retinue
retinue
retire, -tired, -tiring
retirement
retisent   reticent
retoric   rhetoric
retoricul   rhetorical
retort, -ed, -ing
retrace, -traced, -tracing
retract, -ed, -ing
retractable
retrase   retrace
retread, -treaded, -treading
retreat, -ed, -ing
retred   retread
retreive   retrieve
retrench, -ed, -ing
retrenchment

retribushun   retribution
retribution
retrieve, -trieved, -trieving
retrievable
retrieval
retriever
retroactive, -ly
retrograde, -graded, -grading
retrogreshun   retrogression
retrogress, -ed, -ing
retrogression
retrogressive, -ly
retro-rocket
retrospect
retrospective, -ly
return, -ed, -ing
reunion
reunite, -nited, -niting
rev, revved, revving
revalie   reveille
revaluation
revalue, -ued, -uing
revalueation   revaluation
reveal, -ed, -ing
reveille (bugle call)
revel, -elled, -elling
revelation
reveller (festivity)
revelry, -ries
revenew   revenue
revenge, -venged, -venging
revenue
reverberate, -rated, -rating
reverberation
reverberatory
revere, -vered, -vering (respect)
reverence
reverend
reverense   reverence
reverent, -ly
reverie (daydream)
reversal
reverse, -versed, -versing
reversion
revert, -ed, -ing
revertabul   revertible
revertible

review, -ed, -ing (survey)
   review   revue (theatre)
revile, -viled, -viling
revise, -vised, -vising
   revishun   revision
revision
revival
revivalism
revive, -vived, -viving
revocation
revoke, -voked, -voking
revolt, -ed, -ing
   revolushun   revolution
revolution
revolutionary, -ries
revolutionise, -nised, -nising
   revolutionry   revolutionary
revolve, -volved, -volving
revolver
revue (theatre)
   revue   review (survey)
   revulshun   revulsion
revulsion
reward, -ed, -ing
rhapsodical, -ly
rhapsodise, -dised, -dising
rhapsody, -dies
rhesus
rhetoric
rhetorical, -ly
rheumatic
rheumatism
rheumatoid arthritis
rhinestone
rhino, -nos
rhinoceros, -roses, -ros
rhododendron
rhombus, -buses, -bi
rhubarb
rhyme, rhymed, rhyming (verse)
rhythm
rhythmical, -ly
rib, ribbed, ribbing
ribald
ribaldry
ribbon
rice

rich, -ly
riches
Richter scale
rick, -ed, -ing
rickets
rickety
rickshaw
ricochet, -ed, -ing
   ricshore   rickshaw
rid, rid or ridded, ridding
   ridance   riddance
riddance
riddle, -dled, -dling
ride, rode, ridden, riding
rider
ridge, ridged, ridging
ridicule, -culed, -culing
ridiculous, -ly
   ridiculus   ridiculous
   ridul   riddle
   rie   rye (grain)
   rie   wry (askew)
Riesling
rife
riffraff
rifle, -fled, -fling
rift
   riful   rifle
rig, rigged, rigging
right, -ed, -ing (correct)
   right   rite (ceremony)
   right   write (inscribe)
righteous, -ly
rightful, -ly
right-handed
right-winger
rigid, -ly
rigidity
rigmarole
rigor mortis
rigorous, -ly
   rigorus   rigorous
rigour
rig-out
   rigul   wriggle
rile, riled, riling
rim, rimmed, rimming (edge)

rime, rimed, riming (frost)

   rime   rhyme (verse)

rind

ring, ringed, ringing (surround)

ring, rang, rung, ringing (bell)

   ring   wring (squeeze)

ringbark, -ed, -ing

ringer

   ringer   wringer

ring-in

ringleader

ringlet

ringtail possum

ringworm

rink

rinse, rinsed, rinsing

riot, -ed, -ing

riotous, -ly

   riotus   riotous

rip, ripped, ripping

ripcord

ripe, riper, ripest

ripen, -ed, -ing

rip-off

ripper

ripple, -pled, -pling

   rippul   ripple

> If the word is not under **ri-**
> look under **re-**.

rip-roaring

rip-tide

rise, rose, risen, rising

risk, -ed, -ing

   riskay   risqué

riskily

risky, -kier, -kiest

risqué

rissole

   rist   wrist

   rit   writ

rite (ceremony)

   rite   right (correct)

   rite   write (inscribe)

   riter   writer

   rithe   writhe

   ritten   written

ritual,-ly

rival, -valled, -valling

rivalry, -ries

river

rivergum

rivet, -ed, -ing

rivulet

   ro   roe (fish)

   ro   row (boat

roach, -ches

road (street)

   road   rode (did ride)

roadblock

roadworthiness

roadworthy

roar, -ed, -ing (noise)

   roar   raw (uncooked)

roast, -ed, -ing

rob, robbed, robbing

robber

robbery, -ries

robe, robed, robing

   robery   robbery

robin

robot

robust, -ly

rock, -ed, -ing

rocker

rockery, -ries

rocket, -ed, -ing

rocketry

rock'n'roll

rock-wallaby

rococo

rod

   rodayo   rodeo

rode (did ride)

   rode   road (street)

rodent

rodeo, -deos

   rodio   rodeo

roe (fish)

   roe   row (boat)

   roge   rogue

   rogish   roguish

rogue, rogued, roguing

roguery, -gueries

roguish,-ly
role (character)
roll, -ed, -ing (turn)
roll bar
rollcall
roller
roller-skate, -skated, -skating
rolling-pin
rollick, -ed, -ing
rollmop
roll-up
roly-poly
Roman Catholic
romance, -manced, -mancing
romantic, -ly
romanticise, -cised, -cising
romanticism
romanticist
Romany, -nies (gipsy)

| rombus | rhombus |
| rome | roam |

romp, -ed, -ing
rondo, -dos
roneo, -ed, -ing

| rong | wrong |

roo (kangaroo)

| roo | rue (regret) |
| roodiment | rudiment |

roof, roofs
roofless
roof-rack

rooful	rueful
rooge	rouge
rooin	ruin
rooinous	ruinous

rook, -ed, -ing
rookery, -ries
rookie

| rool | rule |
| roolet | roulette |

room, -ed, -ing

| roomatism | rheumatism |
| roomer | rumour |

roomy, -mier, -miest

roon	ruin
roopee	rupee
roorul	rural

| roose | ruse |

roost, -ed, -ing
rooster
root, -ed, -ing (plant)

| root | route (way) |

ropable
rope, roped, roping
ropeable
ropeway
ropey
ropy, ropier, ropiest

| ror | roar (noise) |
| ror | raw (uncooked) |

rort
rosary, -ries

| rosay | rosé (wine) |

rose, rosed, rosing (flower)
rosé (wine)
rosella
rosemary

| rosery | rosary |
| roset | rosette |

rosette
rosewood

| rosie | rosy |

rosily

| rost | roast |

roster
rostrum, -trums, -tra
rosy, rosier, rosiest
rot, rotted, rotting
rotary
rotate, -tated, -tating
rotation
rote (routine)

| rote | wrote (did write) |

| roten | rotten |
| roter | rotor |

rotisserie
rotor
rotten, -ly
rotund, -ly
rotundity

| roudy | rowdy |

rouge, rouged, rouging
rough, -ly

roughage

roughen, -ed, -ing

roughshod

   rought   wrought

   roulet   roulette

roulette, -letted, -letting

round, -ed, -ing

roundabout

rounders

roundly

round-up

rouse, roused, rousing

rouseabout

rout, routed, routing (defeat)

route (way)

   route   root (plant)

   routeen   routine

routine

rove, roved, roving

rover

row, -ed, -ing (boat)

   row   roe (fish)

   rowdie   rowdy

rowdily

rowdy, -dier, -diest

rowel, -elled, -elling

rowlock

   rownd   round

   rowse   rouse

   rowt   rout

royal, -ly

royalist

royalty, -ties

rub, rubbed, rubbing

rubber

rubbish

rubbishy

rubble

rubella

   ruber   rubber

rubicund

   rubie   ruby

   rubish   rubbish

rubric

   rubul   rubble

ruby, -bies

ruck, -ed, -ing

rucksack

   ruckshun   ruction

ruction

rudder

ruddy, -dier, -diest

rude, ruder, rudest (rough)

   rude   rued (regret)

rudely

rudeness

   ruder   rudder

rudimentary

rudiments

   rudy   ruddy

rue, rued, ruing (regret)

   rued   rude (rough)

rueful, -ly (pity)

   ruf   rough (coarse)

   ruffen   roughen

ruffian

ruffle, -fled, -fling (annoy)

   rufful   ruffle

   rufian   ruffian

   rufige   roughage

   rufle   ruffle

   ruful   rueful

rug, rugged, rugging

rugby

ruin, -ed, -ing (destroy)

   ruin   rune (letter)

ruination

ruinous, -ly

   ruinus   ruinous

rule, ruled, ruling

ruler

rum

   rumatism   rheumatism

rumba

rumble, -bled, -bling

   rumbul   rumble

rumen, -mina

   rumer   rumour

   rumige   rummage

ruminant

ruminate, -nated, -nating

rummage, -maged, -maging

rumour, -ed, -ing

rump

rumple, -pled, -pling
  rumpul   rumple
rumpus
run, ran, run, running
runabout
rune (letter)
  rune   ruin (destroy)
rung (did ring)
  rung   wrung
               (squeezed)

run-in
runner
runner-up
runny
run-off
run-of-the-mill
run-on
runt
runway
  rupcher   rupture
rupee
rupture, -tured, -turing
rural, -ly
ruse
rush, -ed, -ing
  Rushun   Russian
  rusit   russet
rusk
russet
Russian roulette
rust, -ed, -ing
rustic, -ally
rusticity, -ties
rustle, -tled, -tling
rustproof
rusty, -tier, -tiest
rut, rutted, rutting
ruthless, -ly
rye (grain)
  rye   wry (askew)
rye-grass
  ryme   rhyme
  rythm   rhythm

Ss

Sabath	Sabbath
Sabbath	
sabbatical	
sabbaticul	sabbatical
sabel	sable
saber	sabre
Sabin vaccine	
sable	
sabot	
sabotage, -taged, -taging	
saboteur	
sabre, -bred, -bring	
sabre-toothed	
sac (bag)	
sac	sack (hessian)
sacarin	saccharin
saccharin	
sacerdotal, -ly	
sachay	sachet
sachel	satchel
sachet	
sack, -ed, -ing	
sackarin	saccharin
sackcloth	
sacrament	
sacramental, -ly	
sacred, -ly	
sacredness	
sacrement	sacrament
sacrifice, -ficed, -ficing	
sacrificial, -ly	
sacrifise	sacrifice
sacrifishul	sacrificial
sacriledge	sacrilege
sacrilege	
sacrilegious, -ly	
sacrilige	sacrilege
sacriligus	sacrilegious

sacrosanct	
sad, sadder, saddest	
sadden, -ed, -ing	
saddle, saddled, saddling	
saddleback	
saddler	
saddlery, -ries	
saden	sadden
sadler	saddler
sadlery	saddlery
sadism	
sadist	
sadistic, -ally	
sadul	saddle
safari, -ris	
safe, safer, safest	
safegard	safeguard
safeguard	
safekeeping	
safely	
safety, -ties	
saffire	sapphire
saffron	
safire	sapphire
safron	saffron
saftie	safety
sag, sagged, sagging	
saga	
sagacious, -ly	
sagacity, -ties	
sagasity	sagacity
sagayshus	sagacious
sage, sager, sagest	
Sagittarius	
sago	
said	
sail (boat)	
sail	sale (sold)
sailsman	salesman
sailboard	
sailcloth	
sailor	
sailplane, -planed, -planing	
saint, -ly	
sainted	
sainthood	
saintliness	

sake	
sakred	sacred
sakson	Saxon
saksophone	saxophone
salaam	
salacious, -ly	
salad	
salamander	
salami	
salamy	salami
salaried	
salary, -ries (wage)	
salary	celery (food)
salasious	salacious
sale (sold)	
sale	sail (boat)
saleability	
saleable, -ly	
saleabul	saleable
salene	saline
salesgirl	
saleslady, -dies	
salesman, -men	
salesmanship	
salesroom	
saleswoman, -women	
saleyard	
salie	sally
salience	
saliense	salience
salient, -ly	
saline	
salinity	
saliva	
salivary	
salivate, -vated, -vating	
salivation	
sallow	
sallowish	
sally, -lies	
sally, -lied, -lying	
salm	psalm

For all other **sall-** words,
look under **sal-**.

salmon
salmonella

salon	
saloobrius	salubrious
saloon	
saloot	salute
salow	sallow
salt, -ed, -ing	
saltbush	
saltcellar	
saltery	psaltery
saltseller	saltcellar
salubrious, -ly	
salubrius	salubrious
salud	salad
salutary	
salutation	
salute, -luted, -luting	
salvage, -vaged, -vaging (save)	
salvage	selvedge (edge)
salvager	
salve, salved, salving	
salver	
salvidge	salvage (save)
salvidge	selvedge (edge)
salvo, -vos, -voes	
sal volatile	
samantic	semantic
samba	
same	
samon	salmon
samovar	
Samoyed	
sampan	
sample, -pled, -pling	
sampler	
sampul	sample
samurai	
samuri	samurai
sanatarium	sanitarium
sanatorium, -toriums, -toria	
sancshun	sanction
sanctification	
sanctify, -fied, -fying	
sanctimonious, -ly	
sanctimonius	sanctimonious
sanction, -ed, -ing	
sanctity, -ties	
sanctuary, -ries	

sanctum, -tums		sapwood	
sand, -ed, -ing		sarcasm	
sandal		sarcastic, -ally	
sandalwood		sarcofagus	sarcophagus
sandbag, -bagged, -bagging		sarcophagus, -gi, -guses	
sandbank		sardeen	sardine
sandblast, -ed, -ing		sardine, -dines	
sandfly, -flies		sardonic, -ally	
sandpaper, -ed, -ing		sargent	sergeant
sandpiper		sari	
sandshoe		sarong	
sandsoap		sarsaparilla	
sandstone		sartorial, -ly	
sandul	sandal	sary	sari
sandwhich	sandwich	saserdotal	sacerdotal
sandwich, -wiches		sash	
sandwitch	sandwich	sashay (trip)	
sane, saner, sanest (not mad)		sashay	sachet (bag)
sane	seine (net)	sashiate	satiate
sanely		sassafras	
saneness		Sassenach	
sang		Satan (devil)	
sangfroid		Satanic, -ally	
sanguinary		Satanism	
sanguine, -ly		Satanist	
sangwin	sanguine	satay	
sanitarium, -tariums, -taria		satchel	
sanitary		sate, sated, sating	
sanitation		sateen (cotton)	
sanitorium	sanatorium	satellite	
sanity		Saten	Satan (devil)
sank		saten	sateen (cotton)
		saten	satin (silk)
		Saterday	Saturday
		satiabel	satiable

For all other **sank-** words,
look under **sanct-**.

sanskrit		satiable, -ly	
Santa Claus		satiate, -ated, -ating	
Santa Klaus	Santa Claus	satiation	
sap, sapped, sapping		satin (silk)	
saper	sapper	satinwood	
sapience		satire (sarcasm)	
sapiency		satire	satyr (a god)
sapient, -ly		satiric	
sapling		satirical, -ly	
sapper		satirist	
sapphire		satisfacshun	satisfaction
sappling	sapling	satisfaction	

satisfactorily
satisfactory

satisfactry	satisfactory
satisfiabul	satisfiable

satisfy, -fied, -fying
saturate, -rated, -rating
saturation
Saturday
Saturn (planet)

saturn	sauterne (wine)

saturnine, -ly
satyr (a god)

satyr	satire (sarcasm)

sauce (liquid)

sauce	source (origin)

saucepan
saucer

saucerer	sorcerer
saucery	sorcery

saucily
sauciness
saucy, -cier, -ciest
sauerkraut
sauna
saunter, -ed, -ing
saurian
sausage

sausy	saucy

sauté, -téed, -téeing
sauterne (wine)

sauturn	sauterne

savage, savaged, savaging
savagely
savagery, -ries

savana	savanna

savanna
savant
save, saved, saving
saveloy
saver (keeper)

saver	savour (taste)
savier	saviour
savige	savage
savigery	savagery
savigry	savagery

saving
saviour

savoir-faire
savory, -vories (herb)
savour, -ed, -ing (taste)

savour	saver (keeper)

savoury, -vouries (tasty)
savoy
savvy
saw, sawed, sawing (cut)

saw	soar (rise)
saw	sore (hurt)
sawcer	saucer
sawcey	saucy
sawdid	sordid

sawdust
sawmill

sawna	sauna
sawnter	saunter

sawpit

saws	sauce (liquid)
saws	source (origin)
sawser	saucer
sawsey	saucy

saxhorn

saxofone	saxophone
saxofonist	saxophonist

Saxon
saxophone
saxophonist
say, said, saying

sayance	seance

say-so
scab, scabbed, scabbing
scabbard

scabees	scabies

scabies
scaffold
scaffolding
scalar
scald, -ed, -ing (burn)

scald	scold (chide)

scale, scaled, scaling

scaliwag	scallywag

scallop, -ed, -ing
scallywag
scalp, -ed, -ing
scalpel
scalper

scalpul	scalpel	scepter	sceptre
scamp		sceptic	
scamper, -ed, -ing		sceptical, -ly	
scan, scanned, scanning		scepticism	
scandal		sceptre	
scandalise, -lised, -lising		scerge	scourge
scandalmonger		scermish	skirmish
scanner		schedule, -uled, -uling	
scanshun	scansion	schematic, -ally	
scansion		scheme, schemed, scheming	
scant		schemer	
scantness		schism	
scanty, scantier, scantiest		schismatic	
scapegoat		schizofrenia	schizophrenia
scapula, -lae		schizoid	
scar, scarred, scarring		schizophrenia	
scarab		schizophrenic	
scarce, scarcer, scarcest		schnapper	
scarcely		schnapps	
scarceness		scholar	
scarcity, -ties		scholarly	
scare, scared, scaring		scholarship	
scarecrow		scholastic, -ally	
scaremonger		scholasticism	
scarf, scarfs, scarves		school, -ed, -ing	
scarify, -fied, -fying		schoolboy	
scarlet		schoolgirl	
scarp		schooner	
scarper		sciatic	
scarsity	scarcity	sciatica	
scary, scarier, scariest		science	
scate	skate	scientific, -ally	
scathing, -ly		scientist	
scatter, -ed, -ing		scimitar	
scatterbrain		scintillate, -lated, -lating	
scatty, -tier, -tiest		sciolism	
scavenge, -venged, -venging		scion	
scavenger		scissors	
sceme	scheme	scitsofrenia	schizophrenia
scenario, -narios		sclerosis, -ses	
scene (view)		scoff, -ed, -ing	
scene	seen (to see)	scolar	scholar
scenery, -neries		scolarship	scholarship
scenic, -ally		scolastic	scholastic
scent (perfume)		scold, -ed, -ing (chide)	
scent	cent (coin)	scold	scald (burn)
scent	sent (to send)	scollop	

scone

  scool   school

scoop, -ed, -ing

scooter

scope

scorch, -ed, -ing

score, scored, scoring

scorer

scorn, -ed, -ing

scornful, -ly

Scorpio

scorpion

  scorpiun   scorpion

Scotch

scotch, -ed, -ing

scot-free

Scotsman, -men

Scotswoman, -women

Scottish

scoundrel

  scoundrul   scoundrel

scour, -ed, -ing (scratch)

  scour   scow (barge)

scourge, scourged, scourging

scout, -ed, -ing

scow (barge)

  scow   scour (scratch)

scowl, -ed, -ing

  scowndrel   scoundrel

  scowt   scout

scrabble, -bled, -bling

  scrabbul   scrabble

scrag, scragged, scragging

scraggly, -glier, -gliest

scraggy, -gier, -giest

scram, scrammed, scramming

scramble, -bled, -bling

  scrambul   scramble

scrap, scrapped, scrapping

scrapbook

scrape, scraped, scraping

scraper

scrappily

scrappy, -pier, -piest

  scrapy   scrappy

scratch, -ed, -ing

scrawl, -ed, -ing

scrawny, -nier, -niest

scream, -ed, -ing

screamer

scree

screech, -ed, -ing

screed

screen, -ed, -ing

screenplay

screw, -ed, -ing

screwball

screwdriver

  screwtinise   scrutinise

screwy, screwier, screwiest

scribal (writer)

scribble, -bled, -bling (write)

scribbler

  scribbul   scribble

scribe, scribed, scribing

scrim

  scrimage   scrimmage

scrimmage, -maged, -maging

scrimp, -ed, -ing

scrip (receipt)

  scripcher   scripture

script (handwriting)

scriptural, -ly

Scripture

scrofula

scrofulous, -ly

scroll

  scroo   screw

  scrotem   scrotum

scrotum

scrounge, scrounged, scrounging

scrounger

  scrownge   scrounge

scrub, scrubbed, scrubbing

scrubber

scrubby, -bier, -biest

scruff

scruffy, scruffier, scruffiest

scrum, scrummed, scrumming

  scrumage   scrummage

scrummage

  scrumpshus   scrumptious

scrumptious, -ly

scrumptiousness

scrumshus   scrumptious
scrunch, -ed, -ing
scruple, -pled, -pling
scrupul   scruple
scrupulosity
scrupulous, -ly
scrupulousness
scrutinise, -nised, -nising
scrutiny, -nies
scuba
scud, scudded, scudding
scuff, -ed, -ing
scuffle, -fled, -fling
scuful   scuffle
scul   scull (row)
scul   skull (head)
sculery   scullery
scull, -ed, -ing (row)
scull   skull (head)
scullery, -leries
scullion
scullyon   scullion
sculpcher   sculpture
sculpt, -ed, -ing
sculpter   sculptor
sculptor
sculptress
sculptural, -ly
sculpture, -tured, -turing
scum, scummed, scumming
scummy, -mier, -miest
scungie   scungy
scungy
scurf
scurge   scourge
scurie   scurry
scurilus   scurrilous
scurrilous, -ly
scurrulus   scurrilous
scurry, -ries
scurry, -ried, -rying
scurvey   scurvy
scurvily
scurvy, -vier, -viest
scury   scurry
scuttel   scuttle
scuttle, -tled, -tling

scuttlebutt
scuttul   scuttle
scythe, scythed, scything
sea (ocean)
see   see (look)
sea-anemone
seaboard
seabord   seaboard
seafarer
seafaring
seafood
seagoing
seagull
seahorse
seal, -ed, -ing
sealant
sealer
sea-level
sealing (close)
sealing   ceiling (roof)
seam, -ed, -ing (join)
seam   seem (appear)
seaman, -men (sailors)
seamanship
seamen   semen (seed)
seamstress
seamy -mier, -miest
sean   scene (view)
sean   seen (to see)
seance
seanse   seance
seaplane
sear, -ed, -ing (burn)
sear   seer (prophet)
search, -ed, -ing
searcher
searchlight
search-warrant
sea-scout
sea-shell
seashore
seasickness
seaside
season, -ed, -ing
seasonable, -bly
seasonabul   seasonable
seasonal, -ly

seat, -ed, -ing
seawards
seaweed
seaworthiness
seaworthy
sebaceous

  sebashus   sebaceous
  secaters   secateurs
secateurs
secede, -ceded, -ceding

  secesshun   secession
secession

  secetary   secretary
seclude, -cluded, -cluding

  seclushun   seclusion
seclusion
second, -ed, -ing
secondary, -arily
secondary boycott
second-class
second-degree
second-hand
secondly
second-rate

  secondry   secondary
seconds

  secratery   secretary
secrecy, -cies

  secreshun   secretion
  secresy   secrecy
secret, -ly
secretarial
secretariat

  secretariul   secretarial
secretary, -ries
secrete, -creted, -creting
secretion
secretive, -ly

  secretry   secretary
  secshun   section
sect

  sectar   sector
sectarian
sectarianism
section
sectional, -ly

  secter   sector

sector
secular, -ly
secularism
secularist
securable

  securabul   securable
secure, -cured, -curing
security, -ties

  sed   said
  sedament   sediment
sedan
sedate, -dated, -dating
sedation
sedative
sedentary

  sedentery   sedentary
  seder   cedar
sedge
sediment
sedimentary
sedimentation

  sedimentery   sedimentary
  sedishun   sedition
  sedishus   seditious
sedition
seditious, -ly

  seditive   sedative
seduce, -duced, -ducing
seducer

  seducshun   seduction
seduction
seductive, -ly
seductiveness
sedulous

  sedulus   sedulous
see, saw, seen, seeing (look)

  see   sea (ocean)
seed, seeded, seeding (plant)

  seed   cede (yield)
seediness
seedling
seedy, seedier, seediest

  seefarer   seafarer
  seefood   seafood
  seege   siege
  seegull   seagull
seek, sought, seeking

seel	seal	seismologist	
seelant	sealant	seismology	
seeler	sealer	seize, seized, seizing	
see-level	sea-level	seizure	
seeling	ceiling (roof)	sekaters	secateurs
seeling	sealing (close)	sekond	second
seem, -ed, -ing (appear)		sekrete	secrete
seem	seam (join)	seks	sex
seeman	seaman (sailor)	sekshun	section
seemly, -lier, -liest		sekstant	sextant
seemstress	seamstress	seksual	sexual
seemy	seamy	seksy	sexy
seen (to see)		sekt	sect
seen	scene (view)	sektor	sector
seenery	scenery	sekular	secular
seenic	scenic	sekure	secure
seenile	senile	sekwel	sequel
seep, -ed, -ing		sekwense	sequence
seepage		sekwin	sequin
seepige	seepage	Selcius	Celsius
seequel	sequel	seldom, -ly	
seer (prophet)		selebrate	celebrate
seer	sear (burn)	selebrity	celebrity
searsucker	seersucker	seleckshun	selection
seersucker		select, -ed, -ing	
seesaw		selecter	selector
seese	cease	selection	
seesfire	ceasefire	selective, -ly	
seeshore	seashore	selectivity	
seesun	season	selector	
seet	seat	seler	cellar (room)
seethe, seethed, seething		seler	seller (goods)
seeweed	seaweed	selerity	celerity
seeze	seize	selery	celery (food)
seezure	seizure	selery	salary (wage)
sege	sedge	selestial	celestial
segment		self, selves	
segmentation		self-addressed	
segregate, -gated, -gating		self-aggrandisement	
segregation		self-assurance	
segregationist		self-centred	
seige	siege	self-confessed	
seine (net)		self-confidence	
seine	sane (not mad)	self-confident	
seismagraf	seismograph	self-conscious, -ly	
seismic		self-contained	
seismograph		self-defence	

self-denial
self-destruct
self-determination
self-employed
self-evident, -ly
self-fertilisation
self-government
self-image
  self-imidge — self-image
self-important, -ly
self-interest
selfish,-ly
selfishness
selfless, -ly
self-made
self-opinionated
self-pollination
self-possessed
self-raising flour
self-respect
self-righteous, -ly
self-rule
self-sacrifice
self-service
self-sown
self-starter
self-sufficient
self-willed
  selibacy — celibacy
  selibat — celibate
  selibrate — celebrate
sell, sold, selling (goods)
  sell — cell (prison)
seller (goods)
  seller — cellar (room)
  sellofane — cellophane
  sellophane — cellophane
sell-out
  sellullar — cellular
  selluloid — celluloid
  sellulose — cellulose
  sellvage — salvage (save)
  sellvedge — selvedge (edge)
  Selsius — Celsius
  selular — cellular
  seluloid — celluloid
  selulose — cellulose

selvage (edge)
selvedge (edge)
  selvedge — salvage (save)
  semafor — semaphore
semantic
semaphore, -phored, -phoring
semblance
  semblanse — semblance
semen (seed)
  semen — seamen (sailors)
semester
semibreve
  semicercul — semicircle
semicircle
semicircular
semicolon
semiconductor
semidetached
seminal, -ly
seminar
seminary, -aries
  seminery — seminary
semiprecious
  semipreshus — semiprecious
semiquaver
Semite
  semitery — cemetery
Semitic
semitone
semitrailer
semolina
  sena — senna
  senario — scenario
  senat — senate
senate
  senater — senator
senator
senatorial
  senatoriul — senatorial
send, sent, sending
sender
senile
  senilitey — senility
senility
senior
seniority, -ties

senna
  senotaf   cenotaph
  sensability   sensibility
  sensabul   sensible
sensation
sensational, -ly
sensationalise, -ised, -ising
sensationalism
sensationalist
  sensatise   sensitise
sense, sensed, sensing
  senser   censer (incense)
  senser   censor (books)
  senser   sensor (device)
  senshual   sensual
  senshur   censure (blame)
sensible, -bly
sensibility, -ties
  sensibul   sensible
sensitise, -tised, -tising
sensitivity, -ties
sensor (device)
  sensor   censer (incense)
  sensor   censor (books)
  sensorey   sensory
  sensorious   censorious
sensory, -orily
sensual, -ly
sensualist
  sensualitey   sensuality
sensuality, -ties
sensuous, -ly
  sensus   census
sent (to send)
  sent   cent (money)
  sent   scent (perfume)
  sentenary   centenary
sentence, -tenced, -tencing
  sentenchus   sententious
  sentennial   centennial
sententious, -ly
  senter   centre
sentience
sentient, -ly
  sentigrade   Centigrade
  sentigram   centigram
sentiment

sentimental, -ly
sentimentalism
sentimentalist
sentimentality, -ties
  sentimeter   centimetre
sentinel, -nelled, -nelling
  sentipede   centipede
  sentor   centaur
  sentral   central
  sentralise   centralise
  sentrey   sentry
  sentrifugal   centrifugal
  sentifuge   centrifuge
  sentripetal   centripetal
sentry, -tries
  sentupul   centuple
  senturion   centurion
  sentury   century
  senyor   senior
  senyority   seniority
sepal
separable, -bly
  separabul   separable
separate, -rated, -rating
separately
separation
separationist
separator
  seperabul   separable
  seperate   separate
  seperation   separation
  sephalitis   cephalitis
sepia
sepoy
sepsis
September
septennial, -ly
  septer   sceptre
septet
septic
septicaemia
  septisemia   septicaemia
septuagenarian
sepulchral, -ly
sepulchre
  sepulchrul   sepulchral
  sepulker   sepulchre

sequel	
sequence	
sequense	sequence
sequenshul	sequential
sequential, -ly	
sequester, -ed, -ing	
sequestration	
sequin	
ser	sir
seraf	seraph
serafic	seraphic
seramic	ceramic
seranade	serenade
serch	search
seremony	ceremony
seraph, -aphs, -aphim	
seraphic, -ally	
serch	search
sere (dry)	
sere	sear (burn)
serebrul	cerebral
sereen	serene
serees	series
serenade, -naded, -nading	
serendipity	
serene, -ly	
serenitey	serenity
serenity, -ties	
seres	series
sereze	cerise
serf (slave)	
serf	surf (sea)
serfdom	
serge (cloth)	
serge	surge (rush)
sergeant	
serial, -ly (part)	
serial	cereal (grain)
serialisation	
serialise, -lised, -lising	
seribelum	cerebellum
seribrul	cerebral
seribrum	cerebrum
series	
serif	
serimonial	ceremonial
serimonius	ceremonious

serimony	ceremony
serious, -ly	
seriousness	
serius	serious
serjent	sergeant
serloin	sirloin
serly	surly
serman	sermon
sermise	surmise
sermon	
sermount	surmount
sername	surname
serpent	
serpentine	
serplice	surplice (gown)
serplus	surplus (extra)
serprise	surprise
serrate, -rated, -rating	
serration	
serry, -ried, -rying	
sertain	certain
sertainty	certainty
sertax	surtax
sertifiabul	certifiable
sertificate	certificate
sertify	certify
sertitude	certitude
serum, sera, serums	
servant	
servay	survey
servaylanse	surveillance
serve, served, serving	
server	
servery, serveries	
servical	cervical
service, -viced, -vicing	
serviceability	
serviceable, -bly	
serviceabul	serviceable
serviceman, -men	
servicewoman, -women	
serviet	serviette
serviette	
serviks	cervix
servile, -ly	
servility	
servitude	

servival	survival
servive	survive
serviver	survivor
servix	cervix
sesame	
sesayshun	cessation
sese	cease
seseed	secede
seseshun	secession
seshun	cession (yield)
seshun	session (period)
sesless	ceaseless
seson	season
sesonabul	seasonable
sesonal	seasonal
sespit	cesspit
sesquicentenary, -ries	
sesseshun	secession
session (period)	
session	cession (yield)
set, set, setting	
setback	
setee	settee
seter	setter
setul	settle
settee	
setter	
settle, -tled, -tling	
settlement	
settler	
settul	settle
set-up	
seudo	pseudo
seudonim	pseudonym
sevear	severe
seven	
seventeen	
seventeenth	
seventh	
Seventh-Day Adventist	
seventieth	
seventy, -ties	
sever, -ed, -ing	
several, -ly	
severance	
severanse	severance
severe, -verer, -verest	

severely	
severitey	severity
severity, -ties	
sew, sewed, sewn, sewing (stitch)	
sew	sow (plant)
sewage	
sewer (drain)	
sewer (stitcher)	
sewer	sower (planter)
sewerage	
sewerige	sewerage
sewige	sewage
sex, -ed, -ing	
sexiness	
sexist	
sextant	
sextet	
sexton	
sexual, -ly	
sexualitey	sexuality
sexuality	
sexy, sexier, sexiest	
sezarian	caesarian
sfere	sphere
sfericul	sperical
sferoid	spheroid
sfincter	sphincter
sfinx	sphinx
sha	shah
shabbily	
shabbiness	
shabby, -bier, -biest	
shaby	shabby
shack	
shackle, -led, -ling	
shackul	shackle
shaddow	shadow
shade, shaded, shading	
shadow, -ed, -ing	
shadowy	
shady, -dier, -diest	
shaft	
shag, shagged, shagging	
shagginess	
shaggy, -gier, -giest	
shagrin	chagrin
shagy	shaggy

shah
  shak   shack
shake, shook, shaken, shaking
shakedown
shaker
Shakespearian
shake-up
  shakey   shaky
shakily
shakiness
shaky, shakier, shakiest
  shal   shall
  shalay   chalet
shale
  shalet   chalet
shall (will)
  shall   shell (cover)
shallot
shallow, -ly
shallowness
sham, shammed, shaming
shamble, -bled, -bling
shambles
  shambul   shamble
shame, shamed, shaming
shamefaced, -ly
shameful, -ly
shameless, -ly
  shampane   champagne
shampoo, -ed, -ing
shamrock
  shamy   chamois
  shandeleer   chandelier
  shandie   shandy
shandy, -dies
shanghai, -haied, -haiing
shank
shan't (shall not)
  shant   shan't
shantung
shanty, -ties
shape, shaped, shaping
shapeliness
shapely, -lier, -liest
  shaperon   chaperone
  sharade   charade
shard

share, shared, sharing
sharebroker
sharefarmer
shareholder
shark
sharkskin
sharp, -ly
sharpen, -ed, -ing
sharpener
sharper
sharpness
sharpshooter
sharpwitted
  shasee   chassis
shashlik
  shater   shatter
  shatow   chateau
shatter, -ed, -ing
shave, shaved, shaven, shaving
shaver
shawl
sheaf, sheaves
shear, sheared, shorn, shearing (cut)
  shear   sheer (thin)
shearer
shearwater
sheath, sheaths
sheathe, sheathed, sheathing
sheave, sheaved, sheaving
shed, shed, shedding
  shedule   schedule
  sheef   sheaf
  sheek   chic (smart)
  sheek   sheik (ruler)
sheen
sheep, sheep
sheep-dip
sheepdog
sheepish, -ly
sheepishness
sheep-run
sheepskin
sheer, -ed, -ing (swerve)
sheer (thin)
  sheer   shear (cut)
sheet, -ed, -ing
  shef   chef

sheik (ruler)

  sheik   shake (move)

sheila

  sheild   shield

shekel

  shel   shell

  shelac   shellac

shelf, shelves

  shelfish   shellfish

shell, -ed, -ing (cover)

she'll (she will)

  shell   she'll

shellac, -lacked, -lacking

shellfish, -fishes, -fish

shell-shocked

shelly, -lier, -liest

shelter, -ed, -ing

shelve, shelved, shelving

shemozzle

shenanigan

she-oak

  sheperd   shepherd

shepherd, -ed, -ing

shepherdess

sherbet

  sherbut   sherbet

  sherie   sherry

sherif (Muslim leader)

sheriff (law man)

sherry, -ries

  shery   sherry

  sheth   sheath

  sheves   sheaves

  shevron   chevron

shibboleth

  shic   chic (smart)

  shic   sheik (ruler)

  shicanery   chicanery

shickered

shied

shield, -ed, -ing

  shiffon   chiffon

shift, -ed, -ing

shiftiness

shiftless, -ly

shifty, -tier, -tiest

  shiling   shilling

shillelagh

shilling

shimmer, -ed, -ing

shimmery

shimmy, -mies

shimmy, -mied, -mying

shin, shinned, shinning

shindig

shine, shone, shined, shining

shiner

  shingel   shingle

shingle, -gled, -gling

shingles

  shinguls   shingles

shiny, shinier, shiniest

ship, shipped, shipping

shipment

  shipreck   shipwreck

  shipright   shipwright

shipshape

shipwreck, -ed, -ing

shipwright

shiralee

shirk, -ed, -ing

shirker

shirr, -ed, -ing

shirt

shirty

shish-kebab

  shivalrey   chivalry

  shivalrus   chivalrous

shiver, -ed, -ing

shivery

  shnaps   schnapps

shoal, -ed, -ing

shock, -ed, -ing

shocker

shod

shoddily

shoddiness

shoddy, -dier, -diest

  shodie   shoddy

  shody   shoddy

shoe, shoes

shoe, shod, shoeing (footwear)

  shoe   shoo (scare)

shoehorn

shoelace	
shoemaker	
shoeshine	
shoestring	
shofer	chauffeur
shogun	
sholder	shoulder
shole	shoal
shoo, -ed, -ing (scare)	
shoo	shoe (footwear)
shood	should
shook	
shoot, shot, shooting (gun)	
shoot	chute (channel)
shooter	
shoot-out	
shop, shopped, shopping	
shopkeeper	
shop-lift, -ed, -ing	
shop-lifter	
shop-soiled	
shop-steward	
shore, shored, shoring (sea)	
shore	sure (certain)
shorely	surely
shorety	surety
shorn	
short, -ly	
shortage	
shortbread	
shortbred	shortbread
shortcake	
short-change, -changed, -changing	
short-circuit, -ed, -ing	
shortcoming	
shorten, -ed, -ing	
shortfall	
shorthand	
shortidge	shortage
shorts	
short-sighted	
short-sited	short-sighted
short-wave	
shot	
shotgun	
shot-put	
shot-putter	

should	
shoulder, -ed, -ing	
shoulder-blade	
shout, -ed, -ing	
shove, -ed, -ing	
shovel, -ed, -ing	
shoveler (bird)	
shoveller (bird), (person)	
shovinism	chauvinism
shovinist	chauvinist
show, showed, shown, showing	
showboat	
showdown	
shower	
showery	
showily	
showjumper	
showjumping	
showman, -men	
showmanship	
show-off	
showt	shout
showy, showier, showiest	
shrank	
shrapnel	
shred, shredded, shredding	
shredder	
shreek	shriek
shrew	
shrewd, -ly	
shrewish, -ly	
shriek, -ed, -ing	
shrift	
shrike	
shrill	
shrimp	
shrine	
shrink, shrank, shrunk, shrinking	
shrinkage	
shrinkige	shrinkage
shrivel, -elled, -elling	
shroo	shrew
shrood	shrewd
shroud	
shrowd	shroud
shrub	
shrubbery	

shrug, shrugged, shrugging
shrunk
shudder, -ed, -ing
   shuffel — shuffle
shuffle, -fled, -fling
shun, shunned, shunning
shunt, -ed, -ing
shunter
   shurbet — sherbert
   shurk — shirk
   shurt — shirt
shush, -ed, -ing
shut, shut, shutting
shutdown
shut-eye
shut-out
   shuttel — shuttle
shutter
shuttle, -tled, -tling
shuttlecock
   shuttul — shuttle
   shuttulcock — shuttlecock
   shutul — shuttle
   shuve — shove
   shuvel — shovel
shy, shied, shying
shy, shyer, shyest
shyly
shyness
shyster
   sianide — cyanide
   siatic — sciatic
   sibernetics — cybernetics
sibilant, -ly
sibling
   sicamore — sycamore
   sicedelic — psychedelic
   siciatry — psychiatry
   sicick — psychic
sick
sicken, -ed, -ing
sickie
sickle
sickliness
sickly, -lier, -liest
   sickul — sickle
   siclamate — cyclamate

   siclamen — cyclamen
   sicle — cycle
   siclic — cyclic
   siclist — cyclist
   siclone — cyclone
   siclotron — cyclotron
   sicoanalise — psychoanalyse
   sicological — psychological
   sicology — psychology
   sicopant — sycophant
   sicopath — psychopath
   sicosis — psychosis
   sicosomatic — psychosomatic
   sicotherapist — psychotherapist
   sicotic — psychotic
   sicul — cycle
side, sided, siding
sideboard
   sidebord — sideboard
sidelight
sideline
   sidelite — sidelight
   sider — cider
sideshow
sidestep, -stepped, -stepping
sidetrack, -ed, -ing
sideways
   sidel — sidle
sidle, -dled, -dling
   sie — sigh
siege, sieged, sieging
sienna
   sience — science
   siense — science
   sientific — scientific
   sientist — scientist
sierra
siesta
sieve, sieved, sieving
   sieze — seize
   sifer — cypher
   sifilis — syphilis
   sifon — syphon
sift, -ed, -ing
   sigar — cigar
   sigaret — cigarette
sigh, -ed, -ing

sight, -ed, -ing (view)

sight	cite (quote)
sight	site (place)

sightless, -ly
sightly, -lier, -liest
sightseeing
sightseer
sigma
sign, -ed, -ing (mark)

sign	sine (maths)

signal, -ed, -ing
signatory, -ries

signatry	signatory

signature

signefy	signify

signet (ring)

signet	cygnet (swan)

significance

significanse	significance

significant, -ly
signification

signifie	signify

signify, -fied, -fying
signpost

signul	signal

sign-writer

sikedelic	psychedelic
sikey	psyche

Sikh

sikiatrist	psychiatrist
sikiatry	psychiatry
sikick	psychic
siksty	sixty
silabul	syllable
silabus	syllabus

silage
silence, silenced, silencing
silencer

silense	silence

silent, -ly

silestial	celestial
silf	sylph

silhouette, -etted, -etting
silica
silicon (element)
silicone (synthetic)
silicosis

silie	silly
silige	silage
silinder	cylinder
silindricul	cylindrical

silk
silken
silkiness
silk-screen
silkworm
silky, -kier, -kiest
silky oak
sill

sillabul	syllable

silliness
silly, -lier, -liest
silo, -los

silogism	syllogism

silt, -ed, -ing

siluet	silhouette

silver, -ed, -ing
silverfish, -fish, -fishes
silverside
silversmith
silvery

sily	silly
simbiosis	symbiosis
simbiotic	symbiotic
simbol	cymbal (music)
simbol	symbol (sign)
simbolicul	symbolical
simbolise	symbolise
simbolism	symbolism
siment	cement
simer	simmer
simetry	symmetry
simfoney	symphony

simian
similar, -ly
similarity, -ties
simile

similer	similar

simmer, -ed, -ing

simmetry	symmetry
simpathetic	sympathetic
simpathise	sympathise
simpathy	sympathy
simpel	simple

simper, -ed, -ing		singsong	
simple, -pler, -plest		singular, -ly	
simple interest		singularity, -ties	
simpleton		singuler	singular
simplicity, -ties		sinic	cynic
simplification		sinical	cynical
simplify, -fied, -fying		sinema	cinema
simplisity	simplicity	sinimatograf	cinematograph
simplistic, -ally		sinisism	cynicism
simply		sinister, -ly	
simposium	symposium	sink, sank, sunk or sunken, sinking	
simptom	symptom	sinker	
simptomatic	symptomatic	sinkhole	
simpul	simple	sinod	synod
simpulton	simpleton	sinonim	synonym
simulate, -lated, -lating		sinonimus	synonymous
simulation		sinopsis	synopsis
simulator		sinoptic	synoptic
simultaneous, -ly		sinoshure	cynosure
simultaynius	simultaneous	sinse	since
sin, sinned, sinning		sinsere	sincere
sinagog	synagogue	sinserity	sincerity
sinamon	cinnamon	sintax	syntax
since		sinthesis	synthesis
sincere, -cerer, -cerest		sinthesise	synthesise
sincerely		sinthetic	synthetic
sincerity, -ties		sinue	sinew
sinchromesh	synchromesh	sinuous, -ly	
sincronise	synchronise	sinus, -nuses	
sine (maths)		sinusitis	
sine	sign (mark)	sinuus	sinuous
sine camera	cine camera	sip, sipped, sipping	
sinecure		sipet	sippet
sinema	cinema	sipher	cipher
sinematograf	cinematograph	siphon, -ed, -ing	
sinepost	signpost	sippet	
sinew		sipress	cypress
sinewy		sir	
sinful, -ly		sirca	circa
sing, sang, sung, singing		sircharge	surcharge
singe, singed, singeing		sire, sired, siring	
singel	single	siren	
singer		siringe	syringe
single, -gled, -gling		sirloin	
single-handed		sirosis	cirrhosis
single-minded		sirup	syrup
singlet		sirus	cirrus

sisal

sise	size
sism	schism
sismic	seismic
sismograf	seismograph
sismologist	seismologist
sissers	scissors

sissy

sist	cyst
sistem	system
sistematic	systematic
sistematise	systematise

sister
sister-in-law, sisters-in-law
sisterly

sistern	cistern

sit, sat, sitting

sitadel	citadel

sitar

sitation	citation

site, sited, siting (place)

site	cite (state)
site	sight (view)
sitely	sightly
siteseeing	sightseeing
siteseer	sightseer
sitey	city
sithe	scythe
sitie	city

sit-in

sitizen	citizen
sitric	citric
sitrus	citrus

sitter
situate, -ated, -ating
situation

sive	sieve
sivere	severe
sivic	civic
sivilian	civilian
sivilisation	civilisation
sivilise	civilise
sivilitey	civility

six
six-shooter
sixteen
sixteenth

sixth, -ly
sixtieth
sixty, -ties
size, sized, sizing
sizeable, -bly

sizeabul	sizeable
sizemic	seismic
sizers	scissors
sizul	sizzle

sizzle, -zled, -zling
sizzler

sizzul	sizzle
skane	skein

skate, skated, skating
skateboard
skater

skedule	schedule
skee	ski
skeem	scheme

skein
skeletal
skeleton

skeletul	skeletal
skematic	schematic
skeme	scheme
skeptic	sceptic
skepticism	scepticism
skepticul	sceptical
skerick	skerrick
skermish	skirmish

skerrick

skert	skirt

sketch, -ed, -ing
sketcher
sketchily
sketchiness
sketchy, sketchier, sketchiest
skew, -ed, -ing
skewer
ski, skis, ski
ski, skied, skiing
skid, skidded, skidding
skiff

skil	skill
skilet	skillet

skilful, -ly
skilfulness

skilite   skylight
skill
skilled
skillet
skillion
skillyun   skillion
skim, skimmed, skimming
skimp, -ed, -ing
skimpily
skimpiness
skimpy, skimpier, skimpiest
skin, skinned, skinning
skin-deep
skindiver
skindiving
skiney   skinny
skinflint
skinhead
skink
skinny, -nier, -niest
skip, skipped, skipping
skiper   skipper
ski-pole
skipper
skirmish
skirt, -ed, -ing
skiscraper   skyscraper
skit (making fun)
skite, skited, skiting (boast)
skitsofrenia   schizophrenia
skittel   skittle
skittish, -ly
skittle, skittled, skittling
skivvy
skol, skolled, skolling
skua
skue   skew
skulk, -ed, -ing
skull (head)
skull   scull (row)
skullcap
skunk

> For all **skw-** words,
> look under **squ-**.

sky, skied or skyed, skying
skydiver

skylark
skylight
skyline
skylite   skylight
skyrocket
skyscraper
slab
slack, -ly
slacken, -ed, -ing
slacks
slag, slagged, slagging
slain
slake, slaked, slaking
slaken   slacken
slalom
slam, slammed, slamming
slander, -ed, -ing
slanderer
slanderous, -ly
slane   slain
slang
slangy
slant, -ed, -ing
slap, slapped, slapping
slapdash
slapstick
slash, -ed, -ing
slasher
slat
slate, slated, slating
slater
slatern   slattern
slather, -ed, -ing
slattern, -ly
slaughter, -ed, -ing
slaughterhouse
Slav
slave, slaved, slaving
slaver
slavish, -ly
slavishness
Slavonic
slawter   slaughter
slay, slew, slain, slaying (kill)
slay   sleigh (sledge)
sleazy, -zier, -ziest
sled, sledded, sledding

sledge
sledge-hammer
sleek, -ly
sleekness
sleep, slept, sleeping
sleeper
sleepily
sleepiness
sleepless, -ly
sleep-out
sleepy, sleepier, sleepiest
sleet
sleeve
sleeved
slege   sledge
sleigh (sledge)
sleight (skill)
sleight   slight (small)
slender, -ly
slept
sleuth
slew
sli   sly
slice, sliced, slicing
slick, -ly
slide, slid, sliding
slight, -ly (small)
slight   sleight (skill)
slim, slimmed, slimming
slim, slimmer, slimmest
slime
slimily
sliminess
slimy, slimier, slimiest
sling, slung, slinging
slink, slunk, slinking
slinky, slinkier, slinkiest
slip, slipped, slipping
sliper   slipper
slipknot
slipnot   slipknot
slipper
slippery, -perier, -periest
sliprale   sliprail
sliprail
slipshod
slip-stitch

slipstream
slipway
slise   slice
slit, slit, slitting
slite   slight
slither, -ed, -ing
sliver
slo   sloe (fruit)
slo   slow (not fast)
slob
slobber, -ed, -ing
slobbery
sloe (fruit)
sloe   slow (not fast)
slog, slogged, slogging
slogan
sloop
sloose   sluice
slooth   sleuth
slop, slopped, slopping
slope, sloped, sloping
slopily   sloppily
sloppiness
sloppily
sloppy, -pier, -piest
slopy   sloppy
slosh, -ed, -ing
slot, slotted, slotting
sloth
slothful, -ly
slouch, -ed, -ing
slough (skin)
sloven, -ly
slovenliness
slow, -ed, -ing (not fast)
slow   sloe (fruit)
slow   slough (skin)
slowch   slouch
slowcoach
slow-motion
sludge
sludgy, sludgier, sludgiest
slue   slew
sluff   slough
sluggard
sluggardly
sluggish, -ly

sluice, sluiced, sluicing
slum, slummed, slumming
slumber, -ed, -ing
slump, -ed, -ing
slung
slunk
slur, slurred, slurring
  slurie   slurry
slurp, -ed, -ing
slurry
slush
slushy, -shier, -shiest
slut
sluttish, -ly
sly, slyer, slyest or slier, sliest
slyly
slyness
smack, -ed, -ing
small
smallgoods
smallpox
small-time
smarmy
smart, -ed, -ing
smart, smarter, smartest
smart alec
smarten, -ed, -ing
smartly
smash, -ed, -ing
smasher
smattering
smear, -ed, -ing
  smeer   smear
smell, smelled or smelt, smelling
smelly, smellier, smelliest
smelter
smidgin
smile, smiled, smiling
smirch, -ed, -ing
smirk, -ed, -ing
smite, smote, smiting
smith
smithereens
  smithey   smithy
smithy, smithies
smitten
smock, -ed, -ing

smog
smoggy, smoggier, smoggiest
  smogy   smoggy
smoke, smoked, smoking
smoke-bush
smoker
smokescreen
smokestack
smoko
smoky, smokier, smokiest
  smolder   smoulder
smooch, -ed, -ing
smoodge, smoodged, smoodging
smooth, -ed, -ing
smoothly
smoothness
smorgasbord
smother, -ed, -ing
smoulder, -ed, -ing
smudge, smudged, smudging
smug, smugger, smuggest
  smuge   smudge
smuggle, smuggled, smuggling
smuggler
  smuggul   smuggle
  smugle   smuggle
smugly
  smurch   smirch
  smurk   smirk
smut
smuttily
smuttiness
smutty, smuttier, smuttiest
  smuty   smutty
snack
snaffle, -fled, -fling
  snafful   snaffle
snag, snagged, snagging
snagger
snail
snake, snaked, snaking
snakebite
snaky, snakier, snakiest
  snale   snail
snap, snapped, snapping
snapdragon
  snaper   snapper

snapper
snappily
snappiness
snappy, -pier, -piest
snapshot

snapy   snappy
snare, snared, snaring
snarl, -ed, -ing
snatch, -ed, -ing
sneak, -ed, -ing
sneaker

sneek   sneak
sneeker   sneaker
sneer, -ed, -ing
sneeze, sneezed, sneezing
snib, snibbed, snibbing
snick, -ed, -ing
snicker, -ed, -ing
snide

snif   sniff
snifel   sniffle
sniff, -ed, -ing
sniffle, -fled, -fling

snifful   sniffle
sniger   snigger
snigger, -ed, -ing
snip, snipped, snipping (cut)
snipe, sniped, sniping (shoot)
sniper

snipet   snippet
snippet
snitch, -ed, -ing
snivel, -elled, -elling
sniveller

snivul   snivel
snob
snobbery
snobbish, -ly
snood
snook
snooker, -ed, -ing
snoop, -ed, -ing
snoopy
snooze, snoozed, snoozing
snore, snored, snoring
snorkel

snorkle   snorkel

snorkul   snorkel
snort, -ed, -ing
snout
snow, -ed, -ing
snowball

snowey   snowy
snowflake
snow job
snowline
snowman, -men
snowplough
snowshoe, -shoed, -shoeing

snowt   snout
snowy, snowier, snowiest
snub, snubbed, snubbing
snuff, -ed, -ing
snuffle, -fled, -fling
snug, snugger, snuggest
snuggle, -gled, -gling
so (in this way)

so   sew (stitch)
so   sow (pig, plant)
soak, -ed, -ing
so-and-so
soap, -ed, -ing
soapbox
soapie
soap opera

soappy   soapy
soapstone
soapy, soapier, soapiest
soar, -ed, -ing (fly)

soar   sore (hurt)
sob, sobbed, sobbing
sober, -ed, -ing
sobriety

sobrikay   sobriquet
sobriquet
so-called
soccer
sociability
sociable, -bly

sociabul   sociable
social, -ly
socialisation
socialise, -lised, -lising
socialism

socialist
socialistic, -ally
socialite
society, -ties
socioeconomic, -ally
sociologist
sociology
  sociul — social
sock, -ed, -ing
  socker — soccer
socket
  sockit — socket
sockeye
sod
soda
soda-water
sodden
  soden — sodden
sodium
sodomite
sodomy
sofa
  sofar — sofa
  sofen — soften
  sofism — sophism
  sofist — sophist
  sofisticate — sophisticate
  sofistication — sophistication
  sofistry — sophistry
soft, -ly
softball
soften, -ed, -ing
soft-pedal, -alled, -alling
soft-soap
software
  softwear — software
soggily
sogginess
soggy, -gier, -giest
  sogie — soggy
  sogy — soggy
  soia — soya
soil, -ed, -ing
  soiray — soiree
soiree
  soiya — soya
  sojern — sojourn

sojourn, -ed, -ing
  soke — soak
solace, -aced, -acing
solar
  solareum — solarium
solarium, -laria
  solass — solace
  solatude — solitude
sold
solder, -ed, -ing
soldier, -ed, -ing
soldierly
sole (shoe)
  sole — soul (spirit)
solecism
  soled — solid
  soleful — soulful
  solem — solemn
solemn, -ly
solemnisation
solemnise, -nised, -nising
  solemnitey - solemnity
solemnity, -ties
solenoid
  soler — solar
  solesism — solecism
solfa, -faed, -faing
  solger — soldier
solicit, -ed, -ing
solicitation
  soliciter — solicitor
solicitor
solicitous, -ly
solicitude
  solicitus — solicitous
solid, -ly
solidarity, -ties
  solidifi — solidify
solidification
solidify, -fied, -fying
solid-state
  solilokwy — soliloquy
soliloquy, -quies
  solisit — solicit
  solisitor — solicitor
  solisitus — solicitous
solitaire

solitary, -taries
solitude

soljer	soldier

> For **soll-** words,
> look under **sol-**.

solo, -los
soloist
solstice

solstiss	solstice

solubility, -ties
soluble, -bly

solubul	soluble
solushun	solution

solution
solvable
solve, solved, solving
solvency

solvensy	solvency

solvent

somber	sombre
sombraro	sombrero

sombre, -ly
sombrero
some (few)

some	sum (total)

somebody, -bodies
somehow
someone

somersalt	somersault

somersault
something
sometime
somewhat
somewhere
somnambulism
somnolence

somnolense	somnolence

son (boy)

son	sun (star)

sonar
sonata

soner	sonar

song
songster
songstress
sonic

sonic boom

sonick	sonic

son-in-law, sons-in-law
sonnet
sonny, -nies
sonorous, -ly

sonorus	sonorous
soo	sue
soocher	suture
soocrose	sucrose
sooet	suet
sooflay	souffle

sook
sooky
soon

soop	soup

soot (chimney)

soot	suit (clothes)

sooth (truth)
soothe, soothed, soothing (calm)
soothsayer

soovenir	souvenir

sop, sopped, sopping

sope	soap

sophism
sophist
sophisticate, -cated, -cating
sophistication
sophistry, -ries
soporific
sopping
soppy, -pier, -piest
soprano, -pranos, -prani
sorbet

sorce	sauce (liquid)
sorce	source (origin)

sorcerer
sorceress
sorcery, -ceries

sord	sword

sordid, -ly

sordust	sawdust

sore, sorer, sorest (hurt)

sore	saw (cut)
sore	soar (rise)
sorel	sorrel
sorey	sorry

sorghum
    sorgum   sorghum
    sorie   sorry
    sorna   sauna
    sornter   saunter
sorority, -ties
    sorow   sorrow
sorrel
sorrow
sorrowful, -ly
sorry, -rier, -riest
sort (type)
    sort   sought (looked)
    sortee   sortie
sortie, -tied, -tieing
    soshable   sociable
    soshal   social
    soshalise   socialise
    sosietey   society
    sosige   sausage
so-so
sot
    soto vochay   sotto voce
sotto voce
soufflé
sough (rustling sound)
    sough   sow (pig)
sought (looked)
soul (spirit)
    soul   sole (shoe)
sound, -ed, -ing
soundbox
sounding-board
soundproof
soundtrack
soundwave
soup
sour, -ed, -ing
source (origin)
    source   sauce (liquid)
souse, soused, sousing
south
south-east
south-easter
south-eastern
southerly
southern

Southern Cross
southward, -ly
south-west
south-wester
south-western
souvenir
sovereign
sovereignty, -ties
    soverin   sovereign
soviet
    sovrenty   sovereignty
sow, sowed, sowing (pig, plant)
    sow   sew (stitch)
sown (planted)
    sown   sewn (stitched)
    sownd   sound
    sowr   sour
    sowth   south
soy
soya
spa
space, spaced, spacing
spaceship
spacious, -ly
spade, spaded, spading
spadework
    spagetti   spaghetti
spaghetti
span, spanned, spanning
    spaner   spanner
spangle, -gled, -gling
    spangul   spangle
Spaniard
spaniel
spank, -ed, -ing
spanner
    Spanyard   Spaniard
    spanyel   spaniel
spar, sparred, sparring (fight)
spare, spared, sparing (extra)
spark, -ed, -ing
sparkle, -kled, -kling
sparkler
    sparkul   sparkle
    sparow   sparrow
sparrow
sparrowhawk

sparse, sparser, sparsest
sparsity
Spartan
  spase   space
  spashus   spacious
spasm
spasmodic, -ally
spastic, -ally
spat (did spit)
  spatal   spatial
spate (sudden)
spatial, -ly
spatter, -ed, -ing
spatula
spawn, -ed, -ing
spay, -ed, -ing
speak, spoke, spoken, speaking
speakeasy, -easies
speaker
spear, -ed, -ing
spearmint
spec (gamble)
  spec   speck (spot)
special, -ly
specialisation
specialise, -lised, -lising
specialist
speciality, -ties
specialty, -ties
species, -cies
specific, -ly
specification
specify, -fied, -fying
specimen
specious, -ly
speck, -ed, -ing (spot)
  speck   spec (gamble)
speckle, -kled, -kling
spectacle
  spectacul   spectacle
spectacular, -ly
spectator
  specter   spectre
spectre
spectroscope
spectrum, -tra
speculate, -lated, -lating

speculation
speculator
speech
speed, sped, speeding
speedometer
speedway
  speek   speak
  speer   spear
  spekul   speckle
  spel   spell
spell, spelt or spelled, spelling
spellbound
spencer
spend, spent, spending
spendthrift
sperm
  spern   spurn
  spert   spurt
  speshal   special
  speshalist specialist
  speshus   specious
  spesify   specify
  spesimen   specimen
spew, -ed, -ing
sphere
spherical, -ly
spheroid
sphinx
  spi   spy
spice, spiced, spicing
spick-and-span
spicy, spicier, spiciest
spider
spidery
spiel, -ed, -ing
spigot
spike, spiked, spiking
spill, spilt or spilled, spilling
spillage
  spillige   spillage
spin, spun, spinning
spina bifida
spinach
  spinaker   spinnaker
spinal
spindle, -dled, -dling
spin-dry, -dried, -drying

spine

spinifex

  spinige   spinach

spinnaker

spinner

spin-off

spinster

spiny, spinier, spiniest

spiral, -ralled, -ralling

spire

  spirel   spiral

  spirichual   spiritual

  spirichualist   spiritualist

spirit, -ed, -ing

spiritual, -ly

spiritualism

spiritualist

spirituality, -ties

  spise   spice

  spisy   spicy

spit, spat, spitting

spite, spited, spiting

spiteful, -ly

spitfire

spittle

spittoon

  spittul   spittle

spiv

splash, -ed, -ing

splashdown

splatter, -ed, -ing

splay, -ed, -ing

spleen

  splender   splendour

splendid, -ly

splendour

splice, spliced, splicing

splicer

splint

splinter, -ed, -ing

  splise   splice

split, split, splitting

split-level

splurge, splurged, splurging

splutter, -ed, -ing

spoil, spoilt, spoiling

spoilage

spoilsport

spoke

spoken

spokesperson

sponge, sponged, sponging

sponger

spongy, -gier, -giest

  sponser   sponsor

sponsor, -ed, -ing

sponsorship

spontaneity, -ties

spontaneous, -ly

  sponteneity   spontaneity

spoof, -ed, -ing

spook, -ed, -ing

spool

spoon, -ed, -ing

spoonbill

spoonerism

spoon-feed, -fed, -feeding

spoor (trail)

  spoor   spore (germ)

sporadic, -ally

spore, spored, sporing (germ)

  spore   spoor (trail)

sporran

sport, -ed, -ing

sportive, -ly

sportsman, -men

sportswoman, -women

spot, spotted, spotting

spotlight, -ed, -ing

  spotlite   spotlight

spouse

spout, -ed, -ing

  spowse   spouse

  spowt   spout

sprain, -ed, -ing

  sprane   sprain

sprang

sprat

sprawl, -ed, -ing

spray, -ed, -ing

spread, spread, spreading

spread-eagle, -gled, -gling

  spred   spread

spree

sprie   spry
sprightly, -lier, -liest
spring, sprang, sprung, springing
springboard
springbok, -boks
spring-clean, -ed, -ing
spring-loaded
springy, -gier, -giest
sprinkle, -kled, -kling
sprinkler
  sprinkul   sprinkle
sprint, -ed, -ing
sprit (pole)
sprite, -ly (elf)
sprocket
  sproose   spruce
sprout, -ed, -ing
  sprowt   sprout
spruce, spruced, sprucing
spruce, sprucer, sprucest
sprung
spry, spryer, spryest
spud, spudded, spudding
spume, spumed, spuming
spun
  spunge   sponge
spunk
spunky, spunkier, spunkiest
spur, spurred, spurring
spurious, -ly
  spurius   spurious
  spurm   sperm
spurn, -ed, -ing
spurt, -ed, -ing
sputnik
sputter, -ed, -ing
sputum, sputa
spy, spies
spy, spied, spying
squabble, -bled, -bling
  squabul   squabble
squad
squadron
squalid, -ly
squall, -ed, -ing
squalor
squander, -ed, -ing

square, squared, squaring
squarely
square-rigged
squash, -ed, -ing
squat, squatted, squatting
squatter
squattocracy
squaw
squawk, -ed, -ing
squeak, -ed, -ing
squeal, -ed, -ing
squeamish, -ly
squeeze, squeezed, squeezing
squelch, -ed, -ing
squib, squibbed, squibbing
squid, squids, squid
squiggle, -gled, -gling
squiggly
  squiggul   squiggle
squint, -ed, -ing
squire, squired, squiring
squirm, -ed, -ing
squirrel
squirt, -ed, -ing
squiz, -ed, -ing
  squod   squad
  squodron   squadron
  squolid   squalid
  squonder   squander
  squosh   squash
  squot   squat
stab, stabbed, stabbing
stabilisation
stabilise, -lised, -lising
stabiliser
stability, -ties
stable, -bled, -bling
  stabul   stable
staccato
stack, -ed, -ing
stadium, -dia, -diums
  staf   staff
staff, -ed, -ing
stag
stage, staged, staging
stagecoach
  stager   stagger

stagflation

stagger, -ed, -ing

staghorn

stagnant, -ly

stagnate, -nated, -nating

stagnation

staid, -ly (calm)

  staid   stayed

                  (stopped)

  staidium   stadium

stain, -ed, -ing

stainless, -ly

stair (step)

  stair   stare (look at)

staircase

stairwell

stake, staked, staking (post)

  stake   steak (meat)

stalactite

stalagmite

stale, staled, staling

stale, staler, stalest

stalemate, -mated, -mating

  stalion   stallion

stalk, -ed, -ing (hunt)

  stalk   stork (bird)

stall, -ed, -ing

stallion

stalwart, -ly

  stalwert   stalwart

stamen

  stamena   stamina

  stamer   stammer

stamina

stammer, -ed, -ing

stamp, -ed, -ing

stampede, -peded, -peding

stance

stanchion

  stanchun   stanchion

stand, stood, standing

standard

standardise, -dised, -dising

stand-by

  standerd   standard

stand-in

stand-offish, -ly

standstill

  stane   stain

stank

  stanse   stance

stanza

staple, -pled, -pling

stapler

  stapul   staple

star, starred, starring

starboard

  starbord   starboard

starch, -ed, -ing

star-crossed

stardom

stare, stared, staring (look at)

  stare   stair (step)

starfish, -fishes, -fish

stargaze, -gazed, -gazing

stargazer

stark, -ly

starkers

starling

start, -ed, -ing

  startch   starch

starter

startle, -tled, -tling

starvation

starve, starved, starving

stash, -ed, -ing

  stashun   station

  stashunry   stationary

  stashunry   stationery

state, stated, stating

stateliness

stately, -lier, -liest

statement

stateroom

statesman, -men

stateswoman, -women

static, -ally

station, -ed, -ing

stationary (still)

stationer (sells paper)

stationery (paper)

statistical, -ly

statistician

statistics

statistishun — statistician
stattic — static
statuary, -aries (statues)
statue
statuesk — statuesque
statuesque, -ly
stature
status
status quo
statute
statutory (law)
statutry — statutory
staunch, -ed, -ing
stave, staved, staving
stawk — stalk
stay, stayed, staying
stead
steadfast, -ly
steadily
steady, steadied, steadying
steady, steadier, steadiest
steak (meat)
steak — stake (post)
steal, stole, stolen, stealing (rob)
steal — steel (metal)
stealth
stealthily
stealthy, -thier, -thiest
steam, -ed, -ing
steam-engine
steamer
steamroller
sted — stead
stedfast — steadfast
stedy — steady
steed
steel, -ed, -ing (metal)
steel — steal (rob)
steely
steep, -ed, -ing
steeple
steeplechase
steepul — steeple
steer, -ed, -ing
steerage
steerige — steerage
steersman, -men

stelth — stealth
stem, stemmed, stemming
stench
stencil, -cilled, -cilling
stenografer — stenographer
stenografy — stenography
stenographer
stenography
stensil — stencil
step, stepped, stepping, (pace)
stepladder
steppe (plain)
stereo, stereos
stereogram
stereophonic
stereotype, -typed, -typing
sterile, -ly
sterilisation
sterilise, -lised, -lising
steriliser
sterio — stereo
steriofonic — stereophonic
steriotype — stereotype
sterling
stern, -ly
sternum
stethoscope
stetson
stevedore, -dored, -doring
stew, -ed, -ing
steward
stewardess
sti — sty
stich — stitch
stick, stuck, sticking
sticker
stickler
stick-up
sticky, stickier, stickiest
stickybeak
stif — stiff
stifen — stiffen
stiff
stiffen, -ed, -ing
stiffener
stifle, -fled, -fling
stiful — stifle

stigma, -mas, -mata
stigmatise, -tised, -tising
 stikler   stickler
 stil   still
stile (steps)
 stile   style (type)
stiletto, -tos
 stilish   stylish
 stilist   stylist
still, -ed, -ing
stillbirth
stillborn
still-life
stilt
stilted, -ly
stilton
 stilus   stylus
 stimie   stymie
stimulant
stimulate, -lated, -lating
stimulation
stimulator
stimulus, -li, -luses
sting, stung, stinging
stingray
stingy, -gier, -giest
stink, stank, stunk, stinking
stinker
stinkhorn
stinkpot
stint, -ed, -ing
stipend
stipendiary, -ries
stipple, -pled, -pling
 stipul   stipple
stipulate, -lated, -lating
stipulation
stir, stirred, stirring
 stirling   sterling
stirrup
 stirup   stirrup
stitch, -ed, -ing
stoat
stock, -ed, -ing
stockade, -aded, -ading
stockbroker
stock-car

stocking
stockman, -men
stockpile, -piled, -piling
stocktaking
stockwhip
stocky, -kier, -kiest
stodgily
stodgy, -gier, -giest
 stogy   stodgy
stoical, -ly
stoicism
 stoisism   stoicism
stoke, stoked, stoking
stoker
stole
stolen
stolid, -ly
stoma, stomata
stomach
stomach-ache
 stomick   stomach
stone, stoned, stoning
stonefish
stonemason
stoneware
stony, stonier, stoniest
stood
stooge, stooged, stooging
stool
stoop, stooped, stooping
stop, stopped, stopping
stopcock
stope, stoped, stoping
stopgap
stoppage
stopper
stopwatch
store, stored, storing
storey (floor)
 storey   story (tale)
 storie   storey (floor)
 storie   story (tale)
 storige   storage
stork (bird)
 stork   stalk (hunt)
storm, -ed, -ing
stormily

stormy, -mier, -miest
story, -ries (tale)
   story   storey (floor)
stout, -ly
stove, stoved, stoving
stow, -ed, -ing
stowaway
   stowt   stout
straddle, -dled, -dling
   straf   strafe
strafe, strafed, strafing
straggle, -gled, -gling
straggler
straight (line)
   straight   strait (passage)
straightaway
straighten, -ed, -ing
straightforward, -ly
strain, -ed, -ing
strainer
strait (passage)
   strait   straight (line)
straiten
straitjacket
straitlaced
strand
   strane   strain
strange, stranger, strangest
strangle, -gled, -gling
strangler
stranglehold
   strangul   strangle
strangulate, -lated, -lating
strangulation
strap, strapped, strapping
strapper
strasbourg
strata
stratagem
strata title
   strate   straight (line)
   strate   strait (passage)
   strategie   strategy
strategic, -ally
strategist
strategy, -gies
stratification

stratify, -fied, -fying
   stratigem   stratagem
   stratosfere   stratosphere
stratosphere
stratum, strata
straw
   strawberie   strawberry
strawberry, -ries
stray, -ed, -ing
streak, -ed, -ing
streaky, streakier, streakiest
stream, -ed, -ing
streamer
streamline, -lined, -lining
   streek   streak
   streem   stream
street
strength
strengthen, -ed, -ing
strenuous, -ly
   strenuus   strenuous
streptomycin
stress, -ed, -ing
stretch, -ed, -ing
stretcher
strew, strewed, strewn, strewing
striate, -ated, -ating
striation
   strick   strict
stricken
strict, -ly
stricture
stride, strode, striding
stridence
strident, -ly
strife
strike, struck, stricken, striking
strikebound
strikebreaker
   striknun   strychnine
strine
string, strung, stringing
stringency
   stringensy   stringency
stringent, -ly
stringer
stringy, -gier, -giest

strip, stripped, stripping
stripe, striped, striping
stripling
stripper
striptease
strive, strove, striven, striving
strobe
stroboscope
strode
stroke, stroked, stroking
stroll, -ed, -ing
stroller
strong, -ly
stronghold
  stroo   strew
strop, stropped, stropping
  stroppie   stroppy
stroppy, stroppier, stroppiest
strove
struck
  struckcher   structure
structure, -tured, -turing
strudel
struggle, -gled, -gling
struggler
  strugul   struggle
strum, strummed, strumming
strummer
strumpet
strung
strut, strutted, strutting
strychnine
  stu   stew
  stuard   steward
stub, stubbed, stubbing
stubble
stubbly
stubborn, -ly
  stuben   stubborn
stucco, -coes, -cos
stuck-up
stud, studded, studding
student
  studie   study
studied
studio, -dios
studious, -ly

  studius   studious
study, studies
study, studied, studying
  stuf   stuff
stuff, -ed, -ing
stuffily
stuffy, -fier, -fiest
  stufy   stuffy
  stuko   stucco
  stultifie   stultify
stultify, -fied, -fying
stumble, -bled, -bling
  stumbul   stumble
stump, -ed, -ing
stump-jump plough
stun, stunned, stunning
stunner
stunt, -ed, -ing
stuntman, -men
  stupefie   stupefy
stupefy, -fied, -fying
stupendous, -ly
  stupendus   stupendous
stupid, -ly
stupidity, -ties
  stupify   stupefy
stupor
  sturdie   sturdy
sturdily
sturdy, -dier, -diest
sturgeon
  sturgun   sturgeon
  sturling   sterling
  sturn   stern
  stuter   stutter
stutter, -ed, -ing
stutterer
  stuward   steward
St Vitus dance
sty, sties
style (type)
  style   stile (steps)
stylish, -ly
stylist
stylistic, -ally
stymie, -mied, -mieing
styptic

suage	sewage
suave, -ly	
suavity, -ties	
sub, subbed, subbing	
subaltern	
subcomitee	subcommittee
subcommittee	
subconscious, -ly	
subconshus	subconscious
subcontinent	
subcontract, -ed, -ing	
subcontractor	
subculture	
subcutaneous, -ly	
subdivide, -vided, -viding	
subdivishun	subdivision
subdivision	
subdue, -dued, -duing	
subeditor	
suberb	suburb
suberban	suburban
subgigate	subjugate
subgroup	
subheading	
subjecshun	subjection
subject, -ed, -ing	
subjection	
subjective, -ly	
subjectivity	
sub judice	
subjugate, -gated, -gating	
subjugation	
subjunctive	
sublimate, -mated, -mating	
sublimation	
sublime, -limed, -liming	
subliminal, -ly	
sublimity, -ties	
sublimminal	subliminal
submarine	
submerge, -merged, -merging	
submishun	submission
submission	
submissive, -ly	
submit, -mitted, -mitting	
submurge	submerge
subnormal, -ly	

subordinate, -nated, -nating	
subordination	
suborn, -ed, -ing	
subpena	subpoena
subpoena, -naed, -naing	
subscribe, -ribed, -ribing	
subscriber	
subscription	
subsection	
subsekwent	subsequent
subsequent, -ly	
subservience	
subservient, -ly	
subset	
subside, -sided, -siding	
subsidence	
subsidie	subsidy
subsidise, -dised, -dising	
subsidy, -dies	
subsist, -ed, -ing	
subsistence	
subsistense	subsistence
subsistent, -ly	
subsoil	
substance	
substandard	
substanshul	substantial
substantial, -ly	
substantiate, -ated, -ating	
substation	
substitute, -tuted, -tuting	
subtefuge	subterfuge
subterfuge	
subterranean	
subtitle, -tled, -tling	
subtitul	subtitle
subtle, -tly	
subtlety, -ties	
subtracshun	subtraction
subtraction	
subtropical	
suburb	
suburban	
suburbia	
subversion	
subversive	
subvert, -ed, -ing	

subway
succeed, -ed, -ing
success
successful, -ly
succession
successive, -ly
successor
succinct, -ly
succour, -ed, -ing (aid)
succulent, -ly
succumb, -ed, -ing
such

| suchure | suture |

suck, -ed, -ing
sucker (dupe)

suckshun	suction
suckulent	succulent
suckum	succumb

sucrose

sucsede	succeed
sucseshun	succession
sucses	success
sucseser	successor
sucsesful	successful
sucsint	succinct

suction
sudden, -ly
suds
sue, sued, suing
suede

| suer | sewer |

suet (meat)

| sufer | suffer |

suffer, -ed, -ing
sufferance

| sufferanse | sufferance |

suffice, -ficed, -ficing
sufficiency
sufficient, -ly

| suffiks | suffix |
| suffishensy | sufficiency |

suffix
suffocate, -cated, -cating
suffocation
suffrage
suffragette
suffuse, -fused, -fusing

suffusion

sufocashun	suffocation
sufocate	suffocate
sufrajet	suffragette
sufrance	sufferance
sufrige	suffrage
sufuse	suffuse

sugar
sugary

| sugeschun | suggestion |
| sugest | suggest |

suggest, -ed, -ing
suggestive, -ly
suicidal
suicide, -cided, -ciding

| suiside | suicide |

suit, -ed, -ing (clothes)

| suit | suet (meat) |

suitability
suitable, -bly
suitcase
suite (rooms)

| suiter | suitor |

suitor
sulk, -ed, -ing
sulky, sulkier, sulkiest
sullage
sullen, -ly
sully, -lied, -lying
sulphur
sulphuric
sultan
sultana

| sultrie | sultry |

sultriness
sultry, -trier, -triest
sum, summed, summing (total)

sum	some (few)
sumbody	somebody
sumhow	somehow
summarine	submarine

summarise, -rised, -rising
summary, -ries (short)

| summary | summery (warm) |

summation
summer

summerhouse
  summerise   summarise
summery (warm)
  summery   summary
                 (short)
summit
summon, -ed, -ing (call)
summons, -monses (court)
sumo
sums
sump
sumptuous, -ly
sun, sunned, sunning (star)
  sun   son (boy)
  sun inlaw   son-in-law
sunbake, -baked, -baking
sunburn, -ed, -ing
sundae (ice-cream)
Sunday (day)
sundeck
sunder, -ed, -ing
sundial
sundown
sundowner
sundries
sundry, -rily
sunfish, -fishes, -fish
sunflower
sung
sunglasses
sunk
sunken
sunlamp
sunny, -nier, -niest
sunshine
sunspot
sunstroke
suntan, -tanned, -tanning
sup, supped, supping
super
superannuate, -ated, -ating
superannuation
superb, -ly
supercharge, -charged, -charging
supercilious, -ly
superficial, -ly
  superfishul   superficial

superfluity, -ties
superfluous, -ly
  superfosfate   superphosphate
superhuman, -ly
superimpose, -posed, -posing
superintendent
superior, -ly
superiority
superlative, -ly
superman, -men
supermarket
supernatural, -ly
supernumerary, -aries
superphosphate
superpower
supersaturate, -rated, -rating
supersede, -seded, -seding
supersonic
superstructure
supervise, -vised, -vising
  supervishun   supervision
supervision
supervisor
supervisory
  supervisry   supervisory
supine, -ly
  suple   supple
  suplement   supplement
  suport   support
  suposition   supposition
supper
supplant, -ed, -ing
supple, -pler, -plest
supplement
supplementation
supplementary
suppliant, -ly
supplier
supply, -plied, -plying
support, -ed, -ing
supporter
supposable, -bly
  supposabul   supposable
suppose, -posed, -posing
supposition
suppository, -ries
suppress, -ed, -ing

suppression
suppressive
suppurate, -rated, -rating
suppuration
supremacy

supremasy	supremacy

supreme, -ly

supres	suppress
supreshun	suppression
suprintend	superintend
supul	supple
sur	sir

surcharge, -charged, -charging
surcingle

> For other **surc-** words,
> look under **circ-**.

sure, -ly (certain)

sure	shore (sea)
sureptishus	surreptitious

surety, -ties
surf, -ed, -ing (sea)

surf	serf (slave)

surface, -faced, -facing
surfboard

surfeet	surfeit

surfeit, -ed, -ing
surfer
surfie

surfis	surface

surge, surged, surging

surgen	surgeon

surgeon
surgery, -geries
surgical, -ly
surly, -lier, -liest

surly	surely

surmise, -mised, -mising
surmount, -ed, -ing
surname

surogat	surrogate

surpass, -ed, -ing
surplice (garment)

surplis	surplice

surplus (extra)
surprise, -prised, -prising
surrealism

surrealist
surrender, -ed, -ing

surreptishus	surreptitious

surreptitious, -ly
surrogate
surround, -ed, -ing

surtaks	surtax

surtax
surveillance
survey, -veys
surveyor
survival
survive, -vived, -viving
survivor
susceptibility
susceptible, -bly
suspect, -ed, -ing
suspend, -ed, -ing
suspender
suspense
suspicion
suspicious, -ly

suspishun	suspicion

sustain, -ed, -ing

sustayn	sustain

sustenance

sustenanse	sustenance
sut	soot
sutable	suitable
suter	suitor
suthen	southern
sutlety	subtlety
sutul	subtle

suture, -tured, -turing
swab, swabbed, swabbing
swaddle, -dled, -dling

swade	suede

swag
swagger, swaggered, swaggering
swagman, -men
swain
swallow, -ed, -ing
swam
swamp, -ed, -ing
swampy, -pier, -piest
swan
swank, -ed, -ing

swap, swapped, swapping
  sware   swear
swarm, -ed, -ing
swarthy, -thier, -thiest
swashbuckler
swastika
swat, swatted, swatting
swathe, swathed, swathing
sway, -ed, -ing
swear, swore, sworn, swearing
sweat, -ed, -ing
sweater
sweatshop
swede
sweep, swept, sweeping
sweeper
sweepstake
sweet, -ly (taste)
  sweet   suite (rooms)
sweetbread
sweeten, -ed, -ing
sweetener
  sweethart   sweetheart
sweetheart
swell, swelled, swollen, swelling
swelter, -ed, -ing
swerve, swerved, swerving
  swet   sweat
  sweter   sweater
  swich   switch
swift, -ly
swill, -ed, -ing
swim, swam, swum, swimming
swimmer
swimsuit
swindle, -dled, -dling
  swindul   swindle
swine
swing, swung, swinging
swipe, swiped, swiping
swirl, -ed, -ing
swish, -ed, -ing
switch, -ed, -ing
switchboard
swivel, -elled, -elling
  swob   swab
swollen

  swollow   swallow
  swomp   swamp
swoon, -ed, -ing
swoop, -ed, -ing
sword
swordfish
  sworm   swarm
sworn
swot, swotted, swotting
swum
  swurl   swirl
  swurve   swerve
  syanide   cyanide
sybarite
sybaritic, -ally
sycamore
  sycedelic   psychedelic
  syche   psyche
  syciatrist   psychiatrist
  syciatry   psychiatry
  sycick   psychic
  syclone   cyclone
  sycoanalise   psychoanalyse
  sycoanalisis   psychoanalysis
  sycofant   sycophant
  sycological   psychological
  sycologist   psychologist
  sycology   psychology
sycophant
sycophantic, -ally
  sycosis   psychosis
  sycotherapist   psychotherapist
  sycotherapy   psychotherapy
  sycotic   psychotic
Sydney
Sydneysider
  syfilis   syphilis
  sygnet   cygnet
  sylable   syllable
  sylf   sylph
  sylinder   cylinder
syllabic, -ally
syllable
syllabus, -buses, -bi
syllogise, -gised, -gising
syllogism
syllogistic, -ally

sylph
sylvan
  sylvun   sylvan
symbiosis
symbiotic, -ally
symbol (sign)
  symbol   cymbal (music)
symbolic, -ally
symbolise, -lised, -lising
symbolism
symbolist
  symfony   symphony
symmetrical, -ly
symmetry, -tries
sympathetic, -ally
  sympathey   sympathy
sympathise, -ised, -ising
sympathiser
symphonic
symphony, -nies
symposium, -siums, -sia
symptom
symptomatic
  synagog   synagogue
synagogue
  synanym   synonym
synchromesh
synchronisation
synchronise, -nised, -nising
synchronous, -ly
  synchronus   synchronous
syncopate, -pated, -pating
syncopation
syndical
syndicalism
syndicate, -cated, -cating
syndication
syndrome
  synic   cynic
  synical   cynical
synod
synodal
  synonimus   synonymous
synonym
synonymous, -ly
synopsis, -ses
synoptic, -ally

syntactical, -ly
  syntaks   syntax
syntax
synthesis, -ses
synthesise, -ised, -ising
synthesiser
synthetic, -ally
  sypher   cipher
syphilis
syphilitic
syphon, -ed, -ing
syringe, -ringed, -ringing
syrup
syrupy
system
systematic
systematical, -ly
systematisation
systematise, -tised, -tising
systemic, -ally
systole
  sythe   scythe
Szechuan
Szechwan

Tt

tab, tabbed, tabbing
  tabacco — tobacco
tabard
tabasco
  tabasko — tabasco
tabby, -bies
  tabel — table
  tabie — tabby
table, -bled, -bling
tableau, -leaux, -leaus
tablespoon
tablespoonful, -fuls
tablet
  tablit — tablet
  tablo — tableau
tabloid
  tabloyd — tabloid
taboo, -boos
taboo, -booed, -booing
  tabul — table
tabular
tabulate, -lated, -lating
tabulation
  taby — tabby
tachometer
tacit, -ly
taciturn
tack, -ed, -ing
  tackie — tacky
tackle, -led, -ling
tackler
  tackometer — tachometer
  tackul — tackle
tacky, -kier, -kiest
taco
tact
tactic
tactical, -ly

tactician
tactics
tactile
  tactyle — tactile
tadpole
taffeta
  tafita — taffeta
tag, tagged, tagging
tail (end)
  tail — tale (story)
tailgate
tailor, -ed, -ing
tailor-made
taint, -ed, -ing
taipan
take, took, taken, taking
takeover
  taks — tax
  taksation — taxation
  taksi — taxi
talc
talcum powder
tale (story)
  tale — tail (end)
talent
talented
  talie — tally
talisman, -mans
talk, -ed, -ing
  talk — talc
talkative, -ly
talkback
tall
tallboy
tallow
tallowwood
tally, -lies (score)
tally, -lied, -lying (score)
  tally — telly (T.V.)
Talmud
talon
  talor — tailor
  talow — tallow
tamale
tamarind
  tamborine — tambourine
tambourine

tame, tamed, taming	tare	tear (rip)
tame, tamer, tamest	target	
tameable	targit	target
tam-o'-shanter	tarie	tarry
tamper, -ed, -ing	tarif	tariff
tampon	tariff	
tan, tanned, tanning	tarmac	
tanbark	tarnation	
tandem	tarnish, -ed, -ing	
tang	tarot	
tangenshul — tangential	tarow	tarot
tangent	tarpaulin	
tangential, -ly	tarpollun	tarpaulin
tangerine	tarragon	
tangible, -bly	tarrif	tariff
tangibul — tangible	tarry, ries	
tangle, -gled, -gling	tarry, -ried, -rying	
tango, -gos	tartan	
tango, -goed, -going	tartar	
tangul — tangle	tartare sauce	
tanjent — tangent	tarter	tartar
tank	tartily	
tankard	tarty	
tanker	tasit	tacit
tannin	tasiturn	taciturn
tantalise, -lised, -lising	task	
tantamount	taskmaster	
tantamownt — tantamount	tassel, tasselled, tasselling	
tantrum	tassul	tassel
tap, tapped, tapping	taste, tasted, tasting	
tap-dancing	tastebud	
tape, taped, taping	tasteful, -ly	
taper, -ed, -ing	tasty, -tier, -tiest	
tape-recorder	tatoo	tattoo
tapestry, -tries	tattle, -led, -ling	
tapeworm	tattoo, -toos	
tapioca	tattoo, -tooed, -tooing	
tapistry — tapestry	tattul	tattle
tappet	tatty	
taproot	taudry	tawdry
tar, tarred, tarring	taught (teach)	
tarantella (dance)	taught	taut (tight)
tarantula (spider)	taught	tort (law)
tardie — tardy	taunt, -ed, -ing	
tardily	Taurus	
tardy, -dier, -diest	taut, -ly (tight)	
tare (weight)	taut	taught (teach)

taut	tort (law)
tautological, -ly	
tautology, -gies	
taven	tavern
tavern	
tawdrily	
tawdry, -drier, -driest	
tawny, -nier, -niest	
tax, taxed, taxing	
taxable	
taxabul	taxable
taxation	
tax-deductible	
taxi, taxis	
taxi, taxied, taxiing	
taxicab	
taxidermy	
taxie	taxi
taxonomy, -mies	
tea (drink)	
tea	tee (golf)
teach, taught, teaching	
teachable, -ably	
teachabul	teachable
teacher	
tea-chest	
teacup	
teal	
team, -ed, -ing (group)	
team	teem (rain)
teamster	
teapot	
tear (crying)	
tear, tore, torn, tearing (rip)	
tear	tare (weight)
tear	tier (row)
tearful, -ly	
tearjerker	
tease, teased, teasing	
teaspoon	
teat	
teath	teeth (noun)
teathe	teethe
tea-tree	
tech	teach
techer	teacher
technical, -ly	

technicality, -ties	
technician	
technicolour	
technique	
technocracy	
technological, -ly	
technologist	
technology	
tecneek	technique
tecnical	technical
tecnicality	technicality
tecnishun	technician
tecnocrasy	technocracy
tecnology	technology
tedious, -ly	
tee, teed, teeing (golf)	
tee	tea (drink)
teech	teach
teek	teak
teel	teal
teem, -ed, -ing (rain)	
teem	team (group)
teenager	
teese	tease
tee-shirt	
teet	teat
teeter, -ed, -ing	
teeth (noun)	
teethe, teethed, teething	
teetotal, -ly	
teetotaller	
teflon	
tekneek	technique
teknical	technical
teknicality	technicality
teknicolor	technicolour
teknishun	technician
teknocrasy	technocracy
teknology	technology
tekst	text
tekstile	textile
teksture	texture
telecast, -ed, -ing	
telecommunication	
telefone	telephone
telefonist	telephonist
telefoto	telephoto

telegraf — telegraph
telegram
telegraphic
telegraphist
telegraphy
teleks — telex
telepathic
telepathist
telepathy
telephone, -phoned, -phoning
telephonic, -ally
telephonist
telephoto lens
teleprinter
telescope, -coped, -coping
televise, -vised, -vising
televishun — television
television
telex
telifone — telephone
telifonist — telephonist
teligram — telegram
teliphoto — telephoto
teliscope — telescope
telivise — televise
telivishun — television
tell, told, telling
teller
telltale
telly, tellies (T.V.)
temerity
temper, -ed, -ing
tempera
temperament
temperamental, -ly
temperance
temperanse — temperance
temperate, -ly
Temperate Zone
temperature
tempest
tempestuous, -ly
tempestuus — tempestuous
template
temple
templut — template
tempo, -pos

temporal, -ly
temporarily
temporary
temporise, -rised, -rising
tempory — temporary
temprament — temperament
tempratcher — temperature
tempremental — temperamental
tempt, -ed, -ing
temptation
tempter
temtation — temptation
tenable, -bly
tenabul — tenable
tenacious, -ly
tenancy
tenansy — tenancy
tenant
tend, -ed, -ing
tendency, -cies
tendenshus — tendentious
tendentious, -ly
tender, -ed, -ing
tenderfoot, -foots, -feet
tenderly
tendon
tendril
tenement
tenet
teniment — tenement
tenis — tennis
tennis
tenon
tenor
tenpin bowling
tense, tensed, tensing
tense, tenser, tensest
tenshun — tension
tension
tent
tentacle
tentative, -ly
tenterhook
tenth
tenuous, -ly
tenure
tenuus — tenuous

tenyer	tenure	terribul	terrible
tepee		terrier	
tepid, -ly		terrific, -ally	
teracota	terracotta	terrify, -fied, -fying	
terain	terrain	terrine	
terarium	terrarium	territorial, -ly	
terazo	terrazzo	territory, -ries	
terban	turban	terror	
terbid	turbid	terrorise, -rised, -rising	
terbine	turbine	terrorism	
terbo	turbo	terrorist	
terbulent	turbulent	terse, terser, tersest	
terf	turf	tersely	
tergid	turgid	tertiary, -ries	
teribul	terrible	tertle	turtle
terier	terrier	terylene	
terific	terrific	teselate	tessellate
terifie	terrify	teselation	tessellation
teritry	territory	tespoon	teaspoon
terjid	turgid	tessellate, -ated, -ating	
terkey	turkey	tessellation	
terkwoise	turquoise	test, -ed, -ing	
term		testament	
termagant		testicle	
terminable, -ly		testicul	testicle
terminabul	terminable	testifie	testify
terminal, -ally		testify, -fied, -fying	
terminate, -nated, -nating		testimonial	
termination		testimony, -nies	
terminology, -gies		testis, testes	
terminus, -ni, -nuses		test-tube	
termite		testy, -tier, -tiest	
termoil	turmoil	tetanus	
tern (bird)		tete-a-tete	
tern	turn (move)	tether, -ed, -ing	
ternip	turnip	tetragon	
teror	terror	tetrahedron, -drons, -dra	
terorist	terrorist	texchur	texture
terpentine	turpentine	text	
terpitude	turpitude	textbook	
terrace, -raced, -racing		textile	
terracotta		textual, -ly	
terrain		texture, -tured, -turing	
terrarium, -rariums, -raria		thach	thatch
terrazzo		thalidomide	
terrestrial, -ly		than	
terrible, -bly		thank, -ed, -ing	

thankful, -ly		theosophical, -ly	
thankless, -ly		theosophist	
thanksgiving		theosophy	
that, those		therapeutic, -ally	
that's (that is)		therapey	therapy
thats	that's	therapist	
thatch, -ed, -ing		therapy, -pies	
thaw, -ed, -ing		therd	third
thay	they	there (at that place)	
theater	theatre	there	their
theatre			(possessive)
theatrical, -ly		there	they're (they
theft			are)
their (possessive)		thereabouts	
their	there (at that	thereby	
	place)	therefore	
theirs (possessive)		therem	theorem
theirs	there's (there	therein	
	is)	thereof	
theism		thereon	
theist		there's (there is)	
theistic, -ally		theres	theirs
theif	thief		(possessive)
theives	thieves	theres	there's (there
theiving	thieving		is)
thematic, -ally		theretic	theoretic
theme		thereticul	theoretical
themselves		therey	theory
then		thereupon	
thence		therewith	
thense	thence	therise	theorise
theocracy, -cies		therist	theorist
theocrasy	theocracy	therm	
theocrat		thermal, -ly	
theodolite		thermodynamic, -ally	
theological, -ly		thermometer	
theologian		thermometrical,-ly	
theology, -gies		thermonuclear	
theolojun	theologian	thermoplastic	
theorem		thermos	
theoretic		thermostat	
theoretical, -ly		thermostatic, -ally	
theorise, -rised, -rising		Thersday	Thursday
theorist		therst	thirst
theorm	theorem	thersty	thirsty
theory, -ries		therteen	thirteen
theosofie	theosophy	therty	thirty

thesaurus, -sauri
these
thesis, -ses
   thesorus   thesaurus
Thespian
they'd (they had)
   theyd   they'd
they'll (they will)
   theyll   they'll
they're (they are)
   theyre   they're
they've (they have)
   theyve   they've
   thi   thigh
thick, -ly
thicken, -ed, -ing
thickener
thicket
thickhead
thickness
thickset
thickskinned
thief, thieves
thieve, thieved, thieving
thievish, -ly
thigh
thimble
   thimbul   thimble
   thime   thyme
thin, thinned, thinning
thin, thinner, thinnest
thine
   thiner   thinner
thing
thingamajig
think, thought, thinking
think-tank
thinly
thinner
thinness
third, -ly
third-degree
   thirm   therm
   thiroid   thyroid
thirst, -ed, -ing
thirstily
thirsty, -tier, -tiest

thirteen
thirteenth
   thirtie   thirty
thirtieth
thirty, -ties
this, these
   thisis   thesis
   thisle   thistle
   thisorus   thesaurus
thistle
thistledown
   thisul   thistle
   thitha   thither
thither
   tho   though
thong
   thor   thaw
   thoraks   thorax
thorax, thoraces, thoraxes
thorn
thorny, -nier, -niest
thorough, -ly (absolute)
   thorough   through (pass)
thoroughbred
thoroughfare
   thort   thought
those
thou (you)
though (but)
thought (did think)
thoughtful, -ly
thoughtless, -ly
thousand
thousandth
   thowsand   thousand
thrall
thrash, -ed, -ing
thread, -ed, -ing
threat
threaten, -ed, -ing
   thred   thread
three
three-dimensional
threepence
three-quarter
threesome
thresh, -ed, -ing

threshold	
thret	threat
threw (did throw)	
threw	through
	(between)
threwout	throughout
thrice	
thrift	
thrifty, -tier, -tiest	
thrill, -ed, -ing	
thriller	
thrips, thrips	
thrise	thrice
thrive, throve, thrived, thriving	
thro' (through)	
throat	
throb, throbbed, throbbing	
throe (spasm)	
throe	throw (toss)
thrombosis, -oses	
throne (chair)	
throne	thrown (tossed)
throng, -ed, -ing	
throo	threw (tossed)
throo	through
	(between)
throte	throat
throttle, -tled, -tling	
throttul	throttle
through (pass)	
through	thorough
	(absolute)
through	threw (tossed)
throughout	
throve	
throw, threw, thrown, throwing (toss)	
throw	throe (spasm)
throwaway society	
thrown (tossed)	
thrown	throne (chair)
thrum, thrummed, thrumming	
thrush	
thrust, thrust, thrusting	
thud, thudded, thudding	
thug	
thuggery	
thuggish, -ly	

thum	thumb
thumb, -ed, -ing	
thump, -ed, -ing	
thunder, -ed, -ing	
thunderbolt	
thunderclap	
thunderous, -ly	
thunderstruck	
thundery	
thundrus	thunderous
thurer	thorough
thurerbred	thoroughbred
thurerfare	thoroughfare

> For **thurm-** words, look under **therm-**.

Thursday	
thurst	thirst
thurteen	thirteen
thurty	thirty
thus	
thwart, -ed, -ing	
thwort	thwart
thyme (plant)	
thyroid	
tiara	
tibia, tibiae, tibias	
tic (twitch)	
tick, -ed, -ing (sound)	
ticker	
ticket	
tickle, -led, -ling	
ticklish	
tickul	tickle
ticoon	tycoon
tic-tac	
tidal	
tiddler	
tiddlywinks	
tide, tided, tiding (ocean)	
tide	tied (bound)
tidie	tidy
tidily	
tidings	
tidul	tidal
tidy, tidied, tidying	
tidy, tidier, tidiest	

tie, tied, tying
tier, (row)
  tier   tear (crying)
  tier   tire (weary)
  tier   tyre (wheel)
  tif   tiff
tiff
tiffin
  tifoid   typhoid
  tifoon   typhoon
  tifus   typhus
tiger
  tigeress   tigress
tight, -ly
tighten, -ed, -ing
tightrope
tights
tigress
tiki
tile, tiled, tiling
till, -ed, -ing
tiller
tilt, -ed, -ing
timber, -ed, -ing (wood)
timbre (sound)
timbrel
  timbrul   timbrel
time, timed, timing (clock)
  time   thyme (plant)
timekeeper
timeless, -ly
timely, -lier, -liest
timepiece
timetable
timid, -ly
timidity
timorous, -ly
  timorus   timorous
timpano, -ni
tin, tinned, tinning
  tinchur   tincture
tincture, -tured, -turing
tinder
tinderbox
tine
tinea
tinge, tinged, tingeing

tingle, tingled, tingling
  tingul   tingle
  tinie   tiny
tinker, -ed, -ing
tinkle, -led, -ling
  tinkture   tincture
  tinkul   tinkle
tinny, -nier, -niest
tin-pot
tinsel, -selled, -selling
tinselly
  tinsul   tinsel
tint, -ed, -ing
tintack
tiny, tinier, tiniest
tip, tipped, tipping
  tipe   type
  tipewriter   typewriter
  tipical   typical
  tipify   typify
  tipist   typist
  tipografy   typography
tipple, -led, -ling
tipsily
tipsy, -sier, -siest
tiptoe, -toed, -toeing
tiptop
  tipul   tipple
tirade
  tiranical   tyrannical
  tiranise   tyrannise
  tirant   tyrant
  tiranus   tyrannous
  tirany   tyranny
tire, tired, tiring (weary)
  tire   tier (row)
  tire   tyre (wheel)
tiresome
  tiresum   tiresome
'tis (it is)
  tis   'tis (it is)
  tis   tizz (anxiety)
  tishoo   tissue
tissue, -sued, -suing
tit
titan
titanic

titavation	titivation	todstool	toadstool
titbit		todul	toddle
tite	tight	tody	toddy
titen	tighten	toe, toed, toeing (foot)	
tites	tights	toe	tow (pull)
tithe, tithed, tithing		toey	
titian		tofee	toffee
titillate, -lated, -lating		toff	
titillation		toffee (sweet)	
titivate, -vated, -vating		toffy (rich)	
titivation		tog, togged, togging	
title, -tled, -tling (name)		together	
titrate, -trated, -trating		togetherness	
titter, -ed, -ing		toggle, -gled, -gling	
tittillate	titillate	toggul	toggle
tittle (dot)		toheroa	
tittle-tattle, -tled, -tling		toi	toy
titul	title	toil, -ed, -ing	
titular		toilet	
tizz (anxiety)		toiletrain	toilet-train
to (towards)		toiletry, -tries	
to	too (also)	toilet-train	
to	two (number)	token	
toad		toksic	toxic
toadfish		toksin	tocsin (alarm)
toadstool		toksin	toxin (poison)
toady, toadies		tol	toll
toady, toadied, toadying		told	
toast, -ed, -ing		tole	toll
toaster		tolerable, -bly	
toastmaster		tolerance	
toastmistress		toleranse	tolerance
tobacco		tolerant, -ly	
tobacconist		tolerate, -rated, -rating	
tobaco	tobacco	tolerense	tolerance
tobogan	toboggan	toll, -ed, -ing	
toboggan		tolrabul	tolerable
tobogganist		tomahawk	
tocsic	toxic	tomahork	tomahawk
tocsin (alarm)		tomarto	tomato
tocsin	toxin (poison)	tomato, -toes	
today		tomb	
toddle, -dled, -dling		tomboy	
toddler		tombstone	
toddy, -dies		tome	
tode	toad	tomfoolery	
todler	toddler	tomorow	tomorrow

tomorrer	tomorrow	topografer	topographer
tomorrow		topografy	topography
ton		topper	
tonal, -ly		topple, -pled, -pling	
tongs		toppul	topple
tongue, tongued, tonguing		topsail	
tongue-tied		topside	
tongue-twister		topsoil	
tonic		topsy-turvy	
tonight		tor (hill)	
tonite	tonight	tor	tore (ripped)
tonnage		tor	tour (trip)
tonne		torch	
tonnige	tonnage	torcher	torture
tonsher	tonsure	torchlight	
tonsil		torchlite	torchlight
tonsillectomy, -mies		tore (ripped)	
tonsillitis		tore	tour (trip)
tonsure, -sured, -suring		toreador	
too (also)		torent	torrent
too	to (towards)	torid	torrid
too	two (number)	torism	tourism
took		torment, -ed, -ing	
tool, -ed, -ing		tormenter	tormentor
toom	tomb	tormentor	
toomstone	tombstone	torn	
toon	tune	tornado, -does, -dos	
toor	tour	tornament	tournament
toot, -ed, -ing		torney	tawny
tooth, teeth		tornt	taunt
toothache		torpedo, -does	
toothake	toothache	torpedo, -doed, -doing	
toothbrush, -brushes		torper	torpor
toothcomb		torpid, -ly	
toothless		torpidity	
toothpaste		torpor	
toothy, -thier, -thiest		torque	
tootle, -tled, -tling		torrenshul	torrential
tootul	tootle	torrent	
top, topped, topping		torrential, -ly	
topas	topaz	torrid, -ly	
topaz		torshun	torsion
topic		torsion, -ally	
topical, -ly		torso, -sos	
topknot		tort (law)	
topless, -ly		tort	taught (teach)
topmast		tort	taut (tight)

tortilla
tortoise
tortoiseshell
  tortology — tautology
tortuous, -ly
torture, -tured, -turing
torturer
  tortus — tortoise
  tortuus — tortuous
toss, tossed, tossing
toss-up
  tost — toast
tot, totted, totting
total, -talled, -talling
totalisator
totalitarianism
totality, -ties
totally
tote, toted, toting
totem
  toter — totter
totter, -ed, -ing
tottery
  totul — total
touch, -ed, -ing (feel)
touchdown
touché (good point)
touchily
touchline
touchstone
touch-type, -typed, -typing
touchy, -chier, -chiest
tough, -ly
toughen, -ed, -ing
toupee
tour, -ed, -ing (trip)
  tour — tor (hill)
  tour — tore (ripped)
tourer
tourism
tourist
tournament
  tournikay — tourniquet
tourniquet
tousle, -sled, -sling
tout, -ed, -ing
tow, -ed, -ing (pull)

tow — toe (foot)
toward
towards
towel, -elled, -elling
tower, -ed, -ing
  towl — towel
town
town-planner
township
  towring — towering
  towsl — tousle
  towt — tout
toxic, -ally
toxicity
toxin (poison)
  toxin — tocsin (alarm)
toy, -ed, -ing
  toyl — toil
  toylet — toilet
trace, traced, tracing
tracer
tracery, -ries
trachea, tracheae
trachoma
track, -ed, -ing
  trackshun — traction
tracksuit
tract
tractable, -bly
  tracter — tractor
traction
tractor
trade, traded, trading
trade-in
trademark
trader
tradesman, -men
tradeswoman, -women
  tradishun — tradition
tradition
traditional, -ly
traduce, -duced, -ducing
traducer
  traduse — traduce
traffic, -ficked, -ficking
trafficable
trafficator

trafficker
  trafic   traffic
tragedian
tragedienne
tragedy, -dies
tragic
tragical, -ly
tragicomedy, -dies
trail, -ed, -ing
trailblazer
trailer
train, -ed, -ing
trainee
trainer
traipse, traipsed, traipsing
trait
  traiter   traitor
traitor
traitorous, -ly
  traitrous   traitorous
trajectory, -ries
  trajectry   trajectory
  trajedy   tragedy
  trakia   trachea
  trakshun   traction
tram, trammed, tramming
tramcar
tramline
trammel, -melled, -melling
tramp, -ed, -ing
trample, -pled, -pling
trampoline, -lined, -lining
  trampul   trample
  tramul   trammel
trance, tranced, trancing
  trane   train
  trankwil   tranquil
  trankwility   tranquillity
tranquil, -ly
tranquilliser
tranquillity
transact, -ed, -ing
transaction
transactor
transceiver
transcend, -ed, -ing
transcendent

transcendental, -ally
transcribe, -scribed, -scribing
transducer
  transe   trance
  transend   transcend
transept
transfer, -ferred, -ferring
transferal
transference
transfigure, -ured, -uring
  transfiks   transfix
transfix, -ed, -ing
transform, -ed, -ing
transformation
transformer
transfuse, -fused, -fusing
transfusion
transgress, -ed, -ing
transgression
transgressor
transient, -ly
  transishun   transition
  transister   transistor
transistor
transit, -sited, -siting
transition
transitional, -ly
transitory
translate, -lated, -lating
translation
translator
translucent, -ly
transmigrate, -grated, -grating
transmigration
transmigratory
  transmishun   transmission
transmission
transmit, -mitted, -mitting
transmitter
transom
transparency, -cies
  transparensy   transparency
transparent, -ly
  transperant   transparent
transpire, -spired, -spiring
transplant, -ed, -ing
transplantation

transport, -ed, -ing	treasure, -ured, -uring
transporter	treasurer
transportation	treasure-trove
transpose, -posed, -posing	treasury, -uries
transsexual	treat, -ed, -ing
transversal, -ly	treatable
transverse, -versed, -versing	treatise
transvestism	treatiss treatise
transvestite	treatment
trap, trapped, trapping	treaty, -ties
trapdoor	treble, -bled, -bling
trapeze	trebul treble
trapezium, -zuims, -zia	trecherus treacherous
trapper	trechery treachery
trappings	tred tread
trapse traipse	tree
trase trace	treecul treacle
trash	treet treat
trashy, trashier, trashiest	treetis treatise
trate trait	treetment treatment
trater traitor	treety treaty
traterus traitorous	trefoil
trauma, -mata, -mas	trek, trekked, trekking
traumatic	trekker
travail, -ed, -ing (labour)	trellis
travale travail	tremble, -bled, -bling
travel, -elled, -elling (tour)	trembly, -blier, -bliest
traveller	trembul tremble
travelog travelogue	tremendous, -ly
travelogue	tremendus tremendous
traverse, -versed, -versing	tremer tremor
travesty, -ties	tremolo, -los
travesty, -tied, -tying	tremor
trawl, -ed, -ing	tremulous, -ly
trawler	tremulus tremulous
trawma trauma	trench, -ed, -ing
trawmatic traumatic	trenchant, -ly
treacherous, -ly	trend
treachery, -eries	trendiness
treacle	trendy, -dier, -diest
tread, trod, trodden, treading	treo trio
treadle, -dled, -dling	trepidation
treadmill	treshure treasure
treason	treshury treasury
treasonable, -bly	treson treason
treasonous, -ly	trespass, -ed, -ing
treasonus treasonous	trespasser

tress		trimaran	
tressul	trestle	trimester	
trestle		trimmer	
trevally		trinity, -ties	
tri	try	trinket	
triad		trio, trios	
trial		trip, tripped, tripping	
triangel	triangle	tripartite	
triangle		tripe	
triangul	triangle	triple, -pled, -pling	
triangular, -ly		triplet	
tribal, -ly		triplicate, -cated, -cating	
tribalism		tripod	
tribe		tripple	triple
tribul	tribal	triptick	triptych
tribulation		triptych	
tribunal		tripul	triple
tribune		trise	trice
tributary, -ries		trisicul	tricycle
tribute		trite, triter, tritest	
tributry	tributary	tritely	
trice, triced, tricing		triumf	triumph
triceps		triumph	
trick,-ed, -ing		triumphal	
trickery, -eries		triumphant, -ly	
trickle, -led, -ling		trivia	
trickster		trivial, -ly	
tricky, -kier, -kiest		triviality, -ties	
tricolour		trod	
tricycle		trodden	
trident		troff	trough
tried		trofy	trophy
triel	trial	troglodyte	
triennial, -ly		troika	
triennium, -enniums, -ennia		trolie	trolley
trifecta		troll, -ed, -ing	
trifle, trifled, trifling		trolley, -leys	
trifler		trollop	
triful	trifle	trolop	trollop
trigger, -ed, -ing		troly	trolley
trigonometrical, -ly		trombone	
trigonometry		trombonist	
trilby, -bies		troo	true
trillion		trooant	truant
trilogy, -gies		trooly	truly
trim, trimmed, trimming		troop, -ed, -ing (soldier)	
trim, trimmer, trimmest		troop	troupe (band)

trooper
  troos   truce
  trooth   truth
  troothful   truthful
trophy, -phies
tropic
tropical, -ly
  trorma   trauma
  trormatic   traumatic
trot, trotted, trotting
troth
trotter
troubadour
trouble, -bled, -bling
troublemaker
troublesome, -ly
troubleshooter
trough
trounce, trounced, trouncing
troupe (band)
trousers
trousseau, -seaux, -seaus
trout
trowel, -elled, -elling
  trownce   trounce
  trowsers   trousers
  trowt   trout
truancy
  truansy   truancy
truant
  trubul   trouble
truce
truck, -ed, -ing
truckie
truculence
  truculense   truculence
truculent, -ly
trudge, trudged, trudging
true, truer, truest
true-blue
  truf   trough
truffle
  truful   truffle
  truge   trudge
truism
  trulie   truly
trump, -ed, -ing

trumpery, -ries
trumpet
trumpeter
truncate, -cated, -cating
truncheon
  trunchon   truncheon
trundle, -dled, -dling
  trundul   trundle
trunk
  truseau   trousseau
truss, -ed, -ing
trust, -ed, -ing
trustee
trustful, -ly
  trustwerthy   trustworthy
trustworthy
trusty, trustier, trustiest
truth
truthful, -ly
try, tries
try, tried, trying
  tryce   trice
  trycycle   tricycle
  trype   tripe
tryst
  tryte   trite
  tryumph   triumph
tsar
T-shirt
tuan
tub, tubbed, tubbing
tuba, -bas, -bae (instrument)
tubby, -bier, -biest
tube, tubed, tubing
tuber (plant)
tuberculosis
tuberculous
tubular
  tuch   touch
  tuchy   touchy
tuck, -ed, -ing
tucker
Tuesday
  tuf   tough
  tuffen   toughen
tuffet
tuft, -ed, -ing

tug, tugged, tugging
tugboat
   tuishun — tuition
tuition
   tuk — tuck
   tuksedo — tuxedo
tulip
tulle
tumble, -bled, -bling
tumbler
tumbleweed
   tumbul — tumble
   tumer — tumour
tumescent
tumour
tumult
tumultuous, -ly
   tumultuus — tumultuous
tuna (fish)
tundra
tune, tuned, tuning
tuneful, -ly
tuner (radio)
   tung — tongue
tungsten
tunic
   tunige — tonnage
tunnel, -nelled, -nelling
   tunnul — tunnel
turban
turbid, -ly
turbine
turbojet
turboprop
turbot, -bots, -bot
turbulence
   turbulense — turbulence
turbulent, -ly
tureen
   turet — turret
turf, turfs, turves
turgid, -ly
turgidity
   turjid — turgid
turkey, -keys
Turkish
   turkwoise — turquoise

   turm — term
turmeric
   turminabul — terminable
   turminal — terminal
   turminate — terminate
   turminus — terminus
   turmite — termite
turmoil
turn, -ed, -ing (rotate)
   turn — tern (bird)
turncoat
   turnikay — tourniquet
   turniket — tourniquet
turnip
turnout
turnover
turnstile
turntable
turpentine
turpitude
turquoise
turret
   turse — terse
   turshury — tertiary
turtle
turtledove
turtleneck
   turtul — turtle
   Tusday — Tuesday
tusk, -ed, -ing
tussle, -sled, -sling
tussock
   tusul — tussle
tutelage
   tutelige — tutelage
   tuter — tutor
tutor
tutorial
   tutoriul — tutorial
tutu
tuxedo, -dos
twaddle, -dled, -dling
twain
twang
twangy
tweak, -ed, -ing
tweed

tweek	tweak	tyfoon	typhoon
tweet		tyfus	typhus
tweeter		tympanic	
tweezers		tympanum, -nums, -na	
twelfth		type, typed, typing	
twelth	twelfth	typecast, -cast, -casting	
twelve		typeface	
twentieth		typescript	
twenty, -ties		typeset, -set, -setting	
twice		typesetter	
twich	twitch	typewriter	
twiddle, -dled, -dling		typhoid	
twidul	twiddle	typhoon	
twig, twigged, twigging		typhus	
twiggy		typical, -ly	
twilight		typify, -fied, -fying	
twilite	twilight	typist	
twill (fabric)		typographical, -ally	
'twill (it will)		typography	
twill	'twill (it will)	tyranical	tyrannical
twin, twinned, twinning		tyrannical, -ly	
twine, twined, twining		tyrannise, -nised, -nising	
twinge, twinged, twinging		tyranny, -nies	
twinkle, -kled, -kling		tyrant	
twinkul	twinkle	tyrany	tyranny
twin-set		tyre (wheel)	
twirl, -ed, -ing		tyre	tire (weary)
twist, -ed, -ing		tyro, -ros	
twitch, -ed, -ing		tzar	
twitcher			
twitchy			
twitter, -ed, -ing			
two (number)			
two	to (towards)		
two	too (also)		
two-dimensional			
two-faced			
twopence			
twostep			
two-time, -timed, -timing			
two-tooth			
'twould (it would)			
twould	'twould		
two-up			
twurl	twirl		
tycoon			
tyfoid	typhoid		

Uu

ubikwity	ubiquity
ubiquitous, -ly	
ubiquity	
U-boat	
ubote	U-boat
uda	udder
udder	
ufologist	
ug	ugh
ug boot	
ugh	
uglee	ugly
ugliness	
ugly, -lier, -liest	
ugly duckling	
ukelele	
ukulele	
ulcer	
ulcerate, -rated, -rating	
ulceration	
ulcerous, -ly	
ullage, ullaged, ullaging	
ulsa	ulcer
ulserate	ulcerate
ulserayshun	ulceration
ulserus	ulcerous
ultamatum	ultimatum
ulteeria	ulterior
ultemo	ultimo
ulterior, -ly	
ultimate, -ly	
ultimatum, -tums, -ta	
ultimit	ultimate
ultimo	
ultra	
ultramareen	ultramarine
ultramarine	
ultrasound	

ultraviolet	
ululate, -lated, -lating	
umber	
umberella	umbrella
umbilical cord	
umbilicus, -bilici	
umbra, -brae	
umbrage	
umbrageous, -ly	
umbrella	
umbridge	umbrage
umpire, -pired, -piring	
umpyre	umpire
umpteen	
umpteenth	
unable	
unabul	unable
unaccompanied	
unaccountable, -bly	
unaccustomed	
unacustumed	unaccustomed
unakumpneed	unaccompanied
unanimity	
unanimous, -ly	
unanimus	unanimous
unapproachable, -bly	
unaprochibul	unapproachable
unassuming, -ly	
unattached	
unattended	
unatural	unnatural
unavailing, -ly	
unavaleing	unavailing
unaware	
unawares	
unawear	unaware
unbalance, -anced, -ancing	
unbecoming, -ly	
unbecuming	unbecoming
unbeknown	
unbeknownst	
unbeleif	unbelief
unbeleiver	unbeliever
unbeleiving	unbelieving
unbelief	
unbeliever	
unbelieving, -ly	

unbend, -bent or -bended, -bending
  unbenown   unbeknown
unblinking, -ly
unblushing, -ly
unborn
unbosom, -ed, -ing
unbounded, -ly
  unbownded   unbounded
  unbrideld   unbridled
unbridled
unburden, -ed, -ing
uncalled-for
uncanny, -nily
unceremonious, -ly
uncertain, -ly
uncharitable, -ly
uncharted
uncircumcised
uncle
unclean, -ly
uncomfortable, -ly
  unconfortibul   uncomfortable
uncommon, -ly
uncommunicative, -ly
  uncomon   uncommon
uncompromising, -ly
unconcerned, -ly
  uncondishunal   unconditional
unconditional, -ly
unconnected, -ly
unconscionable, -bly
unconscious, -ly
  unconshunibul   unconscionable
  unconshus   unconscious
unconstitutional, -ly
unconventional, -ly
  uncooth   uncouth
uncouth, -ly
uncover, -ed, -ing
unction
unctuous, -ly
  uncumftibul   uncomfortable
uncut
  uncuver   uncover
undaunted
undecided
undefined

undemonstrative, -ly
undeniable, -bly
  undeniabul   undeniable
under
under-age
underarm
undercarriage
  undercarridge   undercarriage
  underclose   underclothes
underclothes
undercoat
  undercote   undercoat
undercover
  undercurent   undercurrent
undercurrent
undercut, -cut, -cutting
  undercuver   undercover
underdeveloped
underdeveloping
underdevelopment
  underdevelopt   underdeveloped
underdog
underdone
  underdun   underdone
  underestamate   underestimate
underestimate, -mated, -mating
underexpose, -exposed, -exposing
  underexposhur   underexposure
underexposure
  underexpows   underexpose
underfoot
undergo, -went, -gone, -going
undergraduate
  undergrajuate   undergraduate
  undergroth   undergrowth
underground
undergrowth
underhand
  underite   underwrite
underlay, -laid, -laying
underlie, -lay, -lain, -lying
  underlieing   underlying
underline, -lined, -lining
underling
  underly   underlie
underlying
undermine, -mined, -mining

underneath
   underneeth   underneath
undernourish, -ed, -ing
   undernurish   undernourish
underpants
underpass
underpin, -pinned, -pinning
underplay, -played, -playing
underprivileged
underproof
   underprufe   underproof
   underscaw   underscore
underscore, -scored, -scoring
undersecretary, -taries
undersell, -sold, -selling
undershot
undersign
   undersine   undersign
understand, -stood, -standing
understanding
   understait   understate
understate, -stated, -stating
understatement
   understayt   understate
understood
understudy, -studied, -studying
   undertaik   undertake
   undertaiker   undertaker
undertake, -took, -taken, -taking
undertaker
under-the-counter
   undertoan   undertone
   undertoe   undertow
undertone
undertow
   underware   underwear
underwear
underworld
underwrite, -written, -writing
undesirable, -bly
   undesiribul   undesirable
undeveloped
   undevelupt   undeveloped
   undew   undue
   undewlate   undulate
   undewly   unduly
undo, -did, -done, -doing

   undoo   undo
undoubted, -ly
   undowted   undoubted
undress, -dressed, -dressing
undue
undulate, -lated, -lating
undulation
undulatory
unduly
   undur   under
undying
   undyou   undue
unearned
unearned income
unearth, -ed, -ing
unearthly
uneasily
uneasiness
uneasy, -easier, -easiest
   unecessary   unnecessary
uneducated
   uneekwell   unequal
   uneesy   uneasy
   uneeven   uneven
   unekwivacal   unequivocal
unemployed
unemployment
unequal, -ly
   uneque   unique
unequivocal, -ly
unerring, -ly
   unesesary   unnecessary
uneven, -ly
unevenness
unfailing, -ly
unfair, -ly
   unfaling   unfailing
   unfare   unfair
unfamiliar, -ly
unfamiliarity
unfeeling, -ly
   unfemilyer   unfamiliar
unfinished
unfit, -fitted, -fitting
unflagging, -ly
   unflapibul   unflappable
unflappable, -bly

unfold, -ed, -ing
  unforchinate — unfortunate
unforeseen
unforgettable
unformed
  unforsean — unforeseen
unfortunate, -ly
unfounded, -ly
  unfowld — unfold
  unfownded — unfounded
unfrock, -ed, -ing
unfurl, -ed, -ing
ungainliness
ungainly
  unganely — ungainly
  ungarded — unguarded
ungodliness
ungodly
ungracious, -ly
  ungrashus — ungracious
unguarded, -ly
unguent
ungulate
unhappily
unhappiness
unhappy, -pier, -piest
unhealthily
unhealthiness
unhealthy, -thier, -thiest
unheard-of
  unhelthy — unhealthy
  unherdoff — unheard-of
unhinge, -hinged, -hinging
  unhinj — unhinge
  unholey — unholy
unholy, -lier, -liest
  unholesum — unwholesome
uni
unicameral
unicellular
  uniceluler — unicellular
unicorn
  unidirechunal — unidirectional
  unifacation — unification
unification
uniform, -ly
uniformity, -ties

unify, -fied, -fying
  unike — unique
unilateral, -ly
  unilatrel — unilateral
unimaginable, -ably
  unimaginabul — unimaginable
unimpeachable, -ably
  unimpeechibul — unimpeachable
  unimployed — unemployed
  unimprooved — unimproved
unimproved
uninhibited
uninspired
uninspiring
union
union card
unionisation
unionise, -nised, -nising
unionist
unionistic
Union Jack
unique, -ly
uniqueness
  unirve — unnerve
unisex
unisexual, -ly
unisexuality
unison
unit
Unitarian
Unitarianism
unitary
unite, united, uniting
unit trust
unity, -ties
universal, -ly
universal suffrage
universe
university, -ties
unkempt
  unkemt — unkempt
unkind, -ly
  unkined — unkind
  unkle — uncle
unknit, -knitted, -knitting
unknown
unlawful, -ly

unlearned, -ly
unlearnt
unleash, -ed, -ing
unleavened
  unleesh — unleash
  unlerned — unlearned
  unlernt — unlearnt
  unles — unless
unless
unlettered
unlike
unlikelihood
unlikely
  unlikelyhood — unlikelihood
unlimited
unlisted
unload, -ed, -ing
  unlode — unload
unlooked-for
unluckily
unluckiness
unlucky
  unluckyly — unluckily
unmake, -made, -making
unmanageable, -bly
  unmanagebul — unmanageable
unmanliness
unmanly
unmannerliness
unmannerly
  unmenchunabul — unmentionable
unmentionable, -bly
unmistakable, -bly
  unmistakabul — unmistakable
unmitigated, -ly
  unmooved — unmoved
unmoved
unnatural, -ly
unnecessary, -rily
unnerve, -nerved, -nerving
  unnesesarily — unnecessarily
  unnesesary — unnecessary
  unobtrusif — unobtrusive
unobtrusive, -ly
unofficial, -ly
  unofishel — unofficial
unorganised

  unorgenized — unorganised
unpalatable, -bly
  unpalatabul — unpalatable
  unparaleled — unparalleled
unparalleled
  unparraleled — unparalleled
unpicked
unplaced
  unplaised — unplaced
unpolished
unpopular, -ly
unpopularity
  unpopuler — unpopular
unprecedented, -ly
  unpresidented — unprecedented
unprincipled
  unprinsipled — unprincipled
unprintable
  unprintibul — unprintable
  unprofeshunel — unprofessional
unprofessional, -ly
  unproffessinal — unprofessional
  unkwalified — unqualified
unqualified
unquestionable, -bly
  unquestionibul — unquestionable
unravel, -elled, -elling
  unravell — unravel
unreal, -ly
unrealistic, -ally
  unreckonized — unrecognised
  unredeamed — unredeemed
unredeemed
  unreel — unreal
  unreelistic — unrealistic
  unreesenibul — unreasonable
  unrekwited — unrequited
  unrelaited — unrelated
unrelated
unrelenting, -ly
  unreleived — unrelieved
unrelieved
  unremiting — unremitting
unrepeatable, -bly
  unrepeetibul — unrepeatable
unrequited, -ly
unrest

unrivalled
  unriveled — unrivalled
  unrooly — unruly
unruffled
  unrufled — unruffled
unruly
unsafe, -ly
  unsaif — unsafe
  unsaterated — unsaturated
unsaturated
  unsavery — unsavoury
unsavoury
unscathed
unschooled
unscrew, -ed, -ing
unscrupulous
  unskru — unscrew
  unskuled — unschooled
unseasonable, -bly
unseat, -seated, -seating
  unseesenibul — unseasonable
  unseet — unseat
unsecured
  unsecurred — unsecured
unseemliness
unseemly
  unseemlynes — unseemliness
unseen
unselfish, -ly
  unsellfish — unselfish
unserviceable
  unservisabul — unserviceable
  unsetled — unsettled
unsettled
unshakable, -bly
unshakeable, -bly
  unshakibul — unshakeable
  unshore — unsure
unsightly
  unsitely — unsightly
  unskild — unskilled
unskilled
unsociability
unsociable, -bly
unsolicited
  unsolisited — unsolicited
  unsoshabul — unsociable

unsound, -ly
  unsownd — unsound
unspeakable, -bly
  unspeekabul — unspeakable
unspoilt
  unspoylt — unspoilt
unstable, -bly
  unstabul — unstable
unsteady, -dily
  unstedie — unsteady
unstructured
  unstruxured — unstructured
unstudied
  unstudyed — unstudied
  unsubstanshul — unsubstantial
unsubstantial, -ly
unsung
unsure
unswerving, -ly
  unswurving — unswerving
  untangel — untangle
untangle, -gled, -gling
untapped
untenable, -bly
unthinkable, -bly
  unthinkabul — unthinkable
unthinking, -ly
  untidie — untidy
untidiness
untidy, -died, -dying
untidy, -dier, -diest
untie, -tied, -tying
until
  untill — until
untimely
unto
  untoo — unto
untold
untouchable
  untouchabul — untouchable
  untooward — untoward
untoward, -ly
  untroo — untrue
  untrooth — untruth
untrue
untruth
unturned

unushual	unusual	upholster, -ed, -ing	
unusual, -ly		upholsterer	
unutterable, -bly		upholstery, -ries	
unutterabul	unutterable	upill	uphill
unvale	unveil	upkeep	
unveil, -ed, -ing		uplift	
unvoiced		up-market	
unvoised	unvoiced	upold	uphold
unwarented	unwarranted	upolster	upholster
unwarranted		upon	
unweeldy	unwieldy	upper	
unwelcome, -ly		upper case	
unwellcum	unwelcome	upper chamber	
unwholesome, -ly		uppercut	
unwieldiness		upper hand	
unwieldy		upper house	
unwiling	unwilling	uppermost	
unwilling, -ly		upright	
unwillingness		uprising	
unwind, -wound, -winding		uprite	upright
unwined	unwind	uproar	
unwitting, -ly		uproarious, -ly	
unworldliness		uproot, -ed, -ing	
unworldly		uprore	uproar
unworthily		upset, -set, -setting	
unworthiness		upshot	
unworthy		upside down	
unwritten		upstage, -staged, -staging	
up, upped, upping		upstairs	
up-and-coming		upstaje	upstage
up-beat		upstanding	
upbrade	upbraid	upsurge, -surged, -surging	
upbraid, -ed, -ing		upsurje	upsurge
upbringing		upswing, -swung, -swinging	
up-country		uptaik	uptake
updait	update	uptake	
update, -dated, -dating		up-tempo	
upeld	upheld	uptight	
uper	upper	uptite	uptight
up-end, -ended, -ending		up-to-date	
upgrade, -graded, -grading		up-too-date	up-to-date
upgraid	upgrade	upturn, -ed, -ing	
upheaval		upward, -ly	
upheevul	upheaval	upwards	
upheld		upwood	upward
uphill		uranic	
uphold, -held, -holding		uranium	

Uranus
urban (town)
urbane, -ly (civilised)
urbanity, -ties
urchin
urea
  urear   urea
ureter
urethra, -thrae, -thras
urethral
urge, urged, urging
urgency
urgent, -ly
urinal
urinary
urinate, -nated, -nating
urination
urine
  urinel   urinal
urinous
  urj   urge
  urjensy   urgency
  urjent   urgent
urn (jug)
  urn   earn (gain)
urogenital
  urojenital   urogenital
urology
  urolojy   urology
ursine
usability
usable
usableness
  usabul   usable
usage
  usaje   usage
use, used, using
useable
  useabul   useable
used
useful, -ly
usefulness
useless, -ly
uselessness
usher
usherette
usual, -ly

  ushuel   usual
  ushuelly   usually
usurp, usurped, usurping
usurpation
usurper
usury, -ries
  utalisation   utilisation
ute
utensil
  utensle   utensil
uterine
uterus, uteri
utilisation
utilise, -lised, -lising
utilitarian
utilitarianism
utility, -ties
utmost
utopia
utopian
utopianism
  utta   utter
utter, uttered, uttering
utterly
uttermost
U-turn
  uttur   utter
  uturus   uterus
uvula, -las, -lae
uxorious, -ly
uxoriousness

Vv

vacancy, -cies
  vacansy   vacancy
vacant, -ly
vacate, -cated, -cating
vacation
vaccinate, -nated, -nating
vaccination
vaccine
  vaccuum   vacuum
  vacency   vacancy
vacillate, -lated, -lating
  vacseen   vaccine
  vacsinate   vaccinate
  vacsination   vaccination
  vacsine   vaccine
vacuity, -ties
vacuous, -ly
vacuum
vacuum-packed
vacuum-sealed
  vacuus   vacuous
vagabond
vagary, -ries
vagarious
  vagarius   vagarious
  vage   vague
vagina, -nas, -nae
vaginal
vagrancy, -cies
  vagransy   vagrancy
vagrant, -ly
vague, vaguer, vaguest
vaguely
  vail   vale (valley)
  vail   veil (cover)
vain, -ly (proud)
  vain   vane (blade)
  vain   vein (blood)

vainglorious, -ly
  vainglorius   vainglorious
vainglory
  vajina   vagina
  valadation   validation
  valantine   valentine
  valay   valet
vale (valley)
  vale   veil (cover)
  valedicshun   valediction
valediction
valedictory
  valedictry   valedictory
valentine
  valer   valour
  valerus   valorous
  valese   valise
valet, -leted, -leting
valiant, -ly
valid, -ly
validate, -dated, -dating
validation
validity, -ties
valise
valley, -leys
  valor   valour
valorous, -ly
  valorus   valorous
valour
valuable, -bly
valuation
value, -ued, -uing
valuer
valve, valved, valving
valvular
  valy   valley
  valyu   value
  valyubul   valuable
  valyuless   valueless
vamoose, -moosed, -moosing
vamp, -ed, -ing
vampire
van
vandal
vandalism
  vandul   vandal
vane (blade)

vane	vain (proud)	veal	
vane	vein (blood)	vector	
vaneer	veneer	veel	veal
vangard	vanguard	veemense	vehemence
vanglorius	vainglorious	veement	vehement
vanguard		veer, -ed, -ing	
vanilla		vegatation	vegetation
vanish, -ed, -ing		vegetable	
vanity, -ties		vegetabul	vegetable
vankwish	vanquish	vegetarian	
vanquish, -ed, -ing		vegetarianism	
vantage		vegetate, -tated, -tating	
vapid, -ly		vegetation	
vaporise, -rised, -rising		vegetative, -ly	
vaporiser		vegtabul	vegetable
vaporous, -ly		vehemence	
vapour		vehement, -ly	
variability		vehicle	
variable, -bly		vehicular	
variabul	variable	veicular	vehicular
variance		veil, -ed, -ing (cover)	
varianse	variance	veil	vale (valley)
variant		vein (blood)	
variation		vein	vain (proud)
varicolored	varicoloured	vein	vane (blade)
varicoloured		veks	vex
varicose		veksashus	vexatious
varied		vektor	vector
variegate, -gated, -gating		Velcro	
varietal, -ly		veldt	
variety, -ties		vellum	
various, -ly		velocipede	
varius	various	velocity, -ties	
varnish, -ed, -ing		velodrome	
vary, varied, varying		veloor	velour
vascular, -ly		velour	
vase		velum	vellum
vasectomy, -mies		velt	veldt
vaseline		velvet	
vasillate	vacillate	velveteen	
vast, -ly		velvety	
vat, vatted, vatting		venal, -ly	
Vatican		venality, -ties	
vaudavil	vaudeville	vend, -ed, -ing	
vaudeville		vender	vendor
vault, -ed, -ing		vendetta	
vaunt, -ed, -ing		vendor	

veneer
venerability
venerable, -bly
  venerabul   venerable
venerate, -rated, -rating
veneration
venereal
  venerial   venereal
venetian blind
  venew   venue
vengeance
vengeful, -ly
  vengense   vengeance
venial, -ly
venison
venom
venomous, -ly
  venomus   venomous
venous (of veins)
  venous   Venus (planet)
vent, -ed, -ing
  ventalation   ventilation
ventilate, -lated, -lating
ventilation
ventilator
ventral, -ly
ventricle
  ventricul   ventricle
  ventrilokwism ventriloquism
ventriloquism
ventriloquist
venture, -tured, -turing
venturer
venturesome, -ly
venturous, -ly
  venturus   venturous
venue
Venus (planet)
  venus   venous (of
             veins)
veracious, -ly (honest)
  veracious   voracious
             (greedy)
veracity, -ties
veranda
  verashus   veracious
  verasity   veracity

verb
verbal, -balled, -balling
verbalise, -lised, -lising
verbally
verbatim
  verbel   verbal
verbena
verbiage
  verbige   verbiage
verbose, -ly
verbosity
verdant, -ly
verdict
verdure
verdurous
verge, verged, verging
verger
  vergin   virgin
  verie   vary
verifiable, -bly
verification
  verifie   verify
verify, -fied, -fying
verily
verisimilitude
veritable, -bly
vermicelli
vermilion
vermin
verminous, -ly
vermouth
vernacular, -ly
vernal, -ly
vernier
versatile, -ly
versatility
verse, verses (poem)
  verses   versus (against)
versification
versify, -fied, -fying
version
versus (against)
  versus   verses (poems)
vertebra, -brae
vertebrate
  verteks   vertex
vertex, -tices

vertical, -ly
vertiginous, -ly
   vertiginus   vertiginous
vertigo, -goes
verve
very, -rier, -riest
   vesa   visa
vespers
vessel
vest, -ed, -ing
vestal
   vestibul   vestibule
vestibule
vestige
vestigial, -ly
vestment
   vestrie   vestry
vestry, -tries
   vestul   vestal
vesture, -tured, -turing
vet, vetted, vetting
   vetenary   veterinary
   vetenry   veterinary
veteran
veterinary, -ries
veto, -toes
veto, -toed, -toing
vex, -ed, -ing
vexation
vexatious, -ly
   veza   visa
   vi   vie
via
viability
viable, -bly
   viabul   viable
viaduct
vial (tube)
   vial   vile (bad)
   vialate   violate
   vialin   violin
viand
viaticum, -ca, -cums
vibes
vibrant, -ly
vibrate, -brated, -brating
vibration

   vibrater   vibrator
vibrator
viburnum
vicar
vicarage
   vicarige   vicarage
vicarious, -ly
   vicarius   vicarious
vice
vice-chairman, -men
vice-chancellor
vice-president
   vicer   vicar
viceregal, -ly
   viceroi   viceroy
viceroy
vice versa
vicinity, -ties
vicious, -ly (evil)
   vicious   viscous (thick)
vicissitude
   vicount   viscount
   victer   victor
victim
victimisation
victimise, -mised, -mising
victor
Victorian
victorious, -ly
   victorius   victorious
victory, -ries
victual, -ualled, -ualling
victualler
video
videophone
videotape, -taped, -taping
   vidio   video
vie, vied, vying
   vieing   vying
Vietnamese, -ese
view, -ed, -ing
viewer
viewfinder
viewpoint
   viger   vigour
vigil
vigilance

vigilanse — vigilance
vigilant, -ly (watchful)
vigilante (law enforcer)
vigneron
vignette, -gnetted, -gnetting
vigoro
vigorous, -ly
   vigorus — vigorous
vigour
   viksen — vixen
   vilafication — vilification
   vilain — villain
vile, viler, vilest (bad)
   vile — vial (tube)
vilely
vilification
   vilifie — vilify
vilifier
vilify, -fied, -fying
   vilige — village
villa
village
villager
villain
villainous, -ly
villainy, -nies
   villanus — villainous
vim
vinaigrette
vindicate, -cated, -cating
vindication
vindictive, -ly
vine
vinegar
vinegary
vineyard
   vinigar — vinegar
vino
vintage, -taged, -taging
   vintige — vintage
   vinul — vinyl
vinyl
viola
violate, -lated, -lating
violation
violator
violence

violense — violence
violent, -ly
violet
violin
viper
viperous, -ly
   viperus — viperous
virago, -goes, -gos
viral
virgin
virginal, -ly
virginity
Virgo
virile
virility, -ties
virtual, -ly
virtue
virtuoso
virtuous, -ly
   virtuus — virtuous
virulence
   virulense — virulence
virulent, -ly
virus, viruses
visa, -saed, -saing
visage
vis-a-vis
viscera
viscosity
viscount
viscountess
viscous, -ly, (thick)
   viscous — vicious (evil)
   viscuus — viscous (thick)
   vise — vice
   vise-chairman — vice-chairman
   vise-president — vice-president
   visera — viscera
   viseregal — viceregal
   viseversa — vice versa
   vishiate — vitiate
   vishun — vision
   vishunry — visionary
   vishus — vicious (evil)
visibility, -ties
visible, -bly
   visibul — visible

visinity	vicinity
vision	
visionary, -ries	
visionry	visionary
visissitude	vicissitude
visit, -ed, -ing	
visitant	
visitation	
visiter	visitor
visitor	
viskosity	viscosity
vista	
visual, -ly	
visualise, -lised, -lising	
visuul	visual
visuulise	visualise
vital, -ly	
vitality, -ties	
vitamin	
vitel	vital
vitiate, -ated, -ating	
viticulture	
vitreous, -ly	
vitrification	
vitrifie	vitrify
vitrify, -fied, -fying	
vitriol	
vitriolic	
vituperate, -rated, -rating	
viul	vial (tube)
viul	vile (bad)
vivacious, -ly	
vivasious	vivacious
viva voce	
vivid, -ly	
vivisecshun	vivisection
vivisect, -ed, -ing	
vivisection	
vivisectionist	
vixen	
vocabulary, -ries	
vocal, -ly	
vocalisation	
vocalise, -lised, -lising	
vocalist	
vocation	
vocational, -ly	

vociferous, -ly	
vociferus	vociferous
vodka	
voge	vogue
vogue	
voice, voiced, voicing	
void, -ed, -ing	
voiige	voyage
voile	
voise	voice
volatile	
volatility	
volcanic, -ally	
volcano, -noes, -nos	
voley	volley
volishun	volition
volition	
volley, -leys	
volley, -ed, -ing	
volleyball	
volt	
voltage	
voltaic	
voltmeter	
voluble, -bly	
volubul	voluble
volume	
volumetric, -ally	
voluminous, -ly	
voluminus	voluminous
voluntarily	
voluntary, -taries	
volunteer, -ed, -ing	
voluptuous, -ly	
voluptuus	voluptuous
vomit, -ed, -ing	
voodoo, -doos	
voodoo, -dooed, -dooing	
voodooism	
voracious, -ly (greedy)	
voracious	veracious (honest)
voracity	
vorasious	voracious
vortex, -texes, -tices	
vortical, -ly	
vosiferus	vociferous

votary, -ries
vote, voted, voting
voter
votive, -ly
vouch, -ed, -ing
voucher
vouchsafe, -safed, -safing
vow, -ed, -ing
  vowch   vouch
  vowcher   voucher
vowel
  vowul   vowel
voyage, -aged, -aging
voyager
  voyd   void
voyeur
voyeurism
  voyse   voice
  vue   view
vulcanise, -nised, -nising
vulcanism
vulcanite
  vulcher   vulture
vulgar, -ly
vulgarism
vulgarity, -ties
vulnerability
vulnerable, -bly
  vulnerabul   vulnerable
vulpine
vulture
vulva, -vae, -vas
  vurb   verb
  vurchoo   virtue
  vurchual   virtual
  vurchuus   virtuous
  vurgin   virgin
  vurtue   virtue
  vurtuous   virtuous
  vye   vie

Ww

wack whack
wad, wadded, wadding
waddle, -dled, -dling
waddy, -dies (club)
  waddy wadi (channel)
wade, waded, wading
wader
wadi, -dies (channel)
  wadi waddy (club)
  wadle waddle
  wadul waddle
  wafe waif
wafer
wafery
waffle, -fled, -fling
  waful waffle
wag, wagged, wagging
wage, waged, waging
wager
waggish, -ly
waggle, -gled, -gling
waggly
wagon
wagtail
  wagul waggle
wahine
waif
wail, wailed, wailing (cry)
  wail wale (welt)
  wail whale
      (mammal)
wainscot, -scotted, -scotting
wainwright
waipiro
waist (body)
  waist waste
      (squander)
waistband

waistcoat
waistline
wait (stay)
  wait weight
      (amount)
waiter
  waitey weighty
waitress
waive, waived, waiving (forgo)
  waive wave (ocean)
waiver (law)
  waiver waver (sway)
wake, woke, woken, waking
wakeful, -ly
waken, -ened, -ening
  waks wax
  walabey wallaby
wale, waled, waling (welt)
  wale wail (cry)
  wale whale
      (mammal)
walk, -ed, -ing
walkabout
walkathon
walker
walkie-talkie
walkout
walkover
wall
wallaby, -bies
wallaroo
wallet
walleyed
wallflower
wallop, -ed, -ing
wallow, -ed, -ing
wallpaper
wall-to-wall
walnut
  walop wallop
  walow wallow
walrus, -ruses
  walts waltz
waltz, -ed, -ing
wampum
wan, wanner, wannest (pale)
  wan won (win)

wand
wanda (ghost)
wander, -ed, -ing (walk)
   wander   wonder (think)
wanderer
wanderlust
wane, waned, waning
wangle, -gled, -gling
wangler
   wangul   wangle
want, -ed, -ing
wanton, -ly (lewd)
   wanton   won ton
                 (dough)
war, warred, warring
   warant   warrant
   warantee   warranty
waratah
warble, -bled, -bling
warbler
war cry
ward
warden
wardress
wardrobe
ware (goods)
   ware   wear (cover)
   ware   where (place)
warehouse
   warehowse   warehouse
   warey   wary
   warf   wharf
warfare
warhead
warily
wariness
   warior   warrior
warlike
warlock
warm, -ed, -ing
warm-blooded
warmonger
warmongering
warmth
warn, -ed, -ing (signal)
   warn   worn (tired)
warp, -ed, -ing

warrant, -ed, -ing
warrant officer
warrantor
warranty, -ties
warren
warrigal
warrior
wart (lump)
   wart   wort (plant)
wart-hog
   warves   wharves
wary, warier, wariest
was
wash, -ed, -ing
washboard
washer
washing soda
wash-out
wasn't (was not)
   wasnt   wasn't
wasp
waspish, -ly
wassail
wassailer
wastage
waste, wasted, wasting (squander)
   waste   waist (body)
wasteful, -ly
wasteland
wastrel
   wat   watt (power)
   wat   what (question)
watch, -ed, -ing
watchdog
watchful, -ly
watchman, -men
watchword
   wate   wait (stay)
   wate   weight
                 (measure)

water, -ed, -ing
waterbed
water-buffalo
water-closet
watercolour
watercolourist
water-column

watercourse
watercress
waterfall
waterfowl
waterfront
waterfrontage
watergate
waterhole
watering-can
watering hole
waterlily
waterlog, -logged, -logging
waterloo
watermark
watermelon
water-pistol
water-polo
waterproof
water-rat
water-repellent
watershed
water-ski, -ski'd or skied, -skiing
watertable
watertight

| watertite | watertight |

water-tower
water-vapour
waterway
waterwheel
waterworks
watery

| watige | wattage |

watt (power)

| watt | what (question) |

wattage
wattle, -tled, -tling
wattlebird
wave, waved, waving (ocean)

| wave | waive (forgo) |

waveband
wavefront
wavelength
waver, wavered, wavering (sway)

| waver | waiver (law) |

wavily
waviness
wavy, -vier, -viest

wax, waxed or waxen, waxing
waxen

| waxflour | waxflower |

waxflower
waxplant
waxwork
way (method)

| way | weigh (amount) |
| way | whey (liquid) |

waybill
wayfarer
waylay, -laid, -laying
way-out
wayward, -ly

| waywerd | wayward |

we (us)

| we | wee (little) |

weak, -ly (feeble)

| weak | week (time) |

weaken, -ed,-ing
weakling
weakly, -lier, -liest (feebly)

| weakly | weekly (time) |

weal (hurt)

| weal | wheel (disc) |

wealth, -ily
wealth tax
wealthy, -thier, -thiest
wean, -ed, -ing
weaner
weapon
wear, wore, worn, wearing (cover)

wear	ware (goods)
wear	where (place)
wearey	weary

wearisome, -ly
weary, -rier, -riest
weary, -ried, -rying
weasel

| weat | wheat |

weather, -ed, -ing (rain)

| weather | wether (geld) |
| weather | whether (if) |

weatherboard
weathercock
weathervane
weave, wove or weaved, weaving

weave	we've (we have)	weja	ouija
web, webbed, webbing		welch, -ed, -ing	
webfoot, -feet		welcher	
webfooted		welcome, -comed, -coming	
wed, wedded or wed, wedding (join)		weld, -ed, -ing	
we'd		welder	
wed	we'd (we had)	welfare	
Wedensday	Wednesday	welfare state	
wedge, wedged, wedging		well, better, best	
wedge-tailed eagle		we'll (we will)	
wedgie		well-appointed	
wedlock		well-balanced	
Wednesday		well-being	
wee, weer, weest (small)		well-born	
weed, weeded, weeding		well-bred	
weediness		well-connected	
weedul	wheedle	well-disposed	
weedy, -dier, -diest		well-grounded	
week (time)		well-heeled	
week	weak (feeble)	well-informed	
weekday		well-known	
weeken	weaken	well-meaning	
weekend		well-off	
weekender		well-preserved	
weekling	weakling	well-read	
weekly, -lies (time)		well-rounded	
weekly	weakly (feebly)	well-to-do	
weel	weal (hurt)	welsh, -ed, -ing	
weel	wheel (disc)	welt	
weelbarow	wheelbarrow	welter	
weeld	wield	welth	wealth
ween	wean	wen (swelling)	
weep, wept, weeping		wen	when (at what time)
weeping willow			
weet	wheat	wench	
weevil		wend, wended, wending	
weeze	wheeze	wenever	whenever
weft		Wensday	Wednesday
wege	wedge	went	
weigh, -ed, -ing		wepon	weapon
weight, -ily		wept	
weightiness		wer	weir (dam)
weightlessness		werd	weird
weighty, -tier, -tiest		were (was)	
weild	wield	were	where (place)
weir (dam)		we're (we are)	
weird, -ly		were	we're (we are)

wereabouts	whereabouts
wereas	whereas
werefore	wherefore
weren't (were not)	
werent	weren't
weresoever	wheresoever
wereupon	whereupon
werever	wherever
werewithal	wherewithal
werewolf, -wolves	
werey	weary
werisum	wearisome
werk	work

> For other **werk-** words,
> look under **work-**.

werld	world

> For other **werl-** words,
> look under **worl-**.

werm	worm

> For other **wer-** words,
> look under **wor-**.

Wesleyan
west
West End
westerly, -lies
western
westerner
Westernise, -nised, -nising
westernmost
Westminster system
westward
westwardly
westwards
wet, wetted, wetting (soak)
wet, wetter, wettest

wet	whet (sharpen)

wether, -ed, -ing (geld)

wether	weather (rain)
wether	whether (if)
wetherboard	weatherboard
wethercock	weathercock
wethervane	weathervane

wetsuit
wettex

we've (we have)	
weve	weave (cloth)
weve	we've (we have)
weevel	weevil

whack, whacked, whacking
whacko
whale, whales (mammal)
whale, whaled, whaling
whaleboat
whalebone
whaler
whaler shark
wham, whammed, whamming
wharf, wharves, wharfs

wharfey	wharfie

wharfie
what (question)

what	watt (energy)

whata
what-d'ye-call-it
whatever
whatnot
whatsoever
wheat
wheat germ
wheatmeal

whedul	wheedle

wheedle, -dled, -dling
wheel (disc)

wheel	weal (hurt)

wheelbarrow
wheelchair
wheeler-dealer

wheet	wheat

wheeze, wheezed, wheezing
wheezy, -zier, -ziest
whelk
whelp
when
whenever
where (place)

where	ware (goods)
where	wear (cover)

whereabouts
whereas
wherefore
wheresoever

whereupon
wherever
wherewithal
| wherl | whirl (spin) |
| wherl | whorl (circle) |
wherry, -ries
whet, whetted, whetting (sharpen)
| whet | wet (soak) |
whether (if)
| whether | weather (rain) |
| whether | wether (geld) |
whew
whey (liquid)
| whey | way (method) |
| whey | weigh (measure) |
which (what)
| which | witch (magic) |
whichever
whiff
whiffle, -fled, -fling
while, whiled, whiling (time)
| while | wile (trick) |
whilst
whim
whimper, -ed, -ing
whimsey, -sies
whimsical, -ally
whimsicality, -ties
whimsy, -sies
whine, whined, whining (complain)
| whine | wine (grape juice) |
whinge, whinged, whingeing
whinny, -nies
whinny, -nied, -nying
whip, whipped, whipping
whipbird
whipcord
whiplash
whippersnapper
whippet
whipping boy
whip-round
whirl (spin)
| whirl | whorl (circle) |
whirligig

whirlpool
whirlwind
whirr, whirred, whirring
whisk, whisked, whisking
whisker
whiskey, -keys (U.S., Irish)
whisky, -kies (Scotch, Canadian)
whisper, -ed, -ing
whist
whistle, -tled, -tling
whistler
| whisul | whistle |
whit (jot)
| whit | wit (humour) |
white, whiter, whitest
whitebait, -bait
whitecap
white-collar
white-elephant
white ensign
white-eye
whitefish, -fishes, -fish
white flag
white lie
white light
white pointer
white slave
whitewash
whither (where)
| whither | wither (shrivel) |
whiting
whitlow
whittle, -tled, -tling
| whitul | whittle |
whiz, whizzed, whizzing
who
whoa (stop)
| whoa | woe (sorrow) |
who'd (who would)
| whod | who'd |
whodunit
whoever
whole (all)
| whole | hole (opening) |
wholegrain
wholehearted
wholemeal

whole number
wholesale, -saled, -saling
wholesome, -ly
who'll (who will)
   wholl   who'll
wholly (entirely)
   wholly   holy (good)
whom
   whom   womb (uterus)
whoop (cry)
   whoop   hoop (ring)
whoopee
whooping cough
whoops
whoops-a-daisy
whoosh
whop, whopped, whopping
whopper
whore, whored, whoring
   whore   who're
who're (who are)
whorl (circle)
   whorl   whirl (spin)
whorled
who's (who has)
   whos   who's
whose (possessive)
whosoever
   whur   whirr
   whurl   whirl (spin)
   whurl   whorl (circle)
who've (who have)
   whove   who've
why, whys
   wich   which
                       (question)
   wich   witch (magic)
wick
wicked, -ly
wickedness
wicker
wickerwork
wicket
wicket-keeper
wide, wider, widest
wide-angle
widely

widen, -ed, -ing
widespread
widgie
widow, -ed, -ing
widower
width
wield
   wierd   weird
wife, wives
wig, wigged, wigging
wiggle, -gled, -gling
wiggly
   wiggul   wiggle
wigwam
wilco
wild, -ly
wildcat, -catted, -catting
wildcat strike
wilderness
wildfire
wild flower
wildfowl
wild-goose chase
wildlife
Wild West
wile (trick)
   wile   while (time)
wilful, -ly
wiliness
will, willed, willing
willingness
will-o'-the-wisp
willow
willowy
willpower
willy-nilly
   wilst   whilst
wilt, wilted, wilting
wily, -lier, -liest
   wim   whim
   wimen   women

> For other wi- words,
> look under **whi-**.

wimple, -pled, -pling
win, won, winning
wince, winced, wincing

winch, winched, winching
wind, -ed, -ing (air)
wind, wound, winding (turn)
windbag
windbreak
windcheater
winder
windfall
wind gauge
windjammer
windlass
windmill
window
window-dressing
window-shop, -shopped, -shopping
windpipe
windrow
windscreen
windsock
windsurf, -ed, -ing
windsurfer
wind-tunnel
windvane
windward
windy, windier, windiest
wine, wined, wining (grape juice)

wine	whine
	(complain)

wing, winged, winging
winger
wingspan
wingspread
wink, -ed, -ing
winkle, -kled, -kling
winnings
winnow, -ed, -ing
winnower
winsome, -ly
winsomeness
winter
wintery
wintry

wip	whip

> For other **wip-** words,
> look under **whip-**.

wipe, wiped, wiping

wipe-out
wiper
wire, wired, wiring
wireless
wirrah

wirl	whirl (spin)
wirl	whorl (circle)
wirr	whirr

wiry, wirier, wiriest
wisdom
wisdom tooth, -teeth
wise, wiser, wisest
wisecrack
wisecracker
wish, wished, wishing
wishbone
wishful, -ly
wishy-washy

wisk	whisk

> For other **wis-** words,
> look under **whis-**.

wisp, wisped, wisping
wisteria
wistful, -ly
wistfulness
wit (humour)

wit	whit (jot)

> For other **wit-** words,
> look under **whit-**.

witch (magic)

witch	which
	(question)

witchcraft
witchdoctor
witchetty grub
witch-hunt
witch-hunting
with
withdraw, -drew, -drawn, -drawing
withdrawal
withdrawal sympton
withdrawn

withdroo	withdrew

wither, -ed, -ing (shrivel)

wither	whither (where)

withers
withhold, -held, -holding
withholder
within
   withold   withhold
without
withstand, -stood, -standing
witness, -ed, -ing
witticism
   wittisism   witticism
witty, -tier, -tiest
wives
   wiz   whiz
wizard
wizened
   wo   whoa (stop)
   wo   woe (sorrow)
wobbegong
wobble, -bled, -bling
wobble board
   woble   wobble
   wobul   wobble
   wod   wad
   wodle   waddle
   wodul   waddle
woe (sorrow)
   woe   whoa (stop)
woebegone
woeful, -ly
   woft   waft
   woful   woeful
   wolet   wallet
wok
wolf, wolves
wolfish, -ly
wolfhound
wolfram
wolf spider
wolf-whistle, -led, -ling
   wolop   wallop
   wolow   wallow
wolves
   wom   womb
woman, women
womanise, -nised, -nising
womaniser
womanish, -ly

womanly
womb
wombat
women
women's lib
women's liberation
womera
won (win)
   won   one (number)
wonder, -ed, -ing (think)
   wonder   wander (walk)
wonderful, -ly
wonderland
wonderment
wondrous, -ly
   wondrus   wondrous
wonky, wonkier, wonkiest
wont (accustomed)
   wont   want (need)
   wont   won't (will not)
won't (will not)
won ton (dough)
   wonton   wanton (lewd)
woo, wooed, wooing
wood (timber)
   wood   would (will)
woodblock
woodcarving
woodchip
woodchuck
woodcut
wooden, -ly
woodenness
woodwind
woodwork
woody, woodier, woodiest
wooer
woof, -ed, -ing
woofer
wool
wool classer
wool classing
woolclip
   woolen   woollen
   woolf   wolf
wool-gatherer
wool-gathering

woolgrower
wool-growing
woollen
woollies
woolly, -lier, -liest
woolshed
wool-stapler
wool-stapling

woom	womb
wooman	woman

woomera

woond	wound

woozily
wooziness
woozy

wop	whop (hit)
wor	war
worble	warble
worbul	warble

word, worded, wording

worden	warden

wordily
wordiness
wordless, -ly
word processor

wordrobe	wardrobe

wordy, -dier, -diest
wore

worf	wharf
worfair	warfare

work, worked, working
workable
workaday
workaholic
workbench
workbox
worker
work force
workhorse
workhouse
working capital
working class, -classes
working model
working party, -parties
workman, -men
work-out
works committee

workshop
work-to-rule

worl	whirl (spin)
worl	whorl (circle)

world (earth)

world	whirled (spun)

world-class
worldliness
worldly, -lier, -liest
worm, wormed, worming

worm	warm (heat)

wormhole
wormwood
wormy, wormier, wormiest
worn (tired)

worn	warn (signal)

worn-out

worp	warp

worrier
worrisome
worry, -ries
worry, -ried, -rying
worse
worsen, -ed, -ing
worship, -shipped, -shipping
worshipper
worst
worsted
wort (plant)

wort	wart (lump)

worth
worthily
worthiness
worthless, -ly
worthwhile
worthy, -thier, -thiest

wos	was

> For other wo- words,
> look under **wa-**.

would (will)

would	wood (timber)

would-be
wouldn't (would not)

wouldnt	wouldn't

wound, wounded, wounding (injure)
wove

woven
wowser
wrack (seaweed)
wraith
wrangle, -gled, -gling
wrangler
  wrangul   wrangle
wrap, wrapped or wrapt, wrapping
wrapper
wrath
wrathful, -ly
wreak, -ed, -ing
wreath, wreaths (flowers)
wreathe, -thed, -thing (encircle)
wreck, -ed, -ing
wreckage
wrecker
  wrek   wreck
wren
wrench, -ed, -ing
wrest, wrested, wresting
wrestle, -tled, -tling
wrestler
wretch
wretched, -ly
  wri   wry
wrick, wricked, wricking
wriggle, -gled, -gling
wriggler
wriggly
  wrigul   wriggle
wright (worker)
wring, wrung, wringing
wringer
wrinkle, -kled, -kling
wrinkly
  wrinkul   wrinkle
wrist
wristpin
wristwatch
writ
write, wrote, written, writing
  write   right (true)
  write   rite (ceremony)
  write   wright (worker)
write-off, written-off, writing-off
writer

writhe, writhed, writhing
written
wrong
wrongdoing
wroth
wrought
wrought iron
wrung
wry, wrier, wriest
  wun   one (number)
  wun   won (win)
  wunce   once
  wunder   wonder
  wunse   once
  wur   whirr
  wurl   whirl (spin)
  wurl   whorl (circle)
wurley
wurlitzer
wurrung
wurrup
wye, wyes

X-axis
X chromosome
  X cromosome   X chromosome
  xenofobia   xenophobia
xenophobe
xenophobia
xenophobic
  xerograf   xerograph
  xerografic   xerographic
  xerografy   xerography
xerograph
xerographic
xerography
  xeroks   xerox
xerox
Xmas
X-ray
X-ray tube
xylocarp
  xylofone   xylophone
  xylograf   xylograph
  xylografer   xylographer
  xylografic   xylographic
  xylografy   xylography
xylograph
xylographer
xylographic
xylography
xyloid
xylophagous
xylophone
xylophonic
xylophonist

Yy

y	why
yabber	
yabbie	yabby
yabby, yabbies	
yacht	
yachting	
yack	yak
yahoo	
yahweh	
yak, yakked, yakking	
yakka	
yam	
yandie	yandy
yandy	
Yang	
yank, yanked, yanking (pull)	
Yank (American)	
yap, yapped, yapping	
yard	
yardarm	
yardstick	
yarmelke	
yarmulke	
yarn, -ed, -ing	
yarran	
yaw, -ed, -ing	
yaw	yore (long ago)
yaw	your
yaw	you're (you are)
yawl	
yawn, -ed, -ing	
yaws (disease)	
yaws	yours
Y-axis	
yay	yea
Y chromosome	
Y cromosome	Y chromosome
ye	

yea	
yeah	
yeald	yield
year	
yearbook	
yearling	
yearly, -lies	
yearn, -ed, -ing	
yeast	
yeasty, yeastier, yeastiest	
yeeld	yield
yeer	year
yeest	yeast
yell, -ed, -ing	
yellow	
yellowcake	
yellowish	
yellow pages	
yellow peril	
yelosih	yellowish
yelow	yellow
yelp, -ed, -ing	
yen, yenned, yenning	
yeoman, -men	
yern	yearn
yes, yeses	
yes-man, -men	
yesterday	
yesteryear	
yet	
yeti	
yety	yeti
yew (tree)	
yew	ewe (sheep)
yew	you (person)
yewse	use
yewshual	usual
yewshuul	usual
yewsual	usual
yewsuul	usual

> For other **ye-** words,
> look under **u-**.

Yiddish	
yield, yielded, yielding	
Yin	
yippee	

yob	
yodel, -delled, -delling	
yodeller	
yodle	yodel
yodul	yodel
yoga	
yogert	yoghourt
yogert	yoghurt
yogert	yogurt
yoghourt	
yoghurt	
yogurt	
yogi, -gis	
yogism	
yoicks	
yoke, yoked, yoking (frame)	
yoke	yolk (egg)
yokel	
yokle	yokel
yokul	yokel
yolk (egg)	
yoman	yeoman
Yom Kippur	
yonder	
yoo-hoo	
yore (long ago)	
yore	yaw (move)
yore	your
yore	you're (you are)
yors	yours
yorker	
Yorkshire pudding	
yot	yacht
you (person)	
you	ewe (sheep)
you	yew (tree)
you'd (you would)	
youd	you'd
you'll (you will)	
youll	you'll
young	
youngster	
your (possessive)	
your	yaw (move)
your	yore (long ago)
your	you're (you are)
you're (you are)	

youre	you're
yours	
yourself, -selves	
youth, youths	
youthful, -ly	
you've (you have)	
youve	you've
yowey	yowie
yowie	
yowl, yowled, yowling	
yoyo, -yos	
yuan	
yuckey	yucky, yukky
yuckie	yucky, yukky
yucky, yuckier, yuckiest	
yuk	
yukky, yukkier, yukkiest	
yule (Christmas)	
yule	you'll (you will)
yummy, yummier, yummiest	
yung	young
yungster	youngster
yurn	yearn
yuse	use
yuseful	useful
yusual	usual
yusuul	usual
yutensle	utensil
yutensul	utensil
yuterine	uterine
yuteris	uterus
yuterus	uterus
yuth	youth
yutilise	utilise
yutopia	utopia

For other **yu**- words,
look under **u**-.

Zz

zabaglione
zany, -nier, -niest
zap, zapped, zapping
   zar   tsar
zeal
zealot
zealotry
zealous, -ly
zebra
zebra crossing
zebu
   zeel   zeal
   zefer   zephyr
   zelot   zealot
   zelous   zealous
Zen
zenith
zenithal
   zenofobia   xenophobia
   zenophobia   xenophobia
   zepher   zephyr
zephyr
   zeplen   zeppelin
zeppelin
   zercon   zircon
zero, -ros
zero, -roed, -roing
   zeroks   xerox
zero population growth
   zerox   xerox
zest
zestful, -ly
   zigote   zygote
zigzag, -zagged, -zagging
zilch
zillion
   zilofone   xylophone
   zilophone   xylophone

zinc
zing
   zink   zinc
zinnia
Zion
Zionism
Zionist
Zionistic
zip, zipped, zipping
zip-fastener
zipper
zippy, -pier, -piest
zircon
zirconium
zither
zodiac
zodiacal
zombie, -bies
zombiism
   zomby   zombie
zone, zoned, zoning
zonk, zonked, zonking
zoo
   zoochiney   zucchini
   zoochini   zucchini
   zoologey   zoology
zoological, -ly
zoologist
zoology, -gies
zoom, zoomed, zooming
zot, zotted, zotting
zucchini, zucchini, zucchinis
Zulu, -lus, -lu
Zuni, -nis, -ni
zwieback
zygote